SAGE was founded in 1965 by Sara Miller McCune to support the dissemination of usable knowledge by publishing innovative and high-quality research and teaching content. Today, we publish over 900 journals, including those of more than 400 learned societies, more than 800 new books per year, and a growing range of library products including archives, data, case studies, reports, and video. SAGE remains majority-owned by our founder, and after Sara's lifetime will become owned by a charitable trust that secures our continued independence.

Los Angeles | London | New Delhi | Singapore | Washington DC | Melbourne

CHINA'S
TRANSFORMATION

CHINA'S
TRANSFORMATION

The
SUCCESS
STORY
and the
SUCCESS
TRAP

Manoranjan
MOHANTY

SAGE

Los Angeles | London | New Delhi
Singapore | Washington DC | Melbourne

First published in 2018 by

SAGE Publications India Pvt Ltd
B1/I-1 Mohan Cooperative Industrial Area
Mathura Road, New Delhi 110 044, India
www.sagepub.in

SAGE Publications Inc
2455 Teller Road
Thousand Oaks, California 91320, USA

SAGE Publications Ltd
1 Oliver's Yard, 55 City Road
London EC1Y 1SP, United Kingdom

SAGE Publications Asia-Pacific Pte Ltd
3 Church Street
#10-04 Samsung Hub
Singapore 049483

Published by Vivek Mehra for SAGE Publications India Pvt Ltd, typeset in 10/12 pt Adobe Garamond by Diligent Typesetter India Pvt Ltd, Delhi, and printed at Chaman Enterprises, New Delhi.

Library of Congress Cataloging-in-Publication Data

Name: Mohanty, Manoranjan, author.
Title: China's transformation : the success story and the success trap / Manoranjan Mohanty.
Description: Thousand Oaks : SAGE Publications India Pvt Ltd, [2018] | Includes index.
Identifiers: LCCN 2017032993 | ISBN 9789386602848 (print hb) | ISBN 9789386602855 (e-pub) | ISBN 9789386602862 (e-book)
Subjects: LCSH: China—Economic conditions—2000 | China—Economic policy—2000- | China—Politics and government—2002-
Classification: LCC HC427.95 .M64 2018 | DDC 330.951—dc23 LC record available at https://lccn.loc.gov/2017032993

ISBN: 978-93-866-0284-8 (HB)

SAGE Team: Rajesh Dey, Alekha Chandra Jena, Syeda Aina Rahat Ali and Ritu Chopra

To

Bidyut

My closest critic for over five decades

Thank you for choosing a SAGE product!
If you have any comment, observation or feedback,
I would like to personally hear from you.

Please write to me at **contactceo@sagepub.in**

Vivek Mehra, Managing Director and CEO, SAGE India.

Bulk Sales

SAGE India offers special discounts
for purchase of books in bulk.
We also make available special imprints
and excerpts from our books on demand.

For orders and enquiries, write to us at

Marketing Department
SAGE Publications India Pvt Ltd
B1/I-1, Mohan Cooperative Industrial Area
Mathura Road, Post Bag 7
New Delhi 110044, India

E-mail us at **marketing@sagepub.in**

Get to know more about SAGE

Be invited to SAGE events, get on our mailing list.
Write today to **marketing@sagepub.in**

This book is also available as an e-book.

Contents

List of Tables

List of Figures

Preface

This is a study of the momentous transformation that has taken place in China, especially in rural China, since the reforms were launched by Deng Xiaoping in December 1978. The focus is on the nature of the development strategy and the State and the party that formulate and implement policies. It decodes the ideological and political formulations such as 'socialist market economy' and finds out what it entails in concrete terms. It presents an analysis of the effects of the policies on the peasants, workers and women as well as on people's health and education. It takes China's development experience of three decades and examines the policies and practices not only in general but also as they unfolded in a rural area in coastal China.

Explaining the great success story of China's reforms is the main objective of this effort. The way the Communist Party of China (CPC) leadership used the State machinery and the market forces for its 'reform and open door' policy framework, and evolved appropriate strategies from time to time, provided the clue to this success. Testimonies to the success of China are the fast growth of its economy, a substantial rise in people's livelihood, a vast expansion of urban infrastructure and a rise of its prestige and influence in the world. With reforms, a set of problems emerged, many of which had serious dimensions. Inequality of income and wealth, regional disparities, urban–rural gap, distress migration from the countryside, environmental degradation as well as corruption and social alienation were some of the stark problems. While the CPC leader Jiang Zemin had focused on achieving economic growth, Hu Jintao and his successor Xi Jinping paid serious attention to tackling these problems to make development equitable and sustainable. My study shows that the compulsions of the success story of growth are so strong that it was difficult to change the main development path to achieve a desirable level of equity and sustainability. This is what I have described as a 'success trap' that China seems to be currently grappling with.

In China, however, there are welcome initiatives to promote a 'new development philosophy' that is not dictated by a high-growth obsession. Hu Jintao's 'scientific development outlook' and Xi Jinping's 'four comprehensives' advocating balanced, coordinated, open, green and shared development promise to have long-term, positive consequences. However, my argument is that the reform path of China is so grounded in the premises of the European Industrial Revolution and it has generated so strong sociopolitical forces at home that a major change in the development path is unlikely. But all indications point to a strong and prosperous China as a rising world power in the coming decades, trying to cope with the sociopolitical problems in its own way.

This is not a work of an economist but of a student of politics interested in development studies and socialist systems. Development is seen here as a multidimensional process of change, rather than economic growth. Hence, we look at the role of the State and the party, social groups and classes, and social development issues. I have shown how the policies initiated by Deng Xiaoping in a framework of building socialism with Chinese characteristics gradually led to the emergence of a capitalist society and economy, even though the CPC constantly reaffirms its commitment to socialism. To understand the process on the ground, we take up questions relating to grassroots governance, rural industrialization, rural–urban relationship, women's rights, and trends in public health and education. In all these respects, we examine how the development path had produced negative consequences for common people despite the great achievements made in terms of economic growth and infrastructure development.

This is not the product of a systematic survey. This is based on field visits over more than 30 years. During my visits routed through the Wuxi government, facilitated by the central authorities of China, I was accompanied by an interpreter-cum-guide. During short trips on my own—going to Wuxi every time I passed through Shanghai—I managed to visit places and meet officials and scholars independently. So while some pieces of information provided are systematic and official, some are my own impressions. Nevertheless, all of them were vetted against the official documents of the Wuxi government or the Central government publications as well as other reports and studies in China and abroad. The rural area that I chose to study became a suburban area and then an integral part of the metropolitan district of Wuxi. However, that process was typical all over China and was, therefore, a useful window to understand the overall reform process.

I have done detailed analysis of ideological and theoretical questions in contemporary China elsewhere. In this book, I wanted to closely examine the sociopolitical process at the grass-roots level while understanding the national development strategy. In course of this study, many intricacies of

China's multi-tier administration and complexities of the party–government –enterprise interaction became clear to me. I was able to appreciate the uniqueness of many institutional processes such as the urban–rural linkage, reallocation of household labour and accountability in the production process. I have tried to explain the policies, especially the innovations made in the course of the reforms, the difficulties that emerged in the process and the initiatives taken to overcome them.

Acknowledgements

Over the past 38 years of research on China's reforms and Wuxi, I have been receiving support from numerous scholars, officials and institutions in India, China, Europe and the USA. Here, I will be able to mention only a few of them.

Professor Ji Xianlin, an eminent Indologist of Peking University, had arranged my first visit to China in 1979, and his colleague, Professor Liu Guonan, accompanied me to many places, including Wuxi, for a month. They are no more. I shall be ever grateful for their help. Their successors Ma Jiali, Hu Shisheng, Sun Sihai, Wang Shuying and Jiang Jingkui have been of immense help during the past three decades.

The Indian Council of Social Science Research (ICSSR) has been the main source of support for the fieldwork done in China in 1979, 1985 and 1993. The Ford Foundation grant to the Institute of Chinese Studies (ICS) helped me to make research visits in 2002 and 2006. During the past three decades whenever I visited China to attend any conference, I made it a point to add a trip to Wuxi and gather up-to-date information. I also availed opportunities to visit Wuxi under the ICSSR exchange programme with the Chinese Academy of Social Sciences (CASS). The Institute of World Politics and Economy, Institute of Rural Development and Institute of Asia-Pacific Studies of CASS were generous with me, providing materials and arranging discussions and field visits. China Institute of Contemporary International Relations, Chinese People's Institute for World Affairs, China Institute of International Studies, China Reforms Forum, and National Development and Reforms Commission have been extremely cooperative helping me on many occasions.

Professor Wu Xian of CASS was with me when I stayed in a peasant's home in Hela in 1980. Professor Sima Jun of CASS Institute of World Economy and Politics had accompanied me to Wuxi in 1985 and shared his expert analysis of Chinese and Indian economic policies. I can never forget their help.

I had many long discussions with CASS economist Sun Beijun in the 1980s to understand the fast-changing socio-economic process in China. He had taken me to meet the great economist Chen Hansheng, discussion with whom contributed enormously to my understanding. I pay tribute to them.

Some eminent scholars in contemporary China with whom I have interacted closely and whose ideas have influenced my studies include sociologist Ma Rong of Peking University, political economist Wen Tiejun of Renmin University, rural policy expert Li Chenggui, demographer Cai Fang of CASS, Asian Cultural Studies expert Yao Chaocheng of Shenxi Finance and Economics University, intellectual historian Huang Chih-lien of Hong Kong Baptist University and political thinker Wang Hui of Tsinghua University.

Professors Wang Dehua of Shanghai Academy of Social Sciences and Zhou Xiaohong of Nanjing University have been of great help in facilitating my research in Wuxi.

I am most grateful to the Wuxi Municipal Foreign Affairs Office for always responding positively to my requests to visit, sometimes on a very short notice. The Jiangnan University and its earlier form, Wuxi Light Industry College, Vice-President Cherry Cai and her colleagues have been most gracious towards me throughout this period.

Hela Township leadership has been my greatest point of support, knowing fully well that I did not always agree with their policies. I especially thank Zhang Weinan for continuous help for decades. The family of Lao Mo and her husband Ding Maoshen who had hosted me in their home in 1980 and whom I had visited many times later, including a visit to their new high-rise apartment building, shaped my understanding of changes taking place in China.

My research was mainly conducted at the University of Delhi and ICS where colleagues were of constant help, facilitating, monitoring and complaining about the delay in finalizing the book. I record my gratitude to the late Professor V. P. Dutt for his encouragement, support and trust in my work. My friends late Giri Deshingkar, Mira Sinha-Bhattacharjea and G. P. Deshpande contributed enormously to the making of my academic life including this work. As my teachers, colleagues and friends, Tan Chung and Huang Ishu have had great influence on my thinking. ICS Chairperson Patricia Uberoi read a draft of this work some time back and had given extremely valuable suggestions. She had also accompanied me to Wuxi on one trip. Her support has been invaluable. ICS colleagues C. V. Ranganathan, Vinod Khanna, Kishan Rana, Ravi Bhoothalingam, Sreemati Chakrabarti, Sabaree Mitra, Hemant Adlakha, Brij Tankha, M. V. Rappai and Virendra Verma have been constant source of encouragement all these years. Madhavi Thampi as editor, *China Report*, gave useful comments on the women chapter (Chapter 8) before publishing an earlier version. Alka Acharya as Director, ICS, took special steps to help me with research assistance in the final stage of the work. ICS has emerged as an excellent place of collective academic endeavour in India.

I have been a beneficiary of it. I am most grateful to its director, faculty and staff, both present and past.

I was lucky to have excellent research assistants, many of whom are established scholars today. I remember the contribution made by Professors Arttatrana Nayak, Kamal Sheel, Sreemati Chakrabarti and Gopa Joshi at early stages of my research. I thank Ritu Aggarwal and Anurag Mohanty for their sustained help. I also recall the able assistance of Sanjeev Kumar. Madhusudan Chaube continues to be a great help in both Delhi and Beijing.

The research scholar whose assistance during the past three years helped me to actually complete the manuscript is Bhim Subba from University of Delhi's Department of East Asian Studies, currently ICS–Harvard-Yenjing doctoral fellow. I cannot adequately express my thanks to him.

Over the years, I have done research on aspects of this book in several different institutions—University of Oxford (1988), International Institute for Asian Studies, Amsterdam (1990), Center for Chinese Studies, University of California, Los Angeles (1998, 2001 and 2003), Orfalea Center for Global and International Studies, University of California, Santa Barbara, (2007–11), India China Institute, New School of Social Research, New York (2014). I particularly remember the late UCLA Professor Richard Baum who was very excited about my Wuxi research and we fruitfully worked together on grass-roots politics in China and India. My old friends, famous scholars Mark Selden at Cornell and Kjeld-Erik Broadsgaard in Copenhagen, have extended their valuable support whenever I needed.

The final shape to this work was given at the Council for Social Development. I am grateful to CSD President Professor Muchkund Dubey for his many insightful suggestions and his constant prodding to complete this work. Professor K. B. Saxena always set the high intellectual and political standards which put me on guard. The secretarial assistance of Suraj Pal was helpful. I thank colleagues and staff of the CSD for their consistent support.

Eminent scholars Mark Juergensmeyer and Sucheng Chan, my friends from Berkeley days (the late 1960s), and the Odia poet and social activist Rabindranath Sahoo, my friend from Ravenshaw days (the late 1950s) have been constant inspirations for all my work. With this book in hand, I can now face them better.

My visits to Wuxi accidentally brought together Che Abhijit Sahoo and Mao Wenjun who eventually set up a happy family and a flourishing business in India and China. Wenjun's parents besides being great hosts also helped me in understanding Chinese society much better than I could have done otherwise. I thank her brother Mao Wenfei who accompanied me to Wuxi a few times.

The SAGE team that took minute care at every stage to process this work deserve my sincere thanks.

I owe much gratitude to the two anonymous reviewers for their detailed comments and suggestions which helped me enormously to prepare the final manuscript.

In June 1979, Bidyut, our children Berkeley Sanjay and Jinee Lokaneeta, and I made our first visit to China and enjoyed the beauty of Wuxi. Bidyut was also with me in 2016 and we experienced the momentous transformation. In recent years, Berkeley and Brinda, Jinee and Sangay, and our granddaughters Adya and Raeva were asking impatiently about the conclusion of the familiar China reform book which was going on and on. I am pleased to end their anxiety.

My late father Bichitrananda Mohanty whose birth centenary we are observing this year saw this work in progress with great interest and did not mind being left alone often at home. I remember him with gratitude.

Thank you all.

Of course, there are many limitations and gaps in this work for which none else but I am responsible.

Manoranjan Mohanty

1

Introduction

The Story of China's Reforms

People in contemporary China constantly talk of 'two centenaries'—the centenary of the founding of the Communist Party of China (CPC) in 2021 and of the founding of the People's Republic of China (PRC) in 2049. These are not just emotive ideas for nationalist mobilization as would seem from the slogan of realizing the 'Chinese dream of national rejuvenation' given by Xi Jinping at the start of his term. They represented concrete economic and social goals for the particular stages of China's transformation. The goal set for 2020 by the CPC leadership in 2002 was to build 'a moderately well-off society in all respects' by doubling the 2010 per capita income. By the middle of the twenty-first century, China aspired to become a medium-level developed country. These goals link up the goals of the Chinese revolution and Mao Zedong's vision with the visionary agenda of reforms initiated by Deng Xiaoping and followed by his successors, Jiang Zemin, Hu Jintao and Xi Jinping. Domestic and international initiatives of Xi Jinping throughout his regime were specifically geared towards achieving China's transformation and fulfilling the goals of the 'two centenaries'. My effort in this book is to understand the nature of the transformation since the launching of the reforms and assess its implications.

The Chinese economic reforms have been regarded as a great success story and the whole world is talking about the 'rise of China'. China became the world's second largest economy after the USA in 2010. The relative decline in China's rate of growth since 2012 from double digits to 6–8 per cent has been accepted as a 'new normal' by the Xi Jinping regime to pursue structural reforms and achieve goals of equity and sustainability. Chinese people themselves celebrate this experience as 'China's peaceful development', 'new Long March' and 'Second Revolution'. Yet, China's fourth-generation leadership led by Hu Jintao and fifth-generation leader Xi Jinping, even while upholding the glorious record of the overall strategy of 'reforms and open door', have tried to shift the focus of the policies to tackling the problems that have arisen in the course of the reforms. This book analyses the remarkable successes achieved in the course of the reforms and the problems that this development path has generated. Xi Jinping's predecessor Hu Jintao's stress on following a 'scientific outlook on development', solving the problem of 'five imbalances' (between urban and rural, coastal and western, economic and social development, ecology and economy, and domestic and international), 'enhancing the governing capacity of the CPC' and above all the central guiding objective announced in 2006 of building 'a harmonious society' were all part of the new perspective. Acknowledging the seriousness of the 'three rural problems' in contemporary China and announcing a programme of 'building a new socialist countryside' in 2006 was the leadership's frank admission of the magnitude of problems despite the remarkable economic achievements during the previous three decades. As a response to this accumulated crisis, despite major successes, the CPC announced its programme of promoting a new outlook of 'scientific development' at the Seventeenth Party Congress in 2007. The CPC's Eighteenth Party Congress in November 2012 made this point even clearer. It not only celebrated the achievements of the 'glorious decade' of the Hu Jintao–Wen Jiabao leadership but also admitted serious problems facing China on many fronts.[1] Xi Jinping, as the CPC general secretary and China's president, has not only acknowledged the major achievements of the reform period but also admitted serious challenges while putting forth his agenda. During his first term as the CPC leader, he took a number of initiatives to consolidate the achievements of the previous decades and address many challenges confronting China at home and abroad. His ideas formulated in the course of the Third Plenum of the CPC Central Committee (CC) in 2013 when the key decision was made to deepen market reforms until the Sixth Plenum in 2016 when his core position as the leader was formally affirmed had come to be articulated as the 'four comprehensives'.[2] That Xi was determined to address the problem of corruption and social alienation along with the economic problems became even more pronounced as he continued to establish his firm leadership in all the major State, party, economic and military institutions and launched the famous anti-corruption campaign to catch both 'tigers and flies'. His many global and regional initiatives including the One Belt, One Road and Asian Infrastructure Investment Bank (AIIB), active role in BRICS, steady promotion of economic globalization are meant to enhance China's external influence.

I have been a witness to this great transformation during the past three decades and more. Since my first visit in 1979, I have closely watched the reforms process, especially the changes in rural areas. Through my periodic trips to Wuxi in Jiangsu Province in the eastern coastal region and extensive interviews in the field and by visiting other areas including some less developed regions, I have tried to understand the nature of this success story. I wish to tell the success story recounting the tremendous improvements in people's livelihood and the vastly developed infrastructure. The new pride and self-confidence that the Chinese middle classes as well as common people emit due to the achievements of the reform period are indeed remarkable. But, I will also identify, without underestimating the successes, the problems, some rather serious, which have arisen in the course of the reforms. I would like to point out that the reforms process has raised the living standards of the Chinese, enormously improved urban infrastructure, vastly increased the industrial and military power of China and secured a pride of place for the country in the world community. But, at the same time, it has produced its own complex dynamics consisting of achievements as well as problems. Its own compulsions make it extremely difficult for the Chinese leaders to depart from the already stabilized path of development, which cannot be easily altered. In other words, the reforms strategy has produced what I would like to call a 'success trap'. By about 2006, I was convinced that China had landed itself in such a situation, and the political leadership, intellectuals, cadres and many citizens in China that I interacted with were already talking about these problems. The common refrain was: 'The party did not know what to do about the problems!' That was a clear indication of a 'trap'—a difficult situation out of which it was not easy to get out. My subsequent visits to China, even more frequently than before, have confirmed this understanding. And that nuanced assessment of China's development experience—one by a student of politics—I wish to present in this book.

At a time when many developing countries are enthusiastically announcing their desire to emulate the Chinese reforms model, it is very important to grasp the totality of the Chinese experience—both the success story and the success trap. Indian leaders, who launched economic reforms in 1991, constantly referred to the Chinese experience to justify their policies of liberalization, privatization and globalization. Indian politicians, corporate chiefs, bureaucrats, professionals and the media have been so excited by the success of China's reforms that for every policy, they constantly urged Indian people to emulate China. The finance minister of the United Progressive Alliance (UPA led by the Congress party) government P. Chidambaram often cited the Chinese example in many matters. Ever since the National Democratic Alliance (NDA led by the Bharatiya Janata Party [BJP]) came to power in 2014 with Prime Minister Narendra Modi as the leader, China was the reference point for India's goal of achieving high growth rate. The Western advocates of globalization constantly cited the Chinese reforms as vindication of their approach to development and asked for even faster and deeper reforms. In this situation, it was very important to read the whole story including the experience of the pre-reform period under Mao in a fresh perspective, so that policy-makers everywhere can avoid some of the pitfalls of the Chinese experience while learning many positive, valuable lessons. Perhaps the world can appreciate the nature of the new policies initiated in China after 2002 first by the Hu Jintao regime and later by the Xi Jinping leadership which, in my opinion, frankly acknowledged and squarely addressed the problems. There was greater awareness of the problems and stronger initiatives undertaken. But there was enough evidence to show that China still remained in the 'success trap'—enjoying many successes and experiencing many problems. The several 'new normals' including the slower rate of growth and the 'four comprehensives' were Xi's way of addressing critical problems. These bold steps did present new possibilities. Indeed, by 2021, China would be a stronger and more prosperous country and by 2049, a relatively developed and powerful country in the world. But whether the civilizational and sociopolitical goals set out in the course of revolution and reform would be achieved is an open question. As I argue in this book, despite the bold and innovative policy changes, in both reform objectives and the role of the party and government agencies which formulated, adopted and implemented them on the ground, the structural-political nature of the development path adopted by China during the reform period was such that they had inherent limitations leading to the success trap.

We can, thus, restore some balance in the world development discourse on various dimensions of development theory and address the issues of justice, equity, participation and sustainability in building a better society while not ignoring the nature and magnitude of economic growth that can foster them.

There are three parts of the argument presented here. One is to recognize the many achievements of China in the course of the reform policies. Second is to acknowledge the serious problems that the people and the regime confront. But, the third and equally important argument is the main concern of this book. That is to point out the reasons as to why efforts to tackle the problems while pursuing this path continued to face obstacles. These three parts together provide some lessons for development theory. The study showed that the structural logic of the development path was too powerful to allow the policy initiatives to successfully address problems such as inequality and un-sustainability. This is the story that unfolds in my narrative of China's reforms both seen from a rural, suburban grass-roots vantage point and from seeing China as a whole.

This is not a comprehensive account of China's economy, society or polity, though it may present a certain dynamic picture of them during the reform period. It is a study of

1. the Chinese development path after 1978,
2. the agencies—the party and the State—which formulated, implemented and monitored it and
3. some select spheres of the operation of the strategy related to workers in rural enterprises, women, social sector and the changed profile of villages.

The study of these aspects draws from my fieldwork in Wuxi and analysis of national-level reports, documents and studies. The aim is to propose an argument about the development path, its power and its limitations. As I point out throughout the book and present in the concluding chapter, it not only presents an assessment of the Chinese development path but also presents a critical perspective on the global development history since the European Industrial Revolution. The decoding of socialism with Chinese characteristics—State-guided market economy with many unique features— is the running theme of this work.

Presented as a narrative of a 'success story and a success trap', the study as a whole and each chapter keep three sets of questions in mind:

1. Questions raised in contemporary *development theory* at a time when globalization and neoliberalism have confronted crises, and new challenges and civilizational issues are raised about the dominant development path all over the world.
2. Questions raised by contemporary students of *politics* when preoccupation with governance has relegated issues of power and freedom to the background and there is a resurgence of questions of freedom, equality and justice all around us.
3. Questions in contemporary *Marxism* when triumphant claims of capitalism have been challenged by new discourses on socialism in the twenty-first century, aiming at eliminating class, caste, gender, ethnic, racial and religious domination; establishing new relations of harmony between humans and nature; and practising democracy at all levels.

The Success Story

'Rise of China' became the talk of the world press when Goldman Sachs predicted in 2003 that China would surpass the USA in gross domestic product (GDP) by 2041 to become the largest economy of the world, emerging as the second largest by 2016.[3] (Actually, China beat the forecast by becoming the second largest economy in 2010.) In its report entitled *Dancing with Giants: China, India and the Global Economy*, the World Bank came out with scenarios of continuing high growth rate of China whose growth they described as the 'largest growth "surprise" ever experienced in the world economy' which would have major impact on the world economy.[4] Chinese economy had grown, on an average, at the annual rate of over 9 per cent during the 20-year period, 1995–2005—an experience unparalleled in world history. The per capita income of the Chinese in 2001 crossed the US$1,000 mark which was more than four times of what it was in 1980, thus fulfilling the target fixed by Deng Xiaoping, the architect of China's reforms. The target of doubling the per capita income to US$2,000 in 10 years was achieved in 2010 when it reached US$2,500 (at current prices US$4,514) and of crossing the US$5,000 mark by 2014 (at current prices US$7,593). Thus, there were many indicators of the tremendous measure of economic success achieved by China (Table 1.1). This success was symbolized by the grand scale of the hosting of the 2008 Olympics in Beijing and Shanghai Expo in 2010. The way China coped with the global financial crisis in 2008 by introducing a huge stimulus package amounting to US$586 billion or RMB4 trillion was yet another sign of China's ability to handle difficult economic emergencies. Meeting the challenge of severe acute respiratory syndrome (SARS) epidemic in 2003 and effectively responding to the massive losses of humans and property in the Wenchuan earthquake in 2008 and many such accomplishments also showed the performance capabilities of a political and administrative leadership in China.

In fact, the Chinese themselves consciously talked about 'rise of China'. Chinese theoretician Zheng Bijian initiated the discourse on 'peaceful rise of China' in 2003, stressing the fact that the economic growth, increase in living standards and the growing prestige of China in world forums had been accomplished through peaceful development of China during the reforms period.[5] Soon the discourse acquired widespread attention in China and abroad. The formulation was slightly altered to talk about China's peaceful 'development' (*fazhan*) rather than 'rise' (*qilai*), thus avoiding the threatening connotation of 'rise of a big power'. But, clearly, there was an acknowledgement of the fact that after over a century of struggle against domination

Table 1.1:
Human development indicators: China, India and the USA

	China	*India*	*USA*
Human development index (country rank)			
2000	87	115	6
2005	81	128	12
2010	89	119	4
2015	90	131	10
Human development index (trends)			
1975	0.527	0.413	0.868
1980	0.407	0.345	0.843
1990	0.495	0.410	0.878
2000	0.590	0.463	0.907
2005	0.637	0.507	0.923
2010	0.689	0.547	0.934
2015	0.738	0.624	0.920
Life expectancy at birth (years)			
1970–75	63.2	50.7	71.5
2005	71.9	62.9	77.4
2010	73.5	64.4	79.6
2015	76	68.3	79.2
Infant mortality rate per thousand ('0000) live births			
1970	85	127	20
2000	32	69	7
2005	23	56	6
2010	16	50	7
2015	9.2	37.9	5.6
Under-five mortality rate			
1970	120	202	26
2000	40	96	8
2005	27	74	7
2010	18	63	8
2015	10.7	47.7	6.5
2004 GDP (US$ billion)	1,931.7	691.2	11,711.8
2011 (2005 PPP in US$)	9,970.6	3,976.5	13,238.3
2013 (2011 PPP in US$ billion)	15,643.2	6,558.7	16,230.2

(Table 1.1 Continued)

(Table 1.1 Continued)

	China	India	USA
GDP per capita (PPP in US$)			
2005	6,757	3,452	41,810
2009	6,828	3,296	45,989
2011 (2005 PPP in US$)	7,418	3,203	42,486
2013 (2011 PPP in US$)	11,525	5,238	51,509
Annual growth rate (GDP %)			
1975–2005	8.4	3.4	2
1990–2005	8.8	4.2	2.5
2008–12	9.3	6.9	1.7
Human poverty index rank (2006)	26	55	16
Population below income poverty line (%)			
1900–2003 (PPP US$1)	16.6	34.7	—
2000–09 (PPP US$1.25)	15.9	41.6	—
2002–11 (PPP US$1.25)	13.1	32.7	—
National poverty line (%)			
1990–2003 (PPP US$1)	4.6	28.6	—
2000–09 (PPP US$1.25)	2.8	27.5	—
2002–12 (PPP US$1.25)	2.8	29.8	—
Improved sanitation facilities (% of population access)[a]			
1990	47.5	16.3	99.5
2005	64.9	30.6	99.8
2010	70.8	35.5	99.9
2015	76.5	39.6	100
Population undernourished (%)[a]			
1991	24	23.7	—
2005	15.6	21.2	—
2010	12.5	15.7	—
2015	9	15	—

Sources: UNDP, *Human Development Report* (New York, NY: Palgrave Macmillan, 2006, 2007–08, 2010, 2011); UNDP, *Human Development Report* (New Delhi: Academic Foundation, 2013, 2014, 2015, 2016); IMF, *World Economic Outlook Database*, April 2011, 2012, http://www.imf.org/external/pubs/ft/weo/2012/01/weodata/index.aspx (accessed on 23 September 2012).

Note: [a]World Bank, *World Development Indicators*, 2012, 2014, 2015 (updated on 16 February 2017).

and humiliation by the West, China had emerged as a world power.[6] In June 2013, when Chinese President Xi Jinping met US President Obama in California, they jointly proclaimed a framework statement on a new way of handling relations among great powers in the twenty-first century, which was reiterated during Obama's visit to China in November 2014. That China figured as the main challenger to the USA in economic and security spheres became clear from the many statements and exchanges between US President Donald Trump and Chinese President Xi Jinping.

The economic indicators adequately confirmed the scale of achievements. People's livelihood measured in per capita income has grown substantially (Table 1.1). Industrial production has grown continuously at varying but high rates since 1995. By 2005, China was world's number one producer of many industrial products, including steel, coal, electricity, cement, chemical fibre, woven cotton fabrics and television sets, besides being the leading producer of sugar, cereals, meat, tea and fruits. The human development indicators have shown remarkable improvement. Even though the country's rank for the Human Development Index has fluctuated, the index itself has registered a rising trend (Table 1.1). Life expectancy and literacy have improved tremendously and there is a significant decline in poverty as well as infant mortality.[7] On the US$1-a-day criterion on measuring poverty, the number had fallen from an estimated 400 million in 1980 to about 82 million in 2014, according to official figures.[8] It declined further to 43 million in 2016 and as announced by Premier Li Keqiang at the Twelfth National People's Congress (NPC), the goal was to lift all of them above the poverty line by 2020.[9] The volume of foreign trade increased several fold. China experienced a large trade surplus in the fourth decade of the reforms. The Chinese foreign exchange reserve reached US$1,000 billion in 2005 and has continued to reach new heights—nearly US$3,500 billion in 2015 year-end (Table 1.2). There were many other indicators of China's economic success (see Tables 1.1 and 1.2).

Visitors to China cannot miss the great change that has taken place during the past four decades. The Shanghai I first visited in 1979 was so different from what stood on the ground in 2006 and in 2016. I remember the vast agricultural fields of Pudong that I drove through in the 1980s. In 1987, the planning office in Pudong showed me a video of their future city. In 2004, when I attended the first World Congress of China Studies in the Convention Hall in Pudong facing the Jinmao Tower, the prevailing feeling of excitement all around over the great transformation that had taken place was boundless. The momentous changes that have taken place in the city of Wuxi and its villages including the houses and living amenities of the people are absolutely amazing. The peasant household which had hosted me in

Table 1.2:
China's vital statistics: 2008–15

Categories	2008	2009	2010	2011	2015
GDP (100 million yuan)	314,045	340,903	401,513	473,104	685,505
Growth rates (%)	9.6	9.2	10.4	9.3	6.9
Urban employed people (10,000 people)	32,103	33,322	34,687	37,102	40,410
Year-end foreign exchange reserves (100 million US$)	19,460	23,992	28,473	38,811	34,231.5
Growth rates (%)	27.3	23.3	18.7	11.7	−13.66
Agriculture (output of grains: 10,000 tons)	52,871	53,082	54,648	57,121	62,912
Growth rates (%)	5.4	0.4	2.9	4.5	2.37
Industrial value added (100 million yuan)	130,260	135,240	160,722	188,470	236,506
Growth rates (%)	9.9	8.7	12.1	10.4	1.13
Imports (100 million US$)	11,326	10,059	13,962	17,435	16,795.4
Exports (100 million US$)	14,307	12,016	15,778	18,984	22,734.7
New entrants into education (10,000)					
General tertiary education	608	640	662	682	737
Secondary vocational education	812	869	870	814	601
Senior secondary education	837	830	836	851	796
R&D investment (100 million yuan)	4,616	5,802	7,063	8,687	14,220
Medical technical workers (10,000 people)	517	554	588	620	800
Per-capita disposable income					
Rural (yuan)	4,761	5,153	5,919	6,977	11,421
(%)	(8)	(8.5)	(10.9)	(11.4)	(11.2)
Urban (yuan)	15,781	17,175	19,109	21,810	31,194
(%)	(8.4)	(9.8)	(7.8)	(8.4)	(9)
Rate of phone subscribers (100 people %)					
Year-end no. of fixed phone subscribers	25.76	23.62	21.05	21.26	16.80
Year-end no. of mobile phone subscribers	48.53	56.27	64.36	73.55	92.49

Sources: National Bureau of Statistics of China, 'Statistical Communiqué of the People's Republic of China on the 2012 National Economic and Social Development', 22 February 2013. Available at: http://www.stats.gov.cn/english/newsevents/201302/t20130222_26962.html (accessed on 2 June 2017); National Bureau of Statistics of China, 'Statistical Communiqué of the People's Republic of China on the 2013 National Economic and Social Development', 24 February 2014. Available at: http://www.stats.gov.cn/english/PressRelease/201402/t20140224_515103.html (accessed on 2 June 2017); National Bureau of Statistics of China, 'National Data'. Available at: http://data.stats.gov.cn/english/easyquery.htm?cn=C01 (accessed on 17 February 2017). Also www.safe.gov.cn/wpf/portal/english/Data/Forex/ForeignExchangeReserves (accessed on 22 July 2017).

Hela village of Wuxi in 1980 was now dispersed into separate family units and lived in modern comforts in three apartments in the tall, multi-storeyed structures that stood on the village ground on the outskirts of the city. That is the success story of China's reforms measured in universally accepted economic and social indicators. But behind these impressive statistics, there were trends which reveal other aspects.

The Problems

Let us see how the then CPC General Secretary Hu Jintao described the problems facing China in November 2012 in his political report to the Eighteenth Party Congress:

> Unbalanced, uncoordinated and unsustainable development remains a big problem.... The development gap between urban and rural areas and between regions is still large, and so are income disparities. Social problems have increased markedly. There are many problems affecting people's immediate interests in education, employment, social security, health care, housing, the ecological environment, food and drug safety, workplace safety, public security, law enforcement, administration of justice, etc.... Some sectors are prone to corruption and other misconduct, and the fight against corruption remains a serious challenge for us. We must take these difficulties and problems very seriously and work harder to resolve them.[10]

Five years later, though many of these issues had been addressed through concrete policies, as Premier Li Keqiang put it in his Report on the Work of the Government to the Twelfth NPC in March 2017, there were 'many problems and challenges' China faced in pursuing economic and social development. After listing economic problems, he went on to mention the following:

> Environmental pollution remains grave, in particular, some areas are frequently hit by heavy smog.... There are also problems causing public concern in housing, education, healthcare, elderly care, food and drug safety, and income distribution. It is distressing that there were some major accidents in the coalmining, construction and transportation sectors.[11]

While the above is an accurate account of the main problems facing China after nearly four decades of reforms, some concrete examples would give an indication of many of them. In January 2013, people of Beijing city suffered from such an intense smog that they were advised to stay home for three days.

This has become a regular feature. In January 2017, schools were closed for three days for the same reason. In 2009, the Taihu Lake had been polluted with so much algae due to the flow of the waste from the industries surrounding the lake that water supply to the Wuxi city and the neighbouring towns was suspended for nearly a fortnight. The people in this famed region of industrial prosperity in the Yangtze River Delta were supplied drinking water from mobile tanks. The environmental pollution in China has many indicators with China having surpassed the USA as the world's largest emitter of carbon dioxide. The frequent accidents in the coal mines indicate the enormous dependence on fossil fuel for the high rate of industrial growth.

The crisis in the countryside has continued to deepen despite many interventions during the Hu-Wen decade and the decisions under Xi Jinping. It has forced rural citizens to migrate to cities where they are not entitled to the normal health, education and housing amenities that are available to the city people, because they still hold the *hukou* (residence registration) in their village. The decision by the government in 2016 to allow intermediate cities to provide *hukou* facilities has somewhat relaxed this difficult situation. For 2017, the plan was to provide urban residency status to 13 million people. In a country where at least 300 million rural migrants worked in the cities, this was too small a step. In the countryside, health, education and welfare infrastructure which had been provided by the collective and the State during the commune period, as also financed from the income from rural enterprises in the first two decades of the reforms, have shrunk considerably in the absence of adequate financing. No doubt, the countryside has seen vast improvement not only in infrastructure but also in health, education and welfare facilities. However, there is a paradoxical situation in the countryside. The rural rich have access to high-quality hospitals and schools in a nearby city. Due to the strategy of encouraging private sector in health and education which is now in full swing, the well-to-do avail good facilities in social sector, while the same is not easily available to the common people in both cities and villages. The neoliberal policy to offer subsidized health insurance to rural people was grossly inadequate. Despite many notable achievements in health and education spheres, growing inequality in access and the unsatisfactory conditions in the public institutions continued to trouble the common people.

On the political front, not only the incidents of protest have multiplied, but the curbs on civil liberty activities also remain stringent. Tensions in the regions inhabited by minority nationalities have taken the form of violent incidents involving minorities which are promptly suppressed by the security forces. Xinjiang province has witnessed major upsurges of violent protests spreading into other parts of China in the recent years. Xi Jinping's call to build 'an iron wall against terrorism' in Xinjiang in 2017 indicated the seriousness of the situation. Incidents of self-immolation by Tibetans protesting against Chinese domination had crossed 100 in 2012.[12] The Chinese government attributed these occurrences to incitement from abroad, forces loyal to Dalai Lama in the case of the Tibetan incidents. Even though both the minority provinces have experienced a great deal of economic development, still people's alienation continues to grow due to lack of political autonomy.

Thus, despite all the accounts of achievements, there is a deep concern in contemporary China about a number of problems which afflict China even after nearly four decades of success with economic reforms. The most evident problem is the widespread social anxiety which grips the bulk of the population.[13] The effects of reforms are so disparate that a lot of people feel alienated as they perceive others having gained far more than them. Inequality among households and groups has been accentuated to such an extent that China today is one of the most unequal societies of the world (Table 1.3).[14] Contrast this with the situation less than four decades ago when it was one of the most egalitarian societies in history. In 1982, the Gini coefficient of China was 0.30 and it became 0.49 in 2008, though showing some improvement in the situation with 0.47 in 2012[15] and also 0.46 in 2014. Regional disparity both among provinces and between regions within provinces was growing steadily over the years. The Human Development Index for the coastal provinces is five times that of the western provinces.[16] The rural–urban differences in income and social opportunities continue to grow.[17]

Rural reforms of the 1980s which were once described as the 'third revolution in China's countryside'[18] had been neglected to such an extent in the 1990s that in 2003 when Wen Jiabao took over as premier, he described the 'three rural problems' (*san nong wenti*) as the principal challenge. These referred to low productivity in agriculture, low income of peasants and backward infrastructure in the countryside. Peasant income had been declining for four consecutive years since 1997 and the income gap between urban and rural residents had further widened to 3.4:1, and if the facilities that urban residents enjoyed were taken into consideration, the gap would be as high as 6:1. China's rural population which constituted 70 per cent of the total accounted for less than 25 per cent of China's domestic consumption.[19] The pace of urbanization has been accelerated and the urban population accounted for over 51 per cent according to the 2010 Census. But, the basic nature of this disparity remained.

Incidences of mass protest actions continued to rise. The number was 52,000 as reported officially to the NPC in 2003 rising to 76,000 in 2004 and 87,000 in 2005.[20] In 2010, unofficial yet uncontested number of mass incidents stood at 180,000. Of these, more than two-thirds took place in the countryside, mostly involving takeover of farmland for industrial purposes. There were many instances of violent confrontation between villagers and

Table 1.3:

Inequality in China, India and the USA

Countries	Survey Year	Share of Income or Expenditure Poorest 10%	Share of Income or Expenditure Poorest 20%	Share of Income or Expenditure Richest 20%	Share of Income or Expenditure Richest 10%	Gini Index
China	2001	1.8	4.7	50	33.1	44.7
	2005	1.8	5	47.9	32	42.5
	2012[a]	2.05	—	—	31.43	42.16
	2014	—	—	—	37.2[b]	0.469[c,d]
India	1999–2000	3.9	8.9	43.3	28.5	32.5
	2005	3.8	8.6	42.4	28.3	33.4
	2011[a]	3.56	8.26	43.97	29.77	35.1
	2014	—	—	—	—	33.6
USA	2000	1.9	5.4	45.8	29.9	40.46
	2010[a]	1.62	—	—	29.4	40.46
	2014[e]	1.6	5.2	45.1	29.2	0.394[c]

Sources: UNDP, *Human Development Report* (2006, 2010, 2011, 2013, 2015); IMF, *World Development Indicators*, 2012, 2013; OECD, 'Income Distribution and Poverty', 2014.

Notes: [a]Knoema, 'World Data Atlas: World and Regional Statistics, National Data, Maps, Rankings'. Available at: https://knoema.com/atlas (accessed on 3 March 2017).
[b]World Wealth and Income Database, 'Income Inequality, China, 1978–2015'. Available at: http://wid.world/country/china/ (accessed on 5 March 2017).
[c]Gini coefficient.
[d]Hazrat Hassan, 'The Gap Between China's Rich and Poor is Growing', Foreign Policy News, 17 May 2016. Available at: http://foreignpolicynews.org/2016/05/17/gap-chinas-rich-poor-growing/ (accessed on 3 March 2017).
[e]OECD, 'Income Inequality Remains High in the Face of Weak Recovery', 24 November 2016. Available at: http://www.oecd.org/social/OECD2016-Income-Inequality-Update.pdf (accessed on 3 March 2017).

local government or entrepreneurs or their agents in 2005 and 2006 that were reported worldwide.[21] In 2011, the intensity of such incidents was symbolized by cases such as the farmers' protest in Wukan in Guangzhou. Several studies conducted by the CPC organs in 2012 showed that while 60 per cent of the incidents arose out of land takeover issues, nearly 20 per cent of the cases related to environmental degradation, another 20 per cent to labour demands and the rest 10 per cent to corruption.[22]

The special problems faced by women, farmers, workers, ethnic minorities and the youth are indicators of the magnitude of the problems faced by contemporary China. Women's employment trends are unsteady and empowerment process feeble, while many new burdens and pressures currently grip them.[23] Farmers who had laid down the foundation of the reforms in the early

1980s and benefited greatly from them became the main losers in the 1990s and thereafter. The large-scale rural migration to the cities has produced a class of urban people who have lost their rural facilities and are not entitled to urban-resident status. In 2003, for example, as many as 189 million urban residents out of an estimated 524 million did not have the urban *hukou*. In other words, 36.068 per cent rural people who had become migrants had no access to urban amenities.[24] Workers' unrest is now a common occurrence in China. Not only that the large numbers of the retrenched workers who are seeking employment are restive, but even the serving workers in various industries find the working conditions and the wages unacceptable. China's manufacturing success that delivers cheap products throughout the world has meant continuation of 'sweatshop' labour—most of whom are women from backward regions.[25] Xi Jinping regime's focus on structural transformation of the economy by moving fast towards producing for the domestic market and manufacturing high-quality products under the innovation-driven 'Make in China 2025' programme had shown positive results in expanding the service sector and earning global reputation; but it did not address issues of inequality, unemployment and distress migration at least in the short run.

Ethnic minorities live mostly in the western region where special development programmes have been launched in the recent years. But, that does not meet the expectations of the 55 minority nationalities who occupy nearly 60 per cent of the area of PRC, even though they constitute only about 8 per cent of the population. Economic development, cultural autonomy and political power are the core of their demands.[26] The youth was theoretically the most benefited by the enormous modern opportunities generated by reforms and the open door. They availed the vastly expanded educational opportunities, went abroad and enjoyed the new liberal cultural milieu. Many foreign-trained experts were welcomed back to the country with plump jobs and generous facilities. But, the youth as a whole, which is the product of a pampered childhood of one-child families—relaxed in 2016—competitive economy and open-door environment in the era of globalization reacts sharply to the situation of unemployment and urban inconveniences. They may not be rebellious but they manifest discontent openly.[27]

These issues of social dissatisfaction acquire further seriousness when they are seen against the backdrop of the environmental challenge that China faced as a result of the kind of industrial development that went on during the reforms period. Its rate of energy consumption (GDP per unit of energy) grew from 1.3 in 1980 to 5.7 in 2014, and per capita carbon dioxide emission rose from 1.5 tons in 1980 to 7.5 tons in 2013 (Table 1.4). In 2003, China accounted for 16.3 per cent of the world's emissions, second to the USA, which was responsible for 23 per cent. China surpassed the USA in 2010 as

Table 1.4:
Energy and environment

	China	India	USA
GDP per unit of energy use (PPP US$ per kg of oil equivalent) 2011 constant			
1980	1.3[a]	3.3[a]	2.8[a]
1990	2	5	4.8
2000	4.1	6	5.7
2010	4.8	7.8	6.8
2014	5.7	8.4	7.8
Carbon dioxide emission (per capita tons)			
1980	1.5	0.5	20.1
1990	2.1	0.7	19.2
2000	2.7	1	20.2
2010	6.6	1.4	17.5
2013	7.5	1.59	16.4
Share of world total of carbon dioxide emissions			
2003	16.5	5.1	23
2011[b]	28	6	16
Greenhouse gas emissions per capita (tons of carbon dioxide equivalent)			
2005	1.5	0.7	3.7
2010	1.38[c]	1.38	18
Total greenhouse gas emissions (million tons)			
2008	6,803	1,473.73	5,833.13
2009	7,710.50	1,602.12	5,424.53
2010	9,679.3	2,432.1	6,668.8

Sources: UNDP, *Human Development Report* (2006, 2010, 2011, 2013); World Bank Database. Available at: http://data.worldbank.org/indicator/EG.GDP.PUSE.KO.PP.KD (accessed on 15 June 2017).

Notes: [a]GDP per unit of energy use (2000 PPP US$ per kg of oil equivalent) and others are constant 2011 PPP (updated on 16 February 2017)

[b]EPA, 'Global Greenhouse Gas Emissions Data'. Available at: https://www.epa.gov/ghgemissions/global-greenhouse-gas-emissions-data (accessed on 16 February 2017).

[c]*The Guardian*, 'World Carbon dioxide Emissions Data by Country: China Speeds Ahead of the Rest', *The Guardian*, 31 January 2011. Available at: https://www.theguardian.com/news/datablog/2011/jan/31/world-carbon-dioxide-emissions-country-data-co2#data (accessed on 27 April 2014).

the world's number one emitter. Indeed, the Chinese leadership was acutely aware of the magnitude of the environmental crisis and the Eleventh Five-year Plan (FYP) had a specific stipulation of reducing energy use by 20 per cent for every unit of production and meeting strict environmental standards. The same efforts were built into the Twelfth Plan as well beginning in 2011. In fact, Hu Jintao's 'Scientific Outlook on Development' clearly focused on sustainable development together with social justice. The Thirteenth Plan that came into force in 2016 also had a similar orientation. Premier Li Keqiang at the Twelfth NPC in March 2017 informed that the goal for the next year was to reduce energy consumption per unit of GDP by at least 3.4 per cent besides many other environmental measures. Yet, the Chinese government did not seem to be excessively faulted on the environmental issue so as to drastically alter its development strategy for achieving economic growth.[28]

The experience of rapid economic growth has created a new value situation in the society that is characterized by many as one of moral degeneration. The magnitude of corruption has grown to unprecedented proportions. Xi Jinping's signature campaign against corruption, launched in 2013, highlighted the magnitude of this problem. In fact, the CPC leadership had warned about this problem for long. Jiang Zemin regarded it as a 'life and death question' for the party, and Hu Jintao said that it might affect the 'governing capacity' of the party so badly that the party might lose power. Xi Jinping's four-year-old campaign had already led to the punishment given to 240 central-level officials and over a million local cadres for violating party and government rules. But did this eliminate the sources of corruption?

A market economy that operates on a large degree of discretion and in the lack of adequate institutional safeguards presents the vulnerable environment for bribe and illegal deals involving huge amounts of money and other favours. The practice of meting out harsh punishment including summary trials and executions has failed to check the trend which continued to rise. 'Making money' or worshipping Mr Money (*qian xiansheng*) is the new mantra in China to which all other values have been subordinated. The decline of feeling of fellowship towards people and rise of crude individualism are widespread in contemporary China. This is no doubt noted as a serious problem by the CPC which talked about striving for material as well as spiritual civilizations, to which political civilization was added in 2002 at the Sixteenth Party Congress. The slogan of building a 'well-off society' (*xiaokang shehui*) which the party congress gave, however, still emphasized economic growth and material facilities. Perhaps, the notion of building a 'harmonious socialist society' which Hu Jintao started propounding in 2006 partly addressed the issue of human values. But, the new slogan turned out to be pale in the glow of the drive for the 'well-off society'. In 2007, at the Seventeenth Party Congress, the goal was re-articulated as achieving a 'well-off society in all respects' which was reiterated at the Eighteenth Party Congress in 2012. Hu Jintao went a step further to define it as achieving development in five spheres—economic, social, political, cultural and ecological—desperately trying to affirm that development had to be comprehensive. This five-dimensional concept of development has been reiterated by Xi Jinping together with the 'four comprehensives'. Xi's value education and ethical conduct campaign for party members in 2014 tried to give a new orientation to people's aspirations. The fourth comprehensive principle, namely comprehensively practising strict self-discipline by the party members, reiterated at the Sixth Plenum in 2016 did stress party's values. But achieving material prosperity at par with people in the USA and surpassing them had already emerged as the strongest motivation during the reform period. The slogan of the 'Chinese dream' that built up a climate of nationalism found the material base in this economic propensity. This flowed from the ideological line of the reforms that invoke 'taking economic construction as the focus'.

However, this orientation confronted another powerful reality. There is a worldwide upsurge of democratic consciousness on the part of groups, regions and individuals, especially oppressed people seeking fulfilment of their creative potentiality, asserting their dignity and right to self-realization and self-determination. Hence, there has been a continuing resistance to imperialism, neocolonialism and all forms of domination. China's people's democratic revolution was a great inspiration to that process of multidimensional liberation. It is, therefore, natural that people hope for democracy and self-determination in everyday life. There is a clear urge for grass-roots democracy and right to participate in the political process at every level. It is an urge that is directed at reducing class, ethnic, gender, race and caste domination.[29] If China's reforms process had indeed led to re-emergence of such forms of dominance and even newer forms of control and exploitation, then the strategy needed to be thoroughly re-examined on these standards.

The Success Trap

This exercise is not only about the success of the reforms and the problems generated by it but also about why it is difficult to change the course of reforms and why such problems are bound to arise in the course of such reforms. In fact, the CPC's fourth-generation leadership which came to power in 2002 especially President Hu Jintao and Premier Wen Jiabao had frankly spoken about these problems and initiated a number of steps to tackle them. Xi Jinping articulated such problems in different ways. The argument I propose here is that the strategy of development pursued since 1978, especially in its post-1992 phase, has created a 'success trap' in China. The reform process is undoubtedly a success on economic standards as a result of which, to quote Mao Zedong's inaugural speech on 1 October 1949, 'China had stood up' in the world. But, the reforms have also created a 'trap', binding the country firmly to a development path and certain sociopolitical and economic forces from which it is difficult for the Chinese government to take the country out. It should be noted though that Hu Jintao's initiatives put the focus of reforms on 'balanced, coordinated development', and Xi Jinping went a step further in espousing a 'new development philosophy' that was rooted in the 'four comprehensives' and focused on addressing people's problems, thus reorienting the reforms in significant ways. These measures raised hopes of overcoming the 'success trap'. But these steps reckon with the powerful structures of political economy already built over the past four decades.

The emergence of the success trap is clearly discernible in the course of the reform process seen in both the macro and micro perspectives. While many reports on the extent of inequality, regional disparity, corruption and alienation have come out within China as well from abroad, Hu Jintao's own enumeration of the problems in the Report to the Eighteenth Party Congress leaves us in no doubt about the serious magnitude of these issues. Yet, both President Xi Jinping and Premier Li Keqiang have reaffirmed the continuation of the same reform strategy. Calling the reforms 'the biggest dividend for China', Li has also admitted that there was 'great room for improvement' in the country's socialist market economy. In other words, they all see that there are serious problems resulting from the strategy, yet they have to continue on the path at the micro level.

My study of Wuxi in the Yangtze River Delta which is one of the most developed areas of China shows the same trend. Wuxi is a great success story of rural and urban transformation. This middle size, light industry town has become a new power house of high-tech industrial development together with a thriving tourism industry. But, the pollution level in Taihu Lake and the surrounding region, the huge income gap among the residents and between them and the migrant labourers, and the new problems faced by women are some of the fallout of this process.[30] If the Wuxi experience confirms the proposition on China's 'success story' and the 'success trap', then it would be even more applicable to poorer areas where problems are starkly visible.

The trap has been forged by institutional measures in the economy and politics which had actually contributed to the growth of production and profit. It is based on the steadily evolving interest groups or classes of entrepreneurs, managers and professionals with specific identities, interests and networks of support. What we call the trap is considered as a positive foundation of economic development and is appreciated greatly by the forces of globalization in the Western countries who regard market economy, advanced technology and promotion of incentives for entrepreneurs as the most efficient drivers of growth. Even though the Chinese reforms had started much before the World Bank launched the 'structural adjustment programme', they cite the Chinese economic success as the vindication of their prescription of the market economy. This global recognition further consolidates the trap because it exists in the advanced capitalist countries as well following the same logic.

China calls its system 'socialist market economy' to stress that it is a market economy guided or controlled by the Communist Party and the State. Deng Xiaoping had affirmed this position saying that there was no need to fear the growth of capitalism in China because the CPC leadership will always guard against that eventuality. This was the powerful message he delivered during his famous 'southern tour' to special economic zones (SEZs) in February 1992. This provided the impetus to the development of private enterprise in China and growth of the export-oriented economy thereafter. This path is so well-entrenched that it has turned out to be a trap. The nature of the trap is such that even the successive groups of Communist Party leadership have fallen into it and they are unable to change the basic reform policies. In fact, with the capitalists having joined as members of the party and interest groups being recognized for their contribution to China's economic rise, the party's capacity for unravelling the knots in the trap has shrunk. On the contrary, the party authority and State power that backs the economic model hardens and complicates the trap. Thus, the forces of the market economy have trumped the elements of socialism, rendering the governing capacity of the CPC an instrument of sustaining that process.

The dynamics of the socio-economic process will certainly loosen the trap and open it up one day when the problems become serious. The CPC itself may be transformed to acquire a new capacity for innovative socialist development. Hu Jintao's call for adopting a 'scientific concept of development' that takes into account growth of production together with social justice and environmental sustainability and building a 'harmonious society' by addressing the problems causing 'disharmony' or contradictions in the society was a step in that direction. But, unless the leaders realize that they have landed in a success trap and begin to understand why excessive preoccupation with economic growth necessarily leads to such situations of alienation and inequity, attempts to tackle these problems will have only marginal effect and may remain only as propaganda statements. Even momentous announcements of big programmes like the 'building a new socialist countryside' may have limited consequence. The programme had attracted a lot of attention after the Seventeenth Party Congress and the Eleventh FYP. But, it got routine mention and scanty resources thereafter.

If Hu Jintao's initiatives which were designed in direct response to the imbalances and the problems did not succeed in taking China out of the success trap, did the leadership of President Xi Jinping and Premier Li Keqiang indicate a way out? In my view, even though Xi had taken a number of steps to address the economic bottlenecks, sociopolitical problems and organizational flaws in the party and the State organs during his first term, the structural character of the development path remained solidly in force, thus continuing the trends of inequality, alienation and environmental degradation in China. His stewardship of the economy and polity has generated greater self-confidence among the Chinese masses and his leadership has shown new strength of China to the world. Some of his policy initiatives at home and abroad had yielded concrete results. But they were not adequate to take China out of the 'success trap'.

Xi Jinping's policy initiatives were presented in a framework of pursuing the 'Chinese dream of rejuvenating the Chinese nation' and steering the country towards observing the two centenaries coming up in 2021 (founding of the CPC) and 2049 (founding of the PRC). While these were platforms of mobilizing nationalist imagination, there was the need to take concrete action affecting the people's aspirations and problems. Xi took three major initiatives on the domestic front and two initiatives on the international front.

Firstly, and most importantly, Xi Jinping's anti-corruption drive launched in 2013 impacted the whole apparatus of the party and the State. Led by the CC for Discipline Inspection (CCDI) Secretary Wang Qishan, new investigation mechanisms and procedures and prosecutions were enforced at every level. As many as 240 officials at the central level and over a million at the provincial, the county and lower levels were investigated and punished. In 2015, when the party's Fifth Plenum adopted the decision on enforcing rule of law, this drive got further vigour. The annual session of NPC in March 2017 was informed that the anti-corruption campaign had acquired an 'irresistible momentum'.[31] But at the end of four years and more, the system was still not corruption-free. No doubt, a climate of fear was created and many got severe punishment and even a campaign for socialist morality was launched. But the structural roots of corruption that lay in the discretion-driven, profit-seeking market economy persisted.

The second initiative addressed the economy by 'deepening' market reforms and giving them a decisive role. This formulation adopted at the Third Plenum in 2013 was further developed in the strategy and policies of the Thirteenth FYP adopted by the Fifth Plenum in 2015 and launched in 2016. It was reflected in the changes in the land policy which made it obligatory for the village administration to seek approval of the villagers before deciding on land transfers while making it possible for households to sell their contracted land in certain conditions. As many of the rural protests were against the township and village leadership in many areas handing over land to commercial and industrial entrepreneurs arbitrarily and involved corrupt practices, these measures were welcomed by many.

Thirdly, some social policy initiatives of the Xi Jinping leadership were also long overdue. Among them was the decision to relax the one-child policy at the Fourth Plenum of the CPCCC in 2014. It allowed couples to have two children. As we discuss in Chapter 9, this came too late. The one-child policy had already produced many negative consequences that would have long-term consequences for the population structure, distorted composition of the work force and aging society besides many cultural and psychological consequences. Still, there was some truth in the statement that this policy averted a major population explosion in China and contributed to the economic success story.

Reform of the *hukou* system giving access to rural migrants to some basic amenities in some cities partly ameliorated the hardships of a section of the migrants. Reorienting the economy towards being driven by domestic demands, thus pursuing the objective of 'pattern transformation' announced during the Twelfth Plan and reaffirmed during the Thirteenth Plan, was the highlight of the Chinese economy under Xi Jinping. Declaring the 'medium-to medium-high' growth rate of the economy as the new normal—keeping it between 6 and 7 per cent per annum—while addressing to problems of inequality, regional disparity, rural crisis and social sector gaps was one of the critical decisions stressed by the Xi regime.

Fourthly, Xi Jinping's international initiatives acquired global signifi-cance during his first term. The One Belt, One Road (*yidai yilu*) initiative that he announced in 2013 and pursued vigorously since then attracted worldwide attention. The ancient Silk Route linking the land mass of Asia and Europe on the one hand and the maritime route stretching from China's east coast to regions and islands in the Pacific, Indian Ocean, the Gulf and the Atlantic port cities of Europe on the other hand were sought to be linked under this plan. China's offer to invest its capital in the regions on this route on mutually agreed projects had been welcomed by most countries on the route. This project not only utilizes Chinese savings productively and profitably but also contributes to vast expansion of modern infrastructure, thus helping enhancement of global trade and commerce. However, India has refused to participate in this project for strategic reasons. It has found the China–Pakistan Economic Corridor (CPEC)—involving US$56 billion—unacceptable as it passed through parts of Jammu and Kashmir under Pakistan's control.

China took the initiative to set up the AIIB in Beijing with over 40 countries including India joining as founding members. Together with the New Development Bank based in Shanghai under the auspices of BRICS, Xi Jinping's active leadership in Asian and global financial management in the post-2008 environment was clearly pronounced. China under Xi Jinping had become a leading force, playing an influential role in G20. On climate change, President Xi Jinping and President Obama concluded a deal in 2015 which announced some progress in realizing the COP21 goals set for 2030. Xi Jinping's proposal during his first meeting with Obama in the USA in 2013 on 'new norms guiding great power relations in the twenty-first century' had been a constant refrain in his dealings with the USA. Xi reiterated these norms in the course of his telephone conversations with President Trump in February 2017. That they should work on the areas of agreement and expand them, respect each other's core concerns and engage in dialogue on their points of difference were important principles advanced by Xi. However, there were no formal responses to them.

President Xi's global leadership role was evident when he addressed the Davos World Economic Forum at Davos in January 2017 and defended economic globalization and open and free trade. Decrying protectionism was seen as a counter to President Trump's assertions.

Many observers see Xi Jinping's assertive foreign policy as an extension of his stress on Chinese nationalism. Asserting the Chinese sovereign rights over the South China Sea disputed by many countries, expansion of the Chinese naval power in the Indian Ocean is seen in the same vein.

Xi's policies, domestic and foreign, will no doubt consolidate the Chinese nation and the Chinese state apparatus, making it stronger. China would also earn even more recognition in the comity of nations. Whether they address the serious problems of rising inequality, alienation and unsustainability is an open question. Globally, the Chinese seem to be more interested in preserving the existing, unequal, unjust, world economic and financial order, out of which they have benefited greatly. On the other hand, many countries and people's movements around the world are determined to transform the prevailing world order. In fact, BRICS had been conceived to pursue that agenda.

Hence, I would argue that the 'success trap'—continuation of the current development path, celebrating certain successes while living with and grappling with serious problems that arise out of it—is likely to persist under Xi Jinping and beyond.

Lessons for Development Theory

First of all, let us understand why it has become difficult to alter the main orientation of the reform strategy. That would help in capturing some of the lessons in development theory.

Achievement of a high growth rate has become an end in itself. Theoretically, Deng Xiaoping formulated the principle of taking 'economic construction' at the centre of all programmes.[32] This was reiterated throughout the reform period as the principle of 'one centre, two points'. One centre referred to the focus on economic development—something that had been neglected by Mao Zedong according to him. Indeed, China achieved high growth rate in the course of the reforms and that became a source of great pride for the Chinese people spurring a tide of nationalism in contemporary China. A high rate of growth has been regarded by the advocates of liberalization and globalization saying that without producing enough goods and services, any agenda of distribution cannot be undertaken. This GDP-preoccupation itself creates the kind of problems that have appeared in China. The high-growth profile is used by the rulers of China to acquire legitimacy among common people and stress the importance of sociopolitical stability. A development path that is sustained on the basis of stability and legitimacy is bound to perpetuate itself despite other problems that may eventually affect those very foundations.

The Chinese growth has produced an entrepreneurial class consisting of a bourgeoisie in the classical sense of the term as well as a spectrum of modern managers, professionals, shareholders and business people. This class is closely integrated with the Western economic processes and, therefore, is part of the global capitalist process. At the same time, this bloc of entrepreneurs and middle class has been fully intertwined with the party and the State system in China. Jiang Zemin facilitated the political integration of this class with the CPC through his Three Represents formulation which opened party membership to the capitalists. But, it is the functioning of the economy jointly by the State and the market forces which consolidated their power. They are the strong social base of China's political economy, ensuring that the reforms continued on the same path. Their global commitment to supply goods to various markets, acquire raw materials from abroad, procure technology from the advanced countries, perform their role in the multilateral organizations and perform the role of 'a responsible stakeholder' in the global political and economic order have very long-term perspectives. Even though China had refocused the orientation of the economy towards domestic market, its international involvement using its accumulated surplus capital kept its global linkages growing. The One Belt, One Road and other new avenues of Chinese investment were indications of this trend. They very much would require the continuation of the 'medium-to-high-growth' path. The internal policies ranging from innovation to infrastructure had to correspond to those commitments. Therefore, any change in the path is difficult. That is what is captured by the concept of the 'success trap'. It also encapsulates some essential questions raised in the discourse on social transformation during the past two centuries.

The Chinese reforms experience illustrates a fundamental question that has arisen in the course of the global historical development flowing out of the Industrial Revolution. This development was characterized by mass production using modern technology harnessing natural resources that reduced scarcity, facilitated higher standards of living, saved human lives from epidemics and many serious diseases, and enlarged human freedom. Even though colonialism was instrumental in spreading the Industrial Revolution path all over the world causing devastation and wars, still in that process and later these areas got access to modern science. Most post-colonial States, including China and India, chose to adopt the path of development that flowed out of Industrial Revolution. But, that era seems to have been exhausted. The negative consequences of that path are clear today. That path led to the creation of a high-tech, high-consumption, high-energy, high-speed and high-rise life as the inevitable choice which has caused gross inequalities, alienation and destruction of natural environment. Thus, the world is witnessing a civilizational transition which may extend to a century or two in search of an equitable and sustainable world. The great Chinese success story that has landed in a success trap is a stark example of this.

Did socialism which emerged as a challenge to capitalism also fall into the same trap of the Industrial Revolution? Economic growth under State or collective ownership leading to new inequities and environmental decay did not after all move towards creating a society where 'freedom of each was the precondition of freedom of all'.[33] After all, reducing alienation and enlarging the realm of freedom, rather than increasing production for its own sake, was the central idea of socialism. The new questions which were raised by the social movements of the past half-century, the women's movement, the environmental movement and the anti-race and anti-caste movements went beyond the traditional formulations of capitalism and socialism centring around productive forces and class relations and pointedly emphasized on relating them to the people's right to self-realization. This was part of the constant struggle for comprehensive development to achieve economic, political, social, cultural and, above all, ecological conditions of freedom. Did socialism acquire a new definition beyond replacing the class order of capitalism? Thus, the 'success trap' not only addresses some familiar issues of capitalist development in contemporary China[34] and possibilities for socialist transformation[35] but also more consciously takes up the issues raised by creative society, issues of socialist freedom and exploring the Anthropocene in the twenty-first century in the course of this analysis.[36]

The Structure of This Book

With this framework of the study in mind, I have presented the chapters in three parts. The first part has two chapters, giving a macro view and a micro view of the development process. Chapter 2 takes an overview of the reform strategy in China as it evolved from 1978 onwards with focus on the countryside, explaining the features of the policies in each stage. The next chapter looks at this process from a grass-roots vantage point, from a rural area in Wuxi. These two chapters present a relatively comprehensive understanding of the reform strategy in China. How the strategy of State-guided market reforms unfolded in China at different stages during the past four decades is discussed in this part.

In the second part, the focus is on the agencies which formulate and implement these policies. They are the party-led State organs in the Chinese political system. In two chapters, the government and the party organization, structure and their dynamic role under different regimes are analysed at both the macro and micro levels. The changes made in their functioning and their role in implementing the reform policies are examined. To what extent did these remain in the traditional mode of communist organization and whether new norms of governance had guided these changes are addressed. There were periods when the government cadre and the enterprise manager played the key role. But in the later years of Hu Jintao and under Xi Jinping, the party cadre took over the decisive role while promoting market economy. No doubt, there are other major agencies in every society, ranging from family, social groups, cultural and religious organizations and civil society bodies to the corporates, the media and international agencies, not to mention the army which often plays an autonomous role in the polity. Even though there is a focus here on the party-led State apparatus as the main drivers of the reform process, one should always keep the larger social picture in mind. Some of these issues indirectly figure in the subsequent chapters.

The third part continues the effort to see the policies and their performance in certain specific spheres of people's life. We take up rural enterprises and the workers and examine why the approach to industrialization integrally linked to agriculture was replaced by an export-driven manufacturing. Then we look at the conditions of villagers and rural areas where we saw both prosperity and distress. The impact of the reform strategy on women is discussed in depth as it shows potentialities as well as pitfalls of this path of development. The effect of the reforms on health and education is analysed as it is important that economic growth should be assessed mainly in terms of social development. These chapters draw heavily from my fieldwork in Wuxi but are analysed in terms of the national policies and profiles. We make comparative references to India in some places to bring home implications for India.

The three parts are summed up and reflected upon in the conclusion. There, I discuss a few theoretical and policy questions, draw some lessons for development theory and present a few observations on Marxism and politics in the contemporary world.

Notes and References

1. Manoranjan Mohanty, 'Harmonious Society: Hu Jintao's Vision and the Chinese Party Congress', *Economic and Political Weekly* 48, no. 50, 12–16 (15 December 2012).
2. Four comprehensives, discussed in detail in Chapter 5, refer to 'comprehensively building a moderately prosperous society', 'deepening reform', 'governing by rule of law' and 'strictly

governing the party'. These evolved from the Eighteenth Party Congress in November 2012 until the Sixth Plenum of the CPC in November 2016.

3. Dominic Wilson and Roopa Purushothaman, 'Dreaming with BRICs: The Path to 2050' (Goldman Sachs Global Economic Paper No. 98, October 2003). Available at: http://www.goldmansachs.com/our-thinking/archive/archive-pdfs/brics-dream.pdf (accessed on 20 July 2017).

4. L. Alan Winters and Shahid Yusuf, *Dancing with Giants: China, India and the Global Economy* (Washington, DC: World Bank Publications, January 2007).

5. Zheng Bijian, 'A New Path for China's Peaceful Rise and the Future of Asia: Bo'ao Forum for Asia, 2003' in *China's Peaceful Rise: Speeches of Zheng Bijian 1997–2005* (Washington, DC: Brookings Institution Press, 2005).

6. In 2005, PRC's State Council Information Office published an authoritative document. *People's Daily Online*, 'China's Peaceful Development Road', *People's Daily Online*, 22 December 2005. Available at: http://en.people.cn/200512/22/eng20051222_230059.html (accessed on 2 June 2017).

7. Human Development Index of China has steadily improved since 1975. Chinese official figures for poverty reduction are even more impressive from 250 million in 1986 to less than 40 million in 2006. Wen Jiabao, *Report the Work of Government to the NPC* (March 2007). Available at: http://english.cpc.people.com.cn/66102/7320564.html (accessed on 20 July 2017).

8. *Global Times* quoted senior Chinese official Zheng Wenkai on 14 October 2014 to say this. On the World Bank's US$1.25-a-day count, he said that it was nearly 200 million.

9. Li Keqiang, *Report on the Work of the Government,* delivered at the Fifth Session of the 12th National People's Congress of the People's Republic of China on 5 March 2017. The revised poverty line at present is RMB5,000 yuan which is more than US$1 but less than US$2 per day. Available at: http://news.xinhuanet.com/english/china/2017-03/16c_136134017.htm (accessed on 20 July 2017).

10. Hu Jintao, *Firmly March on the Path of Socialism with Chinese Characteristics and Strive to Complete the Building of a Moderately Prosperous Society in All Respects*, Report to the Eighteenth National Congress of the Communist Party of China on 8 November 2012 (Beijing: Xinhua English, 17 November 2012), 5.

11. Li Keqiang, *Report on the Work of the Government,* 10–11.

12. The number crossed 140 in early 2016. See Edward Wong, 'Tibetan Monk, 18, Dies after Self-Immolation to Protest Chinese Rule', *The New York Times* (3 March 2016). Available at: https://www.nytimes.com/2016/03/04/world/asia/china-tibet-self-immolations.html (accessed on 20 July 2017).

13. Rural discontent, urban unemployment and social tensions are documented by Dale Wen, *China Copes with Globalization: A Mixed Review* (San Francisco: International Forum on Globalization, 2005).

14. Inequality measure, the Gini coefficient, shows that there was greater inequality in China after 25 years of reforms than was the case in India (Table 1.3).

15. Xinhuanet, 'China Gini Coefficient at 0.474 in 2012', 18 January 2013. Available at: http://news.xinhuanet.com/english/china/2013-01/18/c_132111927.htm (accessed on 12 September 2014).

16. UNDP, *China Human Development Report 2005* (2005). Available at: http://hdr.undp.org/sites/default/files/china_2005_complete.pdf (accessed on 20 July 2017).

17. Wen Tiejun and Wen Li, *China in Major Strategic Transition* (monograph; Beijing: Renmin University, 2005).

18. Ross Garnaut, Guo Shutian, and Ma Guonan, *The Third Revolution in China's Countryside* (Cambridge: Cambridge University Press, 1996).
19. Wen Tiejun and Li, *China in Major Strategic Transition.*
20. The practice of reporting this was abandoned in the premier's report to the NPC in 2007. The incidents most likely increased further as evidenced by the greater emphasis on building a 'harmonious society'.
21. Edward Cody, 'For Chinese, Peasant Revolt is a Rare Victory', *Washington Post* (13 June 2005). This gives a detailed account of a struggle against land takeover for an industrial park in Huaxi in Zhejiang province in which on one occasion 20,000 peasants confronted a 3,000-strong police force. For a comprehensive discussion of the phenomenon, see Kathy Le Mons Walker, '"Gangster Capitalism" and Peasant Protest in China', *Journal of Peasant Studies* 33, no. 1, 1–33 (January 2006).
22. This figure was given to me in the course of interviews with scholars at the China Reforms Forum, Beijing, in September 2012.
23. The All-China Women's Federation (ACWF), itself a mass organization of the CPC, has been complaining against the negative effects of reforms from time to time. See, for example, ACWF President Mo Wenxiu's speech at the CPPCC on 11 March 2004. We will analyse this issue in the chapter on women's prospects.
24. In 2006, the number was estimated to be more than 250 million.
25. See Wen, *China Copes with Globalization.*
26. Ethnic minority tensions in Xinjiang, Tibet and some other areas continue to cause concerns to the Central government. That is why the Western Region Development Strategy was launched in 2000, and bridging regional disparity has been identified as a major objective.
27. Youth are a major component of the unemployed and the migrants. Youth discontent is very much evident in the chat rooms and popular literature.
28. The Chinese government reportedly pressurized the World Bank to alter its environmental assessment of the Chinese economy or the 'Green GDP' assessment in July 2007. Mitchell Landsberg, 'China Cancels Second Environmental Report', *Los Angeles Times,* 24 July 2007. Apparently the cancelled report had mentioned that 600,000 people would die prematurely every year in China by 2020 due to urban air pollution.
29. Manoranjan Mohanty and Mark Selden, 'Conceptualizing Local Democracy: Democracy, Resistance and Power in Indian and Chinese Countryside', in *Grass-roots Democracy in India and China: The Right to Participate*, eds. Manoranjan Mohanty, George Mathew, Richard Baum, and Rong Ma (New Delhi: SAGE Publications, 2007).
30. Manoranjan Mohanty, 'China's Reforms: The Wuxi Story', *Economic and Political Weekly* 44, nos. 26–27, 308–19 (2009, 27 June).
31. Li Keqiang, *Report on the Work of Government*, 9.
32. Deng Xiaoping, 'Opening Speech at the 12th Party Congress on September 1, 1982', in *Fundamental Issues in Present-day China* (Beijing: Foreign Languages Press, 1987), 4.
33. Karl Marx and Friedrich Engels, *The Communist Manifesto* (1848). (Reprint of 1848 edition: New Delhi: People's Publishing House, 1998).
34. Martin Hart-Landsberg and Paul Burkett, *China and Socialism: Market Reforms and Class Struggle* (New York, NY: Monthly Review Press, 2005). A round table on this book presents an extremely valuable discussion, focusing on how the global emancipatory project was still on in China through the internal debates and student and youth movements. Hari Sharma, 'Introduction', in *Critical Perspectives on China's Economic Transformation* (New Delhi: Daanish Books, 2007).

35. Many Marxist critics of Chinese reforms have contributed to this discourse. Satyananda J. Gabriel, *Chinese Capitalism and the Modernist Vision* (London: Routledge, 2006), 173. Taking a post-structuralist Marxist view, he shows the emergence of a new class process of capitalism in China. He says, 'But no matter what happens in the future, the Chinese social formation has already been sufficiently transformed and linked to the global economy (with dependencies running in both directions) that the genie cannot be put back in the bottle'.

36. For some new thinking on global transformation raising issues of creative society—pursuit of multidimensional freedom to realize creative potentiality of individuals, groups and regions and exploring the Anthropocene—and a new relationship of humans with nature with the former constantly aware of the effects of their work on the latter, see Richard Falk, Manoranjan Mohanty, and Victor Faessel, eds., *Exploring Emergent Global Thresholds: Towards 2030* (New Delhi: Orient Blackswan, 2017).

PART 1

China's Reforms: Overview and a View from Below

2

Development Strategy and the Countryside

Studying the Reforms

To understand China's success story and the manner in which the Chinese leadership grappled with the problems that arose in the reform process, we need to see how the development strategy evolved after 1978. It is important to note that Deng Xiaoping, the architect of China's reforms, laid down two general principles that guided the reform process thereafter. One was a negative principle, while the other was a positive one. The repudiation of the Cultural Revolution model of socialist construction that denounced market was the first principle. The second was to focus on economic construction by mobilizing all resources at home and abroad. These two ideas were embodied in the formulation 'reforms and open door' that was declared as the foundational principle at the Communique of the Third Plenum of the Eleventh CPCCC in 1978. To implement this line of thinking, he presented a guiding principle of policy-making that was superbly practical—'wading through the river by feeling for the stones'. In other words, he advised the leaders to formulate pragmatic policies looking at the prevailing situation. To popularize this idea, he formulated many slogans such as 'emancipating one's mind' meaning renouncing Maoist economic doctrines. Another was actually a quote from Mao from the revolutionary movement, namely 'seeking truth from facts'. This allowed leaders to formulate new policies from time to time, making serious departures from earlier policies.

It is not just the economic policies that Deng Xiaoping laid down, equally significant were the political initiatives. He put political stability as of utmost priority for the party and the State for he thought that it was the precondition for economic growth. This was to be achieved through regular functioning of institutions of the party and the State, rules of tenure and succession. The turbulence of the Cultural Revolution must be avoided at any cost, he believed. Therefore, as the chairperson of the MAC of the CC—the only post he held from the fall of the Gang of Four until he fell sick in 1996—Deng called upon the People's Liberation Army (PLA) to crush the youth demonstrations in Tiananmen Square in June 1989. Many believe that had he not done that, China would have faced a situation of collapse.[1] Deng's successors have continued to stress stability as a primary principle of governance, resorting to many authoritarian measures, even though this may have been one of the fault lines of the development path. We take up this issue in Chapter 3 when we discuss the nature of the Chinese political system.

By 1982, the principles governing China's reforms came to be theorized as 'socialist market economy', legitimately opting for developing a market economy while maintaining the leading role of the State. Gradually, the perspective crystallized and in 1997, the CPC adopted 'Deng Xiaoping Theory of building socialism with Chinese characteristics' as the guiding doctrine for the reforms. It was listed as a major ideological principle after Mao Zedong Thought. Thus, the two original ideas of Deng—using State and market and striving for higher levels of economic growth—remained the guiding mantras for all the successive regimes in China. They also derived legitimacy from Deng's framework to take pragmatic and even radically new initiatives in the subsequent years. As we will see, after 2002, Hu Jintao took major steps to reorient the economic policies towards a balanced development strategy, focusing on social justice and sustainability. The Twelfth Plan declared 'pattern transformation' as its main goal. Xi Jinping went a step further talking of a 'new development philosophy' and steering the economy and polity with his 'four comprehensives' perspective towards coordinated and balanced development.

Yet, Deng Xiaoping's line of thinking fixing high targets of growth for 2020—doubling 1980 level by 2000 and doubling again by 2010 and again by 2020—remained as the guiding norms for all the regimes. So, we can broadly divide the reform period into four phases, even though they may be further divided into specific phases in terms of policies.

Four Periods of Reforms

1978–92: Focus on rural reforms—Deng Xiaoping lays down the main policies for the whole system

1992–2002: Industrial growth through market economy and expanding exports under Jiang Zemin

2002–12: High growth with social and environmental concerns under Hu Jintao

2012–17: Innovation-driven medium-to-high rate of growth with comprehensive economic, political, social, cultural and ecological goals under Xi Jinping

In this chapter and next, we see the unfolding of this four-decade-long history—first in the national policy perspective and then as it evolved in a region. Our vantage point is the Chinese countryside from where we look at the main features of the policies in each period.

The rural vantage point for examining a development process compels us to ask several questions on rural–urban linkages. One set of questions arises from traditional debates on terms of trade and accumulation process. Why farmers had to make sacrifices to finance industrial development and that was done by many authoritarian regimes is a recurring theme in agrarian studies.[2] There are long debates on production relations and productivity as to whether individual farming is more productive than collective farming, cooperative farming and corporate farming. Is the size of land an important factor in productivity as large size farms facilitate mechanized and large-scale farming along European and American lines? What problems does a small farmer in a rural economy face? Is the typical Green Revolution approach to agriculture that stresses technology-driven production process the main path for development? Has it not produced serious environmental crisis, depleting water resources, reducing soil fertility and creating health hazards from use of fertilizers? On the other hand, does distribution of land to rural households who exercise their choice of appropriate technology have a political and economic significance for restructuring society and bringing about a transformation of the feudal order? Do peasants necessarily have to make sacrifices for nation-building by agreeing to low income from their produce and making grains available to the workers in the cities at cheap price? How is agriculture to be financed, from resources from within or with substantial investments by the State? What is a rational proportion between accumulation and consumption in the rural economy? Is rural economy to be conceptualized differently in modern conditions as a diversified economy with agriculture as only one part of it and industry, commerce and social development infrastructure as equally important? We may not take up all these questions in this study. But two things are clear at the end of nearly four decades of Chinese reforms. One is the clear decision to push ahead with urbanization and build an industrial and high-tech society. So, after the first two decades of prosperity in the countryside, the Chinese leaders opted for a different growth model. They celebrate the fact that[3] 56.1 per cent of the country's population lived in the cities in 2015, and their number is estimated to go up to 60 per cent in 2020 by the end of the Thirteenth Plan. Second, after dismantling collective modes of operation by the mid-1990s, the regime was back to promoting a variety of collective, cooperative, public–private and corporate modes in addition to individual ownership in the recent years. At the same time, for compelling ecological reasons, they also went for many traditional and other renewable ways of diversified agricultural production, even while adopting innovation-driven modern technology.

To get a full view of this process, we need to start from the situation prior to reforms. Indeed, a much longer historical view is necessary from the period before the establishment of the PRC. But for practical reasons, we start from the late 1950s, with the institution of people's communes and why it was dismantled by the post-Mao regime. Then we turn to an understanding of the theoretical perspective underlying the reforms during the past four decades and see how it evolved in the course of practice. The reforms unfolded in phases and we analyse the main features of each phase from 1979 until the Twelfth FYP, 2011–15 and the launch of the Thirteenth Plan (2016–20). Thereafter, we examine the main components of the development strategy in general and rural development strategy in particular: production responsibility system, development of the commodity economy and diversification through technological upgradation of the economy.

What Was Wrong with the People's Communes?

The Third Plenum of the Eleventh CPCCC in December 1978 proclaimed a perspective of economic construction oriented towards rapid growth and modernization. Agriculture was the first of the *four modernizations*, the others being industry, science and technology, and national defence. This was to be achieved by the fullest development of productive forces. The Deng Xiaoping regime, which came to power at the Third Plenum, rejected the economic policies of the Mao era, especially the ideas governing the Great Leap Forward and the Cultural Revolution because they neglected the development of production and hence they started the reforms programmes first in the countryside to push ahead with a programme to raise production, labour productivity and rural income. For that purpose, it found the institution of people's communes unacceptable because it did not adequately achieve productivity and efficiency. We need to understand the logic and the limits of the commune system in order to fully appreciate the rural reforms after 1978.

Agrarian question was given top priority after the CPC came to power in 1949. After carrying our land reforms in 1950–52, the party began to experiment with agricultural cooperatives from 1954 and advanced cooperatives in 1956 steadily moving in the direction of collectivization of agriculture. The people's communes were set up in August 1958 as the three-tier system of rural collectives with *people's communes (renmin gongshe)* at the top, *production brigades (shengcan dadui)* at the middle level and *production teams (shengcan dui)* as the lowest unit. The production team became the operative collective for agricultural production in 1961. The brigade was the unit of ownership, accounting only between November 1958 and December 1960 and the commune only for a few months before that. In the course of the Cultural Revolution, the radicals wanted to raise the level of the collective to the brigade. But this was resisted by the liberals led by Deng Xiaoping.[4] Even the 1975 Constitution of the PRC which had been drafted under the shadow of the Cultural Revolution retained the production team as the accounting unit, though allowing the possibility of raising it to the brigade level wherever local conditions permitted. But the team-level collective which was the level of a small village or part of a village too was also found to be an inefficient mode of production by the Deng regime. One critical assessment of the commune experience of the 1958–60 period summarized the problems as 'five winds', namely the wind of communism (extreme egalitarianism), wind of exaggeration (boasting high production figures which were inaccurate), wind of commandism (higher level leaders insisting on implementation of their decisions), wind among rural cadres to seek privileges and wind of giving blind instructions.[5]

Concretely, three sets of negative consequences were cited by the critics of the commune system. Firstly, they pointed out that the entire workforce of the production team was deployed in the agricultural activities, whether all of them were needed for that purpose or not. This meant underemployment of available labour. Thus, after the commune system was disbanded, a great deal of surplus labour was released for other productive work which not only increased the family income but also contributed to more social production.

Secondly, under the commune system, all labourers were paid equal work points for the hours of work, irrespective of the magnitude of contribution they made to production.[6] The Deng regime decried this as 'equalitarianism' under which all peasants *ate from the same big pot or the iron bowl*.[7] In other words, the lazy peasants got the same remuneration for their work as the hardworking ones. There was no incentive for the hardworking, innovative peasant. In the post-reform system, this was changed into a new policy of more pay for more and better work.

Thirdly, the income level of the peasants under the commune system remained depressed. There were two reasons for this. Firstly, the team committee deducted nearly 50 per cent of the income towards capital construction fund, commune reserve fund and the welfare fund and divided the rest by the total number of work points. Thus, the peasant got wages according to his/her work points only after making a significant portion of his/her income as contribution to the collective. Secondly, the prices paid by the State to purchase grains from the commune were low. Therefore, the income of the team also remained low. Thus, the peasant income in China's countryside remained low throughout the commune period as a result of which the peasants' purchasing capacity for other consumer goods remained limited. A countryside with limited demands had implications for the Chinese economy as a whole. As a result of this situation, industrial production did not get the kind of market for which there was a potential in rural China.

Thus, underemployment and irrational allocation of labour, lack of incentives for production and depressed peasant income due to high accumulation rate made the commune system look unproductive and inefficient according to the Deng regime.

This, however, cannot brush aside the rationale of the commune system that was introduced in China in 1958. The decision to set up the communes was preceded by a debate within the CPC as to the desirability of transforming the agricultural cooperatives to the communes so soon. But Mao Zedong argued that after the implementation of land reforms, mutual aid teams and cooperatives, the next logical step was collectivization. The other view was that it was premature to move on to the stage of collectivization without developing the productive forces adequately; therefore, Liu Shaoqi and others were in favour of technological upgradation in agriculture.[8] The debate that preceded the 1958 decision was revived after Mao's death. In retrospect, however, it may be said that the commune experience may actually have facilitated the creation of an environment in which the post-Mao reforms achieved significant measures of success. There are many reasons for this assessment.

Firstly, the introduction of the communes in a way abolished class distinctions in the countryside by collectivizing land ownership. Except for private plots for kitchen gardens amounting to about 5 per cent of the total cultivable land of the village, rest of the land belonged to the village as a whole run by the village committee. Thus, the programme of China's agrarian revolution was continued with this step. Incidentally, in law, the village collective still owned rural land during the reform period, even though many changes in the contract system were introduced from time to time. Secondly, the commune system provided full employment to the villagers. It meant a great deal to women who from 1958 onwards became workers in the agricultural field, earning work points for their own labour.

This was a major sociopolitical development, even though women earned less work points than men. As we see in Chapter 8, that kind of unequal treatment continued during the reform period as well. Full-scale economic employment initiated an unprecedented wave of women's liberation in China. Thirdly, the leadership of the production team deployed groups of labourers for specific agricultural activities, thus taking advantage of the scale of operations, something that got lost when household farming was reintroduced during the reform period. Teams of peasants undertook ploughing, transplanting and so on, achieving greater efficiency. Fourthly, much of the infrastructure building in China's countryside got financed out of the resources of the commune itself. Irrigation projects, land reclamation and fertilizers procurement were done on a collective initiative out of the capital construction or reserve fund of the commune. Without the commune's own funds as well as the intensive use of collective labour, these projects would not have been possible. Many traditional forms of irrigation were utilized and new ones experimented. One of the principles of the commune system was to use indigenous forms of agricultural technology together with modern technology. Agricultural mechanization was also introduced in many places on the commune's own initiative. Mechanization stations to service tractors and providing technological support were also maintained by the communes at the brigade level. In addition to these, providing elementary education to all children and curbing illiteracy was a major programme of the commune. Providing basic health care using both traditional Chinese medicine and modern medicine was a part of the core social programme. In all this, the 'people's militia', a local mass army of men and women, was mobilized not only to provide security and police functions but also to perform economic, social, cultural and educational work. This was the period when physical education and sports became an essential part of the life style of every Chinese. Many experts believed that the rural reforms of the Deng regime achieved spectacular results because of the already-existing agricultural infrastructure of the commune period.[9] After 2009, when PRC celebrated the sixtieth anniversary of its founding, there was a discursive turn on development discourse in China. The Chinese scholars and commentators now on talked about 60 years of China's development, taking into account the achievements made during the first three decades instead of referring to them as wasted decades, especially the 20 years from 1958 when the Great Leap Forward was launched until 1978 when the Third Plenum adopted the reform and open-door line.[10]

On the question of low incomes, it should be pointed out that prices of commodities also remained more or less stable during the commune period.

Besides, the commune provided free education, health facility, childcare and old-age care to the members. As a system, the commune aimed at ensuring that there was no destitution or food insecurity in the village. The team as a whole looked after the elderly and the children. Crop failure in one village in principle could be managed by getting support from another village. That this system had serious lacunae got exposed when there was widespread drought in extensive areas. The procurement quota fixed by higher-level authorities was enforced uniformly, leaving the local leaders little flexible. The commune as an autonomous unit was left to fend for itself. Lack of communication kept the starvation-stricken regions isolated from national attention. It resulted in the severe crisis with great calamities during 1959–60 when this system did break down, leading to massive fatalities with millions of deaths caused by famine in China.[11] The magnitude of the crisis overwhelmed the system of collective measures in place to attend to the distress situation. Finally, the commune system was responsible for laying the foundation for the impressive rate of industrialization of China. The agricultural surplus was used by the State to feed workers and urban residents at relatively low prices and carry on construction of heavy industries. No doubt, it meant enormous sacrifices by the peasantry for the ostensible purpose of creating an industrial base for China.[12]

Debates will continue on the rationale for the people's commune and the larger perspective propelling it, namely the Great Leap Forward. The famine deaths alone are enough to cloud a balanced view on the desirability of coop-erative and collective agriculture. But it is important to take the 20 years of the commune period together with the four decades of reforms and have a comprehensive view of the 60 years of the PRC. On the whole, despite the famine experience, the achievements of China's people's communes cannot be underestimated. The Deng regime, no doubt, reordered the priorities. It decisively opted for high rate of growth in all sectors of the economy and fast increase in family incomes, rather than the preoccupation with building conditions of equality and socialist culture that Mao Zedong had emphasized. Yet, reform policies also produced a rural crisis in the 1990s that defied easy solutions for the next two decades. It has been argued that 'one-dimensional emphasis' on institutional changes like collectivization to the exclusion of economic and technological measures as was the case during the Mao era had necessary limitations, leading to an extractive economy that 'squeezed' the peasants by keeping their access to most basic services almost stagnant.[13] It is, however, debatable whether the economic and technological aspects were totally neglected in Mao's China. But that is the view that formed the rationale behind the post-1978 reforms.

The new priorities in post-Mao China, therefore, were focused on achieving high rate of economic growth through, first, basic restructuring of the political economy at the level of control over means of production, namely land relations in the countryside and ownership and control of industry and commerce in general, second, responding to the market in production and distribution, third, diversification of the economy including rural economy, and fourth, open door to the national and the international economies. Once the broad goals of 'reform and open door' were proclaimed, the specific policies were left to evolve from time to time by trial and error or as Deng put it 'crossing the river by touching the tones'. This is where Deng's overall perspective and stress on pragmatism came to play its role.

Guiding Principles of Reforms: Act Flexible, Pursue Growth

After Deng's death in 1997, the party leadership adopted 'Deng Xiaoping Theory of building socialism with Chinese characteristics' as its 'ideological banner' at the Fifteenth Party Congress in September 1997.[14] Jiang Zemin and Hu Jintao added their theoretical formulations, Three Represents and Scientific Outlook on Development respectively, in the subsequent party congresses. In the course of Xin Jinping's first term of leadership, especially after he was declared as the 'core' at the Sixth Plenum in 2016, references were made to his 'major addresses, and his new vision, thinking and strategies for China's governance'.[15] A more succinct formulation on this theoretical contribution may come either at the Nineteenth Party Congress of the CPC or in the course of his second term and, going by the past practice, it may be put into the Party Constitution at the Twentieth Party Congress in 2022 when he completes his second term. But as the Eighteenth Congress Report and the CPC Constitution clearly showed, Deng had laid down the *primary thesis for the long-term future path of development.* Xi Jinping's eloquent declaration of the Chinese dream also reaffirmed Deng's path of reforms. Deng's contribution is designated as 'theory', whereas Jiang is credited with 'important thought', Hu scientific 'outlook' and Xi a broad range of ideas on governance. In other words, even though a certain pragmatism was built into the reform perspective from the start, it was pragmatism within a perspective that repudiated the Maoist development strategy and was committed to building market economy under the leadership of the CPC.

Although the specific elements of what crystallized as the 'socialist market economy' evolved gradually in the course of practice, certain broad elements of the new perspective were clear right after the Third Plenum of 1978. They were as follows:

1. Economic construction was the main task in building a socialist society.
2. All forms of ownership, private and public, may be encouraged to achieve higher growth.
3. All enterprises should follow 'open-door' principle, function in response to the market taking into account local, national and international conditions and enjoy autonomy in management.
4. Science and technology from all over the world should be used to develop production.
5. Party and under its leadership, the State shall guide the reforms.

Firstly, it rejected class struggle as the key link or focus of building socialism and affirmed economic construction as the new focus. This remained the central preoccupation of the CPC throughout the reform period. Even when political disturbances took place, such as the army action against the Tiananmen demonstrators in June 1989, this focus was not altered. It also survived the ideological and political consequences of the collapse of the Soviet Union. Thus, the framework governing the reforms in Deng's China was described as 'one focus, two points' (*yizhong liangdian*)[16] which remained the constant refrain even when the fourth-generation leadership led by Hu Jintao carried out many adjustments in the economic policies during the third decade of reforms as did the fifth-generation leader Xi Jinping by declaring lower rate of economic growth and several other policies as the 'new normal'. Economic construction was the focus or the central guiding factor in building socialism. Of the two points, one point was 'reforms and open door' (*gaige kaifang*) and another point was adherence to 'four cardinal principles' (*si zhi yuan*). Whereas reforms and open door were announced at the Third Plenum itself, the four cardinal principles were announced by Deng Xiaoping in a speech in February 1979.[17] Even crystallization of 'one focus, two points' as a framework took place only in the late 1980s. It is important to note that Deng's successor Jiang Zemin constantly emphasized economic construction during his stewardship of the CPC during 1989–2002. In his speech celebrating the eightieth anniversary of the founding of the CPC on 1 July 2001, Jiang elaborated his Theory of Three Represents (*sange daibiao*) of which the first was that the party should represent advanced productive forces. (The other two being representation of advanced culture and representation of the fundamental interests of the majority of the people.)[18] The same perspective was reiterated by Hu Jintao on 1 July 2011 celebrating the ninetieth anniversary of the CPC.[19] The Eighteenth Party Congress reiterated the core ideas of Deng Xiaoping, and Xi Jinping spelt them out further in the course of announcing at the Third Plenum new steps of marketization of the economy in 2013. The introduction of 'supply side structural reforms' in 2016 extended the economic focus forward.

It should be noted that even though 'one focus, two points' is reiterated by all and the focus on economic construction has not changed throughout this period, the emphasis on the two points and their specific components has varied in policy pronouncements and implementation. The nature of the important reforms always depended on the specific decisions by the prevailing leadership. For example, the extent of state-owned enterprise reform or the *hukou* reform and the opening to international financial market were carefully reconsidered from time to time. After all, you decide on how to cross the river by feeling the stones. So, flexibility in policy-making was the norm within the broad reform framework.

Secondly, the concept of reform flowed from Deng Xiaoping's critique of Mao's economic policy during the Cultural Revolution.[20] Deng had pointed out that growth of productive forces should be achieved by all means. If collective ownership and State ownership were not leading to higher productivity, then they should be transformed into or combined with or even subordinated to private or other forms of ownership. Thus, institutional changes, especially *changes in the forms of ownership*, became a major aspect of economic reforms in post-Mao China. At the end of the 1990s, even though quantitatively still some 70 per cent of the means of production were under public ownership, the move was on to reform the SOEs. In 2009–10, 70 per cent of the GDP accrued from non-public sector of the economy.[21] Yet, some critical sectors continued to remain in the public sector. But public sector enterprises were functioning as market-oriented entities. The party had decided to maintain macroeconomic control over the entire economy. This was regarded as one of the main 'socialist' elements of China's market economy. But this has also been interpreted as a method of ensuring the development of capitalist market economy with firm support of the State. Besides, even though public sector remained the dominant sector, such public ownership was subject to the same principles of accountability and management as private ownership. Reform of SOEs was a continuing phenomenon in China during the Eleventh and Twelfth

FYPs. However, it should be noted that a whole range of new combinations of ownership systems—individual, group, cooperative, joint stock, shareholding, national, provincial, local, foreign, with diverse financial investments, territorial jurisdictions and sectoral rights—evolved in the course of the reforms.

Thirdly, according to Deng, centralized management of economic activities by the Communist Party and the State was another bottleneck on growth of production. Such management did not respond to the market situation since the old-style management only implemented policies laid down by authorities from above. Moreover, it did not take any responsibility for gains or losses in production. Hence, *management reform* was a major aspect of the new approach. The Third Plenum emphasized strict differentiation of party, government or administration and enterprise management (*dang zheng qiye fenkai*). Party and government agencies were asked not to interfere in the enterprise management. As we shall see later, this played a major role in developing production in the new context. Each production unit became autonomous in taking decisions that were profitable for itself by choosing the appropriate technology, wage policy and production plans in response to the market situation at home and abroad. Each unit, be it the enterprise, the manager or the worker, was subjected to the production responsibility system. In other words, they earned more wages when they achieved higher production and profit for the unit. Their earnings were reduced corresponding to the decline in production and the income of the enterprise.

The fourth aspect of the reform was the *significant role given to science and technology* for raising production. Deng emphasized the need for modernization literally by using new knowledge of techniques of production to achieve higher productivity. He cited the advances made by the West because of their scientific achievement. This attitude to science was reaffirmed by Jiang Zemin on every possible occasion. Hu Jintao extended this line of thinking by unfolding a grand plan of promoting innovation in every sphere. Xi Jinping regime unfolded a new economic plan for 'China 2025' in May 2015 to change the character of Chinese manufacturing from quantity to quality by developing new technologies and achieving excellence in frontiers of science and technology. Deng described science as a primary productive force. This policy led to greater investment in science, encouraging international collaboration in the various fields of science and technology and forging close links between policy-makers and scientists. Jiang Zemin's second representation that talked about advanced culture included advanced science as well. Hu Jintao's 'innovative society' programme vastly increased investments in science laboratories. Xi Jinping made innovation as the first principle of his 'new development philosophy' with great emphasis on science and technology. China's open-door policy provided a major framework to not only import technology from all parts of the world and establish collaborative research programmes but also steadily develop its own scientific capacity for economic, military and environmental purposes.

Hence, the perspective was designated as 'reform and open door', that is, reform of modes of ownership, management and distribution system and at the same time opening the channels for receiving investment in the form of finance capital and technology and participating in international trade and using both to achieve economic development. In passing, one may note that when Hu Jintao promoted the 'Scientific Outlook on Development' from 2003 onwards, he meant by 'scientific' something distinct, stressing comprehensive and balanced development.

Fifthly, Deng Xiaoping had made it amply clear from the very beginning that the party shall continue to guide the reforms and arrest all negative trends. He had struck down what he called the trends of bourgeois liberalization by dismissing Hu Yaobang in 1987 and deployed the PLA to firmly suppress the youth demonstrations at Tiananmen Square in June 1989. Again, he was the one who re-emphasized the introduction of market economy and private enterprise in a big way in the course of his 'southern tour' to SEZs in Spring 1992. He allayed fears of capitalist restoration saying that the Communist Party would always remain in control and tackle problems of polarization and inequality. Whether that has been the case or did the party allow itself to become the instrument to develop capitalism in China would be a matter of debate and we shall come to it later. But his formulation 'socialism with Chinese characteristics' meant, among other things, that the party and State shall guide the reform process and develop market forces under the watch of the government. As mentioned earlier, the Chinese government effectively handled several crisis situations domestically and internationally because of this system. But it has also meant practising authoritarian politics and refusing to concede people's democratic urges, thus creating alienation and tensions.

Justifying Deng's focus on economic growth, CPC theoreticians pointed out that China did not have a phase of capitalist economy in its history as a result of which productive forces remained backward. The scale of production was low and techniques of production in both agriculture and industry remained backward. Therefore, China needed several decades of economic growth just to modernize its economy and develop the productive forces. For this purpose, China needed to import foreign capital and technology and build its economic base. From this viewpoint, Mao Zedong's economic theory of socialism, especially the class struggle approach, was criticized as being idealist, since it sought to build socialist relations of production without adequately developing the material base or the forces of production. Deng, on the other hand, laid out a programme for what he called the 'primary stage of socialism' which would extend at least until the middle of the twenty-first century when the PRC will be a century old.[22] The same was again affirmed by Hu Jintao in a way assuring the private entrepreneurs and the rising middle classes that the present path of socialist market economy would continue for a long time. In other words, even the mid-twenty-first-century reference point was not relevant and China would continue to focus on economic growth far beyond that. Building China as a prosperous and strong country was the main goal. Jiang's successor Hu Jintao retained that perspective but seeking to address new problems facing China by combining that perspective with building a 'harmonious society'.[23] Xi articulated this through his grand proclamation of the 'Chinese dream of rejuvenation of the Chinese nation' and many pronouncements on celebrating two centenaries. The CPC Constitution affirmed Deng's theoretical proposition on China's reform path in one party congress after another.

Deng's reforms triggered the nationalist imagination of the Chinese unambiguously. The Chinese on the mainland and overseas saw in this a magnificent enterprise to build 'a strong country and a rich nation' (*qiangguo fumin*), the vision of the reformers of late nineteenth-century China. Deng's course embodied continuities of Sun Yat Sen's *three people's principles* (people's nationalism, people's rights and people's livelihood) and Mao Zedong's people's democratic revolution to carry out an anti-colonial and anti-feudal transformation. Along the lines of Mao's PRC foundation-day speech on 1 October 1949, 'The Chinese People Have Stood Up', Deng Xiaoping also gave a stirring call in 1980 to double China's gross national product (GNP) and per capita income in 10 years and redouble them by the year 2000. Actually, the Chinese did achieve that even before the deadline. The Jiang Zemin leadership followed the same line of thinking and targeted to double the 2000 level of the GDP and national income per capita by 2010. At the rally celebrating the fiftieth anniversary of the foundation of the PRC on 1 October 1999, Jiang Zemin reiterated the same goal of building a strong and prosperous China. China's successful hosting of the Olympic Games in 2008 was yet another demonstration of China's nationalist claim. The goals and strategy of China's Eleventh FYP (2006–10) were also set to achieve the doubling of the 2000 level of GDP and per capita income by 2010 and further doubling them by 2020 when a 'moderately well-off society' should have been built in China. The Twelfth FYP (2011–15) continued the same refrain, though aiming at what it called 'pattern transformation'. The Thirteenth Plan announced the goal of comprehensively advancing 'innovative, coordinated, green, open and shared development to establish a moderately prosperous society in all respects'. Even with a relatively lower rate of growth, the aspiration—now with many social and environmental concerns—was still inspiring to most Chinese. Thus, the CPC under the leadership of Deng Xiaoping and his successors has continued to champion Chinese nationalism as the underlying principle of the reform policies. The ideological formulation under Deng Xiaoping Theory of building socialism with Chinese characteristics by promoting 'socialist market economy' conveniently provided a language of discourse to justify this in Marxist theory and carry on building the economy. This was necessary for a communist party to build a market economy and compete with the advanced Western economies.[24]

It is important to stress that China's reforms had indigenous roots and were the product of policy debates and political struggles between Mao and his critics. They were not imposed by the World Bank in times of crisis as in the case of India in 1991 and many other countries of the Third World. What is more, China's 'structural adjustment programme' to use the latter-day World Bank terms started with rural reforms unlike in most other countries where they started with removing restrictions on foreign trade, deregulation of industries and privatization of public enterprises. The success of the rural reforms in China in the 1980s energized the entire Chinese economy by creating a rural market for China's industries which at the same time presented an attractive environment for foreign capital. As we will see later, this period did not last long as the reform strategy unfolded from the mid-1990s essentially as a growth process of export-led manufacturing, while the rural economy was left behind in a serious crisis. At that point, there was some convergence with the World Bank package of reforms. However, soon the Chinese planners realized that their model had to avoid not only Soviet-type centrally planned economy and Maoist policies but also what went as the Washington Consensus on the package of globalization, liberalization and privatization. Gradual, State-guided market economy using globalization to promote their economic objectives with stress on economic growth with their social and political concerns remained the defining characteristic of the Chinese reform path.[25]

Let us now see how the reforms evolved from one phase to another, especially in rural China.

Four Phases of China's Rural Reforms

1. 1979–92: Successful Rural Reforms
   a. 1979–84: Unfolding of the reforms: Fast growth of peasant income
      i.   Household responsibility system (HRS)
      ii. Increase in grain procurement price
      iii. Encouragement of township and village enterprises (TVEs)
   b. 1985–92: Big success of diversified economy with TVEs at the centre
      i.   Streamlining of HRS as a national policy
      ii. Long-term contract of land
      iii. Price reforms—State procurement prices raised
      iv. Relaxation of production quotas
      v.   Diversification of rural economy by promoting new rural enterprises, commerce and third industry in general
2. 1992–99: Manufacture for Export
   a. Shift of focus to urban and private economy and access to foreign capital
      i.   Acceleration of reforms and open door after Deng's southern tour
      ii. Fast expansion of private enterprises, foreign-owned enterprises
      iii. Growth of specialized farm households
      iv. Reorganization of rural enterprises
   b. 1999–2002: Responses to rural crisis
      i.   Village–level elections on competitive basis as per 1998 Organic Law
      ii. Privatization of TVEs—inviting multiple sources of investment
      iii. Emphasis on technological upgradation
      iv. Reorganization of rural units, formation of more urban entities (*shi* or city and *zhen* or town) in rural areas
      v.   Emphasis on market competitiveness in the context of accession to World Trade Organization (WTO)
3. High Growth with Social Concerns
   a. 2002–07: Building a new socialist countryside
      i.   Abolition of agricultural tax
      ii. Emphasis on rural infrastructure-building
      iii. Social security measures in the countryside
      iv. Larger funding to county, city and township governments
      v.   Social management and rising tensions

  b. 2007–12: Scientific development and harmonious society
   i. Growth with stimulus in financial crisis
   ii. Enhanced grants for rural government
   iii. Managing migrant labour
   iv. Focus on reducing regional disparities
   v. Pursuing ecological policies
 4. 2012–17: Coordinated Development
  a. Making innovation or science and technology as the key principle of development
  b. Launching new urbanization
  c. Supply-side structural reforms
  d. Restructuring land policies to promote agribusiness and industries
  e. Governance reforms—fighting corruption and raising efficiency and ethical standards
  f. Launching the Belt and Road Initiative

This schematic view of the various phases of reforms may not be exhaustive, but it helps in showing how the central principles of Deng's reform perspective were put into operation. Maintaining the focus on achieving economic growth, the leadership changed policies to meet the contingent situation from time to time.

During the first phase, the *HRS replaced the commune system*. This was a major institutional reform. The second policy measure during this period was the enhancement of the procurement prices with which actually the rural reforms started soon after the Third Plenum. This brought more income to the peasants throughout China, thus creating a legitimating base for the Deng Xiaoping leadership. Thirdly, production quotas were fixed for various crops, particularly grain output, on the basis of which an incentive price structure was organized. Production surpassing the quota brought higher dividends to the peasants. Finally, rural industrialization was made an important element of the rural development strategy. Together, these policies brought about a significant growth in grain output from an annual rate of 2.4 per cent during the period 1952–78 to 5 per cent in 1978–84 and in agricultural production as a whole from 1.9 to 7.4 per cent. The per capita peasant income grew threefold between 1978 and 1985 (see Table 2.1).

Firstly, during the late 1980s, the HRS was put into practice all over the country. The economic gains achieved by this system were cited as the basis of the new policy. The 1 January 1985 document of the CC and the State Council announced *10 policies for the further invigoration of rural economy*. These policies focused on *reforming the prices* and bridging the gap between the State monopoly purchase of grains and the market prices. Secondly,

Table 2.1:
High growth rate 1978–2015

Items	1978	1989	1997	2005	2010	2012	2015	Average Annual Growth Rate 1979–2015	Average Annual Growth Rate 2001–15
GDP (100 MY[a])	364.52	1,699.23	7,897.30	183,084.8	401,202	518,942.1	685,505.8	9.7	9.7
Primary industry[a]	101.84	422.80	1,426.46	2,307.04	40,533.6	52,373.6	60,870.5	4.4	4.1
Secondary industry[a]	174.52	727.80	3,754.30	8,704.67	187,581.4	235,162	280,560.3	11	10.4
Gross output value of agriculture[a]	139.70	653.47	2,378.84	3,945.09	69,319.8	89,453	107,056.4	5.7	4.8
Grain (10,000 tons)	304.765	407.549	494.171	484.022	5,4647.7	58,958	62,143.9	1.9	2
Oil-bearing crops (10,000 tons)	521.8	12,95.2	2,157.4	3,077.1	—	3,436.8	3,537	5.3	1.3
Aquatic products (10,000 tons)	4.654	11.517	36.018	51.076	53.730	5,907.7	6,699.6	7.5	4
Coal (billion tons)	0.618	1.054	1.373	2.205	3.235	3.65	3.75	5	6.9
Crude oil (million tons)	104.05	137.64	160.74	181.35	203.014	207.47	214.5	2	1.8
Natural gas (billion cum)	13.73	15.05	22.70	50.94	94.848	107.13	134.6	6.4	11.3
Crude steel (million tons)	31.78	61.59	108.94	353.24	637.22	723.88	803.82	9.1	13
Cement (billion tons)	65.24	210.29	511.74	1,068.85	1,881.91	2,209.8	2,359.18	10.2	9.6
Civil aviation (million passengers)	2.3	12.83	56.30	138.27	267.69	319.36	436.18	15.2	13.3
Volume of freight handled in major coastal ports (million tons)	198.34	490.25	908.22	2,927.77	5,483.58	6,652.45	7,845.78	10.5	13

Domestic trade: retail sales of consumer goods (100 MY)	155.9	810.1	3125.3	67,177	156,998	210,307.9	300,931	15.3	14.6
Foreign trade: total value (billion US$)	20.64	111.68	325.16	1,421.91	2,974	3,867.12	3,953.03	15.3	15.2
Exports (billion US$)	9.75	52.54	182.79	761.95	1,577.75	2,048.71	2,273.47	15.9	15.9
Imports (billion US$)	10.89	59.14	142.37	659.95	1,396 24	1,818.41	16,795.6	14.6	14.3
Foreign direct investment (billion US$)	—	3.39	45.26	60.33	105.74	111.71	126.27	—	7.8

Sources: National Bureau of Statistics of China, *China Statistical Yearbook*, 2006, 26–30 Table 2.3; 2011 (Table 1-5), 26–30 Table 2.3; 2011 (Table 1-5), 27–37 (see Section 1-7); 2013; 2016 (see Section 1.2).

Note: ᵃ100 million yuan.

during this period, the quota system was relaxed in many areas and *peasants were allowed to sell in the market*. Until then, the State was the only buyer. Thirdly, *diversification of the rural economy* was consciously encouraged during this phase. Development of *rural industries and commerce* and horticulture, fisheries and all possible expansion of the rural economy were encouraged. The objective was to absorb as much surplus rural labour as possible within the countryside. By the end of the 1990s, out of the estimated 200-million surplus labour from agriculture, about 130 million were absorbed in rural industries themselves.[26] This period also saw the decisive recomposition of the rural economy. In 1987, the contribution of agriculture to the total rural output value of the rural economy was surpassed by the contribution of the non-agricultural sector. In 1995, 67 per cent of the total output value was contributed by the rural industries. Other measures during the second phase included conservation and utilization of land and policy on ensuring continuous investment in agriculture.

The next phase began with Deng Xiaoping's southern tour in early 1992. After the Tiananmen episode of 1989 and the collapse of Eastern European regimes and the Soviet Union in 1991, there was a debate within the CPC leadership on the desirability of further enhancing of market reforms and open-door policies. Chen Yun, senior CPC leader, reportedly wanted that the party should maintain its leadership role in the economy at every level and further privatization of the economy should be stopped. However, Deng Xiaoping personally intervened to thwart this trend of thought. In the course of his visits to the SEZs in Shenzhen, Zhuhai and others on the occasion of the tenth anniversary of their launching, he reaffirmed the need to *accelerate the reforms and further open China to the rest of the world*. He said that with the CPC leadership in power, there should be no apprehension about capitalist takeover of China. This triggered a new wave of marketization and foreign investment in China. Gradually, the sanctions imposed by the Western countries in the wake of the Tiananmen incident were overcome and the economy acquired a fresh momentum.

In the later years of this phase, policy measures were also initiated to add a note of caution to the prevailing trends in grain production and rural industrialization. As for grain production, the performance record was one of fluctuating rates of growth. In fact, the Food and Agricultural Organization of the United Nations raised the scare of an impending food crisis in early twenty-first-century China. Of course, China refuted the prophecy of gloom. But it took a number of measures to ensure continuous rise in grain production. Severe restrictions were imposed on utilizing agricultural land for industrial and other urban purposes. During the 1980s, there was a great deal of conversion of agricultural land to non-agricultural purposes. In Wuxi area, there were examples galore in the suburban districts and the counties to move from grain production to cash crops and from agriculture to industry and commerce. Every *xiang* (rural township) wished to become a *zhen* (urban township). Every *xian* (rural county) wanted to become a *shi* (town/city). There was great disappointment whenever pleas of a local party leadership to get an urban status were turned down by the higher authorities. Every peasant wanted to move from grain production to produce vegetables or other cash crops which gave him/her higher income. Every village committee wanted to build industrial plants or hotels and commercial outfits which involved more commercial use of agricultural land. We will see many examples of this trend in the next chapter on the case study of Wuxi. All this meant less and less of land being used for agriculture. In China, already the per capita availability of cultivable land was low (it was one-third of the same in India). With a large populous society with population growing at the rate of 1.9 despite a very successful population control policy, the need for ensuring grain supply cannot be overestimated, hence, the government policy of *maintaining the availability of agricultural land*. In the Thirteenth Plan, designation of agricultural land for grain production was further stabilized by regulation in order to ensure food security in China.

Irrespective of the quantity of land, the need for modernizing agriculture with the help of improved technology was emphasized in the 1990s. The introduction of the *specialized farm households* in the very first phase of the rural reforms had embodied this policy. In the 1990s, agricultural mechanization became a major policy directive. In the course of the first decade of reforms, because of small-scale household agriculture it was not possible to take advantage of modern technology. The families were left to themselves to look after their land. No doubt the village committee especially its director of agricultural operations supervised the production process. But on the whole, mechanization and scientific farming did not make any headway. In the 1990s, this was one of the focal points of rural policies. The township government drew up plans for the entire area, setting up *science and technology* groups in each village, reinvigorating the farm machinery stations and encouraging the formation of new service cooperatives, some for helping production and some for marketing.

Rural industry reforms were another aspect of the new policies in the 1990s. The peak of rural industrialization had been achieved in the mid-1980s. Now, those rural industries which did not stand up to the market competition were asked to be closed down or diversify their production so that they could earn profit. Strict *quality control measures* were laid down for rural industrial products. Units producing poor-quality goods were severely penalized and often their products were burnt in bulk in public. Another important measure was in the realm of ownership structure of the rural industries. Since most of them in the coastal provinces were collectively owned, the new policy asked them to transform into shareholding companies. The idea was that they could have adequate capital in order to acquire new technology and promote marketing. Thus, the *ownership character of rural industries underwent major changes* in the 1990s. The 'Su Nan model' (south of Yangtze River in Jiangsu province) which is the focus of this study still maintained the essential elements of the collective economy. But they also underwent structural changes to become more like joint-stock companies. Many were simply sold to private entrepreneurs. In the process, the rural industries were encouraged to open up and negotiate with foreign investors for buying modern technology from foreign countries, for diversifying their production and for designing a new marketing strategy at home and abroad. As China intensified the negotiations to join the WTO, these changes acquired greater significance.

Another phase was inaugurated with the adoption of the 'decision on agriculture and certain major issues in the rural areas' by the Third Plenum of the Fifteenth CPCCC in September 1999. There was a serious shift of policy with regard to the development of urban entities in the countryside. It supported the growth of cities (*shi*) and towns (*zhen*) in the rural areas so that urban facilities as well as non-agricultural economic activities could grow without restrictions. China had already achieved the quantitative target of producing 490 million tons of grains, surpassing the requirement for 485 million tons, though the problem of fulfilling the objective of producing good-quality grains remained. The new urban-in-rural framework perhaps could facilitate a greater integration of the production process with the market situation which was urgently needed in the light of the stiff competition that would come into play after China joined the WTO. The second decision related to the TVEs. They were asked to transform themselves in both ownership structure and production plans in the new situation arising out of the reforms of the SOEs. The earlier advantages they enjoyed vis-à-vis the products of SOEs now began to shrink with the SOEs becoming more flexible and competitive. In order to compete with the SOEs and also the global market, the TVEs sought more investment and new technology for new products. This compelled most of the TVEs to transform themselves into private enterprises or joint venture or shareholding enterprises. Many TVEs were closed down in this process as well—especially those that had become bankrupt and had no buyers. The private investment led to a high degree of diversification of the economy for they were based on the market demands then and in future. 'Reforms in the taxation system' was yet another decision in the fourth phase. Since 1992, Jiang Zemin had been talking about the problem of overburdened peasants. They paid taxes to the State, land contract fee to the village collective and a variety of fees to the village and the township besides occasional labour for the collective or fees in lieu of that. But it was decided to go slow with these reforms and do it on experimental basis. Yet, another decision was to cut down the size of the personnel at the local government level to not only cut down bureaucracy but also reduce the financial burden on the peasants since the salaries of local officials are paid out of the peasants' contributions. A formal decision was also taken to allow transfer of *hukou* at the county level and below. Thus, a peasant could move from village to a nearby town or city at the county level and register his/her residence there. The earlier rationale for the strict maintenance of a *hukou* system that prevented easy migration was considered superfluous. The rural residents were now free to look for jobs elsewhere. On the other hand, if the local area provided opportunities for employment which catered to the needs of the rural people, they would consider to stay. Yet a total abolition of the *hukou* system was not on the cards. Cities, particularly big ones, had to face the problem of providing health care and educational facilities to their legal residents. Finally, a new stress was laid on the democratic elections for the constitution of the villagers committee where the first multiple-candidate competitive elections had been held in late 1998 in most parts of the country.

The third phase of reforms in the early 2000s presented a new environment in China's countryside—one of prosperity as well as distress. The HRS, rural industries and private industry and commerce had led to a substantial increase of rural income across the board. At the same time, it had created many new trends such as inequalities in income and new social differentiation and gradual neglect of collective welfare. It had produced a new class of rich farmers and entrepreneurs who now operated in agriculture, industry and commerce, rural and urban economy, and the production, as well as the administrative processes. The Chinese rural economy was now integrated with the national economy and had significant linkages with the world economy.

The policies initiated during the 1990s were inadequate to respond to the intensifying crisis in the countryside. The changed status of the TVEs had reduced the funds at the disposal of the local governments and consequently vastly decreased their support to schools and hospitals and other welfare programmes. On the other hand, the village authorities charged more and more fees in order to maintain whatever services they had under their jurisdiction. In the 1980s, agricultural infrastructure had been improved by local authorities out of the profit the village had made from rural industries. Now that was sharply reduced. The employment opportunities which had expanded in the countryside with the TVEs absorbing a major component of surplus rural labour now began to recede. All this affected agricultural production as well. Even grain production fluctuated as China's overall economy continued to grow at a high rate due to rapid growth of manufacturing industries and expansion of exports. By the time of the Sixteenth Party Congress in 2002, China's leaders were talking of rural problems and world press was reporting on rural revolts. Migration to cities, which was natural and for economic reasons so far, increasingly assumed dimensions of distress migration. The booming cities of East China needed labour and they used this easily available mass of cheap labour. But this stream of migrant labour reflected crisis in the countryside. Solving the 'three rural problems' (*san nong wenti*)—the problem of raising production in *agriculture* (*nongye*), problem of low income of *peasants* (*nongmin*) and problem of poor infrastructure including in health, education and social welfare in *countryside* (*nongcun*) became the focus of much discussion in China. The magnitude of the rural crisis is evident from the following statement by Wen Jiabao in his report to the NPC in March 2006:

> First, it has become difficult to further increase grain production and rural incomes. There is downward pressure on grain prices and upward pressure on the prices of agricultural supplies, making it difficult for farmers to increase their earnings and discouraging them from growing grain. Moreover, the total area of useable farmland continues to decrease, and the overall agricultural production capacity is weak. This poses a threat to the nation's food security.[27]

Wen repeated it in March 2007:

> Agriculture, the base of the economy remains weak, and it is now more difficult than ever to steadily increase grain production and keep rural incomes growing.[28]

To address this crisis, the Hu Jintao–Wen Jiabao leadership announced a new slogan of 'building a new socialist countryside'—first at the Fifth Plenum of the CPCCC in 2005 and then with some specified elements as a part of the premier's report to the NPC in 2006. Its detailed policies were slow in taking shape and there seemed to be debates on the basic path that rural transformation should take at the current stage of China's reforms and 'peaceful rise' or 'peaceful development'. Some economists argued for continuing the current line of development, namely the urbanization path, by investing more on urban construction and absorbing the migrant labour in the services, construction and manufacturing activities in the metropolitan and other urban centres, while a large group of scholars and policy-makers advocated the path of rural development by investing more resources in agriculture, rural industries, transport, and health and education to provide employment opportunities and better livelihood in rural areas. The CPC leadership seemed to strike a balance between the two views as evident from the outline of the Eleventh FYP as well as the deliberations in the State and party forums.

At any rate, the policies announced in the first two years of the Eleventh FYP seemed to address the three rural problems directly. Abolition of the agricultural tax (*nongfei*) on the New Year's Day of 2006 was a major event considering that it had existed in one form or the other for nearly 2,600 years and was the principal source of revenue in traditional China. In the late 1990s, some taxes had been merged, and township and village governments were asked to reduce the number of levies on the peasants. But still the burden on the peasants continued to be heavy, while their income remained low. Therefore, this measure was welcomed widely all over China. On the issue of protection of land rights, the leadership had already taken some significant action by passing Land Contract Law and Agriculture Law in 2002, emphasizing the long-term use right of the contracted land and the flexibility of subcontracting. But the provisions in those very laws regarding the transfer of agricultural land to enterprises were violated indiscriminately, causing violent incidents in many places. The Centre issued directives to strictly enforce the provision of approval by the villagers' assembly by two-thirds votes.

The most important aspects of the new policies were larger allocation for agriculture in 2007—391.7 billion yuan, 52 billion yuan more than the previous year—a higher magnitude of support for rural infrastructure development, construction of water conservancy and roads, and facilities for livestock farming. More funding for health and education, especially achieving the targets of nine-year compulsory education, and special funds for the implementation of that programme in the backward areas were some other elements of the new programme. The Eleventh Plan as well as the premier's reports to the NPC did talk about developing secondary and tertiary industries in the countryside, especially the ones related to agricultural processing. But clearly, the emphasis on collective enterprises in rural economy—the TVEs which had transformed the countryside in the 1980s—had passed into history. Yet, there was no indication of closing them down. In fact, even in 2006, there were nearly 2 million rural enterprises employing over 150 million workers and constituting three-fourths of the rural output value and over a quarter of China's exports.

Under the announced perspective of the Twelfth FYP (2011–15) for 'transformation of the pattern of economic development', agriculture did acquire some emphasis. Responding to the 'three rural problems', 'Premier Wen Jiabao announced in his Report on the Work of the Government, in March 2012, that they fully implemented the policy of strengthening agriculture benefiting farmers and enriching rural areas'. Priority was given to irrigation and water conservation projects, improved rural land and increased technological services. According to him, Central government spending on agriculture, rural areas and farmers exceeded 1 trillion yuan in 2011, an increase of 183.9 billion yuan over the previous year. He also reported that many dilapidated houses in rural areas were renovated, potable water for 63.98 million additional rural residents was ensured and new rural areas were electrified covering 600,000 people. However, the momentum which was seen during the early years of the Eleventh Plan under the programme of a new socialist countryside seemed to have faded away. As we will see later, health and education remain neglected and infrastructure development in the countryside remains slow.

The policies under the Eleventh FYP did take note of the plight of the rural migrant labour in the cities and spelt out some important measures to provide them social security to some extent. Even though the *hukou* system continued to remain as a policy, there were further relaxations for the migrant workers. The children of the migrant workers got some educational and health benefits in many cities. In the countryside, a system of providing partial health insurance was introduced to the peasants. Old-age insurance for rural residents covering 358 million people was introduced on a trial basis.[29]

Building a 'harmonious society' involved reducing rural–urban gap and achieving social development in addition to economic development, and it was hoped that from that perspective, the rural population was to gain more than they did in the recent past. But the trend of export-led industrialization persisted throughout the Eleventh Plan. More and more rural areas were taken over by enterprises either for setting up new industries or for developing real estate. In many places, this led to confrontation between the local administration and the peasants. Some of these incidents turned violent, causing deaths of demonstrating peasants. Thus, in addition to the increasing trend of social inequality and regional disparity, farmers' discontent became an expanding phenomenon. Retrenched labour had already become restive, and labour in many factories had resorted to prolonged strikes in many parts of China such as Liaoning. In view of such developments, the CPC leadership decided to focus on social management or, in the official parlance 'social construction' (*shehui jianshi*). The Fourth Session of the Eleventh

NPC in March 2011 formally announced this new emphasis. The goal of 'economic pattern transformation' in the Twelfth Plan and focus on social construction defined the new parameters of building a harmonious society within the perspective of Hu Jintao's scientific development which meant pursuing a path of coordinated, balanced development combining growth with social equity and environmental sustainability. However, in practice, it was not easy to achieve. Xi Jinping gave these efforts a strong push with additional dimensions.

The Thirteenth FYP carried the stamp of Xi Jinping in economic as well as sociopolitical objectives. Lower rate of economic growth between 6 and 8 per cent or medium-to-high rate as they put it was the 'new normal'. Focus on innovation and pursuing 'supply side structural reforms' and greater emphasis on domestic market were given more attention than before.[30] Science and technology in both research and application in all sectors were given utmost importance not only to produce high-quality goods but also to make China 'a talent-rich country of innovation'. Supply-side structural reforms—very differently conceived from the neoliberal supply side reforms that give maximum freedom to entrepreneurs—involved a number of measures to change the structure of the economy. The National Development and Reform Commission (NDRC) report to the Twelfth NPC in March 2017 listed five priority tasks in this regard directed at reforming the real economy—the economy that is concerned with production of the goods and services: cutting overcapacity, reducing excess inventory, deleveraging, lowering costs and strengthening points of weakness.[31] Cutting down excess coal and steel production, reducing the number of housing projects which vastly surpassed the demand, reducing business leverages by mergers and restructuring to tackle the situation of high debts, and taking substantial cost-reduction measures including cutting down enterprise contribution to many welfare schemes were some of the bold steps taken by the regime.[32] As for rural economy, the Thirteenth Plan had a different approach altogether talking of agricultural modernization and new urbanization, rather than the earlier discourse on tackling the 'three rural problems' and building a 'new socialist countryside'.

The Thirteenth Plan focused on technology-driven, integrated agriculture, rural industry and services to assure the required level of food production and improved livelihood for the rural people.[33] A highlight of this approach was the launching of the '100 counties, 1,000 townships and 10,000 villages' pilot demonstration project to integrate primary, secondary and tertiary industries. The earlier focus on diversification of the rural economy now took a new form with much new stress on technological inputs and business processes.

Two steps were initiated on the land rights of rural households and rural migrants. Described as trial reforms, beginnings were made to separate land ownership rights, contract rights and management rights to make land available for commercial and industrial purposes. Without abandoning the system of collective rights of the village over land, there was a declaration to 'grant the rural residents more adequate property rights'.[34] It is well-known that in many parts of China, land transfer by the village leaders had become an issue of resistance by the villagers. The trend now was clear. Land had to be made available, but the contracted farmer should get substantial benefit. As for the rural migrant, Li Keqiang's Report to the Twelfth NPC mentioned that 13 million more migrants in medium-size cities would be given permanent status as urban residents. Undoubtedly, this was a small gesture compared to the presence of over 300 million rural residents in the cities. The Thirteenth Plan aimed at giving urban resident status to 100 million rural migrants. As is well known, without the urban residency, the migrants and their family members are not entitled to health, education, housing and other welfare facilities availed by the registered urban residents. The orientation of the Xi Jinping regime was to go ahead with 'new urbanization', developing counties and towns into cities and integrating chains of cities of different sizes into a modern urban economy. The new urbanization concept stressed the role of technology to build ecologically sustainable, energy-efficient cities that not only provide all modern comforts but also are 'harmonious and beautiful'. Promotion of 'coordinated urban–rural development' was announced as a goal, though the rural–urban income disparity continued to be substantial urban income about three times the rural.[35] Considering the high level of inequality in both urban and rural China, the picture of this disparity would be even more striking in the case of the majority of rural people compared with the urban residents. However, many measures including abolition of absolute poverty—the remaining 43 million according to the official estimates by 2020—increased health insurance, and more investment in building up the rural economy may help this situation to change.

Among the many initiatives launched under Xi Jinping leadership linking up national development with international initiatives and strict energy-saving and anti-pollution environmental measures are conspicuous. The Belt and Road Initiative involving the Silk Road Economic Belt linking Asia and Europe land route and the Twenty-first-century Maritime Silk Road linking Asia with Europa and Africa already made much progress building six economic corridors and six channels.[36] On the energy saving front, Li Keqiang announced the target for reduction of at least 3.4 per cent in energy consumption per unit of GDP during 2017. The proportion of non-fossil energy consumption rose to 13.3 per cent in 2016 and coal consumption dropped by 62 per cent. Many initiatives, such as forming zones for ecological conservation and management, return of farmland to build forest and grassland, absolute ban on increasing chemical fertilizer and constant monitoring of the action plan on developing climate-resilient cities were launched.

Above all, the perspective on development that was popularized under Xi Jinping leadership and became the key to all policies was a comprehensive message to make development 'innovative, coordinated, green, open and shared'. To translate this vision into reality was the main task.

It should be noted that each regime maintained the governing principles of the reforms while changing policies to meet demands of the emerging situation. Let us now analyse the main institutional principles. They are the key ideas which ought to be debated globally.

Features of China's Reforms Strategy

These are not only the main features of the rural reforms, but they also indicate the general orientation of the economic reforms.

1. Household responsibility system
2. Development of market economy coordinated by the State
3. Integrated development of agriculture, industry and services
4. Regulated interaction with global economy

Household Responsibility System

In 1979, in a county in Sichuan Province, some communes decided to lease land to families for cultivation. This was done by the production teams which decided that the concerned households should decide on their own production plans.[37] This was described as contracting of the production output to individual households (*bao chan daohu*). In the meantime, two documents had been issued by the CC in 1979 whose main thrust was to counter egalitarianism and initiate incentive-based work for accelerating production.[38] Thus, the policy changes slowly unfolded in practice and by the end of 1979, at least 15 per cent of the production teams in Anhui province had adopted the production contract system. By the middle of 1980, this experience had been accepted as a new possibility. This practice had started as contracting of production quota in some areas. Later, in many communes, the entire agricultural activity—land, draught animals and farming tools—was also allotted to the households on contract. They would pay a fee to the collective and enjoy the income out of it.

This system took time to spread in China. When I first visited Wuxi's rural area in May 1979, the three-tier commune system was still operating. A year later, in June 1980 also, the transition had not taken place fully, though there were signs of responsibility system emerging in rural industries. By the time of my fieldwork in 1985, the new HRS was operating in full swing. After the September 1980 policy declaration by the CPCCC, there was no doubt that the party wanted this system to be adopted everywhere. By early 1982, only 10 per cent of China's production teams had been operating the commune system and by the end of 1984 as much as 96.56 per cent of all agricultural households had been covered by the HRS.

PRC commentators refuse to call this step 'de-collectivization' of agriculture in China. They point out that land had only been contracted or leased out to individual households, while the ownership still remained with the village collective. (Under law, rural land belonged to the village collective and urban land belong to the national government in China.) However, the situation got gradually complicated with changes in the property laws later. As noted earlier, under the Xi Jinping regime, steps were taken to separate ownership rights and contract rights from use rights to facilitate development of industrial and commercial enterprises in rural land.

The HRS was a major step in reversing the character of the commune economy. Under the new system, the total agricultural land under a village was allotted or contracted to individual households according to the number of working people in a household. Thus, households with more members would get a larger piece of land. The size of land distributed to the household depended on the total amount of cultivable land available in the village as a whole. Thus, it would vary from village to village, township to township and county to county in different parts of China. Suburban and rural areas in a high-density population zone like Jiangsu would have very little land per head. In Hela Township of Wuxi's suburban district, for example, the per capita availability of land was only 0.3 mu, whereas in the suburbs of Xi'an city in Shaanxi province it was 3.5 mu per head. The village committee which is authorized to distribute land and monitor the HRS tried to make an even distribution of land in terms of quality of land. In this, of course, there are always complaints about some influential families getting better land than the others.

There was an interesting parallel between the commune system and the HRS. In 1979, I asked a production team leader: 'Who are the rich families of the village?' Quickly came the reply, 'Those who have more labouring hands' (*duo laodongli duo fu*). In earlier times, a family with more workers earned more work points in a commune. Now under HRS, a larger household got a large piece of land. But now, a much smaller part of the family could be engaged in agriculture on behalf of the whole family and the others could go for commerce or for working in factories. As we will see later, as agricultural income failed to rise satisfactorily and employment in rural enterprises fluctuated, farmers left for cities to work. In many cases, men migrated leaving behind women and children. Production under HRS was no longer the source of assured income. That is why the phenomenon of specialized households and subsequently technology-driven agricultural modernization programmes came up.

As mentioned earlier, the contract was about production quota to begin with. Usually, the higher level authorities fixed the production quota for the immediate lower level, taking into account the average of the three previous years of output. Usually, the quota is settled through negotiations by the two sets of leaders and they may agree on a higher target as well. The provincial government set the quota for each county, the county fixed the quota for each township, the township set the production target for each village and the village committee in turn fixed the quota for each household. If the quota was over-fulfilled, the peasant would get incentive prices from the State and would earn more for its produce. The new purchasing price was far more than the previous price. For the amount above the quota, there was even higher price.

HRS was a part of the wider principle of responsibility that was introduced as a governing principle of the reforms by Deng Xiaoping. In this case, there was responsibility about the performance in production. Under this *responsibility system* (*zeren zhi*), the Deng Xiaoping regime claimed that the principle of 'each according to his/her ability and each according to his/her work' was put into force. The peasant would do his/her best to produce more and would accordingly earn more for his/her work. The same applied to rural enterprises and practically all other spheres of productive work gradually came under the *production responsibility system* (*shengcan zeren zhi*).

The system of production quota underwent much change in subsequent years. The initial incentive for the farming household fulfilling the production quota was to get the incentive price for the grains fixed by the State. But later, the rules were changed, allowing the farmers to sell their produce in the market. Sometimes, that gave them higher returns. But the market situation fluctuated from time to time and the farmers' returns also varied. During the Eleventh Plan, the Central government paid much attention to fixing minimum support prices for the produce of the farmers. But with the overall decline of the rural situation, farmers got little incentive for producing food grains. The main form of quota that remained in operation was the overall production quota for various crops, particularly food grains for provinces, counties and townships. Thus, the initial rationale for the HRS as promoting production incentive steadily weakened. However, the household's autonomy to plan its allocation of labour or who should work in which sector continued as an important element of reforms.

The tenure of lease or contract was only one to three years when the system was started in 1980. But after 'testing the waters', the party CC announced in 1983 that the responsibility system had enormously contributed to the growth of production.[39] It recommended all forms of the responsibility system, including labour contracts, marketing contracts, transport contracts, construction contracts and various other forms of production contracts. Consolidating this structural change further, the CPC leadership announced in 1984 that the contracts could be for longer durations. It extensively dealt with 'prolonging the contracted period of land use and encouraging farmers to increase investments, enrich land fertility and adopt intensive operations'.[40] At this point, the contract period could exceed 15 years and even longer in cases of horticulture, wasteland development, etc. It was pointed out that short-term contracts for one to three years led to intensive cultivation for maximizing quick returns without caring for land fertility and long-term agricultural output, hence the decision for longer contracts. After 1987, in some areas, the period was extended to 30 years. In 1993, the time limit was abandoned in most provinces. The contract was now for an indefinite period to be inherited by the next generation. This was done on the assumption that a household would pay greater attention to improving the productivity of land, planning its long-term economic use together with the family's other productive activities.

The 1984 document on rural reforms took another major decision, allowing one household to subcontract its land to another household. According to the document,

[The] terms of this transfer of contracted land may be agreed by both sides in accordance with the local customs. Under the present system of grain purchase and supply, households that accept the contracted land of the others are allowed to provide the latter with certain amount of food grains at lower price.[41]

Under this arrangement, many households found it more convenient to subcontract their land to 'specialized households'. Those who were not able to engage in agriculture and those who opted for better sources of earning in industry, commerce or some other activity in urban areas also subcontracted their land. Thus, officially, land concentration was encouraged to facilitate growth in production, with able cultivators playing a special role. The law, however, forbade sale or renting of contracted land and land earmarked for personal use or using them for household or personal use or using them for other non-agricultural purposes. The terms of subcontract made it different from 'renting' in that the arrangement had the concurrence of the village committee and the original contract holder got a small share from the subcontract holder mutually agreed to. The original landholder had the right to recover his/her land any time. Except in the case of the specialized households, the relatively poor who took land on subcontract did have an unequal relationship with the main holder of the land contract.

Many of these provisions were clarified and codified in a new law on land contract in rural areas which was passed by the NPC Standing Committee in August 2002 and promulgated on 1 March 2003. It made the term of contract 30 years for arable land, while for grassland it ranged from 30 to 50 years and for forest land 30 to 70 years (Article 20). The rights and obligations of contracting parties and procedures of contracting and subcontracting were clearly stated in this law. That the household had the authority to decide on the production plan and subcontracting ('Right to Circulate Land' under Article 16) without the interference of the village committee was also mentioned in the law.

Since the promulgation of the 1984 policy, the farmers and collectives had the freedom to use their funds as they liked. Farmers were encouraged to invest in enterprises and buy shares anywhere they liked. Thus, the household could plan its economic activity in a multifarious way. It could invest in agriculture and diversify its sources of earning simultaneously. In Hela, most women worked in rural enterprises which were light industries, while men looked after agriculture in the early 1980s. As years passed by, the more qualified men moved to modern industries and some older women looked after the fields. These changes had serious effects on the nature of division of labour among men and women about which we will discuss more in Chapter 8. Here, it is important to note that the household emerged as the autonomous unit of economic decision-making in rural China. Earlier it was the collective or the State which had decided on allocation of labour and capital. The system of joint labour, unified accounting and unified distribution which prevailed during the commune years was now replaced by the household-based decision on all these aspects and more.

There is a long-standing debate as to whether the nature of agricultural production is such that it can be best managed only by a household. The vulnerability to natural conditions, especially weather, the process of plant biology and the fact that only the totality of the production process can be properly evaluated in agriculture unlike in industry are some of the reasons cited by its proponents who quote Lenin in their support.[42] But history presented a multiple variety of examples ranging from community agriculture in both plain and tribal areas and cooperative farming in many parts of the world to corporate agricultural firms which are very different from household farming. But it has to be admitted that during the first two decades, the HRS in China created an environment of enthusiastic farming by the peasants while at the same time making land equitably accessible to the rural households.

When the communes were introduced in 1958, the rural social structure had been shaken up in a major way. It sought to abolish class contradictions in the countryside. The land reforms of 1950–52 had abolished landlordism and had distributed the landlord's land among the landless and the poor peasants. The formation of the agricultural producer's cooperatives (APCs) in 1954 and their advanced form in 1956 had begun the process of transformation of agrarian ownership structure. The collectivization of land ownership turned all households into equal participants in the production process. This was one of the promises of the Chinese people's democratic revolution which was accomplished in the course of the commune period. It had significantly reduced class inequality in rural China. Only those families who had household assets and links with urban economy and culture had certain higher status. But they were targets of political campaigns from time to time. But whether the commune system weakened the institution of family is an open question.

The smoothness with which the rural reforms were implemented after 1978 shows that the institution of family had survived the commune period as a solidly functioning unit. No doubt, each commune member had a separate passbook which recorded his/her work points. To that extent, there was an individualization of rural society in the course of the production process. But then more hands meant more income. A couple needed each other's income. They raised children and often remained in one joint family, pulling their income together. Moreover, the *five relationships* according to

Confucius (father and son, elder brother and younger brother, husband and wife, teacher and disciple, and king and subject) still operated as powerful values despite the Marxist education and CPC ideological campaigns. It is this culture which was one of the targets of the Cultural Revolution which has since been discredited by the post-Mao regime. Hence, culture and the economy converged in both the commune system and the HRS during the reform period. With the rise of income and as a result of the economic calculus of the new economic opportunities, families began to split in the late 1980s between parents and married children and between brothers. But family as a cultural and economic unit continued to persist in contemporary China.[43] The introduction of the one-child norm had made it an even stronger unit as parents and grandparents invested quite a lot in bringing up their one child, and the child in turn was highly attached to the parents. The institution of family thus got reinforced through intimate links between generations, though in the new economic milieu, young couples were increasingly setting up their separate homes. Close family ties continued despite this as seen in the mushrooming of family enterprises in recent years and of course in the patronage that the children of the cadres got to rise in the system.

While the CPC leadership has affirmed the long-term commitment to the household-based contract responsibility system, they have to manage some practical problems. One is the problem of small size of farmland available to each household. This problem of segmentation of land has been handled under the land laws of 1999 and 2003 by authorizing the village committee to adjust the quantum of land with the change in the composition of the household. Small changes are permitted every three years and major changes can be done every five years taking into account deaths in the household, coming to adulthood of children and such other things. A legal problem that persists in this connection pertains to the nature of the parties to the land contracts. These are technically contracts with households, but carried out by individual heads of the households—usually male heads. Thus, the HRS has reinforced the patriarchal character of the Chinese family, even though male and female members have equal share of the contracted land. Moreover, these are administrative contracts between the village leadership and the household that do not have a legal framework. So, the terms of these contracts may vary from area to area. All this is allowed under the 1984 decision which authorized local bodies 'to make minor adjustments while maintaining overall stability of the policy'.

Even though the ownership of land remains with the village collective, the HRS in practice facilitated a new process of change in the property relations in China's countryside. The surplus from agricultural production was appropriated by the peasant household, and the additional income from industrial, commercial and other sources led to a process of accumulation of private property. Those who accumulated more property in this process began to assume the character of a new class.

Thus, the HRS has been the most critical institutional reform in post-Mao China in both economic and social terms. Its political import has been very significant because it contributed to consolidation of household power in society, politics and economy. On the other hand, it is equally significant to note that democratization of the China's grass-roots political process which began in 1998 with competitive elections in the village political structure gave individual citizens rather than families the right to participate. But individuals after all are not abstract entities. They operate in the socio-economic environment. So it was inevitable to see the emergence of competing elite groups in the local political process.

Development of Market Economy Coordinated by the State

Along with restructuring the production relations by introducing the HRS, the Deng regime took another critical decision to systematically develop commodity economy or market forces in all sectors of the economy starting with rural China. They were of the view that much of China's prevailing agriculture still operated as 'natural economy' where local production essentially aimed at meeting the local needs using local resources. The objective thus far was to be self-reliant and self-sufficient in production. This accounted for persistence of low agricultural productivity which according to one estimate rose only by 2 per cent in the first three decades of the PRC.[44] Under the new strategy, the objective was to produce for the market and make profit so that rural income could steadily grow. Market now meant going beyond the local area as far as possible. For this purpose, many specific steps were taken such as diversification of production by growing not only food crops but also cash crops and setting up rural industries and commerce with a view to producing for the market and earning profit. It also involved raising output and income by a rational allocation of family labour and if necessary by hiring labour. Development of such an economy needed employment of technology ranging from traditional to intermediate and advanced modern technology that would improve quality and quantity of production. All this meant making adequate investment in agricultural development and rural economy in general. Open and free market places were to be eventually developed in the countryside where rural produce could be bought and sold by the peasant according to market prices. Industrial goods and other consumer products would be available for the peasants to buy. Thus, commodity circulation was to be promoted, integrating the rural economy with the urban economy.

However, the party leadership wanted to develop commodity economy without completely abandoning the role of planning. The State was to continue to intervene by regulating supply of goods, by fixing production targets for the economic sector and the region and even in monitoring and fixing prices whenever necessary. But in all these respects, the local production units themselves had enormous autonomy and had to bear the consequences of ill-formulated decisions if ever they made them. In the earlier system, these decisions came from above and the lower units only implemented them. At the same time, the State maintained its power to intervene in the new set-up. The framework of socialist market economy adopted in the 1992 Party Congress stipulated a regulated market economy in which the State maintained its power for macroeconomic management while encouraging the full operation of the market economy. Following Deng, Jiang Zemin, Hu Jintao and Xi Jinping—all of them—affirmed the party leadership and State's right to maintain the control over the economy while developing a market economy. This allowed them to take strong measures to address crisis situations as during the East Asian financial crisis in 1997 when they maintained the strength of the Chinese currency. They successfully exercised this power in the wake of the 2008 global economic crisis to control its negative impact on the Chinese economy. It is this authority for macroeconomic control which the Hu–Wen regime used to rectify some of the major problems arising out of the reforms policies and launch balanced policies under Hu Jintao's Scientific Outlook on Development and coordinated development under Xi.[45]

Approach to commodity economy was a central point of debate during the Cultural Revolution.[46] According to Marxist political economy, commodity production developed during the epoch of capitalism. Goods were produced for exchange in the market and became 'commodity'. The capitalist class controlled the production system and manipulated the exchange process to accumulate profit and deny labour their due. Hence, the agenda of the communist was to ultimately abolish the commodity economy. In communism, production was meant for use so that 'each worked according to his/her ability and got according to his/her needs'. In communism, production was not for exchange and profit-making. During the transitional period of socialism, exchange economy persisted in a form that was different from the same under capitalism. But steps were to be taken in a socialist system to restrict commodity economy and create conditions for its eventual abolition in communism. This was the view taken by Mao Zedong in his *A Critique of Soviet Economics*.[47] This view was propagated forcefully by the proponents of the Cultural Revolution.

Many scholars associate the growth of revisionism in Soviet Union with the development of market forces.[48] Following this perspective, the CPC leadership during the Mao era had adopted the guideline of 'seeking all-round development by taking grain as the key link'. The emphasis was on carrying out grain production so as to feed the vast population of China by relying on domestic resources. Those production teams in some communes which decided to go for producing cash crops were criticized as going against the interest of people. The commune took full control of the total produce so that it could distribute the required amount of food grains and supply a fixed quantity to the State for urban consumption and industrial use. During the commune period, rural trade fairs were discouraged as they were seen as developing what was considered as an undesirable commodity economy. The kitchen gardens in the private plots of the households were also seen as capitalist activities. The approach to labour was also different during the commune period. Performing labour was the duty of the socialist citizen—a creative human activity through which every human being realized his/her potentiality. Hence, the worker was exhorted to perform this revolutionary activity for the sake of socialism and the motherland. They were expected to do their best and earn their fixed work points, rather than be money-minded trying to work for material benefits alone.

The work-point system of the commune era was strongly criticized by the Deng regime. According to the latter, the old system did not allow full play of the creative ability of the labourers. According to them, rather than giving an abstract motivation such as building socialism, it was more practical to offer concrete material gains which alone could motivate the workers to work harder and produce more. Thus, the material incentive system became an important aspect of the emerging commodity economy, whereas it was the ideological incentive that was promoted during the commune period. Competition was regarded as a desirable value now. The workers could now compete with one another in showing better results and earning higher wages. The better performers would get promotion to senior jobs. Enterprises were also expected to engage in competition in the market.

The commune system had maintained a *hukou* system under which each member of a household registered a home place that gave him/her entitlements of various kinds, including property rights, access to health and education facilities. Thus, the regime had enforced serious restrictions on migration of labourers from one commune to another. The commune system was based on the principle of a stable pattern of allocation of labour for a specific productive activity according to the plan. For education and after a person was assigned a job outside the home place, he/she was permitted to move out, but generally the *hukou* identity continued in the original place. This system was not only highly restrictive for men and women's right to move from one place to another on free will, but it also retained and consolidated a strong regional or birthplace identity. Under this system, exchange of labour forces was not possible and development of a countrywide labour market did not take place.[49] This came under review when the reform and open-door policy was launched. This practice was regarded by the Deng regime as a part of the closed economy. Yet, there were practical reasons for not abolishing the system altogether. Its abolition would not only open floodgates of rural–urban migration, but it would also be difficult to provide housing, health and education facilities for the rural migrants in the cities. In fact, this problem became very acute in the 1990s and later. Hence, the regime decided to gradually relax the *hukou* system. As mentioned earlier, a major initiative to expedite the relaxation was undertaken only in the Thirteenth Plan beginning in 2016. After the introduction of HRS, the household was given full freedom to decide which members of the family would work on land in the village and which members in other trades, locally or outside the township. Thus, the prevailing situation of underemployment and low-level productivity was sought to be tackled by releasing surplus rural labour for other activities.

According to one estimate, in 1979, almost half the rural labour force was surplus. With the emergence of diversified economy in the countryside, especially in rural industries, nearly 130 million had been absorbed as of 1997. Consequently, labour market grew at a fast pace in the countryside and gradually also in the city. Migration to the city was relaxed, even though the HRS for every Chinese resident continued to exist. Big cities like Shanghai, Beijing and Guangzhou began to have large 'floating population'.[50] Prosperous counties attracted migrant labour from poor regions. In Hela Township, for example, many enterprises employed migrant labour from the less developed 'Subei' region (north of Yangtze River).

Besides developing the labour market, introducing material incentives and expanding the sphere of agricultural production for the market, the reforms strategy included in it several other steps to develop market forces in the rural economy. It took two major initiatives in price reforms. In 1979, the State procurement prices for grains were nearly doubled with a dramatic effect on the rise of peasant income all over China. In the next five years, it was increased almost 20 per cent per year. During the second phase of reforms after 1985, free market sales by the peasants were permitted and procurement quotas from farmers were relaxed and subsequently abandoned in many places. Thus, eventually, the State had to pay almost the market prices and in later years sometimes even higher prices for purchasing food grains from the farmers. However, with further development of the market forces, and WTO obligations coming into force, the farmers did not always get adequate prices for their produce. In the Thirteenth Plan, a commitment was made to address this problem. In the 1980s, the fact that peasants got higher prices for their produce was a significant development in the realm of freedom for the peasant. This could be an indication of changing the terms of trade between agriculture and industry in favour of agriculture. In fact, there was the trend of a favourable turn for the peasants in the 1980s which got reversed in the 1990s when the urban–rural disparity steadily widened. This has been a serious point of debate in many countries where the farmers are engaged in struggles for getting adequate returns for their produce. But this by itself may not enhance the conditions for peasants' freedom. If industry and services get a still higher rate of return and the prices of goods rise correspondingly, the apparent shift in favour of the peasants may not be real. Yet, these measures by the Chinese government in the reform period raised the standard of living of the peasants considerably.

But it was not easy to fully leave the determination of prices to market forces in practice. At certain points, like in 1993, because the State needed money for investment in other spheres, it either paid lower prices compared to the market or it settled for deferred payment. Local governments signed MoUs with farmers for payment to be made later. This was strongly resented by peasants in many areas, leading to peasant demonstrations.[51] Such a trend recurred in the late 1990s and mid-2000s, causing widespread discontent among peasants. That was the context of launching the programme of building a new socialist countryside. Over the decades of the reform period, it has become clear again and again that the State had to continue to play a crucial role in managing the procurement prices of grain as well as industrial raw material such as cotton and sugarcane. In this context, the nature of the State apparatus becomes relevant. A decentralized, participatory decision-making mechanism can respond to contingencies better than a centralized bureaucratic State apparatus. No doubt, there is a role for the State in supervising the price situation, even though prices are to be normally left to the market forces. But what kind of State apparatus is it and through what mechanism does it adequately represent people's needs and wishes become relevant in this context. Pursuit of people's freedom therefore requires relevance of State, market and social organizations—all in coordination and check with one another with processes of representation.

The second step that the State took by way of price reform was on the supply side in restructuring the public distribution system. During the commune period, commerce was totally under collective ownership. Apart from food grains which commune members got as a portion of their work points, they had to buy all other goods from the commune stores. With the reforms, private individuals were allowed to set up their own stores. In a few years, cheaper and better goods became available in rural markets. Villages were allowed to arrange weekly, bi-weekly and daily markets. The centralized distribution system of the commune period was now a thing of the past. But still the State retained the power to intervene and plan appropriate levels of supply of goods. But this was now a decentralized system. The township authorities would negotiate with various sources of supply and respond to specific situations. Administered prices of essential commodities continued to operate; it applied to less and less number of goods. This was applicable more in the urban and suburban areas and the items varied from region to region. Thus, while making prices responsive to the market and developing market institutions in a decentralized fashion, the State maintained its coordinating role.

The idea of developing *agricultural zones* was put forward in the early 1980s as a part of developing market forces. In the 1990s, it took the form of clustering of rural industries in one zone. Steps were taken to make a unified plan for land use in one agricultural zone for comprehensive development of agriculture, industry and commerce and combine agriculture with forestry, animal husbandry and fisheries. Planning of labour power, utilization of natural resources, long-term investment plan as well as assessment of consumer demands were taken into consideration in the concept of an agricultural zone. A zone as a whole can plan what proportion of grains it needed for the local market and what proportion for the outside market. It can plan the industrial crops either for local manufacturing requirements or for supplying to outside industries. It can have a science-and-technology plan either by establishing local training institutes or by taking advantage of the national market of skilled personnel or even with international technical inputs. The idea of the clustering of rural industries had two other modern considerations relating to energy and communication. Supply of power to a cluster of industries may be more efficient than to industries which were dispersed in great distances from each other. The communication links—roads, railways and air routes—could service a cluster more efficiently. Human resources can be better planned too. Such clustering would develop urban markets in rural hinterland. In fact, taking the city to the village has been a common theme in both the Mao era and the reform era.

In fact, spatial planning focusing on zones has been a major characteristic of development thinking in contemporary China. Creation of science-and-technology development zones, industrial parks, SEZs (for foreign investment), collaborative development zones, economic corridors and river delta development zones are some of the examples. As mentioned earlier, 'functional zones' were created under the Thirteenth Plan to make energy-saving and environmental protection plans. This approach allowed experiments as well as concentrated efforts in some aspects of development.

Integrated Development of Agriculture, Industry and Commerce

A major component of the rural reforms was to diversify rural economy and expand the range of productive activities in the countryside. It was based on the understanding that rural economy was more than agricultural economy. Of course, rural society consisted of not only the economy but also culture and arts, knowledge system and many other aspects of life. The rural economy had in it agriculture, industry and commerce and all other production activities which could take place in the rural area. No doubt, a substantial proportion of economy which related to agriculture or using land as a major resource for production defined it as rural. But this proportion was not necessarily to be measured in terms of contribution to the total output value. It could be in terms of the proportion of workforce engaged in agriculture or of land used for agricultural purposes among other criteria. The new concept of the rural may even transcend these criteria. Then agriculture was also not to be confined to food grain production. It included production of oilseeds, vegetables, cotton, sugarcane and other industrial crops. In China, agriculture (*nongye*) generally included animal husbandry (*dongwuye*), fishery (*yuye*), forestry (*linye*) and horticulture (*shuguoye*) as well. During the commune period also, sideline production (*fuye*) was part of the rural economy. Pig raising and poultry farming were done in the private plots of each household. But sideline production at that time was to be subordinated to grain production. If some production teams put too much emphasis on sideline production during the commune period, that was considered as violation of the political line which gave primacy to grain production.

In the context of the rural reforms, all productive activities in the rural economy were encouraged. The new policies left it to the peasants to decide how best they should use their land, labour and capital to maximize their earnings. Of course, the collective did make overall production plans for grain production and in certain cases concerning other economic activities, keeping in view the targets set by the Centre and the provincial authorities. But they were not difficult targets to achieve. In addition to fulfilling the grain production quota, the farmers were encouraged to launch other productive activities. In areas like Wuxi's suburban district fishery was one of the main sources of income. Even during the commune period, a diversified economy existed in this region consisting of grain production, vegetables, fisheries and some rural industries. Being close to a city and with communication lines to Shanghai on one side and to Nanjing on another side, fishery and vegetable farming by the collective had gone on throughout the 1970s. Mulberry plantation for raising silk worms was another economic activity of the collective to provide silk threads to the textile factories in Wuxi. So, it is not true that there was no diversification of rural economy during the commune period. It is, however, true that sometimes the fear of grain shortage obsessed the party leadership to such an extent that they discouraged diversion of labour or land to other economic activities. The Deng regime took corrective measures in this respect. They were of the view that whereas the State would continue to monitor grain production plans to maintain a reasonable rate of growth of food grains in the national scale, the rural economy needed to be energized by promoting all possible rural economic activities. They pointed out that the overall economic development in the countryside would also help agriculture to grow. Farmers would invest a part of their savings in agriculture, and collectives would also divert some funds from earnings from industry and commerce to agriculture. In other words, different sectors of the rural economy would help one another. Thus, a peasant's freedom to grow a crop of his/her choice had to be reconciled with the total requirement of food grains of a large and populous country. But for that purpose, if there is a substantial constraint on the peasant's ability to raise his/her income, then that would be a curtailment of freedom. Several layers of considerations had to be integrated in order to fulfil the rights of different sections of society. Reliance on grain imports while there is potentiality of adequate production within a country has been generally avoided by all countries for not only reasons of vulnerability to external pressure but also sound economic reasons of utilizing local resources for meeting basic needs. However, Chinese leadership stood by their commitment to make China self-sufficient in food grains, and they had basically achieved it by a combination of policies including assigning production quota to provinces. However, even with over 600 million tons of food grains produced in 2016, distribution problems remained.

Of all the aspects of economic diversification, rural industrialization was the most important one. Rural economy was traditionally conceptualized as a more wholesome economy with wide range of agricultural and industrial activities. In China, social scientists such as Fei Xiaotong had constantly pointed out that even the rich and prosperous Yangtze valley countryside became poor in the 1930s when its silk industry declined and the peasant income from the whole process from mulberry plants and silk worms to spinning began to disappear. He therefore advocated what he called 'supplementary economy' or more and more rural enterprises[52]. In fact, Fei was criticized during the Anti-Rightist Campaign and the Cultural Revolution for this viewpoint. Yet, it should be noted that introducing rural industry was an essential component of the commune strategy proclaimed during the Great Leap Forward in 1958. Even earlier, when a fierce debate was on within the CPC leadership regarding the choice between mechanization and collectivization and the two lines of development were upheld by Liu Shaoqi and Mao Zedong respectively, the idea of rural industrialization was already on the scene. The collectivization line won and the communes were set up.[53] But even at that time, some major steps were taken in the direction of agricultural mechanization and rural industrialization. Small, motorized ploughs (hand-pulled power-driven tractors) were introduced in many areas. Each commune had agricultural machine stations to repair agricultural tools and provide expert assistance at various stages of agricultural work. Furnaces were started in every village to produce steel and manufacture agricultural tools. Indeed, there were several lapses. The backyard furnace experiment failed due to incorrect planning and lack of technological input. But in many areas, small agricultural processing units and tool-making plants came up and thrived throughout the commune period. In 1979, however, there was a major, strategic change in favour of promoting rural industries. The policy-makers thought that these enterprises were necessary to absorb local surplus labour. And, indeed, had they not absorbed some 100–150 million of the surplus agricultural labour, the unemployment situation in contemporary China would have been extremely serious.

Secondly, at the end of the 1970s, the collectives had funds at their disposal which they could invest in new rural enterprises, leaving agriculture to the responsibility of the households. The collectives in turn could use the profits from the rural industries for overall development of the rural economy, especially agriculture. Even though there was transformation of collective ownership of rural enterprises into shareholding companies or private firms, the collectives played a significant role in promoting rural industrialization in the first decade of the reforms.

In the third place, the scope of rural industries was expanded, encouraging them to produce many more items in addition to agricultural machine tools and processed products. In 1979, in Hela Commune—that is what it was called then—for example, the rural enterprises produced spare parts for the big industries of Wuxi. Later, they moved to the field of electronics and then to tourism and hotel business which was known as 'third industry'. Thereafter, in the 1990s, there was no limit to the choice of enterprises, provided they could arrange capital from their own resources or from within the country or from foreign sources. But at the same time, and this is important, they were obliged to meet the quality-control, environmental standards and energy consumption stipulations of the State. These latter considerations acquired serious dimensions as the environmental consciousness grew in China and the State set up a number of monitoring institutions at every level to check environmental pollution. The international climate after the Earth Summit in Rio de Janeiro in 1991 had its effect as well. Subsequently the Kyoto Protocol of 1997 and the Johannesburg Summit on Sustainable Development and COP21 or the Paris Conference on Climate Change in 2015 had serious impact on Chinese policy-making. The issues of energy saving and environmental degradation acquired more significance in the Chinese development strategy. For example, when it was realized that many rural industries were known for wasteful and inefficient use of electricity, many of them faced closure. With these stipulations clearly laid down, the Chinese government continued to promote rural industries as a crucial component of its reform strategy for it raised peasant income significantly, provided employment to a large section of surplus labour and improved rural economy as a whole, thus giving a fillip to the entire Chinese economy.

The policy on rural industries was a critical complement of the HRS and the commodity economy. It linked the household to the larger rural and urban economy and in fact to the national and world economy. Rural industrialization was the engine of development of the countryside, raising household income and a region's total income. Commerce and service sector activities in general expanded steadily as market economy developed. During the Thirteenth Plan, a strategic plan was launched with technology, especially IT, and substantial investment to promote integrated development of agriculture, industry and services. In this process, the close interaction with the global economy was an important factor in carrying out the reform strategy.

Closer Interaction with the Global Economy

Deng Xiaoping had clearly laid down the principle of 'open door' as mainly learning from the whole world and taking advantage of the opportunities provided by the whole world, including the capitalist, Western countries. His theoretical line acknowledged that there were three forces which brought about the transition of world history from feudalism to modernity: science and technology, market and management. It was on these issues that an intense debate had taken place in the final stage of the Cultural Revolution. Deng's critics argued that these forces were inherently rooted in capitalist development and would propel the political economy in that direction. Deng rebutted that view saying that there were instruments of modern transformation and every country had to rely on them. He stressed that political parties could use them for their purposes.[54] So, 'open door' was a key component of the 'reforms' as announced by the landmark Third Plenum in 1978. Very early, at the Twelfth Party Congress, Deng had said: 'We shall unswervingly follow a policy of opening to the outside world and actively increase exchanges with foreign countries on the basis of equality and mutual benefit'.[55] That year, the first SEZ was launched in Shenzhen, followed by several others in the east coast. Ten years later, the perspective was reconfirmed when in February 1992, Den Xiaoping visited the SEZs and called for vigorously pursuing the reforms and open door. Starting with welcoming investment by overseas Chinese from Taiwan, Hong Kong and Singapore, this trend acquired massive momentum with Japanese, European, North American and Australian and later Korean capital-seeking opportunities to invest in China. Open door became such a critical factor in China's growth story that in January 2017, Xi Jinping addressing the Davos Forum struck as the most eloquent defender of economic globalization.

Open-door policy was so integral to all aspects of the economy that not only the provinces but also every rural unit, county, township and town set up its Department of International Economic Affairs. Thus, not only Jiangsu province and the prefecture-level Wuxi City but even Hela Township had an office dealing with foreign business. When the national economy was reoriented in the early 1990s to produce for the world market, the rural enterprises tried to produce for export as well. When the TVEs were reorganized for meeting the compulsions of the new environment, many foreign entrepreneurs bought up the rural enterprises. Later, the TVEs were reconceptualized as small and medium-sized enterprises (SMEs) with solid linkages with foreign capital and foreign market. Using foreign investment and generating substantial capital out of the domestic saving, China emerged as the manufacturing hub of the world. The high rate of economic growth was sustained for nearly two decades as a result of this. In 2010, China surpassed Japan as the world's second largest economy. The process advanced to such an extent that structural problems in the nature of the economy became evident. Hence, the Twelfth Plan announced the beginning of a reorientation of the economy. The Thirteenth Plan's focus on orienting the production process towards domestic demands was the outcome of this. Now China was also ready to increase its investment abroad. Xi Jinping's international initiatives, especially the Belt and Road Initiative, reflected the new perspective. China would produce for both the local and the global markets with focus on quality and technological superiority as well as green consciousness. The Thirteenth Plan put the perspective thus:

> We will comprehensively advance bidirectional opening up, facilitate the orderly flow of domestic and international factors of production, the efficient allocation of domestic and international resources, and deep integration of Chinese and foreign markets, and work faster in cultivating new international competitive edges.[56]

The Political Dimensions of the Success Story

The strategy of reforms as it evolved from one phase after another achieved tremendous success in rural China during the period 1979–92 (Table 2.2 and Figure 2.1). Thereafter, as the national development strategy acquired a new focus on industrial production with an export orientation, the gains from the rural reforms began to slowly melt away and by the end of the 1990s, the leadership was already acknowledging the 'three rural problems'. Since 2000, the Chinese planners have explicitly talked about the prevailing 'rural crisis' in the country. The programme of building a new socialist countryside with greater financial allocations during the Eleventh and Twelfth FYPs had continued this programme. But despite the higher allocations, the crisis in the countryside persisted. As noted earlier, the Thirteenth Plan dropped references to the 'three rural problems' and 'building a new socialist countryside' and opted for a technology-driven modernization programme with elaborate interventions on multiple fronts.

Looking at the rural policies as a whole from the time of the Third Plenum when Deng Xiaoping launched the new era of reforms and through the years his nominees and successors Jiang Zemin, Hu Jintao and Xi Jinping steered

Table 2.2:
Trends in people's livelihood 1978–2014

Categories (Yuan)	1978	1989	1997	2005	2010	2012	2014	Annual Average Growth Rate (%) 1979–2014	Annual Average Growth Rate (%) 2001–14
Per capita annual disposable income of urban households	343	1,374	5,160	10,493	19,109	24,565	29,381	7.4	9.2
Per capita net income of rural residents	134	602	2,090	3,255	5,919	7,917	9,892	7.6	7.9
Savings deposit in urban and rural areas	211	5,196	46,280	141,051	303,302	399,551	485,261	24	15.5
Average wage of staff and workers	615	1,935	6,470	18,364	37,147	47,593	57,361	—	—

Sources: National Bureau of Statistics of China, *China Statistical Yearbook*, 2006, 32–33; 2011 (Basic Statistics on People's Living Conditions [Table 10-1]); 2013 (Tables 4-11 and 11-1); 2015 (see Section 1-2).

Figure 2.1:
Trends in people's livelihood 1978–2014 (yuan)

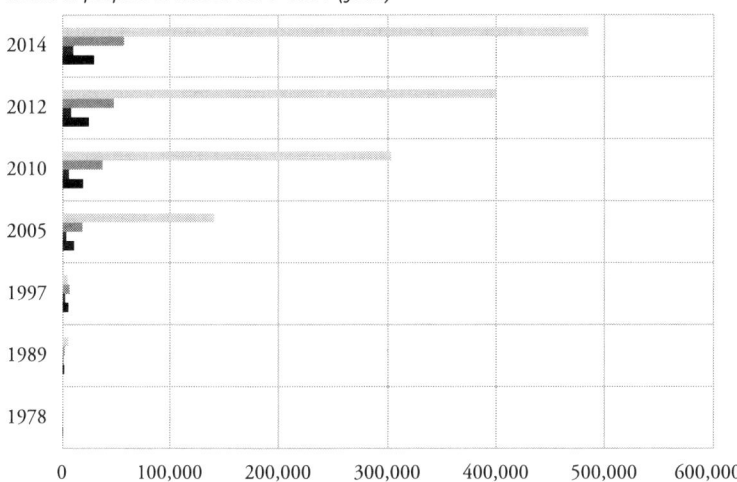

- Saving deposit of urban and rural areas
- Average wages of staff and workers
- Per capita net income of rural households
- Per capita annual disposable income of urban households

Source: National Bureau of Statistics of China, *China Statistical Yearbook,* 2006.

the process further, it can be said that the rural China has undergone a major transformation. There are many indicators of the remarkable successes achieved in the rural economy of China. The per capita output of grain which was 288.13 kg in 1952 and had risen to 326.69 kg in 1980 rose to 405.55 kg in 1999, 408.66 kg in 2010, and 453 kg in 2015.[57] This shows that food grain production did outpace the rise in population. However, it should be noted that the rate of increase in per capita availability declined sharply in the last decade. In the case of cotton, it was 2.29 kg in 1952, 2.76 kg in 1980, 3.05 kg in 1999, 4.5 kg in 2010 and 4.1 kg in 2016.[58] In the case of oil-bearing crops and aquatic products, the increase was very substantial (see Table 2.1). A look at the rise in the income of the rural households during the period since 1985 shows the trend of rapid improvement in the livelihood conditions of the peasants. The net per capita income of the rural household rose from 397.60 yuan in 1985 to 2,210.34 yuan in 1999, 5,919 yuan in 2010 and 10,722 yuan in 2015.[59] During 1985–99, the proportion of remuneration from labour outside the household rose from about 20 per cent to above

30 per cent, the rest coming from household business including farming, animal husbandry, industry and commerce. It is noteworthy that taking China as a whole, still bulk of the household income came from farming, even though the composition of the output value had changed. The rural people's expenditure on consumption had also increased considerably for they were able to pay for better living conditions, even at a higher price (the price index showed a threefold rise during the period 1985–2006). Their savings and credit payments had also gone up from a mere 57.96 yuan in 1985 to 420 yuan in 1999, and the per capita balance of saving deposit to as high as 22,619 yuan in 2010 from 5,076 yuan in 2000.[60] In 2012, the balance of saving deposits was 29,508 yuan.[61]

Thus, there is no doubt that rural China has achieved considerable success in terms of growth of the rural economy and increase in peasant income. That is the success story achieved through the implementation of the reform strategy. The fact that the peasantry in contemporary China has achieved better living conditions and that they enthusiastically implemented the introduction of the rural reforms has to be acknowledged. Better housing and communication facilities and higher living standards had created a new environment in China as a result of the reforms. A new level of political consciousness about rights also grew as was evident in frequent cases of peasant unrest. The introduction of democratic elections at the village level responded to the new awareness in the countryside.

However, by the mid-1990s, it was clear that the reforms had led to increasing inequalities, consumerism and ethical degradation. By the end of the 1990s already, rural distress was being talked about in China just when the world was recognizing China's economic success to which the rural reforms had made a big contribution. China had landed in a 'success trap' in the course of the reforms and the goal of 'socialist freedom' for the Chinese people, especially the people in the countryside, still remained distant.

We try to analyse this success story and the success trap by undertaking a detailed examination of the experience in a rural area in the next chapter.

Notes and References

1. Maya X. Guo, *The Chinese Path and the Chinese School* (Beijing: Foreign Languages Press, 2015), 34. In an interview, a leading theoretician of the reforms Hu Angang said: 'Deng Xiaoping won great credit for his timely and decisive actions in calming the 1989 disturbance and leading China away from the kind of disaster that has been inflicted on the Soviet Union'.

2. Barrington Moore Jr., *Social Origins of Dictatorship and Democracy* (London: Penguin, 1966).

3. *The 13th Five-year Plan for Economic and Social Development of the People's Republic of China (2016–2020)* (Beijing: Central Compilation and Translation Press, 2016), 19.

4. This is a heuristic description to call the Maoists radical and the Deng group liberal. Later on, Deng took the initiative as a radical modernizer, while some of his colleagues such as Chen Yun who wished to go slow with market reforms were regarded as 'conservative' reformers. These are relative terms.

5. Chen Xiwen, *Reform of Rural Economic Structure in China's Economic Transformation over 20 Years* (Beijing: Foreign Languages Press, 2000).

6. Work points referred to the manner of giving a value to a day's work. For example, for eight hours of agricultural work, a male labourer earned 10 work points. However, a woman earned eight work points. The value of each work point was determined by dividing the net income of a production team by the total number of work points earned by all the members of the team.

7. In the reform discourse, the metaphor used in the case of the peasants was the big 'earthen pot' and for the workers the big 'iron bowl' from which they ate.

8. *Socialist Upsurge in China's Countryside* (Beijing: Foreign Languages Press, 1956). It is a collection of the documents of this debate on mechanization and collectivization of agriculture. See also Mao Zedong, 'The Question of Agricultural Cooperation' (speech, 31 July 1955). The speech is also available at: http://afe.easia.columbia.edu/ps/cup/mao_zedong_agricultural_cooperation.pdf (accessed on 5 June 2017).

9. Utsa Patnaik, *The Long Transition: Essays on Political Economy* (New Delhi: Tulika, 1999).

10. Most of the leading scholars of China interviewed by Maya X. Guo reflect this line of thinking, even though they are strong advocates of the reforms. See Guo, *The Chinese Path and the Chinese School.*

11. On the famine deaths in China, Amartya Sen has argued that 30–40 million may have perished due to hunger and starvation during this period. He attributes it to the lack of democratic flow of information in a controlled regime which prevented appropriate relief reaching the scarcity areas. However, there are alternative views on this question. See Peter Nolan, 'Death Rates, Life Expectancy and China's Economic Reforms: A Critique of A. K. Sen', *World Development* 20, no. 9, 1279–1303 (September 1992); Amartya Sen, 'Life and Death in China: A Reply', *World Development* 20, no. 9 (1992): 1305–12. Frank Dikotter has put the figure at nearly 45 million deaths due to mass starvation using recently available Chinese sources. Frank Dikotter, *Mao's Great Famine* (London: Walker Books, 2010).

12. Moore Jr, *Social Origins of Dictatorship and Democracy,* has pointed out how peasantry was squeezed in both Russia and China after the Communist Movement succeeded in capturing power. But in China, during both Mao's and Deng's leadership, peasantry's welfare has been the principal concern of the CPC.

13. Robert Ash, 'Squeezing the Peasants: Grain Extraction, Food consumption and Rural Living standards in Mao's China', *The China Quarterly,* no. 188 (December 2006): 959–93.

14. See Manoranjan Mohanty, 'The New Ideological Banner: Deng Xiaoping Theory', *China Report* 34, no. 1, 101–05 (1998).

15. See, for example, Li Keqiang, *Report on the Work of the Government*, 11.

16. One focus was economic construction and two points were reform and open door and Four Cardinal Principles—socialist road, CPC leadership, Marxism–Leninism–Mao Zedong Thought and dictatorship of the proletariat.

17. Deng Xiaoping, 'Uphold the Four Cardinal Principles (30 March 1979)', in *Selected Works of Deng Xiaoping 1975–1982* (Beijing: Foreign Language Press, 1984).
18. Jiang Zemin, *Three Represents* (Beijing: Foreign Languages Press, 2001).
19. Hu Jintao, Full Text of Hu Jintao's Speech at CPC Anniversary Gathering (July 2011). Available at: http://www.chinadaily.com.cn/china/cpc2011/2011-07/01/content_12818048.htm (accessed on 24 July 2017).
20. For a detailed discussion of Deng's critique of Mao's economic ideas, see Manoranjan Mohanty, 'Power of History: Mao Zedong Thought in Deng's China', in *Ideology Matters: China from Mao Zedong to Xi Jinping*, 90–106 (New Delhi: Aakar Books, 2013).
21. Andrew Szamosszegi and Cole Kyle, *An Analysis of State-owned Enterprises and State Capitalism in China,* (Washington: US–China Economic and Security Review Commission, October 2011), 31.
22. Jiang Zemin, *Political Report to the 15th National Congress of the CPC* (Beijing: Foreign languages Press, 1997). See also Jiang Zemin, *Report to the 16th Party Congress* (Beijing: Foreign Languages Press, 2002).
23. For an articulation of the basic principles of the concept of Harmonious Socialist Society, see *Communiqué of the Sixth Plenum of the Central Committee of the CPC* of 11 October 2006. Available at: http://www.china.org.cn/english/government/183627.htm (accessed on 23 July 2017).
24. Mao Zedong used the method of 'creative application' to formulate the strategy of people's democratic revolution. Deng Xiaoping used 'seek truth from facts' to justify new policies under new circumstances. This formula and the concept of 'emancipation of mind' (*sixiang jiefang*) allowed the next generation similar flexibility in adjusting policies. See Frederic Wakeman, *History and Will: Philosophical Perspectives on Mao Tse-tung Thought* (Berkeley: University of California Press, 1973), Richard Baum, *Burying Mao*, Mohanty, 'Power of History'.
25. How this path of development acquired even more resilience after the 2008 global financial crisis is explained by Justin Yifu Lin, *Demystifying the Chinese Economy* (Cambridge: Cambridge University Press, 2012).
26. Chen Xiwen, *Reform of Rural Economic Structure,* 239.
27. Available at: http://en.people.cn/200603/14/eng20060314_250512.html (accessed on 23 July 2017).
28. Wen Jiabao, *Report on the Work of Government*, 7.
29. Wen Jiabao, *Report on the Work of the Government to the Fifth Session of the Eleventh NPC.* Available at: http://en.people.cn/90785/7759779.html (accessed on 22 July 2017).
30. *The 13th Five-year Plan,* 16–18.
31. National Development and Reform Commission (NDRC), *Report on the Implementation of the 2016 Plan for National Economic and Social Development and on the 2017 Draft Plan for National Economic and Social Development*, delivered at the Fifth Session of the Twelfth National People's Congress on 5 March 2017, 4. Available at: http://online.wsj.com/public/resources/documents/NPC2017_NDRC_English.pdf (accessed on 23 July 2017).
32. Business costs were cut by over a trillion yuan in 2016. Ibid., 5.
33. The plan announced eight major aspects of agricultural modernization: high-quality farmland development, modern seed industry, water-efficient agriculture, agricultural mechanization, intelligent agriculture (using IT), agricultural product quality and safety, development of new types of agribusiness (including family farms and modern managers, and integrated development of primary, secondary and tertiary industries. *The 13th Five-year Plan*, 78–79.

34. NDRC, *Report on the Implementation of the 2016 Plan*, 34.
35. However, there was a slight decline in the urban–rural income ratio from the 2013 level as mentioned in ibid., 29—2013: 2.81; 2014: 2.75; 2015: 2.73; 2016: 2.72.
36. BRI had initiated six economic corridors comprising New Eurasian Continental Bridge, the China–Mongolia–Russia Corridor, the China–Central Asia–West Asia Corridor, the China–IndoChina Peninsula Corridor, the China–Pakistan Corridor and the Bangladesh–China–India–Myanmar Corridor. Six channels refer to highways, railways, airlines, waterways, pipelines, and informations networks. Ibid., 10.
37. Sidney Shapiro, *Experiment in Sichuan: A Report on Economic Reform* (Beijing: New World Press, 1981).
38. *Regulations on the Work in Rural People's Communes* carried in two parts in *Issues and Studies* (August and September 1979). See also some questions concerning the acceleration of agricultural development in Summary of World Broadcasts (SWB) Part III (10 October 1979).
39. Some questions on current rural economic policy, CPC Central Committee, Document No.1, 1983, SWB (14 April 1983) See also the appendix in Liu Suinian and Wu Qungan, eds., *China's Socialist Economy 1949–1984* (Beijing: Beijing Review, 1986).
40. Liu Suinian and Wu Qungan, 'Circular of CPC Central Committee Concerning the Rural Work (1 January 1984)'.
41. Ibid., 657.
42. Chen Xiwen, *Reform of Rural Economic Structure*, 221.
43. See Martin King Whyte and William L Parish, *Urban Life in Contemporary China* (Chicago: University of Chicago Press, 1985) and Patricia Uberoi, *Family and Ethnicity in Yunnan* (New Delhi: Institute of Chinese Studies Monograph, 2006).
44. Ash, 'Squeezing the Peasants'.
45. This is the essence of the Chinese model of development that departed from the Soviet path as well as the Washington Consensus on neoliberal growth according to Lin, *Demystifying the Chinese Economy*, and Guo, *The Chinese Path and the Chinese School*, 57–59.
46. Manoranjan Mohanty, *The Political Philosophy of Mao Tse-tung*. See Chapter two: Theory of Class Struggle in Socialist Society (Delhi: Macmillan, 1978).
47. Mao Zedong, *A Critique of Soviet Economics* (New York, NY: Monthly Review Press, 1979).
48. Charles Bettelheim, *Cultural Revolution and Industrial Organization in China* (New York, NY: Monthly Review Press, 1973); Mao Zedong, *A Critique of Soviet Economics*.
49. One can compare the restrictive character of China's *hukou* system with India's caste system.
50. See Yang Zihui, 'Floating Population and Urbanisation in China', in *Inequality Mobility and Urbanisation: China and India*, ed. Amitabh Kundu (New Delhi: Manak and Indian Council of Social Science Research, 2000); Cai Fang, 'Migration Obstacles, Human Capital and Mobility of Rural Labour Force in China' in *Inequality Mobility and Urbanisation: China and India*, ed. Amitabh Kundu.
51. Kathy Le Mons Walker, 'Gangster Capitalism and Peasant Protest in China', *Journal of Peasant Studies* 33, no. 1, 1–33 (January 2006).
52. Fei Xiaotong, *Peasant Life in China* (London: Kegan Paul, 1939 [1945]); Fei Xiaotong, *Chinese Village Close-up* (Beijing: New World Press, 1983), 95. He says that silk industry existed in Taihu area for over 1,000 years and always contributed to additional income without which peasants would remain poor.
53. Mao Zedong, *Socialist Upsurge in China's Countryside*.
54. See Mohanty, 'Power of History', 90–106.

55. Deng Xiaoping, 'Opening Speech at the 12th Party Congress, 3.
56. *The 13th Five-year Plan*, 201.
57. National Bureau of Statistics of China, *China Statistical Yearbook,* 2011 (Section 13.21); 2016 (Section 12-16).
58. National Bureau of Statistics of China, *China Statistical Yearbook*, 2011; 2016.
59. Ibid.
60. Ibid., Section 10.1 on Basic Statistics on People's Living Conditions.
61. Section 11.1 on Basic Statistics on People's Living Conditions. National Bureau of Statistics of China, *China Statistical Yearbook*, 2013.

3

Hela Township, Wuxi: Transformation of the Land of Rice and Fish

This chapter presents a case study of the transformation process as the reforms unfolded in a rural area of China. I have several purposes in mind. Firstly, it is important to understand the administrative structure at the grass-roots level and the reasons for the changes in it at different points of time. Secondly, it is interesting to note the layers of urban entities ranging from metropolitan Centre to urban districts and cities (*shi*) and towns (*zhen*) within rural areas. Thirdly, this case shows the direction of development by waves of urbanization, industrialization and commercialization as the manifestation of reform and open-door policies. Even though Hela Township is a suburban area in coastal China, there is enough evidence to show that a similar process has taken place in interior rural regions. Fourthly, this profile represents the nature of the debate on the approach to rural transformation. One line of thought advocates steady urbanization along the Wuxi path of the political leadership vigorously developing market forces having close linkages with the global economy. Another line of thought, associated with Wuxi's experiences with the early reform period, calls for larger investment for energizing the rural economy, allowing peasant initiatives and cooperative efforts and promoting self-governing institutions. The former line of urbanization won and Wuxi developed into a twenty-first-century global city and an electronic and IT industry hub.

Some of these issues will be taken up in later chapters. First, an account of Wuxi's reform experience is presented.

Why Hela?

The place of our study is Hela (in Pinyin in the Beijing dialect, it is written as Helie, but in Wuxi dialect, it is pronounced as Hela and that is what we will use throughout this book). Hela People's Commune was renamed as Hela Township in 1983 (*xiang*, translated as township in English, was the traditional rural unit below the county level). It was one of the 10 townships of the suburban district of Wuxi in Jiangsu province of China. It has been subject to further reorganization as a part of the urbanization process to which I will come later.

In the middle of 1979, when I sought the permission of the Chinese authorities to study rural reforms in a Chinese commune, I was recommended Hela Township. Actually, I had shown interest in another commune also in Jiangsu province named Tong Ting about which the Chinese press had carried certain reports. After arriving in Nanjing, capital of Jiangsu, I was given to understand that since that commune was undergoing 'reorganization' (euphemism for personnel changes), I could consider going to another township. I had expressed interest in studying an average commune. That is how I reached Hela on the outskirts of Wuxi. No doubt, this entire region in Jiangsu province was an economically prosperous region. In that sense, no commune in this area would be the representative of the whole of China. But within the south region of Yangtze River, Hela was a middle-range commune that was not among the most developed in Wuxi, and there were some communes which lagged behind Hela too. More than three decades later, Hela remained at the same point of the scale even while making considerable advance as a result of its integration into the city.

Studying rural reforms in the city suburbs had its own limitations. At that time, it was not possible to go and stay in an interior rural area. While conditions for field research quickly became favourable to Western scholars, for scholars going from India it was not easy. Sino-Indian normalization was moving at a snail's pace. But even when the environment of research vastly improved, I decided to stick to Hela and observe the process of change in the subsequent years. Later, I also visited rural areas in other parts of China to get a comparative view. I could witness in Wuxi's suburbs the process of urbanization of the rural area and the emergence of the phenomenon of 'peasant worker'. The rural–urban linkages in the economy, politics and social interaction raised many interesting issues. Moreover, Hela presented a site of the dominant policy on reforms: from agriculture to diversified rural economy with modern rural industries and then assimilated into the urban political economy developing high-tech industries under 'new urbanization'. To that extent, the Hela story spanning over three decades of field observation does give us a glimpse of the main features of the Chinese reform process. Moreover, this study is focused on the sociopolitical aspects of the economic reforms with focus on party, government and society, rather than the technical aspects of agriculture and rural economy. Therefore, choice of a suburban commune was not necessarily a methodological constraint. The Hela account of the 1980s is still the story of much of China's countryside, while its experience of the 1990s and thereafter shows the developing scenario of rural–urban integration and the evolving process of urbanization all over China accompanied by the growth of a rural crisis.

Wuxi has been on the intellectual map of social science research for many years, thanks to the pioneering research by China's most famous sociologist Fei Xiaotong in 1936. His subsequent research visits in 1957 and 1980 to Kaixiangong village on the southeastern side of Taihu Lake have produced most insightful results for social change and development theory.[1] Our study area Hela is on the northern side of the lake on the outskirts of Wuxi city, but it shares many of the socio-economic characteristics of Kaixiangong and we will use Fei's findings as our reference point for some of our important issues under discussion. However, Fei's monumental account is a minute observation of social institutions and practices relating to culture and economic life of the villagers, while my interest in this study is in the politics of the development process. Fei's main arguments that without viable rural industry peasants could not increase their income and without land reforms and cooperative efforts peasant initiative for rural development would not grow remain significant formulations for development discourse in China. Fei illustrated this by showing how the decline of the textile industry in Wuxi region especially in the wake of the challenge of the foreign producers accelerated the process of pauperization in the area and how a cooperative silk factory had tried to reverse that process.[2]

Popularly known as the 'land of fish and rice' (*yu mi zhi xiang*), Wuxi is also famous for its silk production which goes back at least a thousand years. Like Fei Xiaotong's work, another important study has brought focus to Wuxi's silk industry. Lynda S. Bell's *One Industry, Two Chinas* analyses the historical process of the working of the silk industry in modern China and shows how two Chinas—urban and rural—were tied together in this production and marketing processes.[3] Using the rural surveys of the Wuxi villages conducted by the Japanese researchers in 1940 and material based on her own interviews in Wuxi and extensive archival research, Bell has contributed significant insights into the role of elites, peasants and the State in agrarian transformation.[4] Describing how Wuxi became a 'new model sericulture district' by the 1930s, she points out that there was a 'single developmental continuum, in which wealth and power of the silk-industry elites depended on peasant-family production … especially hand labour of peasant women', thus leaving a legacy of 'state policies favouring industry over the countryside'.[5] Perhaps this legacy still had its influence at the beginning of the twenty-first century. Many other studies have contributed to the understanding of the socio-economic history of Wuxi.[6]

In this chapter, we will get acquainted with the region—the city, the district and the township and its later administrative incarnations, the recent development experiences of the people at these levels with special discussion on the policy changes and their consequences. While we take up the specific aspects of the policy changes in the subsequent chapters, here we get an overview of the process of socio-economic transformation that has taken place in this particular region. What was essentially an agricultural economy with a textile industry grew into a flourishing modern industrial hub of China with many new light industries and knowledge economy enterprises along with its traditional environment of natural beauty acquiring new tourist attractions. As we will see, this experience of rapid economic growth also came with its new problems. The process of reorganization of the rural and suburban entities with new economic and political characteristics gives us an insight into the nature of urban–rural linkages that have evolved in China. The changed status of Hela from a rural township to first a town and then a street or sub-district of the city had important implications for the production process, residential rights as well as social welfare.

This account is based partly on interviews with cadres and citizens and information and impressions gathered during periodic visits from 1979 until 2016 and partly on official statistics. It has to be kept in mind that due to the reorganization of the districts, the townships and the towns, the data for the various periods were for the then prevailing units.

Wuxi: The Pearl on Taihu

Wuxi literally means 'no tin', referring to some point in history when the metal tin (*Xi*) deposit in this place had been exhausted (*Wu* meaning 'no') (see Figures 3.1 to 3.3). Wuxi is a medium-sized city in Jiangsu province, located on the northern side of Taihu (Lake Tai). The Yangtze River flows 45 km away on the north with many rivulets linking the river and the city. Wuxi has a history dating back to late Shang and early Zhou periods (eleventh century bc). A county government was set up in Wuxi in 202 bc during the Han dynasty.[7] The Beijing–Hangzhou Grand Canal passes through Wuxi. It is located on the Shanghai–Nanjing Railway, 128 km from Shanghai and 183 km from Nanjing, the capital of Jiangsu province. The Taihu Lake which practically covers three sides of Wuxi city provides its defining characteristics.

In June 2007, Wuxi and Taihu Lake were in world news for the wrong reasons. The waterbed of the whole lake was covered by blue algae because of pollution due to the discharge of chemical waste from the factories surrounding the lake, as a result of which supply of drinking water to Wuxi was suspended

Figure 3.1:
China

Source: http://nexusholidays.com.au/product/china-sampler-11-days-2017/ (accessed on 3 June 2017).

Figure 3.2:
Jiangsu province

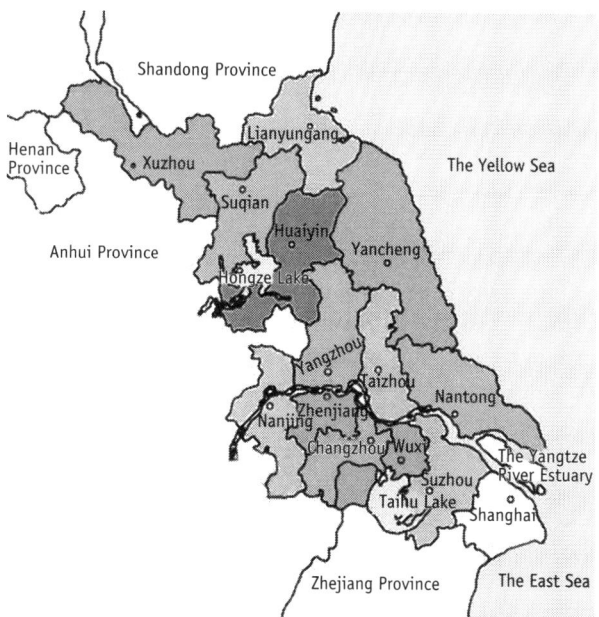

Source: http://www.china-tour.cn/Jiangsu/Jiangsu-Maps.htm (accessed on 3 June 2017).

Figure 3.3:
Wuxi districts

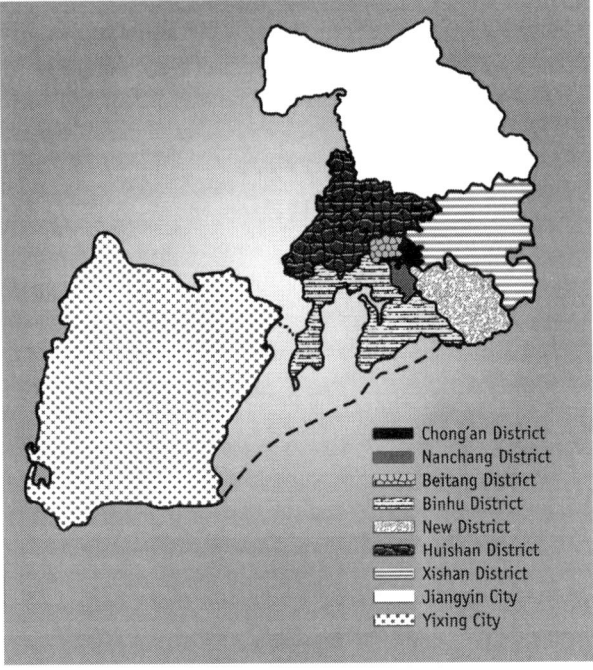

Chong'an District
Nanchang District
Beitang District
Binhu District
New District
Huishan District
Xishan District
Jiangyin City
Yixing City

Source: http://en.wuxi.gov.cn/sitePages/subPages/1300350001336839.html (accessed on 24 April 2017).

for two weeks. Premier Wen Jiabao personally ordered relief measures and took disciplinary action against environment officials and announced strict guidelines for enforcement of environmental standards, leading to closure of several factories. The lake water was treated and water from Yangtze River was diverted to the lake, after which the supply of clean water was resumed.[8]

China's third largest lake Taihu has an area of 2,400 km², covering parts of Jiangsu and Zhejiang provinces. Wuxi's economic and cultural milieu were traditionally set by Taihu, making it the famed 'land of fish and rice'. Charm of Taihu has its uniqueness in every season. Connected with it is Lihu (Li Lake) on the western part with a background of small hills. The famous Liyuan Park (peach garden) is located on the north bank of Lihu with its rock structure, waterways, seasonal flowers and the little pagoda, which is Wuxi's famous insignia dominating the skyline. Among the many other gardens, Meiyuan attracts endless tourists. The three-hill island in the

Taihu Lake and the tortoise head hill (Yuantouzhu hill) on the eastern side are some of the other attractions. Honey peaches of Wuxi have a natural lusciousness in autumn, considered unparalleled in the world. The cherry blossoms in spring drown you in a festival of colours.

This place of history and beauty sought to transform itself into a modern industrial city in the course of the reforms of the 1980s that accelerated on a certain path from the 1990s onwards. The region has made significant strides in that process. It did have a flourishing silk industry in pre-liberation China. Even in the last years of Ming dynasty (1368–1644 ad), a solid foundation had been laid for Wuxi's textile industry. Wuxi silk acquired enormous fame throughout China and even abroad during the past 200 years. In the nineteenth century, development of Shanghai made Wuxi a supporting industrial centre. In the twentieth century, industrial development in Shanghai, Suzhou and Nanjing regions contributed to Wuxi's further development. Therefore, its contemporary leaders pointedly draw inspiration from its past. But it was only during the decades of reforms that Wuxi emerged as the leading centre of China's light industries, manufacturing items ranging from traditional textiles to modern sophisticated electronics and developing service industries. Wuxi's suburbs and rural areas have not only contributed to this growth but have also simultaneously benefited from this process. Yet, people of the region face new problems.

While scrupulously maintaining the traditional scenic spots, Wuxi has also built up many new tourist attractions, capitalizing on people's historical interest. The Tang City, a favourite tourist destination, for example, recreates life and society of Tang China complete with seventh- to ninth-century palace structure, waterways, market place, cultural performances and currencies. Same is with the replica of the Three Kingdoms. They have also created a miniature city of great wonders of the world. Among the modern tourist attractions is the aquarium with many rare collections with a Pacific flavour. The Giant Buddha statue, claimed as the tallest in the world, which has a big park and amazing technological manoeuvres with water fountains was another new attraction at the turn of the century. Many more technological wonders to attract tourists were being planned for the future.[9]

Ever since Wuxi was declared as a fully open city by a State Council decision in 1985, the city has established a number of facilities to invite foreign capital. They included the National Hi-tech Industrial Development Zone, the Wuxi–Singapore Park and the Wuxi Taihu National Tourist Resort Zone. The infrastructure facilities have developed rapidly. The Shanghai–Nanjing Expressway which passes through Wuxi was constructed in record time in the 1990s, reducing access to Shanghai Hongqiao International Airport to only a two-hour ride. Several new bridges and waterways have been constructed. The utilization of all kinds of waterways, small and big canals, rivulets and rivers and lakes is an important part of the modern communication system as it was in the past.

Administrative Organization of the Urban–Rural City

Wuxi is one of the 11 prefecture-level 'cities' of Jiangsu province (Table 3.1).[10] In 1983, Jiangsu like several other provinces underwent administrative reorganization. The guiding principle for this was that cities must serve the countryside and the countryside must serve the cities. Incidentally, a decade later, this principle seemed to have become redundant as the disparity between the rural and the urban people continued to rise and the two-way process had nearly become a one-way process—the city befitting from the linkage far more than the countryside. In the early 1980s, however, in order to integrate rural development with urban development, the city leadership was given a key role. Hence, the jurisdiction of the city was expanded to include the rural counties. Thus, all the counties of Jiangsu were grouped under the 11 major cities (*shi*). Each city is now a greater urban–rural area. After this reorganization at the provincial level, Wuxi consisted of its metropolitan districts and three counties, Wuxi County, Jiangyin city and Yixing city. Gradually, all the three counties became county-level cities (also called *shi*). Thus, Wuxi city is the greater urban–rural area, covering 4,650 km². The metropolitan districts which numbered four in the early

Table 3.1:
Government organizations in rural areas (1999, 2010, 2015)

Level of Organization	1999	2000	2001	2002	2003	2004	2010	2015
Township (*Xiang*) government	10	1	1	1	1	0	—	—
Town (*Zhen*) government	107	101	93	91	84	59	32	30
Villagers committee *Cunmin Weiyuanhui*	2,080	1,821	1,540	1,355	1,272	1,185	579	628
Villagers group	25,198	25,183	24,834	24,392	24,122	23,561	—	—

Sources: Statistics Bureau of Wuxi City, *Wuxi Statistical Yearbook*, 2005, 165; 2011, 163; 2016 (Table 1-01); Statistical Bureau of Jiangsu Province, *Jiangsu Statistical Yearbook*, 2016.

1980s were increased to six in the early 1990s, consisting of Chong'an, Beitang, Wan Chang, Ma Shan, New Districts and the Suburban District (the Suburban District had included parts of Ma Shan and New Districts before). Wuxi County also underwent reorganization with the formation of the Xishan city out of its territory in 1996. As the character of the rural economy changed and urbanization proceeded at a fast pace, the Wuxi city underwent a major reorganization in 2004, and again in 2015, more and more rural units becoming integrated into metropolitan administration.

Designating rural units as urban entities was a continuing trend. Under a proposal from Wuxi leadership confirmed by the State Council, the highest administrative authority of the Central government, Wuxi was further reorganized in 2015. All the former rural units of the original Wuxi County, some of which were townships (rural unit) in the 1980s, becoming towns (urban unit)—parts of the latter including our study area had become street communities—all of them became part of the metropolitan districts of Wuxi. There were now five metropolitan districts (*shi qu*): Xishan, Huishan, Binhu, Liangxi and Xinwu. The new district management committee also continued besides the two county-level cities, Jiangyin and Yixing. Wuxi did not have any rural township after 2004. As we will see later, our study area, the original township of Hela, which had become a street committee of the metropolitan area, was a part of the Binhu District. We should note that even while the steady process of giving urban designations went on, the practice of having rural entities within urban areas continued. The urban–rural linkage existed in this way. But it was a matter of time when these rural units would also transform into urban entities, because the reform path had a clear direction which was one of urbanization. By 2015 year-end, Wuxi city had 32 towns, 51 street communities, 576 village communities (within urban street committees), 593 neighbourhood committees (*zhumin weiyuanhui*; within urban street committees) and 981 villagers committees (*cunmin weiyuanhui*) which are rural areas within the towns.[11]

It should be noted that the county governments aspire to become cities so that they would be allowed by the government to have greater facilities for industrialization and building of infrastructure besides new constructions for residence, commerce and production. Most importantly, urban land is under State ownership and the administration can decide on its use. Rural land is under collective ownership of the village contracted to the rural households, hence the practice of having urban units within rural entities and rural units under urban entities. Xishan city was merged mainly with the urban districts in 2001 (Table 3.2), but it became a freshly reorganized district in 2015. As of 2004, Jiangsu province consisted of 13 cities at the prefecture level, 106 entities at the county level of which 27 were county-level cities—two

Table 3.2:
Wuxi: Administrative divisions (2004, 2010, 2015)

Di Qu/District	Years	Zhen/Town	Jiedao Banshichu/Urban Sub-district Office	Zhumin Weiyuanhui/Neighbourhood Committee	Cunmin Weiyuan hui/Villagers Committee	Area (km²)	Water Area (km²)
Wuxi City Total	2004	59	24	453	1,061	4,787.61	1,502.08
	2010	32	51	567	674	4,627.47	1,335.30
	2015	30	51	593	628	4,627.46	1,289.66
Shi Qu/Urban districts	2004	22	24	298	337	1,622.64	510.44
	2010	7	41	348	214	1,643.88	504.70
	2015	7	41	442	170	1,643.88	488.68
Chong'an district	2004	Metropolitan Area	6	34	8	17.59	—
	2010		6	38	—	16.48	1.04
	2015		6	39	—	16.48	0.97
Nanchang district	2004	Metropolitan Area	6	60	No Villages	22.43	—
	2010		6	55	—	23.90	1.67 (WA)
	2015		6	57	—	23.90	1.65
Beitang district	2004	Metropolitan Area	5	60	—	31.02	—
	2010		5	54	—	31.12	2.24 (WA)
	2015		5	57	—	31.12	2.19
Xishan district	2004	8	Relatively Rural Area, So No Jiedao	33	117	454.36	—
	2010	4	5	39	76	399.11	62.27 (WA)
	2015	4	5	43	75	399.11	56.93

Huishan district	2004	6	No Jiedao	16	134	327.12	—
	2010	2	5	29	80	325.12	49.50 (W/A)
	2015	2	5	55	56	325.12	42.36
Binhu district	2004	5	4	78	72	631.50	—
	2010	1	8	101	9	629.44	371.64 (W/A)
	2015	3	8	104	7	628.14	369.29
New district	2004		3	17	6	138.63	—
	2010	—	6	68	49	218.72	16.34 (W/A)
	2015	—	6	87	32	220.01	15.29
Shi (Xian) county-level city	2004	37	Relatively Rural Area, Formerly Xian	155	724	3,164.96	991.63
	2010	25	10	183	460	2,983.59	830.60
	2015	23	10	151	458	2,983.59	800.98
Jiangyin city	2004	16	Relatively Rural Area, Formerly Xian	64	312	987.53	194.87
	2010	11	6	90	243	986.98	185.70 (W/A)
	2015	10	5	55	243	986.97	171.98
Yixing city	2004	21	Relatively Rural Area, Formerly Xian	91	412	2,177.43	796.76
	2010	14	4	93	217	1,996.61	644.90 (W/A)
	2015	13	5	96	215	1,996.61	629

Sources: Statistics Bureau of Wuxi City, *Wuxi Statistical Yearbook*, 2005, 6–7; 2011, 6–7; 2016 (Table 1-01).

Note: Water area (W/A) refers to the sum of water and water conservancy facilities.

of them were Jiangyin and Yixing in Wuxi—and 54 urban districts, four of them in Wuxi. Of the 1,410 township-level entities, 1,019 were already designated as towns and 281 had become street communities or sub-districts, of which Hela was one.[12]

Wuxi is a medium-sized city with a population of over 4 million, with its non-agricultural or urban population increasing steadily over the years. In 1997, for example, of the total population of 4.32 million, there were 1.73 million living in the metropolitan districts. It increased to 4.47 and 2.79 million respectively in 2004. In 2015, out of 4.8 million, 1.2 million were rural labourers (Table 3.3). The official documentation describes nearly 4.70 million as 'registered population' and 6.46 million as 'permanent residents' in 2012.[13] In other words, as many as over 1.76 million or more than a quarter of the population did not have urban *hukou* in Wuxi. That it attracts much outside labour is due to it flourishing industrial growth as Wuxi is one of the 15 key economic centres in China and one of the 13 relatively large cities besides being one of the 10 major tourist centres. But there is a built-in inequity in access to urban facilities in this process of growth.

Fast Pace of Economic Development: Wuxi's Success Story

Wuxi's economic growth has been spectacular. The GDP growth rate rose to 16.6 per cent during the Sixth FYP (1981–85), showing significant growth in the wages and maintaining a high rate of growth in both right up to the Eleventh Plan (2006–10). But since the reforms started, GDP growth fell below two digits for the first time in the Twelfth Plan period (2011–15) to 9.2 per cent (Table 3.4). That reflected the national trend as medium-to-high growth rate had become the new normal. Wuxi's industries include textile, machinery, electronics, light industry, metallurgy, petro-chemical, building material, food processing and pharmaceutical. In 1997, the GDP of the whole city was 94.78 billion yuan, rising more than five times to 579.33 billion yuan in 2010, and by 2015 year-end, it stood at 852 billion yuan (Table 3.3). The structure of the economy changed vastly during the 1990s and later, with more workers engaged in industry and services rather than in agriculture. Whereas nearly half the workforce was engaged in agriculture and related occupations in 1980, it declined to 22.7 in 2000 and a mere 6 per cent in 2010. On the other hand, the proportion of the workforce engaged in industry rose from 38.3 per cent in 1980 to 48.1 per cent in 2000 and

Table 3.3:
Wuxi: Demographic and economic trends

	1952	1970	1980	1990	1997	2000	2004	2010	2015	Remarks
Population (million), of which					4.32	4.34	4.47	4.66	4.80	Growth rate of non-agricultural population is high
non-agricultural					1.73	1.83	2.79	—	—	
employment (workforce)					2.32	2.21	2.74	3.82	3.90	
GDP (billion yuan)					94.78	117.02	225	579.33	851.82	Fast growth
Primary industry					4.44	4.62	4.42	10.49	13.77	Agriculture not growing much
Secondary industry					56.8	69	137.73	320.87	419.74	Industry growing rapidly
Tertiary industry					33.52	44	82.90	247.95	418.31	Also growing fast
Gross output value of light industry					66.46	72.60	134.49	297.48	376.09	Growing fast
Gross output value of heavy industry					75.68	105.30	323.01	999.62	1078.8	Growing faster
Grain output (million tons)	0.85	1.23	1.46	1.53	1.57	1.27	0.81	0.80	0.72	Declining substantially
Oil-bearing crop (thousand tons)	2.40	13.73	18.5	41.7	39.3	59.1	36.7	11.6	8.6	Clearly not encouraged
Aquatic products (thousand tons)	8.18	10.7	19.18	66.59	81.6	102.5	113.9	121	125.3	Slow progress of a traditional strength
Silkworm cocoons (tons)	5,465	6,124	5,658	2,304	1,139	1,115	603	91	a	Disappearing fast
Tea (tons)	327	1,010	2,023	5,870	4,992	4,898	4,680	6,426	6,710	Continues to be an important produce

Sources: Statistics Bureau of Wuxi City, *Wuxi Statistical Yearbook*, 2005, 10-11; 2011, 13, 25; 2016 (Table 1-05).

Notes: ᵃ2016 statistical yearbook has no data for 2015, but in 2014 it was 73 tons.

Data from 1993 to 2008 are adjusted according to the statistics coverage of the National Economic Census.

Table 3.4:

Annual average rate of growth of selected indicators during FYPs in Wuxi (%)

FYP	Population	GDP	Gross Output Value of Agriculture	Gross Output Value of Industry	Light Industry	Heavy Industry	Grain Production	Average Annual Wages of Staff and Workers
First 1952–56	1.9	4.6	0.4	8.1	6.8	32.2	0.8	0.6
Second 1957–60	0.9	0.5	-1.7	2.1	-0.4	18.9	8.2	1.6
Readjustment period 1961–65[a]	2.2	16.1	16.8	19	15	30.1	17.4	-2.5
Third 1968–72	1.5	5	-1.5	12.7	7.8	23.1	-1.2	0.1
Fourth 1972–76	1.2	9.7	5	12	10.6	13.2	6.6	0.7
Fifth 1976–80	1.4	14.2	0.2	15.5	14.3	13.2	3.4	6
Sixth 1981–85	0.7	16.6	6.2	19.5	14.1	18.6	3.4	9.7
Seventh 1986–90	1.3	10.6	5.9	15.3	12.1	14.3	1.7	17.1
Eighth 1991–95	0.5	24.6	9.7	36.2	28.3	28.2	-0.1	24
Ninth 1996–2000	0.3	11.8	2.9	9.4	22.9	21.1	-3.7	8.8
Tenth 2001–05	0.7	14.4	1.1	19.6	17	31.4	-8.9	18.5
Eleventh 2006–10	0.6	13.6	12.4	15.8	4.2	17.1	0.2	14.1
Twelfth 2011–15	0.6	9.2	8.4	4.7	6.7	2.6	-2.1	9.1

Sources: Constructed on the basis of the data in Statistics Bureau of Wuxi City, *Wuxi Statistical Yearbook*, 2005; 2011, 17–19; 2016 (Table 1.06).

Note: [a] Readjustment policies worked until 1965, after which Cultural Revolution campaigns slowly began, and the turbulent phase continued until 1969.

56 per cent in 2015. Employment in the services in the same years rose from 12.1 per cent to 29.2 per cent and further to 39 per cent of the city's GDP in 2015 (Table 3.5 and Figure 3.4). The development of light industries through TVEs and other enterprises had grown steadily in the 1980s and the early 1990s. In 1995, Wuxi officials happily reported this, saying that the ratio of heavy industry to light industry had risen to 51.6:48.4; the large and

Table 3.5:
Wuxi: Changing composition of employed workforce 1980–2015

Selected Years	Employed Workforce (Total in Million)	Primary Industry (%)	Secondary Industry (%)	Tertiary Industry (%)
1980	2.056	49.6	38.3	12.1
1985	2.367	25.8	56.3	17.9
1990	2.449	22.2	58.6	19.2
1995	2.379	16.5	57.2	26.3
2000	2.210	22.7	48.1	29.2
2004	2.746	12.8	54.8	32.4
2005	2.892	11.8	55.1	33.1
2010	3.823	6	55	39
2015	3.900	4.5	56.3	39.2

Sources: Compiled from Statistics Bureau of Wuxi City, *Wuxi Statistical Yearbook*, 2005, 47; 2011, 47; 2016 (Table 2-07).

Figure 3.4:
Wuxi: Changing composition of workforce 1980–2015 (%)

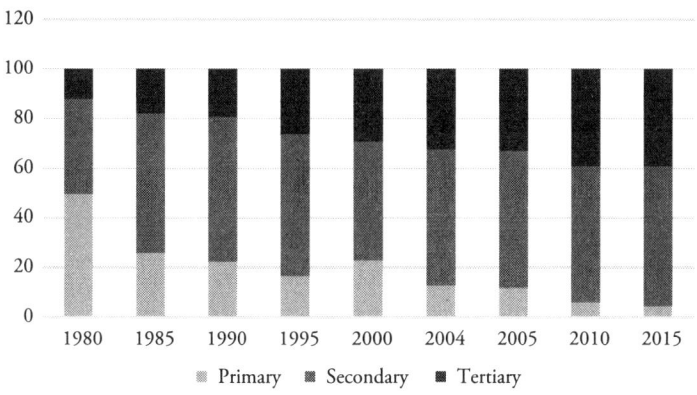

Sources: Compiled from Statistics Bureau of Wuxi City, *Wuxi Statistical Yearbook*, 2005, 47; 2011, 47; 2016 (Table 2-07).

medium-sized enterprises were 32 per cent out of the total, with 48 per cent being small enterprises and the remaining raw material-processing units.[14] In 1995, the rural enterprises contributed two-thirds of the total output value of the whole city. During the period 1981–91, the TVEs registered a yearly 22 per cent rise in their output value. Thus, the Wuxi region had acquired a special reputation for the success of rural enterprises. Their products were not only marketed within the country but also abroad. After the mid-1990s, this situation changed vastly. It was the products of the modern urban enterprises which developed the export market. In 2010, Wuxi had trade relations with 123 countries and regions. The Wuxi municipality has its own import–export corporations which autonomously engage in foreign trade. A large number of quality products in textile, silk, light industry, machinery, electronics, agricultural and sideline products (fishery, animal products and processed foods) are exported to many countries.

The character of the ownership system of enterprises underwent a steady process of change during the 1990s and later with the rise of private enterprises together with corresponding changes in the structure of employment (Table 3.6). It may be noted that urban collective units which provided jobs to 211,800 people, nearly a third of the total number employed in 1980,

Table 3.6:
Changing ownership system and employment pattern

Year	Employment (Millions)	Staff and Workers (Millions)	In the State-owned Units	In the Urban Collective Units	In Other Forms of Ownership	Urban Self-employed	Rural Labourers
1980	2.056	0.592	0.380	0.211	—	0.0013	1.463
1985	2.367	0.740	0.452	0.265	0.022	0.0097	1.618
1990	2.449	0.798	0.480	0.269	0.048	0.016	1.639
1995	2.379	0.783	0.444	0.205	0.133	0.044	1.551
2000	2.210	0.593	0.320	0.086	0.186	0.108	1.509
2004	2.746	0.527	0.209	0.0423	0.276	0.598	1.564
2010	3.823	0.716	0.151	0.0139	0.5363	—	—
2014	3.900	1.179	—	—	—	—	1.223

Sources: Compiled from Statistics Bureau of Wuxi City, *Wuxi Statistical Yearbook*, 2005, 47–48; 2011, 52; 2016 (Table 2-0).

Notes: Data for 2008 and the earlier years are based on the data of urban collective-owned units, data since 2009 are based on the data of non-private urban units. From the beginning of 2011, data are based on the data of staff and workers; staff includes labour dispatch personnel. Data since 2014 are based on the data of employees in non-private urban units (the same as in the following tables).

provided employment only to 42,300 in 2004. In the case of the State-owned units too, there was a decline in employment of workers from 380,300 to 209,000, but it was still a substantial source of employment. On the other hand, the private ownership system in the economy had grown substantially with the non-public units employing 276,000, which was more than the State and collective units put together. This sector had employed only 22,500 in 1985 and experienced rapid expansion after 1992 when Deng Xiaoping gave the call for expanding the market economy during his southern tour to Shenzhen and other SEZs. Table 3.6 also shows the major trend of self-employed urban labour. Their number was miniscule; in 1980, it was only 1,300 which grew to a big number in 2004 to 598,800, again having a sharp rise after 1992. This is the sector of population that had a wide range of differences in income and living conditions. Many of them were migrant labour living in hardship. What remained constant was the massive proportion of rural labourers compared to those in urban employment. The number of rural labourers was 1.466 million while there were only 514,900 urban labourers in 1978. It was still high in 2004 with 1.564 million rural and 527,400 urban. In 2015, there were 1.21 million rural labourers which was still a substantial number, but the urban number had gone up to 2.677 million (Table 3.6). In other words, rural labourers were facing a new situation of finding work when employment in the collective enterprises shrank substantially in the 1990s. Some of them found jobs in the private sector, while many went for self-employment. But a large number remained unemployed or were in search of jobs in the new environment. Thus, whereas the economy recorded impressive growth in GDP, rural population including many in the city faced employment crisis. The registered urban unemployment was 138,221 people in 2015, slightly less than in 2014.[15]

Several important trends in incomes are noticeable if we have 50-year span of analysis (Table 3.7 and Figure 3.5). Firstly, there was a near stagnation of wages from 1952 until 1977 which was also low at only around 500 yuan. It grew 40 times to 20,442 yuan in 2004.[16] Of course, prices of commodities were low and collective social services were available to all during the commune period. And there was an egalitarian environment. But amenities of living were minimal. Secondly, the 1980s witnessed massive growth of income from 550 yuan in 1978 to 2,449 yuan in 1990. This was the period of focus on rural reforms, especially collectively owned rural industries. Thereafter also, the progress was remarkable, crossing the 10,000 yuan mark in 2000, accomplishing much more than Deng Xiaoping's stipulation of fourfold increase. Thirdly, the relatively rural regions Jiangyin and Yixing were not too far behind the incomes in the urban districts until the late 1990s.

Table 3.7:
Trends in average annual wages of workers and staff: 1952–2015 (yuan)

Year	Total Wuxi	Urban Districts	Jiangyin City	Yixing City
1952	507	529	401	355
1957	508	568	420	429
1962	5,515	580	466	451
1970	504	523	478	463
1978	550	574	512	493
1980	699	724	656	639
1985	1,113	1,137	1,086	987
1990	2,449	2,550	2,335	2,119
1995	7,192	7,488	6,998	6,153
2000	10,966	11,988	9,685	8,835
2004	20,442	21,295	20,252	15,956
2010	46,430	49,243	44,076	38,851
2015	71,882	73,254	71,471	65,521

Sources: Compiled from Statistics Bureau of Wuxi City, *Wuxi Statistical Yearbook*, 2005, 51; 2011, 51; 2016 (Table 2-11).

Note: From 1952 until 2000, areas which became a part of Xishan city and then merged with urban districts were included in the total for Wuxi.

Figure 3.5:
Trends in average annual wages of workers and staff: 1952–2015 (yuan)

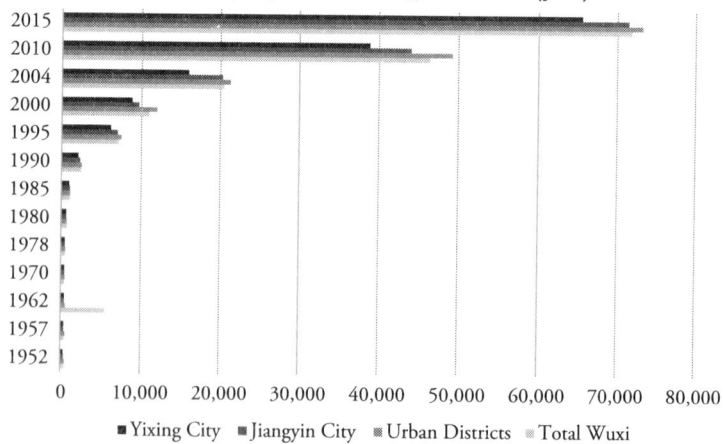

■ Yixing City   ■ Jiangyin City   ▨ Urban Districts   ▨ Total Wuxi

Sources: Compiled from Statistics Bureau of Wuxi City, *Wuxi Statistical Yearbook*, 2005, 51; 2011, 51; 2016 (Table 2-11).

Thereafter, the rural–urban disparities began to widen fast. If we look at the annual average wages of staff and workers in 2004 in terms of where they were employed, then those who worked in the State-owned units got 23,879 yuan—almost double of what was earned by workers in the collective units (12,674 yuan)—and those who worked in the private sector got 18,725 yuan, about one and a half times the wages of the collective workers but less than the wage of the employees in SOEs. That was the average picture, while some in the foreign-owned or joint sector earned much more than the workers of the State-owned units. But in 2004, the average earning of the government employees in Wuxi was 31,525 yuan—higher than those working in enterprises (17,955 yuan) and in other institutions (25,538 yuan).[17] Today, the average wages and salaries of workers have nearly trebled since the early 2000s, with 71,882 yuan in 2015 (Table 3.7).

The living standards improved rapidly during the reforms period as was evident from the rising income as well as the expanding savings (Table 3.7). Simultaneously, the urban–rural gap sharply widened during the 1990s, even though incomes of residents in both rural and urban areas grew steadily. The per capita savings deposits which were substantial from 1985 onwards exceeded the per capita earnings in 2000 and remained so thereafter. In 2015, urban per capita income was 45,129 yuan and for rural residents, it was 24,155 yuan (Table 3.8 and Figure 3.6). As noted earlier, Wuxi's pattern of development has been to urbanize the village communities. Therefore, the

Table 3.8:
Living standards of urban and rural residents: 1978–2015 (yuan per capita)

Year	Disposable Income of Urban Residents	Net Income of Rural Residents	Per Capita Savings Deposits of Residents
1978	340	181	39
1980	456	239	65
1985	958	698	302
1990	1,833	1,496	1,337
1995	5,763	3,976	4,708
2000	8,603	5,256	12,763
2004	13,588	7,115	25,943
2010	27,750	14,002	48,313
2015	45,129	24,155	71,259

Sources: Statistics Bureau of Wuxi City, *Wuxi Statistical Yearbook*, 2005, 74; 2011, 61; 2016 (Table 3-01).

Figure 3.6:
Living standards of urban and rural residents: 1978–2015 (yuan per capita)

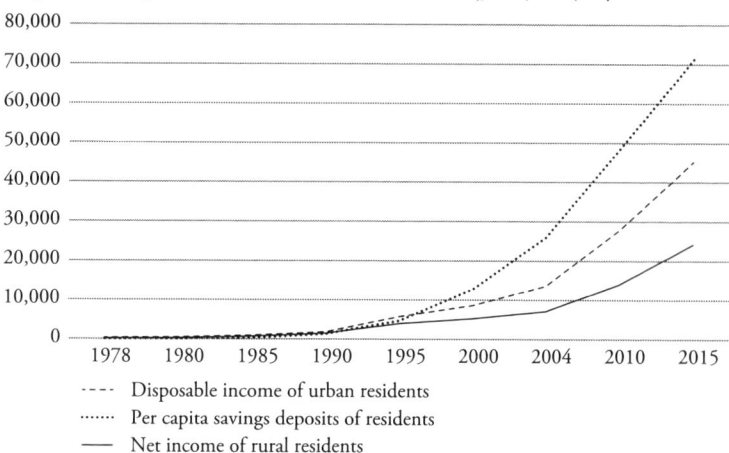

---- Disposable income of urban residents
······ Per capita savings deposits of residents
—— Net income of rural residents

Sources: Statistics Bureau of Wuxi City, *Wuxi Statistical Yearbook*, 2005, 74; 2011, 61; 2016
(Table 3-01).

townships were allowed to be converted into towns. Even the one township that had remained as such after 1999 ceased to exist in 2004. But villagers committees continued within towns, even though their number also declined as many of them became street communities (*jiedao*) or village-level towns. It may be noted that the villagers groups corresponding to the production teams of the commune period continued to exist and perform a crucial role at the village level.

Growing Inequalities

We get a picture of the state of income inequality in Wuxi from Table 3.8. In 2004, nearly a quarter of the population earned below 4,000 yuan, while almost the same proportion were above the 10,000-yuan level. More than 40 per cent were in the middle-income group of 4,000–8,000-yuan bracket. It was noticeable that there were rich people in all the districts and cities. Thus, inequality was pervasive in all the areas. Tables 3.9a and 3.9b show the situation of disparate incomes in the rural areas. It is clear that the rural–urban inequality got accentuated after 2000.

The district where Hela is located reflects many features of the Wuxi city as a whole.

Table 3.9a:
Proportion of per capita annual net income of rural households (2004)

Income Level (Yuan)	Wuxi (Total)	Urban Districts	Jiangyin City	Yixing City
Below 2,000	5.50	4	6	8
2,000–3,000	6.50	6	8	6
3,000–4,000	11	10.50	6	17
4,000–5,000	10.25	12	6	11
5,000–6,000	11	10.50	8	15
6,000–7,000	11.75	10.50	11	15
7,000–8,000	8.75	8	11	8
8,000–9,000	8.50	10.50	10	3
9,000–10,000	5.25	4.50	9	3
Over 10,000	21.50	23.50	25	14

Source: Statistics Bureau of Wuxi City, *Wuxi Statistical Yearbook*, 2005, 91.

Table 3.9b:
Proportion of per capita annual net income of rural households (2010)

Income Level (Yuan)	Wuxi (Total)	Urban District	Jiangyin City	Yixing City
Below 4,000	14	9	NA	5
4,000–5,000	8	4	NA	4
5,000–7,000	22	11	1	10
7,000–9,000	47	23	14	10
9,000–10,000	27	13	6	8
10,000–12,000	59	36	15	8
12,000–14,000	46	20	15	11
14,000–16,000	40	15	11	14
16,000–18,000	41	13	17	11
18,000–20,000	26	12	9	5
Over 20,000	70	44	12	14

Source: Statistics Bureau of Wuxi City, *Wuxi Statistical Yearbook*, 2011, 73.

The District: Urbanization of the Rural

During the past four decades, the grass-roots entities in the countryside have undergone many waves of reorganization. It is important to understand not only the meaning of similar sounding terms but also the rationale behind such changes in nomenclature and status. Our place of study Hela was a people's commune before the reforms. It formally became a *xiang* (township) in 1983 and remained as a basic-level rural administrative unit until 1999 when it was changed into a *zhen* (town) which gave it an urban status. But Wuxi city's urbanization process was going ahead relentlessly incorporating the suburban area into the city's new industrial, commercial and residential areas. In 2004, Hela became a regular unit of a metropolitan district, a *jiedao* (street/sub-district). To complete this story, it should be noted that before 1958, Hela was a *xiang*.

English speakers often find the use of city, township and town confusing because the term itself does not clearly identify the level of the urban or the rural unit. It is even more striking to find urban units within designated rural areas and rural units within designated urban areas. It is important to locate the geographical level which the term refers to. Let us try to clarify this problem because it actually indicates rural–urban linkage and the continuous trend of urbanization in China.

The ongoing process of urbanization meant reorganization of upper-level units at the level of *xian* (county) and *di qu* (districts). As mentioned earlier, Jiangsu province was divided into 13 cities (*shi*) in 1983. The character *shi* is used for city at every level, so one has to find out each time at which level that city was located. Beijing and Shanghai are provincial-level cities. Wuxi, Nanjing and Hangzhou are prefecture-level cities. Then there are county-level cities. A metropolitan or urban area can also be a *shi* or city. For rural China, the entity above the *xiang* level is the *xian* (county). In olden days, the whole of Wuxi city was the Wuxi *xian* (county). From 1983 until the early 1990s, Wuxi had four divisions: Wuxi metropolitan area along with a suburban district, Wuxi County and two county-level cities—Jiangyin *shi* (city) and Yixing *shi* (city). In 2004, Wuxi County ceased to exist and it was integrated with the metropolitan area with many districts (*qu*). Again, there were two kinds of districts in the metropolitan area—*shi qu* (urban districts) and *qu* which were at the level of *zhen* (town) located in the *xian* or the rural county. In 2015, the earlier Wuxi County and the metropolitan areas were integrated and reorganized into four urban districts.

Just as a *shi* (city) can exist at different levels so can a *zhen* (town). There are *xiang*-level towns called *zhen* and there are *cun* (village) towns also called *zhen*. There may be small urban centres which may not have the legal status of a *xiang* or *cun* which may be also called *zhen* or a town. In a *xian* or rural county, there can be both *xiang* (township which is a rural entity) and *zhen* (town). Within a *xiang* (township), there may be *cun* (village) as well as *cun*-level *zhen* (town). Similarly, within a *zhen* (town at the *xiang* level), there can be rural areas or *cun* and urban areas or *zhen* (town at the *cun* level).

The metropolitan area's urban districts are divided into street (*jiedao*) now designated as urban sub-district office (*jiedao banshichu*), and they are further divided into neighbourhood committees (*zhumin weiyuanhui*). But the other districts in the metropolitan area may have both *jiedao* (sub-district) as well as *zhen* (*qu*).

The rationale behind such complex intermixing of rural and urban entities is the reality of the fast pace of urbanization in contemporary China. Declaration of an area as urban changes the nature of ownership. The economic planning acquires industrial direction. Land use is subject to commercial and other regulations. As we will see, the history of Hela's changing status from a grain-producing, mulberry-planting, silkworm-raising community across Liangxi River to an industrial and commercial hub with a modern residential neighbourhood reflected the corresponding administrative change. It is important to note that the same process has taken place even in the remote areas of rural China.

Hela as a *xiang* was part of the suburban district when I first visited Wuxi. So, we start with a picture of the development process in the suburban district and then turn to the profile of Binhu District in which Hela was relocated first as a *zhen* (town) and then as a *jiedao* (street). The suburban district was one of the districts of Wuxi. It consisted of 10 townships (former communes) which together accounted for 108 villages (*cun*), each village having a villagers committee (*cunmin weiyuanhui*). The fact that it is a suburb, that is, with some urban characteristics, is evident from the existence of seven street committees (*jiedao weiyuanhui*) consisting of 94 residents committees (*jumin weiyuanhui*) sometimes also called neighbourhood committees. During the commune period, there were the production teams below the production brigade, and after the reorganization, their counterparts were by and large dissolved, though in some areas work groups did operate. However, in the case of the urban zones, the residents committees continued to function below the street committees and performed the role of being the lowest unit of politics and administration.

During the four decades of reforms, the suburban district of Wuxi vastly changed its landscape and economic characteristics. From one with large-scale agricultural fields, fish ponds, parks, hills and the lake, the new landscape now was dominated by high-rise buildings, industrial plants, flyovers, bridges, hotels and shopping complexes. This district fairly accurately represented the character of transformation of Wuxi and in a sense of China as a whole.

Occupying an area of 150 km², the suburban district had a population of 370,000 in 1996, an increase of 70,000 since 1986. This high percentage of growth over 23 per cent added in 10 years was not due to higher rate of birth but because of establishment of workers and employee colonies which came up along with new enterprises. In 1986, 130,000 were peasants and 170,000 were urban residents. The main orientation with which the suburban district started its reforms was that it should serve the city and benefit by it. Therefore, producing vegetables and food grains for supplying them to the city besides producing a certain amount of food grains for their own consumption continued as a component of its economy. But the development of rural enterprises was encouraged as a part of the national policy to facilitate the overall economic process. The district devised its strategy in such a way that industry and commerce should develop rapidly and out of this development, agriculture should be supported. One of the considerations underlying the strategy was the fact that every year, more and more agricultural land was taken over for construction of industrial and commercial enterprises. Since the district enjoyed autonomy in its economic decision-making, it could utilize its resources including land for most profitable purposes. Hence, in the 1980s, much land was diverted from agriculture to industrial construction. Because of collective ownership of land, such diversions were easy. The composition of the suburban district economy in terms of their output value as of 1996 was as follows: industry—68 per cent, tertiary sector—30 per cent and agriculture—2 per cent, reflecting the trend of urban transformation.

In 1996, the suburban district had a total of 1,200 rural enterprises at the *xiang* and village level, employing 86,000 workers—54 per cent of them were male and 46 per cent were female workers. Women mainly worked in textile units, office jobs, financial and managerial jobs and warehousing units. Only one-fifth of the workers were employed in smaller units with less than 1 million yuan assets. Bulk of them worked in larger units. As for the nature of the rural enterprises, 43 per cent were in the field of machinery and electronics, 30 were textile units, 14 metallurgy enterprises, while the remaining were light industries and food-related units.

After giving tax concessions and other incentives to the rural industries in the 1980s, the Chinese government called upon them to compete with the State enterprises. So, after 1993, the rate of taxation was the same for rural enterprises as well as the urban enterprises. When I visited in 1997, the enterprise leaders were already complaining of the Central government's withdrawal of the special concessions which it had given to the TVEs in the early 1980s.

The fast development of light industries particularly modern enterprises was most noticeable during the preceding two decades. At this time, the tertiary sector grew very fast. The development of hotels, restaurants, banks and the tourism facilities was conspicuous. But as a matter of policy, agriculture was not given up, even though it contributed only a small portion, that is, 2 per cent to the total output value. The district authorities clearly held the view that this proportion in the composition of the economy should be maintained for a long time so that they could fulfil their assigned quotas of grain and other agricultural products which were set from above, while responding to the people's expanding urges for prosperity. This was described as the 'stabilization of the development process', fulfilling the objectives of the Ninth FYP and the targets for the year 2010.

Table 3.10 indicates the high rate of growth achieved by the suburban district during the period of high growth.[18]

The story of the development process in the suburban district was typical of the areas in eastern China which took full advantage of the national policy on reforms. Prior to 1978, the main focus was on grain production. During the Cultural Revolution period, those who paid greater attention to industry, commerce and household sideline production were criticized as 'capitalist roaders'. The State had fixed quotas for grain production for each level. This resulted in inadequate supply of vegetables to the city. There was a large labour force engaged in agricultural production. The production cost remained high. The variety of products was limited. Many such problems were pointed out by the local leaders while referring to the commune period. But it should be pointed out that while stress on grain production was undoubtedly there, diversification of the economy and development of appropriate rural industries were also encouraged in the early 1960s and were part of the overall commune policy. But the thrust on them was now far more pronounced than before.

The perspective that unfolded with the reforms after 1978 asked the countryside to develop on their own and the suburbs to supply vegetables

Table 3.10:
Rate of growth (million yuan)

Values	1978	1986	1994
Total output value	220	1,600	13,239
GNP	110	—	3,890
GNP per capita	—	12,727	24,072

and other needs to the city. Operating under the HRS, the suburb diversified its economy and developed agriculture, industry and commerce.

During the first phase of the reforms, especially in 1979–85, the rural enterprises experienced rapid growth. The suburb took advantage of cheap labour force, both from local sources and from across the Yangtze River— the area in southern Zhejiang which was relatively less developed. To their advantage, the enterprises hired the retired technicians of the industries of Shanghai and Suzhou. As mentioned earlier, Wuxi already had a tradition of industry and commerce. Being the home of the Rong family, the suburban district already was connected with national and international trade.[19] In fact, contemporary China's best-known industrialist Rong Yiren, who was the vice-president of China in 1993–98, was chairperson of China Council of International Trade that played a key role in China's opening up. The suburban district also acquired a lot of second-hand machines to launch its enterprises. Once the rural industries sprang up, some members from practically every peasant household went to work in the industries. Every township and every village tried to set up new enterprises in the early 1980s.

The next phase of reforms in the suburban district started in 1985 and lasted until 1991. Thereafter, the post-1992 impetus for privatization and foreign trade took off. Now the effort was in upgrading the quality of production. The cadres had already accumulated some experience in running enterprises, managers got training and workers developed skills on the job. Hence, a good foundation had already been laid. Farmers had acquired technical skills in a variety of economic activities. The experience with managing rural collective enterprises was compared with that of State-run enterprises, and many lessons were learnt so that these could be managed better. The availability of cheap labour force and land now needed to be integrated with use of modern technology, securing capital from the national and international market. Thus, during the second half of the 1980s, the suburban economy changed from simple production process and what was considered low technology to large-scale and modern production. During this period, many joint ventures with foreign investment came up in different townships including Hela's three-star hotel with Australian collaboration, Meilido Hotel.

The second major phase saw rapid market development after Deng Xiaoping's 1992 southern tour. Initiative and competition were the new creed. The rural enterprises diversified their own production in the wake of fierce competition in the market. In the suburban district of Wuxi, in the initial year of reforms, there was greater demand than supply of various kinds of goods. Now the situation had reversed. The market had more supply of all kinds of goods than was demanded—a phenomenon that became a major problem during the reform period hereafter until the supply-side reforms addressed this in 2016. In this situation, there was more competition faced by the various enterprises. The competition now involved collective enterprises owned by the townships, villages, SOEs and increasing number of private enterprises. By now, the nature of the emerging crisis was becoming clear. The rural enterprises found it difficult to sustain themselves in the face of such competition.

The 1990s saw significant changes in forms of ownership of enterprises. The suburban district encouraged the organization of the shareholding companies. Unlike in Guangdong province where private ownership grew up very fast, in the *Su Nan* (south of Yangtze River) region, collective enterprises still continued as the main form of ownership even in the late 1990s. But they also opened themselves to shareholders. Shares were bought by their own workers, members of the township, other enterprises and companies from within the country and outside. Out of the 1,200 enterprises, 680 units possessing more than three million yuan assets were ready for change in ownership pattern in 1996.

Opening to the national and the world market was the policy after the Fourteenth Party Congress in 1992. In this process, many enterprises got bankrupt because their products were of low quality and they failed in the market. Some loss-making companies were sold out to private individuals or other collectives and companies. When the Fifteenth Party Congress focused on the reform of SOEs in 1997, the policy on the transformation of collective enterprises was already in operation and thousands of rural enterprises had been sold to private entrepreneurs. Thus, 'reform and open door' continued into a new stage of market development in the 1990s in the suburban district (Tables 3.11 and 3.12).

Hela: Commune to Township to Town to Street Community

Hela was one of the 10 townships of the suburban district of Wuxi. Actually, a 1985 publicity brochure of Hela described it as Hela *gongsi*, meaning corporation (Table 3.13). This indicates changing the terms of discourse radically from a commune of Marxist ideology to a modern corporation or company of capitalist market economy. The regime of course would justify the notion of 'corporation' in their framework of socialist market economy.[20]

Table 3.11:
Profile of towns in Binhu district (2004–15)

Zhen/ Town	Years	Total Population	Employed Persons	Land Area (ha)	Cultivated Area Arable (ha)	Financial Revenue (Million Yuan)	Grain Output (Ton)	Remarks
Hela	2004	43, 911	23,514	4,700	760	27.78	3,490	Small area for crops
Xuelang	2004	—	—	—	—	—	—	Small area for crops
	2010	54,012	21,208	—	45	41.43	42	
	2015	110,199	44,357	—	—	109.38	—	
Huazhuang	2004	89,046	43,518	5,329	1,933	43.51	10,693	Larger town, more crops
	2010	93,223	40,658	—	401	90.40	1,093	
	2015	85,971	40,516	—	—	58.96	97	
Taihu town	2004	58,036	34,804	4,212	779	47.01	5,458	Less crops, more income
	2010	92,529	51,557	—	60	65.66	64	
	2015	—	—	—	—	—	—	
Mashan	2004	30,402	19,885	4,788	842	120.21	3,294	Less crops, high-level industrialization, high income
	2010	39,613	27,730	—	446	115.57	2,985	
	2015	40,203	26,131	—	—	128.96	480	
Hudai	2004	34,404	18,224	5,509	818	13.74	5,870	Less crops, more land used for non-agricultural purposes, still less income
	2010	52,895	32,224	—	1,062	61.50	1,987	
	2015	49,951	30,000	—	—	68.42	736	

Sources: Statistical Bureau of Jiangsu Province, *Jiangsu Statistical Yearbook*, 2005, 614–15; Statistics Bureau of Wuxi City, *Wuxi Statistical Yearbook*, 2011, 146–49; 2016 (Table 7-19).

Table 3.12:
Economy and the workforce of towns (Zhen) in Binhu district (2004 and 2010)

Items	Years	Hela Town	Huazhuang Town	Taihu Town	Mashan Town	Hudai Town
Total households (hu)	2004	12,698	23,925	17,978	9,015	11,967
	2010	—	17,602	28,040	15,521	12,151
Total population	2004	43,911	89,046	58,036	30,402	34,404
	2010	—	93,223	92,529	39,613	52,895
Workforce	2004	23,514	43,518	34,804	19,885	18,224
	2010	—	40,658	51,557	27,730	32,224
Persons employed in primary industry	2004	2,334	8,577	2,383	686	2,791
	2010	—	896	38	612	1,578
Employed in secondary industry	2004	16,093	26,734	27,192	13,833	10,573
	2010	—	29,625	20,256	17,500	22,021
Employed in tertiary industry	2004	5,087	8,207	5,229	5,336	4,860
	2010	—	10,137	31,263	9,618	8,625
GDP (million yuan)	2004	2,021	2,920	3,962	2,700	1,051
	2010	—	5,243	4,646	5,321	3,229
Out of which primary industry	2004	32.84	96.1	51.02	60	51.12
	2010	—	85	5.20	79.82	35.06
Secondary industry	2004	896	2,174	2,172.96	1,680	810.59
	2010	—	2,760.53	2,736.50	3,166.09	2,300.78
Tertiary industry	2004	1,092.16	650	1,198.6	960	190.06
	2010	—	2,397.74	1,904.90	2,075.25	893.80
Total financial revenue (million yuan)	2004	277.85	435.18	470.14	1,202.17	137.42
	2010	—	904	656.69	1,155.77	615.01
Average net income per farmer (yuan)	2004	6,855	7,342	8,060	7,337	6,861
	2010	—	18,117	18,161	14,595	14,518
Arable land (ha)	2004	760	1,933	779	842	818
	2010	—	401	60	446	1,062
Total output of grain (ton)	2004	3,490	10,693	5,458	3,294	5,870
	2010	—	1,093	64	2,985	1,987
Total power of farming machinery) (kW)	2004	5,728	12,060	7,071	5,510	8,749
	2010	—	1,355	120	5,757	7,861
Total electricity consumed (million kWh)	2004	111.37	191.12	487.57	2,065	9,708
	2010	—	312.98	403.32	29.326	299.30

Sources: Compiled from Statistics Bureau of Wuxi City, *Wuxi Statistical Yearbook*, 2005, 186–92; 2011, 141–50.

Table 3.13:
Administrative status of Hela

Stages	Period
People's Commune (*Renmin Gongshe*)	1958–83
Township (*Xiang*)	1983–99
Town (*Zhen*)	1999–2003
Street/Sub-district (*Jiedao*)	Since 2004

On the eastern side, Hela is connected with the Wuxi city centre by the Liangxi Bridge at the foot of which the grand new Meilido Hotel dominated the skyline. To the west is the majestic Taihu Lake. The serpentine Liangxi River pats the south edge of Hela, whereas the Huiquan Hill crowns it on the eastern side. With an area of 36 km², Hela had a population of 33,000 and 11,500 households in 1996. Hela Township consisted of 13 administrative villages (formerly production brigades) and 97 *zeran cun* or natural villages or hamlets (formerly production teams). Many of the beautiful spots of the suburban district are located in the Hela Township. The Yihui Park and the Li Yuan (Peach Garden) are located on its eastern and western sides.

In 1978, the suburban district had 15 communes. When the reforms started, the Meiyuan commune was merged with Hela in 1979 so that the entire western suburban area could become an integrated unit. By 1983, the commune structure was fully replaced by the township administrative structure. Similar reorganizations also took place in other communes of the district. Jianfang and Liutang communes were merged to form the new Huan Township. The expanded Nanjing now included Jiangxi, while Lu village merged with Yangmin. Xinan came within the expanded boundary of Liyuan Township and Zhunjiang within Dafu. However, the jurisdiction of Shanbei, Guangyu, Wangzhuan and Yigang Townships was not disturbed. In addition, another formation which was created with the status of a township was called 'scattered area management unit of the district'. Its headquarters are in the heart of the metropolitan area. But it has members in different parts of the suburban district and like the township, it also ran enterprises.

Ecology of Hela

Waterways, hills, residences, shopping complexes, factories and fields constituted the Hela Township. The Liangxi River, rather a rivulet, on the southeastern side links the Taihu Lake (actually its baby lake, Xi Lihu) with the Grand Canal. As in the case of all the waterways in this area, it is used for both navigation and fishing. Long rows of fully loaded boats are strung together and driven by a single motor. Fully loaded boats are a normal sight in this area. The fish brigade, it was still called brigade until 1996 with the status of the village, is located on the western bank of Liangxi River. The Xi Mei road which links the Mei Yuan Park with the Xihu Park runs parallel to the Jiangxi River. Helakou (or Hela gate) near the eastern end of the township is a constantly growing business area. What was a lean and quiet area in 1979 had become in 2006 a bustling activity centre, signalling the steady expansion of the metropolis, and by 2016 had the look of a bustling zone of any global city. The villages around the Helakou have naturally lost maximum land to the city for industries and commerce. For obvious reasons, the adjoining villages are relatively more prosperous compared to the ones that are farther from the city centre. Hela Township's richest villages are Liqiao, Xiemin and Sunjiang. They set up not only plants to provide ancillaries for city industries and the larger market but also shops, restaurants and hotels early in the reform years. Thereafter, many modern industrial units have come up in this area.[21]

The western part of Hela is an expanse of hills, the largest among them being the Longshan (Dragon Hill) range with Hengshan (Straight Hill) and Xishan (Copper Hill) on its south and north respectively, besides a number of smaller hills. In the late 1970s, the hills were full of pine trees and tea plantation. Some slopes were also covered with mulberry trees for raising silkworms. The picture in the late 1990s and after was very different. Hills were cleared for quarries, thus presenting a sight of shaven heads. Much of mulberry land had now been used for orchards or cleared for locating newer and newer industrial plants. It is said that mulberry could be planted in more interior villages, rather than in suburbs which could be used for more profitable purposes. The earlier logic that the mulberry trees in the area fed silk worms providing raw materials for Wuxi's rich tradition of silk production and textile business was now recast.

A road which was concrete laid in the mid-1980s goes through the Hengshan pass by the side of the Dong Hengshan hamlet to the crematorium. Further down this road across the hills lies the Qingxin village, the farthest from the metropolitan area. This is the only village where food grains, that is, rice and wheat continued to be the major products until the late 1990s. Like other villages, Qingxin launched projects of industrialization and commerce in the late 1980s and achieved rapid growth. But throughout the period of my study, the per capita income of this village remained the lowest in the township. It had its agricultural fields, hills and quarries on which rural enterprises came up and vegetable farming also made progress. But in the meantime, other villages made even further progress while this westernmost area continued to lag behind.

The southern and western boarder of Hela is the coastline of the Taihu Lake which is full of orchards of tangerine, peaches and pears and numerous fish ponds. Thus, Hela is richly endowed with plains, as well as hills, river and the lake. As per the 1996 figures, the green hills slopes occupied 16,000 mu, fish ponds 3,000 mu and only 1,360 mu was used for growing vegetables round the year and 800 mu as orchards. The landscape had changed dramatically during the four decades of reforms. Factories, hotels and residential colonies and commercial buildings came up on agricultural fields and hill slopes, filling up even some ponds.

At the same time, because of the rise in family income, there were three waves of house construction during the reform period. The first wave took place in the early 1980s, soon after the reforms started when the commune's restriction on house building was withdrawn and most of the households quickly built new houses to provide reasonable accommodation to the second-generation members of the family. In the middle of 1980, I lived in one such house in Da Ding village in Hela, as a guest of Lao Mo (Madam Mo of the Ding household—more about it later). In 1993, during the second wave, I found the same family and many others in the village living in newer modern houses fitted with technologically designed modern facilities in the same compound or in new places in the same village. Whereas the kitchens earlier mainly used coal, now they had gas and electricity-fitted cooking systems. Earlier they carried the night soil from the latrine to the field to use as manure. Now they had flush latrines. Washing machines and colour televisions became very common in the early 1980s, while more and more families also acquired refrigerators and air-conditioners by the end of the decade. Earlier having a bicycle was a luxury, now more and more families acquired light motorcycles and later, some even owned cars. The third wave of housing appeared when new apartment complexes came up on village land in 2001 onwards. The families of the village were allotted flats in high-rise buildings.

There were strict environmental regulations to prevent pollution of Taihu Lake and the rivers. As per the regulation of the State Council of China, construction of certain kinds of industries within 5 km of the lakeside is prohibited. Still, there have been alarming evidences of pollution of Taihu. As mentioned earlier, the algae pollution was increasing year after year until it assumed slanderous proportion during the summer of 2007. Certain kinds of fishes were not breeding any more the way they used to because the toxic level continued to rise. The water management system seemed to have been upset in recent years as was evident from the fact that every one or two years, there were severe floods in this area during the past two decades.

People and Their Work

Before we look at the population figures (Table 3.14), a clarification is called for. Hela's population figure did not include the residents in the quarters provided by the city government which were located in the territory of Hela. They were city workers who worked in the city-run factories and offices, though they lived in the houses located in the suburban area. Nor does it include those members of the rural family who work in the city and had acquired city residency registration. They may have their houses in the village, but they are enumerated as city workers. In fact, it presents serious problems for statistical calculations. For example, take the case of a family where the husband is a worker in the city-run enterprise and the wife in a TVE; the husband would be counted as a part of urban population and the wife a part of the rural population. Because of having a house in the village, the household would be counted as a rural household, actually peasant household. With the introduction of the HRS, the land can be contracted and subcontracted, while the members may not work on land. Yet, maintaining a piece of land in the village continues to be a much desired asset for most people. They may work in urban enterprises. For certain purposes, the family is regarded as a rural household with some of its members as urban workers. Thus, it gets highly complicated when one tries to work out per capita output or per capita income. If this is complicated for the suburban area, it

Table 3.14:
Population of Hela

Years	Population	Households	Workforce
1979 (*xiang*)	21,236	6,778	110,242
1980	19,672	6,607	9,337
1985	18,400	5,000	8,436
1993	33,000	11,500	—
2001 (*zhen*)	36,000	—	—
2004 (*jiedao*)	43,911	12,698	23,524

is not so easy in a county either. This is because there are towns and urban enterprises in the rural county as well. Even in the case of responsibilities and privileges, urban–rural differentiation may be difficult. For purposes of security, all residents irrespective of where they work, are covered according to internal security zones. For health and educational facilities, some items are common to both but for some purposes such as paying of fees and availing social services, the practice may vary from place to place. Above all, one has to carefully check whether the per capita figure is per capita labour or per capita member of a unit of production, or per capita in terms of population of an area. We have to keep all these questions in mind in understanding the statistical data on Chinese rural situation.

The population of Hela *xiang* declined in the 1980s from over 21,000 in 1979 to a little over 18,000 in 1985 and further down by the end of the decade. This was not due to negative rate of population growth but because the status of members changed from rural to urban workers. (We discuss population growth in a later chapter.) But in the 1990s, with the expansion of economic activities in the township, the number continued to rise. When Hela became a town, more land was allotted for industrial, commercial and residential purposes. Finally, when it was incorporated as a city street, urban housing settlement in Hela was not restricted any more. In 2006, Hela had a new profile with many new modern housing colonies with more and more people living on its territory. This trend continued though subjected to population and migration policies of the city.

In 1996, Hela's population was 33,000. According to the *xiang* leadership, female workers constituted 52 per cent of the workforce in the 1980s. In the 1990s, it was reported to be 50 per cent. This change reflected a changing trend in employment. Initially, more and more women had joined rural enterprises, while men were engaged either in agriculture and fishing or in city enterprises. As the requirement of technical competence became essential, more and more male workers were preferred by the enterprises. We will discuss it in greater detail subsequently.

The decline in the township population was initially because of the city's absorption of more and more peasants into urban jobs as mentioned earlier. This was also partly because of an agreement between the township and the city that whenever the city acquired any township land, the concerned enterprise had to provide employment for at least one person for each mu of acquired land. Often the job was given to the affected family or the village unit. Besides some city workers had moved to the government apartments, thus reducing the population registered with the township. No doubt strict adherence to family planning norms, especially the policy of one-child family until 2015 as well as late marriage, had its impact on the population figures.

The employment opportunities, however, rose dramatically in the early 1990s with the launching of many new enterprises and further diversification of the suburban economy. Rural income continued to rise substantially. So, migration to the city was not on a massive scale. The *xiang* gave number of facilities to its members which the city enterprises could not afford until the early 1990s. The attraction of living in a spacious personal house, close to your relatives in your ancestral place, while earning a good income was still preferred until the urbanization took a big lead and villagers were shifted to skyscrapers.

Over these years, there was a dramatic change in the occupations of the villagers. In 1979, as many as 80 per cent of the workforce was engaged in agriculture, fisheries and other sideline production, while only 20 per cent were engaged in small industries in Hela. Besides grain production, the villagers also grew vegetables and mulberry apart from being engaged in silk-worm culture, pig-raising, poultry, dairy, horticulture and tea plantation. At that time, as many as seven production brigades (villages) were mainly engaged in production of food grains. This picture was drastically changed with the coming of the new economic strategy. The suburban areas were now encouraged to switch to industries and cash crops to benefit out of their proximity to the city. In 1985, the composition of the workforce was very different, as out of 8,436 workers, as many as 6,400 workers or 75.9 per cent were in rural industries, 1,500 workers or 17.8 per cent in fisheries, 250 workers or 2.9 per cent in vegetable growing and the rest 286 or 3.04 per cent were engaged in grain production. It should be noted that many members while working in the factories also looked after their land in spare time. The picture further changed in the 1990s with less and less people engaged in agriculture. In 2004, little less than 10 per cent of the workforce was engaged in the primary industry (farming, fishery, animal husbandry, etc.), while 68.44 per cent were engaged in secondary industry and 21.63 per cent in the tertiary industry. Since the late 1980s, commerce had emerged as a major sector of the economy. The expanding sector of development in this area was what was called the third industry (*di san ye*), referring to tourism, travel, hotel, restaurants, and entertainment. In Wuxi's scenic environment, this industry expanded very fast, inviting foreign investment and deployment of modern technology.

The Production Trends

The total output value of Hela Township had reached 1,050 million yuan in 1992. The first spurt in production took place during 1979–84 when the industrial output value reached 100 million yuan, rising to 270 million yuan in 1987 and over 600 million yuan in 1995. The composition of the economy had changed significantly, the rural industries accounting for 63 per cent, commerce 35 per cent and agriculture and sideline production 2 per cent of the total output value. After the announcement of the Ninth FYP in 1995, Hela Township had decided to raise the proportion of the tertiary sector further to 49 per cent, rural industry reduced to 49 per cent and agriculture and sideline production remained at 2 per cent.

In 1996, Hela had 185 rural enterprises, 20 owned by the township and 265 by the village besides 16 specialized enterprises that were autonomous and professionally managed. Together they possessed fixed assets of 750 million yuan. Hela leadership describes their new path of development as a policy of three-in-one combination, 'taking agriculture as the gold medal enterprise, taking industry as the backbone of the economy and building the third industry (tertiary sector) as the superior enterprises (*youshi qiye*) and coordinating them'. The rural industries of Hela are described as standing on six pillars, namely electronics, machinery, light and textile industries, garments, chemical and metallurgical industries. Hela authorities were never tired of mentioning their quality products—50 products having won quality awards at the provincial and national level, 20 of them such as electronic component, printing machine, kitchen devices, centrifugal pump, umbrellas and gloves were exported to Hong Kong, Southeast Asia and Western Europe. Besides these, the 280 items manufactured in Hela included electric cells, elevators both for passengers and goods, bearings, iron casting tubes, water pumps, woollens and toothpaste.[22] The composition of the products acquired a new character as Wuxi developed into an IT hub and high-quality tourism subsequently.

As indicated earlier, the tertiary industry has developed very fast. In 1996, there were 285 commercial units and 5 market complexes. Mention must also be made of the Meilido Hotel, the Entertainment City, Wuxi Roast Duck Restaurant, Tang Dynasty Food Street and the Unique Wuxi Taihu Pets Centre. There were five joint ventures in Hela involving foreign investment. The township representatives had gone abroad and had set up two enterprises in Australia—hotel resorts on the coast. This trend continued to grow with two-way investments and trade.

On the agriculture and sideline production front, Hela Township showed vegetable production to the tune of about 125,800 ton in 1996. As for horticulture, it produced, among other things, honey peach in 800 mu. It had achieved the status of a 'sparkling project' under which one ton of fish was produced for each mu while maintaining fish pond of 3,000 mu. In addition, the township had built a dairy farm with 100 milking cows and 1,000 pigs and a duck farm with an annual production of 500 million birds. In all, 12 components of sideline production were managed in the *xiang*.[23]

The annual per member income in Hela grew threefold into 1,100 yuan between 1979 and 1983 and rose further to 1,592 yuan in 1986. Ten years later, the figure was not available, but it was not less than 4,000 yuan. In other words, the average real income of a member in the township had risen nearly 10 times over the 20-year period of rural reforms. The *xiang* authorities explained that now the family members had diverse sources of income: agriculture, sideline production, private commerce besides the wages from TVEs and State enterprises. It also became clear that the income disparities were large, some members getting as little as 600 yuan per year and some as high as 600,000 yuan. In our discussion on rural income in village profiles, we return to this question. However, there was unmistakable evidence of dramatic rise in people's living standards as also in the economic growth of the township as a whole.

As a suburban commune, Hela grew into a township with a prosperous economy with a new landscape. Starting as primarily an agricultural suburb with scenic beauty, Hela became the hub of modern industry and commerce in 20 years. Although it had a tradition of textile industry in the pre-liberation times, it was the commune period which had begun the diversification of rural economy. Agriculture, fishery and some rural industries constituted the economy of the commune which was among the relatively prosperous communes of China, though there were even more advanced ones than Hela. But the scale of diversification of the economy was vastly increased with the introduction of the reforms after 1978. Basically, utilizing savings from the commune itself and responding to the market while maintaining the broad framework of collective ownership rural enterprises were expanded in a big way. A small component of agriculture was retained for grain production partly for self-consumption and partly to ensure that a certain quantity of grain was produced from this area for achieving a national target of grain output. But in this township, there was mostly vegetable production and horticulture with a clear focus on expanding industry and commerce. This was seen as one way through which the peasantry acquired greater freedom to advance the productive forces and enhance its income. Peasants and workers of Hela still enjoy their rice and fish—the rich variety that Taihu serves; at the same time, they have opted for modern amenities of living.

This brief account of Wuxi's success story and the grass-roots level picture of a township gives us an idea of how the Deng Xiaoping strategy was implemented in the local level. Three aspects of this process are clear. Firstly, urban–rural linkage was to play an important role for macroeconomic development and pushing ahead industrialization and urbanization out of the savings from rural reforms. Secondly, while grain production was important for the rural economy, diversification into not only cash crops and sideline production such as animal husbandry and fishery but also rural industries and commerce appropriate to the local conditions was extremely important for the dynamic development of the rural economy. Thirdly, opening to the outside world—getting technology and capital and developing two-way exchanges including trade and investment—was very important. But each of them came with problems. The stress on fast economic growth by any means meant ignoring environmental hazards until it became too late. Inequalities grew among households. After the initial spurt in the rise of rural income, its growth lagged behind urban income. More and more intervention by the government became necessary to manage the development process.

It may be said that it was the market economy that has brought about this successful transformation. Some may add that the State and the party policies and their roles in directing the market have led to this remarkable growth. However, unleashing of the market forces had its own cruel logic. Enterprises and peasant households had to cope with the fast-changing environment which necessarily meant a new kind of role by the party and the State at every level. They had to not only launch and monitor market-oriented policies but also tackle problems which arose from time to time, some of them of serious magnitude. This required that the State and the party had to play a special role at the local level while evolving what was later called a 'socialist market economy'. Hence, we turn to a thorough examination of the two major agencies of the reform process, the State and the party and understand the role that they played at the national as well as the grass-roots levels.

Notes and References

1. Fei Xiaotong, *Peasant Life in China* (London: Kegan Paul, 1939 [1945]), 1. He describes the study as 'a descriptive account of the system of consumption, production, distribution and exchange of wealth among Chinese peasants as observed in a village' and stresses the 'equal importance of the traditional and the new forces' in explaining the process of change. Also see Fei Xiaotong, Chinese *Village Close-up* (Beijing: New World Press, 1983) which contains the abridged version of the 1936 study and reports on Fei's visits in 1946, 1957 and 1980 in addition to the research group's findings of a 1980 survey of the village by his colleagues at the Chinese Academy of Social Sciences (CASS).
2. Ibid., 16. The average exports of silk dropped from 20–30 per cent to 17 per cent. For a discussion of the cooperative factory, see ibid., 216–25.

3. Lynda S. Bell, *One Industry, Two Chinas: Silk Filatures and Peasant-family Production in Wuxi County, 1865–1937* (Stanford, CA: Stanford University Press, 2001).

4. Bell's findings challenge the prevailing notions that 'an independent public sphere of local elite activity was emerging in highly commercial areas of China in late Qing times'. She argues instead that 'local elites continued to ally with the state for assistance, protection, and legitimacy whenever possible'. Ibid., 11.

5. Ibid., 13.

6. James C. Shih, *Chinese Rural Society in Transition: A Case Study of the Lake Tai Area, 1368–1800* (Berkeley, CA: Institute of East Asian Studies, University of California, 1992).
   Wuxi's economic development was often described as illustrating the Su Nan model which emphasized the role of collectively owned TVEs in the 1980s as opposed to the Wenzhou model of Hangzhou where the private enterprises played the catalytic role. Many other models have been talked about. See, for instance, the account of the 'Anxi model' in Fujian studied by Thomas P. Lyons, *Poverty and Growth in a South China County: Anxi, Fujian, 1949–1992* (Ithaca: Cornell East Asia Series, 1994), 118. Anxi model of development 'emerged, melding outward-oriented industrialization and village commercialization with continuing emphasis on grain and livestock'. The international economic linkages played the decisive role in this case.

7. Wuxi County was formed by the republican government in 1912, combining Wuxi and Jinkou counties. *Wuxi Shi (History of Wuxi)* (Wuxi: Wuxi chuban she, 2001). Also see Manoranjan Mohanty, 'In the Land of Rice and Fish: Researching Wuxi's Transformation', *Indian Horizons* 43, nos. 1–2 (1994).

8. 'A Review of Pollution and Panic in Wuxi'. Available at: http://www.wuxinews.com. cn/2015-05/09/content_20667898.htm (accessed on 24 July 2017).

9. In 2004, Wuxi had 28 major scenic attractions, each one visited by about 100,000 tourists annually. Statistics Bureau of Wuxi City, *Wuxi Statistical Yearbook*, 2005, 447.

10. Traditionally, it was the case and even now each province in China is divided into several prefectures (*Diji*) and each prefecture is divided into counties. In 2013, there were 333 prefecture-level regions and 286 prefecture-level cities (*Dijishi*) in China like Wuxi city.

11. 'Administrative Division of Wuxi'. Available at: http://en.wuxi.gov.cn/sitePages/channelPages/1300350200330228.html (accessed on 17 March 2017).

12. National Bureau of Statistics of China, *China Statistical Yearbook*, 2006 (Beijing: China Statistics Press, 2006), 3.

13. http://en.wuxi.gov.cn/sitePages/channelPages/1300350200330227.html (accessed on 15 April 2017).

14. Data from interviews with Wuxi city cadres, August 1995.

15. Statistics Bureau of Wuxi City, *Wuxi Statistical Yearbook*, 2016. In 2014, the total registered urban unemployed were 159,749 persons.

16. Even during the commune period, township enterprises had sprung up, making considerable profit for the collective. The profit was said to be 10 million yuan in 1958 which rose to 109 million yuan in 1970. Robert Terrel, *The Jiangsu Miracle: Modernizing China's Most Economically Developed Province* (Beijing: New World Press, 2001), 164.

17. Statistics Bureau of Wuxi City, *Wuxi Statistical Yearbook*, 2005 (Beijing: China Statistics Press, 2005), 56.

18. Data collected from interviews with district cadres. Annual Report of the Hela *xiang* director to the *xiang* people's congress (1996). While the 1986 data were collected in the course of an interview with Jiang Hanling, deputy director of the suburban district on

12 October 1987, the 1996 data were procured through discussions with Zhang Weinan, deputy director of the district in October 1996.

19. Rong family was one of the leading business houses of China during the Republican period, continuing to flourish after 1949. Natives of Wuxi, Rong Desheng (1875–1952) and his brother Rong Zongquan had made Shanghai their industrial base with textiles and flour business and banking. The Wuxi machine tools plant, contemporary Wuxi's signature enterprise, was set up by then in 1948. Rong Desheng's son Rong Yiren (1916–2005) emerged as China's top industrialist, described by Marshal Chen Yi as 'Red Capitalist'. Harassed during the Cultural Revolution, Rong Yiren became economic adviser to Deng Xiaoping at the start of the reforms and set up China International Trust and Investment Corporation (CITIC) in 1978. CITIC became the main mobilizer for Western capital for investment in China. Rong became vice-president of PRC under Jiang Zemin (1993–98). After his death in 2005, he was buried in his home town Xishan, Wuxi. In Rongxiang Street Community Headquarters, there is a museum in his memory. See Ji Honggeng, *Rong Yiren—A Biography* (Beijing: Central Literature Press, 1999 and 2006).

20. Local authorities sometimes were overenthusiastic about such descriptions. But it also reflected the changing political understanding. See Manoranjan Mohanty, 'Changing Terms of Discourse' in *Contemporary Indian Political Theory* (New Delhi: Sanskriti, 2000).

21. In 2001, the following major enterprises were listed in Hela Xiang Brochure as inviting foreign investments: Wuxi Baotong Electronics Co., a Sino-Japanese joint venture that had achieved a sales volume of 14 million yuan in 1999 and exported products to Hong Kong, Taiwan, Southeast Asia and Western Europe; Wuxi Lutong Electronics Technology Co. Ltd, a privately owned enterprise; Wuxi Taihu Machinery Factory, set up in 1966, whose assets reached 12.5 million yuan and whose products had a nationwide market as well as in Southeast Asia—a factory designated by the Ministry of Railways for purchases had 152 workers in 1999; Wuxi Jiangnan Printing Machine Plant, launched in 1980, printing and packaging machines; Wuxi Dajishan Industrial Instrument Factory, a collectively owned factory by the *xiang*, producing kitchen appliances, stainless steel measuring instruments and medical instruments with a market in China and Southeast Asia; Wuxi Xingdi, a leatherwear company owned by a Taiwan merchant since 1993, producing ticket wallets and the like for export to Europe and Southeast Asia (see tables on pages 127–129).

Economic indicators of above-scale industry by county (2015)

Items	Total	Jingyin City	Yixing City	Urban District	Chong'an	Nanchang	Beitang	Xishan	Huishan	Binhu	New District
Number of Enterprises (Unit)	4,988	1,368	897	2,723	7	37	72	649	817	411	729
Deficit Enterprises (Unit)	1,034	242	227	565	1	8	18	131	177	72	158
Gross Industrial Output (Yuan)	145,498,677	57,449,619	27,791,828	60,257,229	58,666	1,524,232	611,727	11,717,103	11,494,335	4,860,584	29,490,009
State-owned Capital (Yuan)	1,397,624	160,912	441,455	795,257	2,550	21,823	251,442	64,541	30,680	94,143	309,673
Hong Kong, Macao, Taiwan and Foreign Capital (Yuan)	12,243,824	2,318,221	932,807	8,992,796	87	20,739	15,768	1,289,322	631,342	307,786	6,698,990
Net Total Profit (Yuan)	8,950,853	3,516,307	1,193,094	4,241,452	4,571	150,584	26,841	614,751	887,496	401,260	1,989,667
Average Employee (Person)	1,253,067	438,402	163,011	651,654	658	10,083	9,357	140,869	115,287	63,043	304,812

Source: Statistics Bureau of Wuxi City, *Wuxi Statistical Yearbook*, 2016 (Table 8.1).

Profile of Wuxi City in 2015 year-end after reorganization

Districts	Area in km²	Population (Persons)	Areas of Jurisdiction
Xishan	399.11	701,500	The Xishan District People's Government is located at No. 1, Xizhou Middle Road, Dongting Residential Street at present. By the end of 2014, the whole district had governed the national-level Xishan District Economic and Technological Development Zone, the Wuxi Xidong New City Business District, 4 towns including Yangjian Town, Ehu Town, Xibei Town and Donggang Town and 5 residential streets including Dongting Residential Street, Anzhen Residential Street, Dongbeitang Residential Street, Yunlin Residential Street and Houqiao Residential Street, counting up to 42 town communities and 76 rural communities (administrative villages)
Huishan	325.12	701,000	The Huishan District People's Government is located at No. 8, Wenhui Road, Huishan New City, Yanqiao Residential Street at present. By the end of 2014, the whole district had governed 1 provincial-level Wuxi Huishan District Economic Development Zone, 5 residential streets including Yanqiao Residential Street, Chang'an Residential Street, Qianqiao Residential Street, Qianzhou Residential Street and Yuqi Residential Street and 2 towns including Luoshe Town and Yangshan Town, counting up to 54 town communities and 56 rural communities,
Binhu	629.44	696,900	Mashan District was repealed, and the original administrative region of Mashan District and 7 towns involving Fangqian Town, Meicun Town, Xin'an Town, Huazhuang Town, Dongjiang Town, Xuelang Town and Nanquan Town of the originally county-level Xishan District were included into the outskirts of Wuxi, renamed as Binhu District, Wuxi. In May 2001, adjustment work was basically finished. At present, the Binhu District People's Government is located at No. 500, Jincheng West Road in Lihu Residential Street. By the end of 2014, the whole district had governed Hudai Town, Mashan Residential Street, Huazhuang Residential Street, Xuelang Residential Street, Liyuan Residential Street, Taihu Residential Street, Helie Residential Street, Rongxiang Residential Street and Lihu Residential Street, counting up to 103 community neighbourhood committees and 7 social neighbourhood committees integrating villages and residential quarters.

Liangxi	65.95	1,010,000	In October 2015, the State Council repealed Chong'an District, Nanchang District and Beitang District of Wuxi and took the administrative divisions of the 3 districts as that of Liangxi District, while the Liangxi District People's Government would be stationed at No. 688, Jiefang South Road, Chong'an Temple Residential Street. The district would have 17 subordinate residential streets: Chong'an Temple Residential Street, Tongjiang Residential Street, Guangruilu Residential Street, Shangmadun Residential Street, Jianghai Residential Street, Guangyi Residential Street, Yinglongqiao Residential Street, Nanchan Temple Residential Street, Qingmingqiao Residential Street, Jinxing Residential Street, Jinkui Residential Street, Yangming Residential Street, Huangxiang Residential Street, Shanbei Residential Street, Beidajie Residential Street, Huishan District and Wuhe Residential Street (of which Beidajie Residential Street and Wuhe Residential Street would jointly work in one office).
Xinwu	2.1872	340,700	In October 2015, the State Council legislated to establish Xinwu District of Wuxi, put Hongshan Residential Street of Xishan District as well as Jiangxi Residential Street, Wangzhuang Residential Street, Shuofang Residential Street, Meicun Residential Street and Xin'an Residential Street of Binhu District in Wuxi under administration of Xinwu District and took the administrative divisions of the six residential streets as that of Xinwu District. The Xinwu District People's Government would be stationed at No. 28, Hefeng Road, Xin'an Residential Street. Xinwu District and the Wuxi High and New Tech Industrial Development Zone would execute management system of unification of district and administration, and adopt operation mode of one set of group, two plates of administrative district and development zone. The district has five parks including the Wuxi National High and New Technology Development Zone, Wuxi Taihu International Science and Technology Park, Wuxi Airport Industrial Park, Wuxi Xingzhou Industrial Park and Wuxi Export Processing Zone as well as six residential streets including Hongshan Residential Street, Wangzhuang Residential Street, Jiangxi Residential Street, Shuofang Residential Street, Meicun Residential Street and Xin'an Residential Street under its command.

Source: http://en.wuxi.gov.cn/sitePages/channelPages/13003502003302228.html (accessed on 17 March 2017).

PART 2

State and Party: Agencies of Reforms

4

Local State and the Agency Trap

The Agency for Reform and Stability

It is the government apparatus from top to bottom that implemented the reforms in China under the guidance and supervision of the CPC. As a unitary State under the rule of the Communist Party, the centralization of power is a basic characteristic of the Chinese political system. The operation of such system in practice in different provinces and regions within provinces varied according to local economic strength and power centres. At the grass-roots level, county and below, this becomes even more complicated. Developed regions exercise more influence in national-level decision-making as do the prosperous areas within provinces. To ensure that no power centre grows against the central leadership, there is a regular policy of transfer of governors and party leaders from province to province and county to county. A party leader at every level and in every institution is the top authority. But the administration is run by the administrative head. As we will see in this chapter and the next, during the reform period, there were times when the party leader was also the administrative head. At other times, the party leader worked behind the scene guiding the administration.

The administrative structure that was built in the PRC acquired a specific character in the aftermath of the Cultural Revolution. It was to disallow all elements of what could be considered sources of social instability and provide the most efficient manner of implementing the central leadership's policies to achieve economic growth. Thus, the State apparatus was the agency of economic development even while a market economy was vigorously promoted. The Communist Party through its branches at every level was the agency of social management and economic growth, guiding and controlling all institutions of the State and society. It derived its legitimacy from the fact that it led the Chinese revolution that defeated foreign domination, achieved China's independence and promised to build a new democracy and a socialist society based on principles of equality. Thus, while the State agency was to provide efficient administration, the party was the source of legitimacy rooted in history. With political victories against imperialism, rise of China's prestige in the world and economic prosperity of people and the country as a whole, there were new avenues to expand legitimacy. The CPC was the flag-bearer of Chinese nationalism during the past hundred years. That was the success story to which the State and the party immensely contributed. But, when along with the successes, political aspirations of common people grew and remained unfulfilled, inequalities accompanied growth, steps to cope with environmental degradation did not work satisfactorily and anti-corruption campaign had only limited success, the contradictory nature of this party–State agency began to show. Along with providing efficiency and high legitimacy, this governance pattern exposed some serious gaps. The implementation of policies, though efficient in many areas, also created new problems. Market economy promoted a logic of its own, bypassing the party norms. This is what we have called an 'agency trap'—the subject of this and the next chapter on government and the party where we analyse the trends in the political structure at the township and village levels. We have used the term 'local state' knowing fully well that the township administration is regarded as the lowest tier of the State under the PRC Constitution—the other local government tiers being county and province above it. Below the township, there is the village (*cun*) which is described as the 'mass organization' or 'community organization'. Article 111 of the PRC Constitution says:

> The residents committees and villagers committees established among urban and rural residents on the basis of their place of residence are mass organizations of self-management at the grass-roots level.

Actually, it is at the village level where the State and society merge and crucial political formation in the power structure takes shape. Cadres acquire experience and recognition first at this level before they move on to higher organs. Entrepreneurs use this realm to build base. This study is focused on the local political process which can serve as a useful window to understand the macro-political process. Since the available information on the local political process and its dynamics is still scarce, even though the body of the field studies continued to expand, this effort has been particularly oriented towards contributing to that field.

Before taking up the local structure, let us have a brief overview of the national-level State apparatus. This apparatus is guided by the party leadership structure which we take up in the next chapter.

As mentioned earlier, achieving a high economic growth through the 'reforms and open-door' policies, without interruption, was the principal preoccupation of Deng Xiaoping and was reaffirmed by Jiang Zemin, the leader chosen by him after the turbulence of the Tiananmen uprising in 1989.

The youth demand for democracy was firmly put down by Deng Xiaoping to maintain social and political stability to facilitate economic growth. Jiang doggedly pursued the line of 'reform and stability' throughout his 13 years of leadership. His successors Hu Jintao and Wen Jiabao (2002–12) and Xi Jinping and Li Keqiang thereafter also put high premium on stability, suppressing dissent and continuing the focus on growth and reforms. However, they confronted far more daunting social, political and environmental problems in a world of increasing tensions and challenges posed by new demands and rising democratic consciousness among people. The CPC and the party-led State were the agencies of both carrying out the growth-centric reforms and handling the sociopolitical problems accompanied by bouts of global economic crises and incidents of violence. The Chinese government leaders like leaders in other countries acquired new capacities, built new institutions at various levels to cope with these challenges and in fact achieved much success in carrying forward their development agenda. Hu Jintao's 'scientific development' and Xi Jinping's many initiatives including 'four comprehensives' and the momentous anti-corruption drive were examples of new interventions. But our study of China at both the macro and grassroots levels shows that the leaderships' absolute commitment to economic growth and social stability did not allow them to undertake the kind of democratization of society and the polity and make appropriate alterations in their development strategy so that they could respond to these problems. On the one hand, the leadership was determined to maintain the high rate or 'a medium-to-high rate of economic growth' as China's Thirteenth FYP envisaged and enjoy the rising status of China as an emerging world power. On the other hand, this path of development generated inequality and tensions at various levels. The degrees of democratization such as the competitive elections at the village level since 1998 and the relatively greater freedom of the media and the freedom of movement to foreigners in China were no doubt positive developments. During the Beijing Olympics in 2008, much of it was appreciated by the whole world. China's hosting of Asia-Pacific Economic Cooperation (APEC), G20 and other world summits did show a new atmosphere of expanding freedom together with rising prosperity of people and most advanced infrastructure. But the limits of this process of political liberalization were also evident. Periodic arrests of journalists and human rights lawyers and activists, expulsion of foreign reporters, suppression of religious dissidents were instances that occurred throughout the reform period. Maintaining stability in the society and polity was declared by all succeeding leaders as the precondition for maintaining steady economic progress. Of course, the Western commentators used such occasions to deride the Chinese 'authoritarian system'. Western social scientists and opinion pollsters measured from time to time the indicators of a democratic polity and gave poor marks to China. But one thing had become clear after three decades of reforms. The overall character of the political regime was not going to change. The party-led State process as an agency of economic, social and political development had evolved as the principal instrument of governance despite continuous restructuring under different regimes. Thus, the party–State apparatus from top to bottom was consciously shaped by successive leaders to be a more efficient, responsive, value-based agency of political management and social transformation within this perspective. The top–down directive to this agency to achieve growth targets and maintain sociopolitical stability was so strong that it could not develop the capacity for exercising participatory, democratic leadership among the people. The irony was that every policy announced its commitment to mobilize creative energy of people at the grass-roots level. Many policies such as the HRS had come up as local experiments—this one in Anhui Province. The 'mass line' framework of Mao Zedong from the Yan'an era which every leader reaffirmed stipulated the principle of 'from the masses, to the masses'.[1] According to this principle, every policy should emerge from people's practice and tested and refined constantly in that process. But the reform strategy aiming at achieving economic growth by stressing social stability made every cadre bit of a policeman. This situation produced what can be called an 'agency trap'. According to my assessment, there was no likelihood of any serious change in this political system in the near future. Since the agency was effective in securing higher economic growth, better living conditions for the Chinese people and higher prestige for China in the global community, it was considered by most people in China as legitimate and functional. It should be immediately pointed out that the question of legitimacy of a political system is always a complicated subject. The absence of free elections and a system of checks and balances in China certainly prompts many observers to withhold judgement on this. But opinion polls by academic institutions within China and organizations outside have confirmed a high degree of satisfaction with the regime.[2] No doubt there would be debates on legitimacy of the Chinese system.[3] There are many attempts to characterize the Chinese government and party officials as 'Leninist aparichi', 'new mandarins', 'meritocratic regime' and so on.[4] But the Chinese State apparatus has been a dynamic organization in many functional and political aspects that defy such terms. As we see in this study, leaders and cadres at every level are called upon to prove performance in realizing the declared goals. Within that specified framework, they have to use imagination, resources and power. We are pointing at a systemic element that may make it efficient and responsive for purposes of growth and stability but not capable enough to steer a transformation process out of the constraints of the same situation.

That the agency of the State and party that they put in shape could only be transformed to a limited extent, improving technical expertise, providing them with the latest infrastructure facilities to work and urging them to follow party's ethical standards, maintaining transparency and rule of law, were all important efforts to make this agency effective. But they were inadequate to meet democratic aspirations such as the right to participate in decision-making. That they could not proceed with competitive elections beyond the village level and hand over power to elected representatives, make government apparatus more autonomous of the party or evolve a system of transparency and accountability in everyday practice was indicative of the situation. As far as the social base of the bureaucracy in China was concerned, there was evidence that it was expanding into more and more classes and regions. But it was still operating from a narrow social and regional base. More on this is discussed in the next chapter.

We will now analyse the nature of the State structure at the local level as it evolved during the reform period making significant changes in the institutional structure that existed before 1978. Then we discuss the operation of the system at the township and village levels.

State in the Reform Era: Deng Xiaoping to Xi Jinping

The CPC exercises State power in China which is a 'unitary multinational state' as stated in the Preamble of the Constitution of the PRC. As 'a socialist state under the people's democratic dictatorship led by the working class and based on the alliance of workers and peasants' (Article 1), the State is politically governed by the CPC 'under the supervision and consultation of democratic parties'. These parties—China Democratic League, Workers and Peasants Party, and Revolutionary Guomindang, most prominent among them—were given more prominence after the reforms were launched as they very much welcomed these policies. They are prominently represented in the CPPCC (Chinese People's Political Consultative Conference) which is also presided by a senior leader of the CPC, usually a member of the Standing Committee of the CPC Politburo.

The Chinese counterpart of a Parliament is the NPC which has over 3,000 deputies and which meets for about a fortnight once a year. The NPC Standing Committee with about 150 members is the critical law-making organ that meets many times during the year. The State Council which is the council of ministers with a premier, vice-premiers, ministers and commissions and bureaus is the executive organ of the State. The head of the State is the president who is elected by the NPC and is the executive head of the State. Since 2012–13, Xi Jinping combines the posts of the president, party general secretary, chair of the MAC as was the case in the early years of the PRC when Mao Zedong occupied these positions.[5] From 1959 until 1966, the chair of the republic was Liu Shaoqi. After the many changes in the Cultural Revolution and later, Jiang Zemin once again combined these positions after Deng Xiaoping retired as chairman of MAC. This system has continued to exist ever since the 1954 Constitution came into force. Xi Jinping reiterated the 'socialist system with Chinese characteristics that integrates the fundamental political system, the basic political systems and the basic economic system' soon after taking over as CPC general secretary in 2012.[6] The three systems referred to are the people's congress system, the party-led system that gives a consultative role for the democratic parties and the socialist ownership system. This basic framework has to be kept in mind while we examine the shifts of emphasis in the State and party functioning under different regimes.[7]

The government structure is led by the party institutions directly by having party leaders occupying the government posts and key decisions first taken and principles laid down by the party CC, following which the State Council formulates specific policies and plans for implementation. Even before the CC meets to discuss and formulate a policy, the Politburo and its Standing Committee engage in numerous consultations and arrive at a recommendation. For example, after the party congress elects a new leadership, they take positions in the State. Xi Jinping was elected as the general secretary in November 2012 at the Eighteenth Party Congress and elected as president by the NPC in March 2013. The tenure of these posts is five years and they can be re-elected for one more term under the rules. The PRC Constitution under Article 79 forbids more than two consecutive terms for the president and the vice-president. Out of the seven members of the Standing Committee of the Politburo, Li Keqiang became premier, Li Yuanchao vice-president, Zhang Dejiang chair of the NPC Standing Committee and Yu Zhengsheng chair of the CPPCC. This united front organ with non-communist parties and individuals in existence since the 1940s is also presided over by a top CPC leader. The NPC also appoints the president of the Supreme People's

Court and chief of the People's Procuratorate. But all of them operate under the supervision of the Central Party leadership—*zhongyang* or Centre.

At the provincial level, it is the governor who is the leader under the supervision of the provincial party secretary. The provincial people's congress has a standing committee which is also the administrative organ of the provincial government. That is the pattern in the levels below, namely county with a director, city with a mayor, district with a director and township with a director. Each of them work under the guidance of the secretary of the party committee at the respective level.

The actual operation of this system varies from regime to regime. Deng Xiaoping led a collective team, though he was the dominant leader as architect of the reforms strategy and has been held up high next only to Mao. He strictly enforced institutional functioning of the State and party bodies, insisting on five-yearly elections in both, annual sessions of the NPC to pass budget and review government work, monthly meetings of the NPC Standing Committee to legislate, annual plenums of the CPCCC, frequent meetings of the Politburo and so on. He set the framework of economy as well as politics as 'socialism with Chinese characteristics'. Jiang Zemin's focus was on achieving high growth with full mobilization of both State and private entrepreneurs. Under his regime, Premier Zhu Rongji focused on trimming the bureaucracy and making it more efficient during his tenure (1998–2003), while his successor Wen Jiabao (Premier 2003–13) stressed on the ability of the government to respond to crisis and day-to-day problems with direct care and concern. Under the regime of Xi Jinping, besides reorienting the reforms strategy for coordinated development, fighting corruption among government officials and party cadres and reflecting communist values in their lifestyle were most conspicuous in his approach to governance. Besides launching a massive anti-corruption campaign under the CCDI, he asked the party cadres to play a new role recalling the campaigns for inculcating communist values in the 1940s.[8] More on this is discussed in the next chapter. These were some steps to break out of the 'agency trap' as well as the 'success trap' the system had fallen into.

As China pursued its high-growth strategy and achieved astounding results in the early years of the twenty-first century, the perspective that Deng Xiaoping had worked out for his successors to follow has baffled many observers. Under the 'one focus, two points' (*yizhong liangdian*) framework, the one point, namely economic development, had been the central preoccupation. That much is clear. But why is it that the 'four cardinal principles'—one of the two points, the other being 'reform and open door'—is sometimes brought into focus to attack leaders and other forces, allegedly supporting 'bourgeois liberalization'? The repression at the Tiananmen Square in June 1989 symbolized the approach to the political management of the economic reforms in Deng's China. It sent out the clear message that the Chinese government would exercise dictatorship to maintain stability which they considered essential for economic growth. Moreover, the leaders assert that the CPC shall continue to wield State power as the ruling party, though it would consult other democratic parties on important issues. Thus, the framework for the coming decades has been often summarized as 'reform, development and stability'—the three interdependent elements of this perspective. This framework crystallized in the Fourth Plenum of the CPCCC in September 1994 and had been reiterated by the Fifth Plenum in September 1995 and spelt out prominently in Premier Li Peng's Report on the Work of the Government presented to the Fourth Session of the Eighth National People's Congress on 5 March 1996.[9] Although the Hu–Wen regime continued this perspective in an overall sense, it added the focus on 'scientific development' or balanced, coordinated development to cope with the problems arising out of this growth-centric strategy. However, it retained the essential character of the State structure that Deng and Jiang Zemin evolved. As we discussed in the earlier chapter, Xi Jinping used the same structure, but creating a new milieu of anti-corruption and ethical conduct with a reduced growth rate as the 'new normal'.

Strengthening democracy in the Chinese political system as a whole and at the grass-roots level in particular was a recurrent theme in all the party congresses. This was the theme in the political report to the Fifteenth Congress of the CPC by Jiang Zemin in September 1997. Talking about the agenda on reforming the political structure, he declared, 'it is imperative that we should uphold and improve this fundamental political system, instead of copying any Western models'.[10] By the fundamental political system, he meant upholding CPC leadership, the socialist system and the people's democratic dictatorship which he described as 'result of struggles waged by the people and the choice of history'. The tasks that Jiang identified in this context were 'to develop democracy, strengthen the legal system, separate government functions from enterprise management, streamline government organs, [improve] democratic supervision system and maintain stability and unity'.[11] But it has been quite clear that free elections at all levels, independent judiciary and free press or the institutions and practices of 'Western liberal democracy' were not on the cards in contemporary China. During the Xi Jinping regime, the theoretical formulation on the political system was articulated in a clear manner. On the one hand, Xi declared that 'the issues of leadership and organizational system are fundamental, comprehensive, stable and permanent'. In other words, no departure from the party-led State system was envisaged. On the other hand, there was need for constant improvement: 'our national governance system and capability still have much room for improvement'.[12] This has been the running theme of Xi Jinping's authoritative speeches and writings throughout as he consolidated his supremacy in the CPC leadership and launched many organizational measures. When it was decided by the Sixth Plenum of the CPCCC in 2016 to designate Xi Jinping as 'core' of the party leadership—a practice given up during the Hu Jintao period—this trend became clear. But this also showed that there were spheres in the country where he was not sure of support for his policies. The assertion that this was 'in the interest of the country and people' showed that Xi Jinping needed to further strengthen his authority to launch new initiatives.[13] This further confirms my argument that the character of this party-led State agency is not likely to change in the near future, thus maintaining the agency trap.

Yet, certain trends in the institutional functioning indicate a positive direction of change. Improving the system of people's congress at every level has been a significant element of political reforms. Regularity of their elections and convening them as well as their standing committees, strengthening their legislative as well as supervisory work and strengthening closer ties between the deputies and people have been emphasized during the reform period.

In this context, the CPC's regular interaction with non-communist political parties has been stressed under the principle of 'long-term coexistence, mutual supervision, treating each other with all sincerity and sharing weal or owe'. In fact, the role of the CPPCC has been institutionalized in a stable manner, enabling the party to try to unite with people of all circles irrespective of political affiliations and develop the broad patriotic, united front for China's development. It should be remembered that the political parties which had aligned with the CPC in fighting the anti-Japanese war and then supported the CPC's line on forming a coalition government before 1949 stayed on in the mainland and continued to collaborate with the CPC in building the PRC. The CPPCC provided the platform for the seven 'democratic parties' and other non-communist forces. The CPPCC is lauded for its historic role in the Preamble to the PRC Constitution which says that it 'will play a still more important role in the country's political and social life …'.[14] They were attacked and sidelined during the Cultural Revolution. After the launching of the reforms, they welcomed the new policies and in return were given an active role in promoting 'reform and open door'.[15]

On grass-roots democracy, there has been a cautious line of thought throughout. Yet, that is the level where foundations are laid for building party and State and creating legitimacy for policies and an ideological line of the central leadership. So, it is important to understand the local sociopolitical process. Jiang Zemin had declared at the 1997 Party Congress that the party would make sure 'that people directly exercise their democratic rights, manage their own affairs…. The grassroots organs of power and self-governing mass organizations in both urban and rural areas should establish a sound democratic system of elections'. Actually, elections to the village committee had in many areas taken place with a degree of competition since 1994. According to one estimate, two-thirds of China's village committees had multiple candidates' elections in 1995. After 1998, this spread to all parts of China. At the township level too, competitive elections (having more than one candidate for each posts) were introduced in some areas. That was an exception. By 2007, it was made clear that the practice of multi-candidate, competitive elections would remain limited to the village committee level. Under the Xi Jinping regime too, there were no indications of raising the level of competitive elections. Prior to 1994, the practice was to decide on a panel of deputies and office-bearers by rounds of consultation between the higher levels and the lower levels. This was changed to more than one candidate filing nominations and the villagers voting for candidates of their choice. But after nearly two decades, after competitive elections were introduced in the village committee, we see a reverse phenomenon due to the milieu of party domination. Even though in theory multiple candidates could compete in a large number of villages, the party nominee got elected and re-elected many times.

This is done in the name of maintaining stability as the party leaders apprehend that competitive elections at the township, county and provincial levels would create conditions of instability. Achieving the growth ambitions and the goals set for the two centenaries—moderately well-off society by 2021 and a strong, prosperous medium-level developed country by 2049—set by Deng Xiaoping and firmly pursued by his successors, they think, required this kind of polity. To maintain the pace of development in that direction, stability has been regarded as the key principle. The question is whether this kind of stability shall not accumulate social tensions which may explode at a future date. This is the nature of the 'agency trap'. This agency of party-led State exercising centralized leadership has achieved tremendous economic successes by maintain social and political stability. So, its authoritarian character which is functional and effective cannot be changed. But it is the same party–State machinery that limits democratic transformation and causes alienation and social tensions. It may be called 'socialist democracy with Chinese characteristics', but it embodies a political contradiction in itself. Theoretical grasp of this phenomenon has been difficult.

Democracy, Stability and Growth

The Western discourse on 'democratization' can hardly appreciate the reasons underlying China's emphasis on stability. For the Western liberals, 'empowerment of civil society' and its active play is the essence of democratization.[16] Competitive party politics, pressure groups operating in the open and participating in the bargaining process and legal institutions governing the social process are some of the crucial features of a civil society. Much of this process may also exist in China in different forms. But from the Western liberal perspective, they fall far short of institutions of democracy. The Western discourse on democracy in China is also not uniform. While some recognize expanding spheres of freedom, others characterize it as 'Leninist authoritarian regime' with high degree of centralization. Some call it the 'Perfect Dictatorship'.[17] What is common to all Western commentaries is the pressure on China for respecting human rights. However, the global mapping of human rights records of various countries exposes the deficit of practically all countries. There is an interesting feature of the discourse on democracy in China. During the Jiang Zemin period the argument for authoritarian control in China was that as a developing country with many problems of development and social management a strong central leadership was needed to achieve fast growth and China 'was not ready' for Western style democracy.[18] Sometime after the Seventeenth Party Congress of the CPC in 2007, we began to notice a different tune asserting that China shall never adopt Western style democracy and shall continue to have a 'socialist democracy with Chinese characteristics'. After the ascendance of Xi Jinping, this line of thinking has become more pronounced.

Since the Fourteenth Party Congress of the CPC in October 1992 where the perspective of socialist market economy and Deng's Theory of building socialism with Chinese characteristics were proclaimed, long-term stability has been the theme. This was partly due to the anxiety of carrying forward the reforms after the passing away of Deng and partly in response to the persisting dissidence activity in China, not to speak of the Western pressures on human rights and other issues. New challenges at home and abroad and the compulsive pressures of achieving nationalist goals made them even more committed to maintaining 'stability' under the current system.

We may add that the theory of 'democratization' has come under attack even in the West. In all societies, power is unevenly distributed among groups. If politics is restricted to those groups who have the ability to take part in the bargaining process, then democracy is denied to the weaker groups. Therefore, many groups working outside the system or against the system also legitimately claim democratic rights, whereas the approach of the liberal theorists would in effect exclude them from the civil society. Even where free and fair elections are the core of democracy, mass mobilization using modern communications have produced populist leaders whose commitment to democratic values are contested by many. The focus on institutional procedures has thus exposed areas of weakness of democracy. Therefore, the theory of democratic transformation has to be broadened to include the creation of structural conditions for democracy while at the same time stressing the need for dissent and political debates, free elections and institutional functioning. In other words, the market theory of democratization is as inadequate as the Soviet theory. The market theory excludes the underprivileged and creates new inequalities. The Soviet theory denies the significance of enabling institutions and procedures of political participation in the name of creating structural conditions of equality. The perspective on democracy advocated by the protagonists of the Cultural Revolution derided existing political institutions of the State and the Communist Party and set up 'revolutionary committees' and conducted politics through mass movements and public debates. That period saw suspension of institutions, thus paving the way for much arbitrary decision-making and indiscriminate persecutions. Therefore, mass movements may at best supplement but cannot replace institutions.[19]

In contrast to the Cultural Revolution period when the NPC met only once, that is, in 1975 after a gap of 10 years, it has been meeting annually since 1978. The PRC Constitution and institutions of State in China are given much significance in contemporary China. There were many functions in 1994 to celebrate the fortieth anniversary of the promulgation of the PRC Constitution and the founding of the NPC. Similarly, the fiftieth and the sixtieth anniversaries of the founding of the PRC were observed not only to mark China's economic achievements but also to focus on the value of the institutions of 'democracy with Chinese characteristics'. The NPC is regarded as the organ of the People's Democratic Dictatorship 'elected by the people and supervised by the people', combining 'democracy with efficiency'. The people's congress system at the national, provincial, county and township levels has been regarded as a key element of socialist democracy with Chinese characteristics. The method of having more candidates than posts in elections has become a common practice at every level. Openly announcing the voting figures indicating how many did not vote for a certain candidate for significant post is no longer a rarity. Involving non-communist parties and individuals with decision-making continues to grow. The National Committee of CPPCC meets at the time of the annual sessions of the NPC and deliberates upon the major policy documents. The role of other demo-cratic parties under the leadership of CPC has increased the plurality at the CPPCC deliberations. For example, the presidium of the fourth session of the Eighth NPC had 16 leaders of non-communist parties, non-party people and from the All-China Federation of Industry and Commerce. It was however only 10 per cent of the 160-member presidium. That has been the normal practice over the years. The CPC leadership over the State is unmistakable. Yet, State apparatus has its distinct significance. As indicated earlier, each regime had its distinct mark on the party–State functioning. The landmark Fourth Plenum of the Fourteenth CPCCC held on 25–28 September 1994 led by Jiang Zemin very clearly reflected the anxiety of the leadership to prepare for the post-Deng era, especially after the Tiananmen uprising. Its focus was on 'strengthening party building'; it reaffirmed the principle of 'democratic centralism', building the party's grass-roots organizations and training and promoting leading cadres with 'political integrity and ability'. This was a response to the growing trend of corruption and crime, moral degeneration and consumerism and economic problems such as inflation and inequities. Despite the high rate of growth across the board, rather than going for wholesale marketization, the need for macroeconomic control has been affirmed as the leading factor to guide market economy. The mass migration to the cities has created a new situation where party units have little control over their members. Party cells had been overrun by the 'evil forces of capi-talism, revival of clans, triads and other underground organizations as well as spread of various religions including Christianity'.[20] It is to counter such trends and promote new cultural works for socialist spiritual civilization, to enforce discipline and to maintain the pace of development that a call has been given to strengthen party leadership.

This framework was worked out by Deng and his colleague Vice-Premier and economic planner Chen Yun together when the former met the latter in Shanghai in the presence of the CPC Politburo Standing Committee members on 24 July 1994 and agreed on an eight-point approach. This was the last reported meeting between the two veterans before Deng fell seri-ously ill and Chen Yun passed away. The points in the agreed framework included stability, the CPC leadership and bringing into play the initiative of the Centre and the localities. Chen himself stated 'five views which were publicized in the Chinese press. These included defending the prestige of the Central authorities, stressing the centrality of agriculture and rural work and opposing indiscriminate 'dissolutions and reforms' (*bo gai*).[21] This indicated that both Deng and Chen Yun were unanimous about 'socialist democracy with Chinese characteristics'. They would not allow political opposition to function, nor would they permit street demonstrations or any attempt to challenge the political authority of the CPC.

The components of the emerging political framework to lead China in the post-Deng years of the twenty-first century slowly became clear. They concerned organizational leadership, the policy perspective and ideological orientation. The CPCCC's Fourth Plenum in 1994 dealt with the first, while the Fifth Plenum which formulated the proposal concerning the formulations of the Ninth FYP (1996–2000) for national economic and social development and the long-term target for the year 2010 clarified the policy perspective. This was further elaborated in Li Peng's Report to the NPC in March 1996. There were indications that the Sixth Plenum, perhaps the last before the Fifteenth Congress of the CPC, would clarify questions of ideology, culture and morality. With that, a comprehensive set of measures would have been laid out to consolidate the leadership of the 'third generation' with Jiang Zemin 'as the core'.

Jiang Zemin held three offices—those of the party general secretary, the president of the State and the chairperson of the Central Military Commission of the party as well as of the State. His speech at the closing session of the Fifth Plenum in September 1995 on *Twelve Major Relationships* had theoretical significance that consolidated his position in the leadership hierarchy in the CPC. It was compared with Mao Zedong's *Ten Major Relationships* of April 1956, where a broad set of considerations combined into formulation of similar policies, avoiding extremes.[22] Although Jiang Zemin was still part of a collective leadership, he had emerged as the most important leader directing the course of development in China along the path of reforms charted by Deng Xiaoping. Since the Fourth Plenum of September 1994, references to party leadership invariably mention 'with Jiang Zemin as the core'. Several instances of changes in regional military command and provincial leadership were clearly seen as steps consolidating Jiang's leadership.

The policy framework of economic development during the Ninth Plan and targets for the period up to 2010 were adopted by the Fifth Plenum in 1995. Among its most important guidelines were as follows:

- Maintain sustained, rapid and sound development of the national economy.
- Energetically promote a shift in the mode of economic growth by making higher economic returns (i.e., expedite privatization).
- Rely on science, technology, education and economy.
- Unswervingly open up to the outside world.
- Integrate the market with macro-control.

These have remained the main principles guiding the later plans and polices, even though new points of emphasis were added by the succeeding leaders.

Within this framework of 'reforms, development and stability', local political process had been reorganized. During the initial years of the first phase (1979–82), the transition was made from the commune system to the *xiang* structure with the introduction of household contract responsibility system in agriculture. During 1982–87, the governmental units were asked to function like entrepreneurial organizations. During this period, the local party leadership left the initiative to the administrative heads or managers of townships and the rural enterprises. After the policy debates of 1989–91, in the wake of Tiananmen, Deng's 'southern tour', early 1992, a new phase of reforms created an economic impetus, leading to a fresh round of administrative restructuring. The diversification of rural economy, mushrooming of rural industries—many of them with foreign collaboration and with a variety of ownership systems—and fluidity of labour and capital had overwhelmed the delicately placed local government. It is in this context that the preparatory meeting of the Fourth Plenum of 1994 noted that over 75 per cent of the party organizations in the rural areas had been paralysed and 30 per cent township and village administrations were not playing their expected role. Therefore, the plenum resolved to strengthen grass-roots level party organizations, and subsequently a circular on that subject was sent out in November 1994. The circular stated the guidelines for party building at the village level and called for a 'systems engineering approach' to administration, ideological education and work style at the township and village levels. Declaring an intention to introduce a dynamic system of participation and representation, the Jiang Zemin leadership passed the revised Grass-roots Democracy Law in 1998. Under this law, competitive elections were started in the village councils in the country as a whole. Even though the practice had emerged in many areas since 1988, it was after 1998 that regular three-yearly elections were conducted in China. That was a part of the centralized, coordinated, political management of rural China under CPC leadership which has been in place since then.

This pattern continued to exist under the regimes of Hu Jintao and Xi Jinping. However, Hu Jintao injected two elements which became constituents of his signature concept, 'scientific outlook on development'. First, in 2003, the CPC Third Plenum stressed that the party must be pro-people, thus recognizing the trend of alienation from common people. In 2004, a major resolution on 'enhancing governance capacity' (*jiaqiang zhizheng nengli*) was adopted at the Fourth Plenum. Governance capacity meant not only efficiency and accountability but also transparency and non-corrupt performance.[23] This, however, did not seem adequate to curb the vast corruption going on in the party and government because of which anti-corruption became the main plank with which the next party leader Xi Jinping started his tenure. Besides governance focus, Hu Jintao put on the agenda the serious problems that had arisen in the course of the reforms and economic growth. He formulated the concept of 'scientific development' to promote balanced and coordinated growth squarely addressing the social inequalities, regional disparities and environmental problems. Hu Jintao's political report to the Eighteenth Party Congress in November 2012 gave ample evidence of it. Through many organizational initiatives, Xi Jinping sought to transform the party into a popular, effective, value-based agency for party's policies.[24] How much of it was also meant to consolidate his personal power over the party, State and military apparatus has been a point of debate among commentators. But they were no doubt serious measures to address some of the corrupt elements in the polity.

With this macro-level understanding of the Chinese political system, we turn to taking a close look at the local political structure at the level of a township to get some idea about the operation of this political process at the grass-roots level.

Replacing the Commune Structure

The rural people's commune (1958–78) had a unified political leadership to manage the collective economy at the grass-roots level (see Table 4.1). It combined the administrative functions with those of economic management, security, education and health. It also had a centralized leadership at the commune level, controlling the brigades and production team. Such a system was regarded by the post-Mao leadership as unhealthy as it led to arbitrary decision-making and lack of accountability. Therefore, one of the major decisions of the Third Plenum of the Eleventh CPCCC in December 1978

Table 4.1:
Rural administrative structure in China

Below the County/Suburban District	
Before 1980	*After 1980*
People's Commune (*Renmin Gongshe*)	Rural Administrative Areas/Township (*Xiang*)
Production Brigade (*Shengcan Dadui*)	Administrative Village (*Cun*)
Production Team (*Shengcan Dui*)	Team/Work Group (*Zeran Cun*/Natural Village)

was to enforce a division of powers among the party, government administration and enterprise management (*dang zheng qiye fenkai*). Thereafter, it was decided to devolve economic decision-making further to the production units. With the introduction of the household contract responsibility system, the peasant households became relatively autonomous decision-making units. Thus, the enterprises at the brigade or *cun*-level were made autonomous. With the full implementation of the rural reforms, the commune was given the old name that it had replaced in 1958 namely, township, which now essentially became an administrative organ. Since 1982, in Wuxi's counties and districts, the township government became the lowest organ of State power. Under the township government, the village (*cun*) committee functioned as a mass or community organization.

In 1979 when I first visited Wuxi, one could see the surviving structure of the commune system which was still not very much affected by the Third Plenum decision. Liu Weibing, the deputy director of Hela People's Commune, was the acting head after the director had been replaced after the launching of the reforms. Liu provided the details of the prevailing political structure of the commune which are a useful point of comparison for discussing the reform structure at the grass-roots level.

Commune Revolutionary Committee *(Gongshe Renmin Weiyuanhui)* and the Commune People's Congress *(Gongshe Renmin Daibiao Dahui)*

During the Cultural Revolution, the new organ of power that was set up in factories, work units and various other spheres was the revolutionary committee. These were gradually replaced starting from 1978. But Hela still called its main organs of power as the commune revolutionary committee in 1979. A year later, it was renamed as the commune management committee which was further replaced by the new structure of the township government in 1982.

The commune revolutionary committee consisted of 32 members including 3 women. It had one chair and five vice-chairs. The other members were described as 'representatives of grassroots'. This committee had as its members three village-level leaders from production brigades and five hamlet-level leaders of production teams. One of them was the director of a factory and another a 'model worker'. The latter, named Zhou Yangyao, had been the leader of a fishing team since 1956. The revolutionary committee had sent six of its members to the Wuxi Municipal People's Congress and one of them to the Jiangsu Provincial People's Congress. This representative was a member of the Jiangsu Province Revolutionary Committee. He was none other than the 'model worker'. One of Hela's Revolutionary Committee members was also elected to the Fifth National People's Congress. It is notable that a village-level leader was a member of all higher bodies including the provincial and national levels.

The 1979 revolutionary committee was elected by the commune people's congress in its Sixth Congress of August 1978. The previous people's congress had met as far back as in 1969. During the intervening period of the Cultural Revolution, the people's congress had not met. It showed the suspension of the institutional process during this period. Incidentally, the leader of the commune was a 'revolutionary rebel'—an aphorism for those who were enthusiastic activists of the Cultural Revolution and supporters of either Lin Biao who dominated the first years of the Cultural Revolution until 1971 or the Gang of Four including Mao's wife Jiang Qing who dominated the last phase (1974–76). He was dropped in 1978. Hence, Liu Weibing became the acting leader.

The commune people's congress in 1978 had 246 representatives. Each village (brigade) sent its quota of representatives which was approximately 10 per cent of its commune members. It was pointed out that in the case of the more 'advanced' brigades, the number of representatives would be more. Since there were no specific criteria for this, the leaders of the concerned brigade did have discretion in such spheres. Women constituted 41 per cent of the representatives. The people's congress had 18 per cent from industry, 3 per cent from commerce, 8 per cent from educational and cultural units, and 69 per cent from agriculture. Thus, the election was not only on the territorial basis, but within a brigade's quota, the various sectors of activity were also represented.

In 1978–79, there was still no multiple candidate election. The commune selection committee, appointed by the higher level, first publicized what should be the requirements of a delegate to the people's congress. Then there were various recommendations from the lower level of the production team. The selection committee would then announce a tentative list and invite comments from people. Then the list was finalized and put to vote. Commune members cast votes on the collective list of the brigade. If they wished, they could also strike off a name indicating their disapproval.

During the Cultural Revolution, voting was a formality according to Liu Weibing; it had changed since 1978. During the 1978 elections, for example, three delegates got only 60 per cent votes indicating their falling base of support, while others got close to 100 per cent.

The commune people's congress ordinarily met once a year. Beginning early 1979, it was to meet twice a year. At the beginning of the year, it met to hear the report of the revolutionary committee on the previous year's work and draw up a programme for the year. The commune people's congress considered (a) production plans for agriculture, forestry and industry; (b) economic and financial plans; (c) capital construction projects involving investments (irrigation, etc.); (d) agricultural mechanization plans; (e) scientific research and (f) welfare of the people.

This was the structure that operated since 1958. Until 1967, the local institutions functioned with some effectiveness. The commune people's congress met at least once a year. The commune committee and production brigade committee regularly met. But during the Cultural Revolution, the decision-making power was concentrated in the hands of the commune leader, the chair of the revolutionary committee. The strength of this committee was too large to make it a collective functional unit. Its composition was in any case influenced by the commune leadership. The election of both representatives to the congress and members of the revolutionary committee was weighed in favour of the nominees of the commune leadership or the still higher organ, the district leadership. Even though the main agricultural activity was conducted by the production team, the lowest collective unit, it had little power. The team leader was chosen by the brigade leadership 'in consultation with the members of the team' or the village and with the approval of the commune leadership. He was under the constant guidance of the brigade leader. The brigade ran some collective farms, industries and commerce. But its plan had to be approved by the commune leadership.

The original objective of the rural people's commune was to ensure grassroots participation in political decisions and the production process. The Cultural Revolution also started off to expand popular participation. But as it degenerated in the course of factional power struggle, the commune acquired a very different character from its original shape. Located as an institutional link between the peasantry and the society, the commune leadership had become the concentrated organ of State power and party authority. It had very little checks, if it committed mistakes. What had been set up as a structure of coordination, working as a process of mass participation, had become the local level of bureaucratic centralism. Hence, the post-Mao regime found a case for reorganization.

Before the full-scale reorganization was implemented, as a transitional step, the commune revolutionary committee was renamed as commune management committee (*Gongshe Guanli Weiyuanhui*). In June 1980, Liu Weibing was still its leader. In March 1980, the commune people's congress had met and had elected a 17-member commune management committee. The process of election was the same as before. But now it was a smaller committee. The commune had now set up nine central offices.

The New Township Government Structure

In 1982, the commune was renamed as township which was the rural administrative unit in China below the county before 1958. The change of name heralded a fundamental restructuring of rural political economy. The township was now the lowest level of the government.[25] It was no longer the unit of integrated economic, cultural and political activities. The principle that the party, government and enterprise management must be differentiated was implemented. Political activities were minimized and now the focus was on increasing production. Every unit was given autonomy and responsibility for production. If they performed better, then they obtained more dividends. If they fell short of targets, then they earned less.

In 1985, the new director of the Hela *xiang* Mr Zhang Weinan and his colleagues explained the changed structure to me.[26] (Now the head of the township government was called *xiang zhang* just as the head of the provincial government was called *sheng zhang* and of city government *shi zhang*. Earlier, the term used was *zhuren* meaning the main responsible person.) The main theme under the changed circumstances was autonomy for production units. In the past, the brigades and the teams had no power to decide their production plans. They used to do according to the plan drawn up for them by the higher authorities, namely the commune, and now they could decide as to what to produce and how. Similarly, the industrial and commercial units had been turned into autonomous companies and the township government provided only guidance to the enterprises and to the villages in planning. But the village had basic authority in economic decision-making. Thus, the political leadership of the township was now separated from the economic process. This was one of the major aspects of the reforms programme. It was stressed that there should be no political interference in economic decision-making and production units like enterprises, families or individuals must respond to the market and maximize their profit by working hard.

Unlike the practice during the commune period, the village committee and the enterprises now enjoyed more power. They took their own decisions. They could have economic exchanges with other units within or outside the township. The mode of distribution of wages was decided by each unit. They could diversify production and go for new products and so on.

The new township government had a variety of functions: taxation, industrial production, commerce, judicial work, financial work, medical and public health, education, and enterprise management. But the functions were performed under different lines of administration of the provincial and county governments.

In 1985, Hela *xiang* headquarters had moved from the Hela village office to a new, impressive building. The offices of the township government had been reorganized. Under the *xiang* director, there were five vice-directors, each in charge of a department, namely industry, agriculture, commerce, finances and office administration. One of them was a woman. (In 1979, she was the leader of the women's federation of Hela Commune.) Then there were six assistants: (a) civil affairs (*min shi*) to help settle disputes among neighbours, do counselling in family tensions, etc.; (b) judicial work; (c) planning and construction (house building, allotting land for factory, etc.); (d) health and education; (e) family planning and (f) financial matters. These are managed by cadres who are appointed by the township director in consultation with the party secretary.

There were three offices under the supervision of the township director: (a) tax office, which collected taxes from enterprises and villages; (b) industry and commerce, which maintained liaison between the township and the suburban district and (c) police station, which maintained peace and security in the region.[27]

There were four autonomous companies (*gongsi*) set up for (a) industry, (b) agriculture, (c) fisheries and (d) sideline production (*fuye*). Earlier, these activities were managed by the Economic Affairs Committee. That committee had now been disbanded because the decision-making power was to be decentralized. These companies were to coordinate the production units and enterprises in their respective areas. There were also two cooperatives under the joint leadership of the *xiang* and a credit cooperative and a supply and marketing cooperative.

In 1987, more details were available about the streamlining of the *xiang* office in Hela. The new adjustment policies of the party were reflected in these changes. Now the work staff had been reduced. The number of vice-directors was now three. The four companies had continued with the Sideline Production Company replaced by Commerce and Tourism Company (*shangye luyou gongsi*) to lead the flourishing hotel and tourism business in Wuxi's suburbs. Another important development was the establishment of the Economic Management Office (*jingji guanli bangongshi*). This was the time when there was a countrywide campaign to improve economic management. So, Hela Township had taken this step. In addition, there was a new office to check the quality of the products of various enterprises; the Office of Inspection of Enterprises was set up in 1987. By then, there were numerous reports about poor quality of products of the rural industries. The higher government authorities also now undertook surprise checks to see whether the enterprises followed the production plan and abided by the law and the regulations.

In the 1990s, several changes were visible in the organization of the township government, reflecting, perhaps, the new accent on managerial efficiency. We go into them in some detail in order to get a comprehensive view of the local administrative process. In mid-1993, instead of five there were four vice-directors. One was in charge of industry, business and foreign economic affairs. Unlike in most countries, in China there were Foreign Affairs Departments and International Trade and Investment Offices in every township. No doubt they were under centralized supervision, but they could take initiatives and foreign business people could contact them directly. There was a section responsible for construction work in rural areas such as building of hospitals, schools, roads and water supply. There was a new woman leader called Tang Shumin taking over the work after her predecessor Madam Shen had been transferred to a neighbouring township. This cadre was also in charge of family planning, education, legal affairs, broadcasting, communication and social affairs including old people's homes. She was also in charge of the township government's office administration.

Another deputy director Chen Daxia was in charge of agriculture and animal husbandry. His department included fisheries—one of the most important activities in this area—vegetable farming, horticulture and another important task namely land management. The division of science and technology, health, entertainment, sports and security was looked after by yet another deputy director, Zhang Qipeng.

The number of assistants was reduced from six to five with a degree of reorganization of the local government office; they were (a) health/medical affairs, (b) social affairs/civic affairs, (c) education and culture, (d) legal affairs and (e) family planning.

Hela Township had three police stations which were divisions under the security office (*gong an bu*) of the district. However, the local police officers were responsible to the township government. In other words, the head of the township government had the responsibility of maintaining peace and order in its territory. At the same time, there was a lateral chain of authority extending to the district, city and provincial levels. Thus, the township director combined the role of a political executive with that of an administrative head besides being a major economic manager in the reform context.

It may be noticed that health and education now had got separate offices, enjoying better attention. However, planning and construction were removed from the assistants' office to that of a vice-director. The practice of having a single office for both the township government and the township party committee continued in Hela. However, in many other townships, the party and government offices operated separately. Thus, in Hela Township, there were four offices: (a) Party and Government Office, (b) Economic Management Office, (c) Audit Office and (d) Finance Affairs Office.

Under the vice-director for industry, there were three corporations (*gongsi*), one each for industry, commerce and export, each having a separate management office. Under the vice-director for agriculture, a fourth corporation was in operation with separate divisions for agriculture, animal husbandry, etc. Unlike the practice in the 1980s, one could notice that greater emphasis was given to commerce and exports, now each having a separate corporation. The corporations besides having their own managers, later re-designated as managing directors, were now under the leadership of a vice-director of the township government. Thus, under the responsibility system, greater accountability was sought to be ensured. As to the degree of autonomy they enjoyed, the picture was not clear. Under the previous system of Economic Affairs Committee, there was collective leadership to which the company was responsible. Now at each level, there was one responsible manager who was required to show performance. This was stipulated under the production responsibility system.

The earlier situation regarding the location of branches of credit cooperative, supply and market cooperative, and industry and commerce unit continued. They were assigned work by the higher levels. The total number of office staff including the responsible cadres in the township government was 145, out of which 40 were women—a proportion much larger than before.

However, the staff strength of the township office was considered too large according to the norms of the State Council. One of the major decisions of the Eighth NPC in 1993 was pruning and streamlining bureaucracy from top to bottom; Premier Li Peng personally took number of measures to enforce the decision throughout the country to be followed even more minutely by Premier Zhu Rongji.[28] In Hela, they decided to reduce the staff strength by 30–50 per cent. They also wanted to employ more young people with higher education who were competent to manage economic affairs. An interesting aspect of the cadre mobility in China during the first two decades of reform period was that the lower the level of administration, the higher was their income. So, a city cadre wanted to go to suburban district or a county to work. A county cadre preferred to work in a township because the per capita income was higher there. Finally, the village paid still higher wages to its cadres than those of the township. It was rather unusual to see this phenomenon of higher salaries for the lower-level cadres that prevailed in China in the heyday of TVEs in the 1980s and early 1990s. In the later decades, as the rural economy lagged behind the urban economy, the rural government cadres got far less than the city cadres.

Thus, local public administration in rural China had undergone a steady process of reorganization in the 1980s and early 1990s. The focus was on economic management rather than political mobilization which was the case in the 1970s. The township administration started off in the early 1980s as a coordination centre of autonomous units of industrial enterprises and household agriculture enabling them to maximize output and make profit. The party interference in management was minimal. But by the early 1990s, the township leadership had acquired a critical role of planning and directing the economy while managing social affairs and responding to economic problems. The party was now more actively engaged in supervising economic management. But the township government had been more professionalized to tackle the modernized economy, the increasing number of joint ventures involving foreign capital, and a volatile mass of consumers. The network of autonomous production units continued but under the reaffirmed leadership of the township level. The national policy of the CPC of emphasizing macroeconomic coordination and sociopolitical stability was reflected at the grass-roots level.

In the post-1992 period, this situation changed at a rapid pace. Privatization of the rural enterprises became the norm. A new rural elite emerged gradually, taking advantage of the economic opportunities on the one hand and political patronage on the other. After 1998, the competitive elections did provide an arena to manage local tensions. But the local elite in many areas took hold of the local party apparatus and dominated the political economy. In the process, rural tensions grew and incidents of mass protest became a frequent phenomenon in the late 1990s and thereafter. Were the local political structures capable of handling this developing situation?

Township People's Congress

In actual practice, the reorganized township put more emphasis on efficient management through division of responsibilities, rather than allowing any elaborate channels of mass participation. Hence, in the new set up, the township people's congress had a reduced membership and a changed role. The new role was to discuss production plans and targets, rather than supervise the performance of the leaders which was part of the task of the old commune people's congress at least in theory.

The new township people's congress of Hela was elected in August 1984, having tenure of three years. According to the 1982 Constitution of the PRC, the tenure of the NPC is five years and that of the provincial people's congress and the local people's congress is three years. The membership of the Hela People's Congress was now 77—a considerable reduction from the previous figure of 246. This was obviously to make the forum manageable for serious discussions. The election procedure was still the same. Representatives were to come from each village and the rural enterprises.

After the elections in 1987, the number of representatives was further reduced to 57, out of whom 12 or about 20 per cent were women. It may be recalled that in 1979, the proportion of women was much higher (41 per cent). By then, some trends were discernible. The accent was on having larger number of young and educated numbers in the responsible bodies. (This was the theme of the special conference of the CPC in September 1985. Since then, those between 35 and 45 years of age were considered as the luckiest. The older ones, as the talk of the town went, had missed the bus.)

Age composition of representatives of Hela *xiang* people's congress in 1987 was as follows:

Below 30 years	30 per cent
30–50 years	60 per cent
Above 50 years	10 per cent

In terms of education, none of the representatives now was below the middle school (ninth class). About 40 per cent of them had crossed the high school level (twelfth class).

The people's congress met once a year—usually towards the end of the year. It heard the report of the director and discussed it in detail. The report not only summed up the activities of various departments of the township government but also laid down the plans for the coming year. The director generally prepared the report in consultation with the party secretary and the director of the district.

One interesting feature of the new people's congress was the stipulation that 40 per cent of the representatives should come from outside the CPC. In fact, the united front organ, the Township People's Political Consultative Conference, had been already activated. The new requirement ensured that people from various opinion groups—inside or outside the party—were associated with the new economic activities. This policy operated at local, provincial as well as national levels. The policy was to mobilize maximum people for economic development.

It is noteworthy that under the new structure, there was no committee rule. The *xiang* director and his team of deputy directors were called upon to face the *xiang* people's congress once a year. The earlier stress on collective leadership through either the commune committee or the commune revolutionary committee was found to be a system that did not put responsibility on any one. Moreover, during the Cultural Revolution, it had led to concentration of power with the chair or secretary without having responsibility for showing economic results. The large-scale participation of masses was seen as having created severe constraints on the leadership's capacity for effective management and innovation. This was the assessment by the Deng regime, hence the new director-oriented system.

Township's Director-oriented System

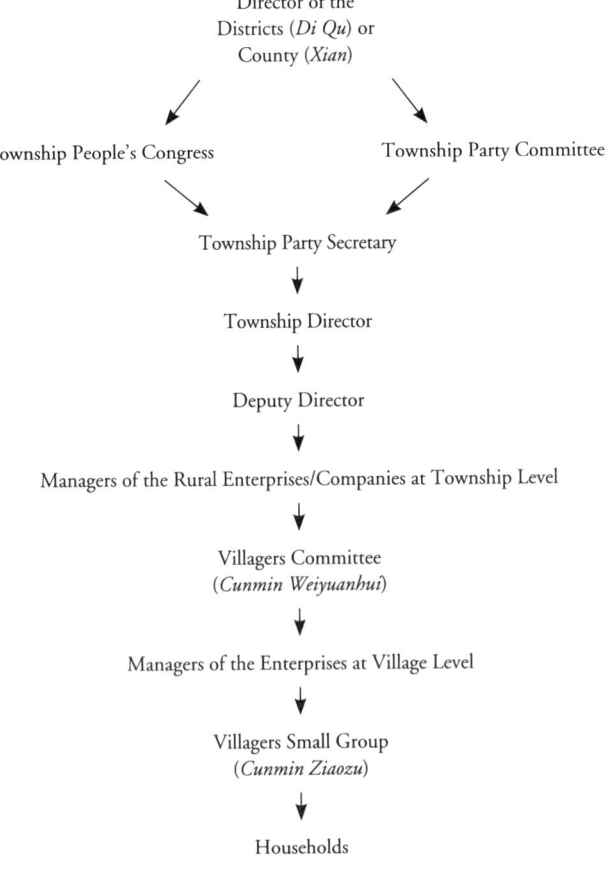

In 1993, I noticed that once again there was a rise in the number of deputies to the *xiang* people's congress. In the elections that took place in November 1992, 172 deputies were elected, 35 per cent of whom were women. The average age of the deputies was 40 years, reflecting the trend of putting young people in responsible positions. There was representation of managers, workers, cadres and others covering the spheres of industry, agriculture, education, science and technology, medical services and culture.

Elections to the *xiang* people's congress were held as per schedule in 1995. It had a reduced number of deputies—only 70 representatives, 30 per cent of whom were women. It elected a new director. The previous director was elevated as party secretary of Hela. As per the norm, the new director was a deputy secretary of the *xiang* party committee. The outgoing director presented the report of the *xiang* government, giving details of the economic performance of the previous year and spelling out the FYP proposals of Hela *xiang* as well as the tasks for the forthcoming year. The director announced continuation of the structural reforms by the way of giving more autonomy to the enterprises. The government could only maintain macro coordination and control, supervising performance trends and providing information to the enterprises. Thus, government organs were to shift their role from direct management to indirect guidance of the enterprises, thus avoiding administrative interference in the affairs of enterprises. Another focus of the report was on improving the science and technology level of the economy. For that purpose, managers and cadres should be periodically trained and technology should be procured from outside while every enterprise should have its own research and development wing.

The Village Level

In the reorganized Township structure, the production brigade of the commune period was renamed *cun* or village, and this was considerably strengthened as a production unit. At the same time, the lowest unit, the production team, which was usually a small village or part of a village and was the collective unit of land ownership, production and distribution during the commune period, was practically dissolved. In place of the team, there were villagers small groups (*cunmin xiaozu*) wherever they were needed. There were many such small groups of farming households in the Wuxi region.

Hela's 13 brigades were renamed as villages. Each village had a villagers committee (*cunmin weiyuanhui*) which had three–five members in 1985, further reduced to two–three members in 1987. At that time, in order to constitute this body, the names of the possible members of the village committee were first suggested by the township government and then the village representatives congress elected them. The congress also elected the director and the deputy directors of the village in the same way. Thus, the higher-level township government still wielded considerable power over the administration of the village under the new system. The introduction of the competitive elections changed this situation after 1998. But still the township government's preference for certain candidates was known to the villagers in most cases. Therefore, villagers' choices were often limited.

But the village level was almost wholly transformed into an economic unit as the economic agenda of the reform period unfolded.[29] Its political and administrative functions were taken over either by the *xiang* government or the party. The village level now had its own companies for agriculture, industry and commerce and it had set up its enterprises. Each was headed by a manager. In villages, where the scale of operations was small, there was only one village director and the company managers were appointed by the township director. They reported to him on their production plans and performance. He evaluated their work and recommended higher or lower bonus.

Below the village level were the villagers groups, still called production teams (*shengcan dui*) in the local parlance. Hela had 90 teams earlier. The 1985 figures stood at 87. But they were further split into many work groups. For vegetable farming, fishing and forestry, the villagers formed work groups, whereas food grain production was carried out by the households. In Hela, 45 production teams continued to operate as collective units growing vegetables. Teams or work groups signed contracts with the village or a marketing unit. Similarly, there were 30 teams in fishing, each divided further into two or three groups. This practice generally continued in the 1990s.

While the teams and the villagers groups worked under the leadership of the village, the village leaders were responsible to the township government whose director was the link between the State or the higher authorities and the village. Thus, between the basic production units, namely the agricultural households, villagers groups and enterprises on the one hand and the State on the other, there was one single channel of mediation, supervision and control, namely the township director.

The Township Director (*Xiang Zhang*)

In China's countryside, the *xiang zhang* or the township director had emerged as the most critical official during the reform period. In China's reformed structure, the *xiang* director was a government official or State cadre (*guojia ganbu*) but was elected by the township people's congress. He/she was the second most powerful cadre in the township, the first being the party secretary. The salaries of the director and the deputy directors were paid by the government. The government appointed them and periodically transferred such cadres from one township to another—but generally within the region. The appointment and the election were part of the interacting process involving the higher and the lower echelons of the party and the government. By government here, we mean the immediate higher level, namely the district or the county. It may also involve the city government (*shi zhengfu*) acting under the direction of the provincial government.

But the picture is more complex due to the nature of the job of the township director. As mentioned earlier, this position carries the responsibilities of an elective office as well as the appointed cadre with multiple tasks. Hence, the director has to either come from the region or be sufficiently familiar with the area.

Hela Township director Zhang Weinan happily reported in 1987 that while earlier the *xiang* directors were appointed by the government, now they were democratically elected by the people's congress. But actually, in his own case what happened was that he was first appointed to the office in November 1983 and when the township people's congress met in August 1984, it 'elected' him and then his appointment was 'approved' by the higher authorities. In other words, the director was basically appointed by the higher authorities. He then organized the composition of the people's congress in such a way that he could count on their support. May be in the prevailing situation if the people knew that he was the nominee of the higher body, then they would formally elect him. In practice, there was no competitive election for the *xiang* director so far.

Both Liu Weibing and Zhang Weinan were from Hela Township. While Liu was earlier the leader of the fishing brigade, Zhang was his deputy. Zhang was a native of Longshan village. Starting as the head of the Longshan production team in 1972, he became the party secretary of the Longshan production brigade in 1976. He moved up as the deputy director of the commune management committee in 1980. After serving as township director, Zhang Weinan moved to the next higher level and became a district cadre—vice-director of the suburban district government in 1993.

The township director had to work under the political and ideological supervision of the party secretary. Actually, the *xiang* director was the deputy secretary of the party committee. But the equation in the changed situation was noticeable. The director, the company managers and the enterprise directors were more important in practical terms than the party secretary at the corresponding level in the mid-1980s. But in all appointments, the township director had to secure the concurrence of the party secretary. Moreover, the party secretary had his separate and parallel channels to supervise, report and influence. He could report to the higher party committee at the district or county level. He could also get reports from the village party units. But the party–government–management differentiation principle was underlined and the party was not to interfere in the economic administration during this period. In any case, since the party had adopted the new economic policies such as 'production according to market needs', 'wages according to the quality and quantity of work' and 'encouragement of private enterprise', the local party leader could not obstruct that process. But in case something went wrong, the party secretary could intervene through the township party committee where the director and the deputy directors were members.

The roles of the *xiang* director in the reforms context were explained by director Zhang in 1987 as follows:

1. Working out the principles and goals for the development of the whole township as to how best to use the land resources, water, forest and human power for agriculture, industry and commerce.
2. Ensuring that all the deputy directors and development leaders were working effectively in their jobs.
3. If there were problems involving more than one department, trying to solve them.

The director was the final authority in economic as well as administrative matters. He/she was responsible for whatever mistakes were committed by himself or others in any department. In 1993, however, the focus clearly was on accelerating the process of growth. As we will see later, this was the result of Deng's call in early 1992.

On the whole, the township director was the key figure in rural administration in the reformed structure. He had to show results in production and if they were impressive, then he could get higher bonus or a promotion. He had to maintain his political support from below by keeping the lower levels happy and carrying the blessings of the higher authorities at the same time. Since there were still no institutionalized mechanisms to conduct politics below and interact with the superior bodies, a great deal depended on the personal rapport of the leaders at various levels.

The director-centric administrative system that evolved in the course of the reforms to provide effective leadership at the township level was vulnerable to falling into the 'agency trap' for two reasons. Firstly, the director was to follow the directives from above and he/she owed his/her office to the higher authorities. He/she was in reality the instrument of central rule rather than a representative of people at the grass-roots level. Secondly, in the market economy where many entrepreneurs and managers dominated the rural scene, he/she was often unable to implement the party policy. The 'consultative' institutions such as the township people's congress and the township party committee were not mass line forums. They were instrumental in legitimatizing and enforcing party policies. But they were needed to enforce 'reform, development and stability'.

Supervision by the District/County Authorities

As we have seen, in the 1990s, Hela was one of the 10 townships in the suburban district, which in all had 110 villages and 936 small groups or production teams. The urban areas within the *xiang* had 6 street offices and they in turn had 65 neighbourhood committees. The new policies were based on the principle of making the economies of the city and the countryside complementary (*Cheng-Xiang Jiehe*). That is why the province of Jiangsu had been administratively reorganized into prefecture-level cities with both urban and rural areas in them.

The district had one director and five deputy directors, one of whom was a woman. Each was in charge of a separate department: (a) industry, (b) agriculture, (c) commerce, (d) culture, education and health and social welfare and (e) city and neighbourhood affairs. They did not have a separate security department, presumably because the Provincial Security Office had its branch in the township. The director and the deputy directors of the district had supervisory roles over the respective spheres in each *xiang* not only through the township director but also through a direct channel. They were elected for a three-year term by the district people's congress which had a membership of 220. Hela had sent deputies to the district people's congress. But this election was also non-competitive. The higher level, namely the municipal government, after studying the situation would put up a panel which was approved by the people's congress.

The main responsibility of the district government was to interpret the policies of the Central Government or the party CC and transmit them to the township and ensure that they were followed. In the light of the policy since 1987 'to reinvigorate the economy' (*Jinyibu gaohuo jingji*), the district authorities were busy enforcing enterprise law, helping in fixing targets and checking quality of production. In 1987, an important stage of rural reform was considered to have been completed with the full implementation of the family contract system and expansion of rural industries. The next task involved adjustment in production structure by raising the technological level. To achieve economic efficiency in the new stage, emphasis was put on improving management. Technology and management in agriculture as well as industry and commerce to promote specialized production were the new slogans. From October 1992 onwards, the focus was on building a 'socialist market economy' by diversifying the ownership system. After the Fifth Party Plenum in 1995, the stress was on consolidation. The district authorities had the responsibilities of supervising the township performances.

This system of local government at the township and village levels continued with shifting points of emphasis under Hu Jintao and Xi Jinping. For the Hu–Wen regime, attending to people's concrete needs by remaining in close touch with them was the focus of the local government. His administration saw the effects of the new post-1992 economic strategy which created the 'three rural problems'. In that situation, the local governments heavily depended on the grants from the Centre even to pay salaries to the cadres. Under Xi Jinping, clear instructions were given to the grass-roots governments to refrain from giving exclusive emphasis on achieving high growth rates. New criteria of successful cadres were popularized, stressing on attending to people's needs, eliminating corrupt practices and living with communist values of integrity, service and discipline. Party exercised leadership directly at every level.

A system of decentralized governance has stabilized in China with a party-led state operating at every level. That it was decentralized was clear from the fact that the decision-making power on economic matters remained with the managers' production units at the local level. However, political power is not decentralized despite multi-candidate elections at the village level. The fact that even the party-designated township leader had to be elected by the township people's congress did provide an occasion for debate and in many places there were challenges to official nominees and even initiatives for recall as provided by law. But the new system had built in elements of centralized power. At the local level, the enterprise managers, the township director and the district director were the new centres of power. Many of them were entrepreneurs and managers themselves. What was conspicuous was the lack of emphasis on channels of mass participation through the people's congress and the committees in decision-making. They were mainly platforms for discussion on party decisions or at best channel of gathering people's views.[30] This system was operated by the party which assumed a new role under each regime, sometimes granting autonomy to economic units and administration, sometimes directly taking over those functions, but always maintaining direct or indirect leadership at the grass-roots level.

That takes us to a closer look at the role of the party.

Notes and References

1. Mao Zedong, 'Some Questions Concerning Methods of Leadership', in *Selected Works of Mao Zedong*, vol. 3 (Beijing: Foreign Languages Press, 1965), 119. See my discussion on how this turns into centralism unless there is strategic dependence on masses in Manoranjan Mohanty, *The Political Philosophy of Mao Zedong* (New Delhi: Aakar Books, 2012), 46–47.

2. If one goes by the opinion polls that the Pew Research Center has conducted from time to time, then more than 50 per cent of the population has always favoured the overall system and the policies. They of course have views on specific policies. See, for example, the one on 10 October 2014, available at: www.pewresearch.org. But such polls do not resolve the questions on legitimacy of regimes.

3. Institute of Sociology, CASS and the Peking University Social Survey Centre have conducted many surveys, none of which show disaffection with the regime or the system.

4. Daniel A. Bell, *The China Model: Political Meritocracy and the Limits of Democracy* (Princeton, NJ: Princeton University Press, 2015). This is an interesting characterization of the Chinese political system that combines Confucian values and Communist Party discipline and commitment, thus possessing a capacity to address complex problems that Western democracies find difficult to handle. Yet, this does not prevent the phenomenon of an 'agency trap' as it does not have the mechanisms of participation, accountability and correction of course in an institutional manner.

5. On the aftermath of the failure of the Great Leap Forward, critical changes took place at the Lushan Plenum of the CPCCC. Among them was Mao's resignation from chair of the republic and Lu Shaoqi taking over that post.

6. Xi Jinping, 'Study, Disseminate and Implement the Guiding Principles of the 18th CPC National Congress (November 17, 2012)', in *The Governance of China* (Beijing: Foreign Languages Press, 2014), 10.

7. It is important to take the official formulations seriously while examining the authoritarian and other elements of the system. Many interesting formulations explain the character of the Chinese State. Building a market economy did not necessarily involve creating a liberal–democratic State. It never meant withdrawal of the State from critical coordination and monitoring role of the State. As institutional reforms proceeded to push market reforms in the late 1990s, the local administration got reorganized with privatization of rural enterprises and reorganization of tax structure. Dali L. Yang thinks that the politics of institutional changes carried out by the early 2000s had already laid down the framework of stable, State-guided, well-functioning market economy. He is right in saying that 'the Chinese leaders have leveraged their political machinery to gradually refit the ship of the state'. Dali L. Yang, *Remaking the Chinese Leviathan* (Stanford: Stanford University Press, 2004), 297. But the final years of Hu Jintao and the first term of Xi Jinping showed that even though the Chinese leaders' capacity for economic management had continued to remain strong, the sources of instability and alienation persisted as exposed in the course of the anti-corruption campaign.

8. Manoranjan Mohanty, 'Xi Jinping and the Chinese Dream', in *Ideology Matters: China from Mao Zedong to Xi Jinping* (New Delhi: Aakar, 2014).

9. Li Peng, *Report on the Work of the Government*, delivered at NPC Session (Beijing: Xinhua Press Release), 5 March 1996.

10. See Jiang Zemin, *Hold High the Great Banner of Deng Xiaoping Theory for an All-round Advancement of the Cause of Building Socialism with Chinese Characteristics to the 21st*

Century, Report delivered at the 15th National Congress of the Communist Party of China (Beijing: Foreign Languages Press, 1997, 12 September).

11. See Jiang Zemin, 'Reforming the Political Structure and Strengthening Democracy and the Legal System', in *Hold High the Great Banner of Deng Xiaoping Theory for an All-round Advancement of the Cause of Building Socialism with Chinese Characteristics to the 21st Century*, Report delivered at the 15th National Congress of the Communist Party of China, (1997, 12 September). Available at: http://www.bjreview.com.cn/document/txt/2011-03/25/content_363499_10.htm (accessed on 7 June 2017).

12. Xi Jinping, 116–17, see note 6.

13. Li Keqiang, *Report on the Work of the Government*.

14. *Constitution of the People's Republic of China* (Beijing: People's Publishing House, 2004), 15. The CPC Constitution also affirms this saying that the CPC adhered to the 'system of multi-party cooperation and supervision under the leadership of the CPC'. But as we have seen, the political environment determined the nature of cooperation with these parties.

15. The eight democratic parties are Revolutionary Committee of the Kuomintang, the China Democratic League, the China Democratic National Construction Association, the China Association for Promoting Democracy, the Chinese Peasants and Workers Democratic Party, the China Zhi Gong Dang, the Jiusan Society and the Taiwan Democratic Self-government League. Yang Fengchun, *Chinese Government* (Beijing: Foreign Languages Press, 2004). According to Yang, they 'participate in state affairs' … 'represent the interests of different groups…', 66–67. It is to be noted that this is different from saying that they participate in the exercise of State power. So theirs is a consultative role.

16. Xi Jinping regime passed a new law regulating the role of foreign NGOs in China for which it was criticized severely in the Western press. See *The Guardian*, 'China Passes Law Imposing Security Controls on Foreign NGOs, 28 April 2016. Available at: https://www.theguardian.com/world/2016/apr/28/china-passes-law-imposing-security-controls-on-foreign-ngos (accessed on 18 April 2017).

17. Stein Ringen, *The Perfect Dictatorship: China in the 21st Century* (Hong Kong: Hong Kong University Press, 2016). The State had become 'radically harder and more ideological' under Xi Jinping, according to this study.

18. Jiang Zemin had, in his *Political Report to the Sixteenth Party Congress in 2002* rejected 'copying of any model of the political systems of the West'. Jiang Zemin, *Political Report to the Sixteenth Party Congress in 2002* (Beijing: Foreign Languages Press, 2002), Section V, para 1.

19. Deng Xiaoping took the decisive step on this issue by 'shifting focus from class struggle to economic construction' at the Third Plenum in 1978. Maintaining steady economic growth by ensuring social stability is the primary goal of the political structure. That is why mass demonstrations have been disallowed during the reform period in China.

20. *Communique of the Fourth Plenary Session of the 14th CPC Central Committee* (Beijing: Xinhua Press Release, 24–28 September 1994).

21. See Zhu Jiamu, 'Chen Yun and Deng Xiaoping in the Initial Stage of Reform and Opening-up'. Available at: http://www.cssn.cn/upload/2013/01/d20130111154110755.pdf (accessed on 4 July 2014).

22. Mao Zedong, 'On the Ten Major Relationships' (1956, 25 April). Available at: https://www.marxists.org/reference/archive/mao/selected-works/volume-5/mswv5_51.htm (accessed on 18 April 2017). He dealt with a broad perspective of policies, dialectically handling the relationship between heavy industries and light industries and agriculture, industrialization in coastal areas and interior, economy and defence, State, collectives and

producers, Centre and local authorities, Han nationality and the minorities, party and non-party forces, revolution and counter-revolution, right and wrong ways of dealing, and China and foreign countries.

23. Mohanty, 'China's Focus on Governance'.

24. Xi Jinping, 'Improve Party Conduct, Uphold Integrity and Combat Corruption', in *The Governance of China* (Beijing: Foreign Languages Press, 2014), 436. See also in the same volume 'Establish and Promote the Conduct of "Three Stricts and Three Earnests"', 421. They refer respectively to being strict in self-development, exercise of power and self-discipline and earnest in making pans, opening up new undertakings and upholding personal integrity.

25. See Lianjiang Li, 'Direct Township Elections', in *Grassroots Political Reforms in Contemporary China*, eds. Elizabeth J. Perry and Merle Goldman (Cambridge, MA: Harvard University Press, 2007).

26. During 1985–87, I met the township director, while the party secretary was shy of meeting me.

27. This information is based on my discussions with the officials of the township.

28. See Yiu-chung Wong, *From Deng Xiaoping to Jiang Zemin: Two Decades of Political Reforms in the People's Republic of China* (Lanham, MD: University Press of America, 2005), 112.

29. This process has been described as 'local state corporatism' by Jean C. Oi, 'The Evolution of Local State Corporatism', in *Zouping in Transition: The Process of Reform in Rural China*, ed. Andrew G. Walder (Cambridge, MA: Harvard University Press, 1998). Local state like the State as a whole is a dynamic, contradiction-ridden power process that cannot be reduced to a dichotomous relationship between State and society as State is after all the aggregate power structure society. Manoranjan Mohanty, 'Duality of the State Process', in *Capitalist State: Critical Essays*, Felicitation Volume in Honour of A. R. Desai, ed. Ghanashyam Shah (Mumbai: Popular Prakashan, 1990). The local state in China confronts a complex web of boundary-spanning contention with people challenging and obeying the authorities and relating to power process in numerous different ways. So, the reorganization of local structures responds to such phenomenon as they unfold from time to time. Kevin J. O'Brien, 'Boundary-spanning Contention in China', in *State and Society in 21st Century China: Crisis, Contention and Legitimation*, eds. Peter Heys Gries and Stanley Rosen (New York, NY: Routledge Curzon, 2004).

30. Does that make China a 'deliberative democracy' as many Chinese scholars have pointed out? See Fang Ning, *China's Democracy Path* (Beijing: China Social Science Press, 2014), 8. After the first decade of reforms, Vivienne Shue had thought that the 'new state corporate power structure in the countryside could well prove a good deal more efficient, as well as more wholeheartedly responsive to the visions of modernization and development … than were the weary localist cadres of the Maoist past' which she had described as 'honeycomb patterns'. Vivienne Shue, *The Reach of the State: Sketches of the Chinese Body Politic* (Stanford: Stanford University Press, 1988), 152. After three decades of reforms, the local political regime may have been effective in achieving economic growth targets but ineffective in responding to socio-political demands, thus the state corporate power structure facing alienation from common people.

5

The Party and Its Governing Capacity

There are many actors on the stage
But the Party is the director of the play.
—A District Party Cadre

Conceptualizing the Party Rule in China

That our discussion on the party follows the functioning of the State and government needs an explanation as most accounts on the Chinese political system from both China and abroad start with the party. Indeed, the CPC is the ruling force in China. But every society, China included, is governed by a state system which is created by a Constitution. Military dictatorships and monarchies are exceptions. Martial law situations are different. But it is important to understand the nature of the State in studying a polity, society or economy. To understand who wields State power, we look at the political forces on the one hand and social forces on the other. In a competitive party system, the political party that wins electoral mandate exercises power for the specific term as stipulated under the Constitution. In a one-party system, we have to understand how the party acquired that role. This is how understanding the historical process of a revolution or freedom struggle becomes important. But equally important is to investigate the social forces that support the ruling party and the State. In studying socialist states or communist party regimes, most observers equate State with government on the one hand and with society on the other. It is important to maintain these distinctions and observe them in a dynamic historical perspective.

Then it would be easy to understand the ruling strategies of modern States. Even though state by definition is organization of power, its ruling strategy always involves a multidimensional strategy of governance. A State uses coercive, responsive and legitimate power to maintain itself and continue. However, their combinations may vary from time to time.[1]

In China, the fact that the CPC general secretary assumed the office of the president of the republic from Jiang Zemin onwards makes this point clear. The same leader also occupying the post of the chairperson of the MAC makes it even clearer. This commission that leads the armed forces exists as both an organization under the CC of the party and a part of the State structure appointed by the NPC. No doubt the Party's National Congress, every five years, formulates the path of sociopolitical development, and politically it is far more significant than the election of the NPC every five years which follows the party congress. But the State Council headed by the premier is also a major player in the State. Its role must not be perceived narrowly as a subordinate agency of implementation. The premier, vice-premiers and most of the ministers are also important members in the party organization. At every level, the cross-cutting membership—same people having posts in the State apparatus and party—makes the party–State interaction functional.

Structure of the CPC
National Congress of the CPC every five years elects
CC and CCDI
CCDI elects
Secretary
CC elects
Politburo, Standing Committee, General Secretary and MAC with a
chairperson and several vice-chairpersons

As for policy formulation, all bodies of the State and the party provided inputs and then the party CC led by the Politburo and its Standing Committee formulated the broad policy framework.[2] On that basis, the State Council formulated policies, and NPC and its Standing Committee made laws. All critical decisions formulating the line or overall perspective or outlook were first taken by the party CC. Just as the decision to launch the Cultural Revolution was formulated by the CC in May 1966, the Third Plenum of the Eleventh CC in December 1978 adopted the 'reform and open-door' framework, guiding the whole stream of reforms thereafter. After each party congress, the CC plenums decide major decisions. For example, the CC's Third Plenum in 2013 adopted the line of 'deepening market economy and allowing it to play a decisive role', relaxed the *hukou* system and altered the 'one-child policy', while the Fourth Plenum in 2014 declared new measures to enforce 'rule of law'. Then the necessary laws and administrative measures were taken by the State organs. The Fifth Plenum in 2015 formulated the outline of the Thirteenth FYP which became the basis for the making of the elaborate plan document adopted by the NPC in March 2016. Once initial decisions are made about a matter, the policies are first put before the public as drafts for public discussion. This happened also in the case of the two critical documents on Norms of Political Life in the Party and Regulations on Intra-party Supervision adopted by the Sixth Plenum of the CC in October 2016 which also declared Xi Jinping as 'the core' of leadership. The initial proposals were formulated by the Politburo in March 2016 and were circulated throughout the country for responses before being finalized. The lower units of the party are asked for their opinions on all matters. Even before initial decisions are made, some units are encouraged or allowed to make experiments in policies. There are cases when the central leadership finds out about experiments in one place or the other and then examines it for taking it as a national policy. From agricultural cooperatives and people's communes to HRS and specialized households, there are many examples of such policy initiatives. These get reflected within the party organs through diverse opinion groups or factions linked to ideological lines or regional base or plain interest groups. Crucial decisions in economic and political matters are routinely discussed in non-CPC forums and their views taken into serious consideration before policies are formulated.

To take the CPC only as a homogenous top–down party is misrepresentation of reality. 'Democratic centralism' may be more centralism and less democracy, mass line may be a mobilizational slogan on most occasions, but making this an essential organizational principle has its significance. This is what Mao Zedong called 'practice as the sole criterion of truth' and 'seeking truth from facts' during the Yan'an period while he formulated a new strategy of revolution suited to Chinese conditions. Mao Zedong described it as a creative application of Marxism–Leninism to the concrete conditions prevailing in China at the time. Deng Xiaoping revived these very concepts to launch reforms and insisted that the party must be innovative, 'feel the stone while crossing the river' and evolve its policies as it went along. He formulated the concept of 'socialist market economy'. But the way to concretely formulate policies within the framework had multiple opinions and even a range of alternative policies out of which the party leadership was to choose and build a consensus within it. Thus, plurality of opinion and variety of experiences from the field are important features of CPC's functioning.

Often commentators refer to the phenomenon of trinity of party–government–army ruling China. Indeed, in the Chinese context, the PLA had been an autonomous force because of the role it played in the course of the Chinese revolution. During the Cultural Revolution, it became evident as Defence Minister Lin Biao used the PLA to attack opponents in the party, and the PLA had actually launched the ideological campaign to popularize his version of the Maoist principles through a mass movement in 1965. Only a military action amounting to a coup led by a section of PLA and the party, against the Gang of Four, defeated them in 1976 and put Deng Xiaoping in power. Deng remained as the chairperson of the MAC even after Jiang Zemin took over as CPC general secretary and president. In June 1989, Deng as MAC chairperson ordered the PLA to crush the youth uprising at Tiananmen. All the CPC leaders including Xi Jinping usually reshuffled the military commanders to maintain their support base. In fact, the party–government–military interaction percolates the whole system. But still China cannot be characterized as a PLA-led polity or a military-dominated political system. There are elaborate political and institutional arrangements and theoretical affirmations to ensure that 'the party commands the gun and the gun shall never be allowed to command the party'.[3]

Understanding the nature of the party-led polity in China also requires an understanding of the actual political and social process as it has evolved over the decades, before and after the launching of the reforms. First of all, the CC and the Politburo have party groups in charge of key policy areas. For example, Xi Jinping heads the party group in charge of reforms. In 2013, when the CC's Third Plenum launched the campaign for 'Comprehensively Deepen Reforms', the CC also set up a special group headed by Xi to conduct and monitor it. Several new groups formulating and supervising important policies ranging from national security to Internet security are headed by Xi. Besides, almost all organizations including enterprises, offices, schools, universities, research institutes, cultural institutions including government departments and army units have party committees. The party secretary in the respective organization is politically more powerful than the formal administrative head. But usually the administrative head is the deputy secretary of the party committee. They work in consultation with one another. The party leader's role is that of a vigilant observer and a general adviser. While the actual decision is made by the administrative authorities, they respect the overall guidance of the party and in the case of deviation from central policy or irregularity, the party leader intervenes and reports to higher authorities.

At every level, there are congresses, conferences and party committees or party branches, even if the number of members is small. Then there are the CPPCC organs which are united front bodies of non-communist parties and groups which exist at every level, right down to the township level which also plays a supervisory or auditing role. With village elections opening up opportunities for debates and voters' mobilization taking place at election time, there are other avenues of vigilance as well. As the Internet expanded in China and social media coverage spread—from 2014 onwards—the party's CCDI entertained anonymous complaints against corrupt practices. With this, the situation has become qualitatively different. It is this institutional framework which may perform the functions of a check and balance system in China. However, it should be pointed out that such arrangements may not always work adequately to achieve the goals of the system in either China or elsewhere.

The CPC from Deng Xiaoping to Xi Jinping

The CPC has functioned with distinct characteristics from one regime to another. Even though there were many shifts during Mao Zedong's lifetime, two things were clear about his leadership of the party. Firstly, he was the unquestioned leader of the party, even when he faced challenges on specific policies on several occasions. Secondly, his mass support was so widespread that he could directly appeal to them to launch policies and campaigns, bypassing institutions of the State and party. This had weakened the organizational functioning of the party during the last decade of his life, especially the decade of the Cultural Revolution.[4]

While Mao drew his legitimacy from his leadership of the revolution which survived bitter criticisms of his policies after his death, Deng Xiaoping promised and delivered concrete economic results to the common people and established his legitimacy. Using his long experience in revolution as well as in government until the Cultural Revolution, Deng gave a perspective on modernization that captured the imagination of the Chinese people. That using State power and party legitimacy China could achieve economic growth through a system of incentives and using global capital, technology and market was his line of thinking. He laid down institutional rules of governance, regularity of convening of State bodies like the NPC and party organizations and conferences, fixed tenures and succession processes through consensus and wide consultation process with non-communist forces in society (see Table 5.1 showing regular convening of Party Congress after 1982). Arrangements such as 'one country, two systems' brought the integration of former colonies such as Hong Kong and Macao and opened up access to Taiwan which appealed to the global civil society. When in crisis, as in the wake of the Tiananmen uprising, he took firm steps but did not reverse the reforms. During the 1992 southern tour, he called for full play of private capital and market forces in developing the economy and declared, 'Do not be afraid of capitalism, the party is there to take care of it'.[5]

The party underwent a major transformation of its social base under the leadership of Jiang Zemin who pulled off all stops to invite foreign capital and

Table 5.1:

CPC Congress and membership since 1945

Party Congress	Year	Chairman/General Secretary	Total Membership
7th	1945	Mao Zedong (Chairman)	1,211,128
8th	1956	Mao Zedong	10,734,384
9th	1969	Mao Zedong	20,000,000
10th	1973	Mao Zedong	28,000,000
11th	1977	Hua Guofeng	35,000,000
12th	1982	Hu Yaobang (General Secretary)	39,650,000
13th	1987	Zhao Ziyang	46,000,000
14th	1992	Jiang Zemin	51,000,000
15th	1997	Jiang Zemin	58,000,000
16th	2002	Hu Jintao	66,000,000
17th	2007	Hu Jintao	73,000,000
18th	2012	Xi Jinping	82,000,000

Sources: http://english.cpc.people.com.cn/; http://english.people.com.cn/90785/7910578.html (accessed on 28 July 2017).

accelerate export-oriented growth. He opened the membership of the CPC to entrepreneurs—described as patriotic forces—who contributed to the development of the motherland. This was a departure from the class background of the CPC members who came from workers, peasants, soldiers and progressive intellectuals. Since party membership was a privilege that brought positions in the party, State or the economy and raised the social status, this had much consequence for the character of the party. Jiang's 'Three Represents' rationalized his initiatives with long-term implications.[6] Premier Zhu Rongji took a number of steps to curb bureaucracy and make the party and government cadres more efficient.

Hu Jintao's main task was not only to maintain the tempo of economic growth but also to address some serious problems that had arisen in the course of reforms. It was under his regime that the party's 'governance capacity' came to the centre of political discourse in China. His predecessor Jiang Zemin did refer to 'fighting corruption' as a 'life and death question for the party'. But Hu went a step further actually warning that the CPC would cease to remain as the ruling party if it failed in governance, that is, fulfilling people's aspirations. It was under his regime that the 'three rural problems' got maximum publicity and measures for 'building a new socialist countryside' were stipulated under the Twelfth FYP. Party being asked to practice the tradition of 'serve the people' and Hu Jintao's scientific development perspective advocating balanced, coordinated development in five sectors—economic, political, social, cultural and ecological—became the new thrust of the party ideology.

But implementing that perspective in practice still eluded the leadership, and that became the focus of the Xi Jinping leadership. On the one hand, he gave the slogan of achieving the 'Chinese dream of great rejuvenation of the Chinese nation' to excite the patriotic imagination of the people. On the other hand, he paid serious attention to rebuilding the party, initiating concrete measures on two fronts. One was his famed anti-corruption campaign in the party under the framework of the CCDI and this spread to all spheres of economy, society and polity as party cadres dominated them all.[7] On the one hand, in 2013, the CC and CCDI issued a 'Work Plan for Establishing a Complete System of Combating Corruption through Both Punishment and Prevention'. On the other hand, each party cadre had to exemplify party values and conduct himself/herself as pro-people, efficient cadres exhibiting austere life style and high ideals.[8] He took many policy measures to reorient the economy and foreign policy and established new consensus points—he called them as 'new normal'—such as moderate growth rate, domestic-demand-driven economy. The new security concept and 'One Belt, One Road' and neighbourhood policy framework were some of his major policy initiatives.

As mentioned before, Xi Jinping's ideas are put in the ideological framework of the party after Deng Xiaoping, Jiang Zemin and referring to his 'major addresses, his new vision, thinking and strategies for china's governance'. Essentially, his line of thought has been encompassed as 'four comprehensives': 'comprehensively build China as an all-round, moderately prosperous society', 'comprehensively deepen reforms', comprehensively enforce rule of law' and 'comprehensively practice strict governance of the party'. Xi Jinping systematically devoted each of the CC plenums Third Plenum in 2013 onwards to focus on each of these issues. The Sixth Plenum held in October 2016 not only declared Xi as the 'core' of leadership, but it also adopted two major political documents which would have long-term effect on the governance capacity of the party.[9] Jiang Zemin had been described as the 'core'—a practice which Hu Jintao did not continue. Using that expression again for Xi Jinping meant that there were forces in the party who did not share his perspective, and there were many questionable trends. Explaining the need for new party norms which replaced the 1980 norms, Xi mentioned a number of serious faults among members, including 'lax discipline, detachment from the people, arbitrariness and inaction, acts of individualism, factionalism, money worshipping and violations linked to formalism, bureaucracy, hedonism and extravagance', besides nepotism, election fraud, selling of positions of power. How serious was the situation can be seen from this statement by him according to official reports:

> In particular, a handful of senior Party officials, overcome by their political cravings and lust for power, have resorted to political conspiracies by working in ostensible obedience, while forming cliques to pursue selfish interests.[10]

One should note that Premier Wen Jiabao was always mentioned along with Hu Jintao and Hu–Wen regime. Currently, Xi was the undisputed leader with Premier Li Keqiang clearly not playing the same kind of role as Wen Jiabao. Not surprisingly, the volume carrying Xi Jinping's selected speeches during 2013–14 is titled *Governance of China*. His many speeches, especially the one titled 'Governing a Big Country Is Like Frying a Small Fish', clearly showed how conscious he was with the present mandate that he had to lead.[11]

The fact that Hu Jintao raised the question of governing capacity of the party and Xi Jinping had gone all out to rebuild the party as a non-corrupt, value-based and effective organization which it had fallen far short of confirms our argument that the party had got into an agency trap. It had become a fairly efficient part of the growth process, but corrupt and incapable of addressing the issues raised in the framework of scientific development, thus alienated from the bulk of the population. Hence, Xi's anti-corruption drive and organizational initiatives could be seen as steps to break out of the agency trap and make the party a transparent, pro-people, effective instrument of participatory development to achieve its goals.

Thus, the party-led system in China needed to be put in perspective so that we can fully comprehend its nature and working.

The Party and the Reforms

The Communist Party's professed objective had been to guide the social process in the direction of socialism and communism. In concrete terms, its duty was to ensure that the policies worked out by the CC were carried out at every level. It did so by supervising the process of decision-making and also through ideological education and propaganda. The promotions and demotions of cadres by and large were made by the party leadership. That role of the party being constant, we have seen three kinds of roles that the party had played before and after the reforms. One, when the party is both the government and the enterprise manager. In other words, the party secretary was also the township director and also manager of an enterprise. In theory, this was the case before the reforms. Even though the party secretary was not always the enterprise leader, he/she was performing a major economic role. As we have discussed earlier, the Third Plenum of 1978 stressed the need of differentiating the three roles. The second situation was what the Third Plenum of 1978 stipulated, namely that the party leader would be a political and ideological leader and would give full autonomy to the local government and the enterprise manager. That was needed because the autonomous manager can then respond to the market situation, take decisions for resource allocation, make production and marketing plans and manage the enterprise keeping those considerations in mind. This situation prevailed in China from 1979 until about 1989, the first decade of reforms. This was the time when rural enterprises bloomed and made a major contribution to the development of the rural economy and the national economy as a whole. The third kind of role was when the enterprise manager was given a special status and the party cadre and the government cadre were following the lead of the managers as the imperatives of economic growth governed the entire system. This was the period when many party cadres were enterprise managers. This trend continued until about 2002 when party cadres were called upon to play a political supervisory role. Still the economic drivers of the polity ruled the system and even when the top leadership under Hu Jintao and Wen Jiabao emphasized the need for pro-people work style and balanced development, the situation in the provinces and below continued to see the dominant role of the economic elite. Many of the party leaders at various levels were business people themselves. Many party leaders had their family members directly managing or owning firms, having stakes in public enterprises or private firms. The linkage with the foreign firms investing in China and Chinese exports to all parts of the globe produced enormous opportunities for the party leaders to make massive profits. Personal relationships and network of alliances—the well-known *guanxi* (relationship) factor in Chinese system—backed by political influence played a major role in getting contracts and launching economic drives. This was a critical factor in achieving growth targets. So 'party as entrepreneur' was a new phenomenon in China. It made China world's second largest economy after the USA. But it also created or accentuated a series of problems.

The Hu–Wen regime acknowledged the magnitude of these challenges and had initiated the process of transforming the nature of the party. But they had not achieved much result. It was left to Xi Jinping to first declare that attaining high growth rate was not the main goal of the CPC, but rejuvenation of the Chinese nation through a strategy of coordinated, balanced, equitable and sustainable development. For this, he revived the idea of the Communist Party as a mass line organization with cadres with honesty and integrity. The anti-corruption campaign therefore was meant not only to punish the corrupt cadres, and establish a transparent and accountable system of governance, but also to reaffirm the political–ideological role of the party. In a way, this was the framework that Deng Xiaoping had envisaged when he spoke of differentiation of the roles of party, government and enterprise. But that was to reduce party interference in day-to-day administration in the government and interference in the enterprise management which had become the practice during the Cultural Revolution. In the case of Xi, having learnt lessons from the past four decades, the policy was to make the party leadership at every level the active participant in decision-making without necessarily ignoring the specialized role of the government cadres and enterprise managers. The drive for building an 'innovation society'—not only in science and technology but also in every sphere that had started under Hu Jintao and re-emphasized by Xi Jinping—and the moral code that Xi has asked all party members and cadres to observe make the new role of the party the leading force in social transformation, rather than either a profit-seeking manager or an apolitical bureaucracy.

If the party's policies had not only led to growth of production and increased peasant income but also reduced disparities with greater involvement of the peasants and workers in the decision-making process, then we could establish that it took China higher up on the freedom scale. The picture however is mixed. Even though agricultural production had grown and peasant income had increased, political participation was very limited at the grass-roots level. The initial years of the commune presented a degree of mass participation. But during the Cultural Revolution, though the slogan was to increase mass participation in decision-making, in practice the head of the commune became even more powerful. The party leadership and the leadership of revolutionary committee became one and the same.

At the local level, the party was to intervene in the rural society by changing the production relations, and it took direct lead in organizing ideological and educational activities. In the early 1950s, the land reforms and the agricultural cooperatives were carried out by the local mass organizations, rather than directly by the party. The commune was also set up as a mass political organ, though under the party leadership. The commune committee and party committee were different. Despite the monopoly of power by the party, its approach was to encourage broader mass involvement. But revolutionary committee during the Cultural Revolution not only blurred the distinction between the party and the State, but it also had representatives of the broader masses in it. Loyalty to the Cultural Revolution line of the party faction at each level was the crucial thing. Thus, factional struggle broke out and the party got isolated from vast sections of the people.

The post-Mao leadership reversed the trend and decided to withdraw the party from government administration and enterprise management. The purpose was to pin responsibility upon administrators and managers so that standing at some distance, the party could evaluate their performance. The assumption was that party interference caused inefficiency. In a system of checks and balances, even though there was greater scope to work efficiently, to work this out in practice was not easy.

From its role in facilitating mass participation in the 1960s, the CPC moved to actively guiding administration and management in the 1970s and then withdrew to a position of external supervision in the 1980s. In a situation of increasing popular demands for democratic rights and dissent, this role increasingly came under scrutiny. Economic policies in the countryside and the general trend of opening up of China to foreigners created a new environment in China.

From the Tiananmen incident in June 1989 until the Fourteenth Congress of the CPC in October 1992, there was considerable debate within the Chinese leadership about the future course of reforms and the role of the party in it. The questions of exercising dictatorship, promoting democratization, the pace of growth of production and the extent of opening up to the outside world and the ideological orientation of the party came for close discussion. There were important domestic and international developments which had serious effects on these debates. The youth movement for democracy had appeared periodically even before the massive demonstrations in the Tiananmen Square. CPC General Secretary Hu Yaobang was removed from his office in January 1987 due to his inability to contain this trend. His successor Zhao Ziyang paid a similar price in the wake of the Tiananmen crisis in June 1989. In labelling the youth demonstrations as 'counter revolutionary rebellion' and crushing it with full military force, the party under Deng Xiaoping's leadership re-established its role as the leading force exercising dictatorship in Chinese society.[12]

The turbulent developments in Eastern Europe in 1990 and the collapse of the Soviet Union in 1991 marked the international climate which the CPC had to cope with. At the time of the Tiananmen demonstrations, there was speculation in the West that the process of collapse of the Chinese Communist regime had begun. One option which some leaders within the CPC seemed to have advocated was that the reforms should be slowed down; international trade and investment curtailed, ideological campaign in Marxism intensified and the party leadership's control over the system strengthened. This line was generally associated with Chen Yun who along with Deng had inaugurated the reforms package at the Third Plenum of the Eleventh CC in 1978. At this point, however, Chen wanted to exercise caution on the nature and pace of reforms. On the other hand, the line associated with Hu Yaobang and Zhao Ziyang envisaged greater liberalization of the polity and the economy. They were for introducing elements of competitive politics in people's congress system, allowing freedom of expression and association, and frank and open debates among intellectuals along with fuller development of the market economy. It is not clear whether they were for giving up the monopoly of power by the CPC.[13]

Deng Xiaoping intervened in this debate and decisively influenced the course of events. This came in the form of Deng's visits to Shenzhen, Wucheng, Zhuhai and Shanghai in January–February 1992. These SEZs were celebrating the tenth anniversary of their founding. Deng not only enthusiastically endorsed the pattern of their development but also gave a call for accelerating the reforms.[14] Deng said,

> [I]f there were no achievements of reform and opening we might not have been able to pass the test of 4 June incident.... The reason our country could continue to be stable after the incident was that Reform and Opening had promoted economic development and had improved people's livelihood and that the Armed Forces and the Government also supported this road, this system and these policies.[15]

This call gave a new momentum to the development of private economy, expansion of foreign investment and the rate of growth. Both Chen Yun and Zhao Ziyang lines were left behind, though certainly their votaries had not disappeared.

It is this perspective which led to the proclamation of the concept of 'socialist market economy' and Deng Xiaoping Theory of 'building socialism with Chinese characteristics' at the Fourteenth Party Congress in October 1992. Deng's formulation suggested that while developing market economy in China, the leadership of the Communist Party and maintaining the State as the 'people's democratic dictatorship' would be emphasized to give a socialist orientation to growth. These political features and the role of the State in microeconomic planning were propounded as some of the 'Chinese characteristics' of market economy.

This perspective permeated right down to the grass-roots level. Developing production, promoting joint enterprises with foreign collaboration became a legitimate part of the development strategy. At the same time, the role of the party cadres was strengthened for accelerating this very economic process.

I could witness the actual operation of this line during my fieldwork in Wuxi and other parts of China in August 1993. As a district-level party leader put it, the Chinese leadership had two guarantees against the Soviet type of collapse—one was the emphasis on increasing people's living standards through growth of production and the other was strict vigilance and control by the Communist Party. The first kept people happy about the system and the second prevented outbreak of disorder right from its inception. The cadre pointed out that Gorbachev had failed on both fronts; on the one hand, the Soviet economy did not deliver the goods so far as the concrete day-to-day needs of Soviet citizens were concerned, and, on the other hand, Glasnost and Perestroika provided outlets to even prompted outbursts of people's discontent, leading to the collapse of the system. Therefore, maintaining stability under party leadership and using full energy for the development of productive forces and people's income levels constituted the new path of China's socialist development. While emphasizing economic development, the party ought to take determined steps to meet people's demands for better livelihood and at the same time pay attention to ethics. For this purpose, there was a need to forcefully develop forces of production to fulfil people's basic needs.

It was this perspective which was further clarified at the CPC Fourth Plenum in September 1994 which announced measures on party building. Jiang Zemin in his closing speech at the Fifth Plenum refined it further in dealing with 12 major relationships, as discussed earlier, highlighting the nature of this phase of China's development. To achieve that, work in a variety of sectors and activities, locally, nationally and internationally, had to be carried on. When Jiang Zemin retired in 2002 leaving his theoretical formulation on Three Represents as a part of the ideological formulation of the CPC, China was on the path of steady economic growth with full mobilization of private capital from home and abroad. And the shift of strategy from rural economy to urban economy, with focus on producing for exports, had been firmly put on track.

As mentioned earlier, the Hu Jintao regime, while maintaining the focus on high rate of growth, began to orient the party towards addressing problems such as rural–urban disparities, rising income inequalities and serious environmental hazards. The Hu–Wen perspective therefore was to combine growth with social and environmental concerns. But the party stayed on the path of high economic growth during most of his tenure. The party acquired global prestige organizing the Olympics in 2008. It successfully handled the global financial crisis of 2008–09 by injecting nearly US$500 billion stimulus package. Inheriting this achievement and the problems, his successor Xi Jinping tried to rebuild the party with many new initiatives giving a new moral–political impetus. How this scenario unfolded at the grass-roots level provides interesting insights into the functioning of this unique party organization.

The Party's Role at the District/County Level

A look at the district-level party affairs indicates that it is a serious checkpoint for monitoring the local political process. Below the district, it is the township which is the active unit supervising the political life of the rural area. The provincial level above the district is concerned with high policies as, for example, it negotiates with the Central government on investments and allocations. But all grants to the townships flow through the district or the county. It is also a key level of promotion for the local cadres. Those who move up quickly to the suburban district or county level may reach the provincial level very fast.

In 1985, the Wuxi suburban district had 7,712 CPC members[16] among its population of 277,000. The membership rose to 8,100 in 1987 when its population was nearly 300,000. The district party structure consisted of the party congress which elected a district party committee which in turn elected a standing committee, a secretary and deputy secretaries. In this case, there was an eight-member standing committee including a secretary and a deputy secretary. (From the district and county levels upwards, there were standing committees because the size of the party committees was large and the standing committee ensured collective authority with continuous functioning.) The district party committee had over 30 members.

The district party committee had under it 10 departments: (a) propaganda, (b) personnel, (c) rural work, (d) discipline inspection, (e) communist youth league, (f) women federations, (g) trade unions, (h) party training, (i) administrative office and (j) militia affairs. Compared with the district government, the district party committee had a different set of activities, leaving the various economic aspects to the former. It may be noted that unlike the district government, the party had a militia affairs department to maintain link with the security forces.

The secretary of the Wuxi Suburban District Party Committee in 1985 was Ding Houxing aged 42. He was holding the post since October 1983 before which he was deputy party secretary and prior to that he was the secretary of a township party committee. This showed the normal channel of mobility of a leader. As was the practice now, the party secretary was not the director of the district government. The director of Wuxi suburban government in 1985 was Rong Dehai aged 38—a college graduate who had been a party secretary of the brigade, then of a commune and finally the deputy director of the district government. He was now also the deputy secretary of the district party committee. Yet, another deputy secretary-level leader was a 41-year-old female member of the party committee who was in charge of the Discipline Inspection Commission of the district. She had been a township party secretary before.

By the middle of 1993, there were some changes at the suburban level. Now the party membership had increased to nearly 15,000, of which about 30 per cent were women. (Note the reference to 30 per cent of women membership in many places.) The Wuxi Suburban District Party Committee now had 21 members; only 5 of them were women. Since the party committee at that level was large, it had a standing committee of nine members in charge of day-to-day work. It should be noted that there were no women in the standing committee. In fact, as one looks at the higher levels of the party and government, women's representation seems to be less and less. The average age of the party committee was 45 years. The educational level of old party members was not high. Most of the leaders had passed only senior middle school or had obtained vocational training. The party congress consisted of 20 per cent of the members as representatives. The suburban district sent 11 representatives to the Wuxi city Party Congress. Since Hela was a medium-level success story, the successful townships of the suburban district seemed to have greater say at the district level.

There was mobility of the party leadership in the region, though the pace was slow. Zhang Weinan who was the township director during 1985–87 had moved up to become a district cadre in 1992. The former party secretary of Hela Township Bao Tie Zhong was new deputy secretary of the suburban district party committee. Another former party secretary of the township Cao Shukun was now vice-director in charge of general affairs, an important responsibility at the district level.

The suburban party committee played a key role in the appointments to the various posts in the district. All the directors of government departments were first nominated by the party committee and then approved by the district people's congress. In making the recommendations, the district party leadership consulted its higher level as well. In addition, the party performed its important role of political and ideological education and monitoring the overall political economy. But during the 1980s, it refrained from directly involving itself in the administrative and the economic activities.

But strict separation of the party from the government and management spheres was impossible because the government leaders and enterprise managers were members of the party committee at their respective levels. What it only meant was that party secretaries would no longer interfere in day-to-day functioning. However, discussion and evaluation of work took place in the party forums. Within this framework, the district party leadership supervised the work at the township level. However, by the mid-1990s, the pattern of party–government interaction was clear. The party was to lead economic work directly and exercise political control over the region.

The membership of the suburban district party had risen to 30,000 in 1996. This was a significant increase due to the fact that while old members did not retire, many new members had joined. The new members were more educated and in the age group of 21–35. The suburban party committee continued to have 11 members which included the director and a deputy director of the suburban district government. The party committee had one general secretary and three deputy general secretaries. The party committee had four departments: publicity, discipline inspection, organization (personnel) and security forces. When I met the suburban district leaders in October 1996, the impact of the Sixth Plenum was most visible. The focus on cultural and civilizational dimensions of socialism was the talk of the day. The party members were discussing measures to combat drugs, gambling and prostitution, which had posed serious dangers to society. Their major concern was to pay equal attention to cultural and economic issues of development. Fighting evil influence of decadent Western ideas was also in the air. This viewpoint was put into the larger framework that was presented at the Fifteenth Party Congress in 1997.

Township Party Committee

Significance of the township party committee lies in the fact that it is the critical rural unit, guiding production as well as administration. The party secretary in a Chinese township is the main leader in the area.[17]

In 1979, the Hela Commune had a total party membership of 678 who had elected 103 representatives to the party congress in 1977. The ratio was about one delegate for seven party members. The township party committee which had 17 members included 1 secretary and 4 deputy secretaries. A rough break-up of the party membership put 400 from agriculture, 40 from commerce, 50 from education and cultural circles and over 100 from industries. (In 1969, the party members in Hela numbered only about 300 and in 1959; they were just above 50 according to Liu Weiping.) Most of the present members were young. Nearly half (47 per cent) were below 30 years, 30 per cent below 50 and the rest 20 per cent over 50.

As per the Cultural Revolution practice, the party committee secretary was the chair of the commune revolutionary committee. But by the middle of 1979, the Hela Party Secretary Wu Decheng was already under criticism for his errors. The Senior Deputy Secretary Liu Weiping was the acting head of the commune as well.

By 1980, there was not much change in the party structure of Hela. Liu Weiping continued as the leader with his formal position still the same, deputy secretary of party committee. He was now called deputy director of the commune management committee. The party membership had risen to 800, perhaps after the readmission of many disgraced members and entry of new young members. The commune party committee membership had come down to 11, starting a trend towards smaller committees. The commune leaders were preparing to convene the commune party congress. They were studying the documents and directives of the central leadership. The leaders studied them first and discussed among themselves. Then they would discuss with party members. Talk of the year was 'to raise the standard of each party member'. It was stressed that 'to guarantee the smooth march of four modernizations, the party had to play a very important role'. The tune played by the Centre, however, was somewhat different at the time. The Centre stressed the separation of the party from administration and enterprise management. The commune party leaders were beginning to mention it, but they did not seem to fully comprehend it. This was accomplished by 1982 and in 1985, the party was playing a different role.

In 1985, the township had 667 party members according to the township director Zhang Weinan. It showed a fall but not necessarily due to expulsion of those criticized for 'leftist' activities during the Cultural Revolution. In the course of the 'party consolidation movement', some may have been stripped of their membership. But the more important reason may be the inclusion of some part of the population in the city register. Hence, some party members would have been listed under their organizations in the city. The township party members would be those who are engaged in township and village economic activities.

The Hela Township Party Committee was now even smaller in size with only seven members including a secretary and a deputy secretary. Party secretary Zhou Shikun was a State cadre earlier who had been transferred to

Hela from another township in June 1984. They were elected at the township party congress in December 1982 for a three-year term. The party congress had 45 representatives elected by the party members. Hela Township Party Congress had sent 6 representatives to the suburban district party congress and one to the provincial party congress.

In 1987, a more complete picture of the township party structure was available. The township party secretary, township director and deputy directors as well as others in the township provided many details to me. By 1987, the Hela Township had an increase in party membership to 825 with more than one-fourth, that is, 217 female members. The rise in the women membership was confirmed by the former chair of women federation, presently a deputy director of the township. This was partly because of new employment opportunities for women in the expanding rural industries and partly because of effective mobilization by an active women leadership.

The age break-up of the members went as follows:

Up to 25 years	16 members
26–35 years	175 members
36–50 years	340 members
51–60 years	144 members
Above 60 years	150 members
Total	825 members

It should be pointed out that even though nearly 300 party members were above 50 years of age, a large majority were below that age. The 36–50 age group 10 years ago would be the 26–40 group which would have been very active during the Cultural Revolution. But they had now come up as beneficiaries of the rural reforms. The stress on the youth was visible in the new age classification making 25 and 35 as dividing lines. Close to 35 were the most favoured cadres for important responsibilities.

The educational composition of the party membership had improved considerably too:

With university education (meaning college attended)	18
Higher Middle School (*Gao Zhong Xue*) and Technical Middle School	226
Middle-school Graduates	340
Lower Middle-school Graduates (*Xiao Xue*)	241
Total	825

The number of those educated in college had increased as also the number of higher secondary graduates. Still a vast number, 231, had attended only until lower middle, that is, sixth class level of education. For peasants, this was not unusual. But for a suburban district, this was a big number. It was expected that in an economically advanced area like Wuxi, the party members would have a higher educational level. But there was a paradox. The reform policies, on the one hand, talked about raising educational standards. On the other hand, the rural industries absorbed young people of the villages after they passed the middle school, giving them higher wages than university graduates!

As of 1993, party membership in Hela Township had expanded still further to 1,163—in other words, a rise of 41 per cent since 1987 when it stood at 825 people only. The percentage of women had increased too. Whereas it was 25 per cent in 1987, now women constituted 38 per cent of the membership. The average age was 45 years, indicating a significant level of recruitment of young people into the party. The member of representatives to the party congress of the township had now increased significantly from 45 to 252 with an average age of 35 years. The tenure of the township party congress was three years and it met twice every year. Of these representatives, 30 per cent were women. Hela had its township-level party elections in December 1992 which elected a new township party committee.

The township party committee continued to be small, though now slightly increased from seven to nine members. Besides the secretary, the party committee had now two deputy secretaries, one of whom was the township director. There were two female members in the township party committee, one of whom was the chair of the women federation.

The township party committee in 1987 had eight members, which was one more than in 1985. Besides one secretary—it was now Bao Tiezhong—it had two deputy secretaries, one of them being the township director Zhang Weinan. The other was Chu Hongzhou who was reported as studying at the Suburban District Party School. (Chu was a school teacher before joining the organization department of the suburban district from where he was transferred to the township.) The remaining five members were (a) one of the deputy directors of the township who was in charge of the township industry department, (b) member in charge of the organization department, (c) a member in charge of discipline inspection, (d) a member in charge of personnel affairs (appointments and related matters) and (e) an advanced cadre. While the district had separate departments in charge of discipline inspection and organization, the township party committee had a member in charge of each. The close link of the party with the township administration was another noticeable feature. Besides the township director, the vice-director in charge of industry was a member. It reflected the fact that industry was a key area of the rural development at the current stage.

Hela Township Party Committee
2 Main Branches
(*Zong Zhibu*)
46 Party Branches
(*Dang Zhibu*)

The party organization was not exclusively territorial. There were territorial units as well as units in enterprises and organizations. In those places where there were at least 50 party members, there was a main branch. In places where there were at least three members, there was a party branch. There was one main branch for the township-level departments and one for the village-level departments. There were 20 branches in factories, 4 for members engaged in agriculture, 4 in the various companies, 7 for members in culture, education and health affairs and 12 other branches. Each branch had a branch secretary as leader. Each branch met twice a month to review economic and political work, study the higher party directive and plan future tasks.

The main branch was a new party institution introduced in 1987. (According to the township party secretary, this did not exist before because their educational level was not advanced.) Between the township committee and the small party branch they, perhaps needed an intermediate level to discuss party affairs. But at the same time, this could increase the points of control.

Meeting in December 1984, the township party congress with its 45 representatives had elected the township party committee for a three-year period. Zhou Shikun was replaced by Bao Tiezhong as party secretary. These elections and replacements were clearly done on the direction of the higher party authorities. Zhou later became deputy director of the Wuxi suburban government. Zhou was also first appointed township party secretary in May 1984 but confirmed by the party congress at the end of that year. He was promoted to the district post in March 1987 and Bao succeeded him. Bao's confirmation by the party congress was to follow.

The list of leaders of Hela Party Committee since the formation of the people's commune in 1958 indicated several interesting trends (see Table 5.2). Firstly, not a single leader continued for a very long time to be able to acquire a strong personal power base. They were either promoted to the district or transferred to another commune or township. Only one

Table 5.2:
Party secretaries of Hela

Year	Name	Position Later Held
1958	Wu Zhao	Deputy Mayor of Wuxi
Thereafter but time not specified	Ding Weicheng	
1965	Ding Shuxia	
1967	Wu Wenhe	Secretary General of Chong'an District Party Committee
1969	Xi Zhide	Director of Mashan District Government
1975	Xia Tingyi	Director of Wuxi Suburban District Bank
1978	Wu Decheng	'Committed Mistakes, Now an Ordinary Cadre'
1983	Zhu Yunan (acting)	Shanbei Township Member, Inspection and Research
1984	Du Guobing	Director, Town Management, Wuxi Suburban District
1985	Zhou Shikun	Deputy Secretary, Wuxi Suburban District Party Committee
1987	Zhang Weinan	Deputy Director, Wuxi Suburban Government
1992	Huang Guiliang	

Source: Information collected through interviews with local cadres in Wuxi.

secretary was identified as having committed mistakes and therefore had now become an ordinary cadre. Not all details were available about all the leaders. But the list with a few details was still interesting.

The fact that the township director was only deputy secretary of the township party committee put him below the party secretary. But their actual relations depended on the personality of the leaders, their political backing at higher levels and the party's policy of the moment. In the 1980s, in Hela, the township director seemed to enjoy better status because of his/her contacts with the higher leadership. Both Liu Weiping and Zhang Weinan had powerful personality and because of their proven expertise in fisheries and local administration, both commanded good deal of influence. Moreover, the party's post-1978 policy was to stress on production and show economic results, so the administrative head enjoyed more autonomy. But in the post-Tiananmen climate, the party functionaries' role acquired more importance.

In most matters, both the leaders, the township director and party secretary, took decisions collectively. But sometimes differences persisted.

That was the reason why there were frequent changes of party secretaries in Hela. As a township director put it: 'This was a shortcoming of our structure; it could be resolved if political and ideological work was unified'. What he perhaps meant was that there should be one person in charge.

The new party secretary of Hela Township in 1993 was Huang Guiliang since December 1992. Huang was the director of Hela Township for three years prior to that and one of the vice-directors in charge of industry and commerce previously. Prior to taking up a township-level office, Huang was the party secretary of Longshan village in the same township. Unlike his predecessors who had not gone to the university and had trained themselves on the job, Huang had graduated from Suzhou University in the neighbouring city of Suzhou in 1989 as a part-time student. The other members of the township party committee as usual included the director of the township and two of the vice-directors. The other five were party cadres in charge of discipline inspection, organizational affairs, propaganda and militia affairs. The secretary of Hela village (one of the 13 villages of Hela Township) Madam Wang Shuzhen was also a member of the party committee.

The composition of the party committee and the allocation of work were clearly oriented towards economic performance. Asked about the focus of party work, invariably the cadres and members mentioned the shift of focus from class struggle to economic reconstruction as was decided in the Third Plenum of 1978. There was even a change of accent in the post-1992 period compared to the role of the party in the 1980s. Earlier, the party was a watchdog and a guide, whereas the reforms were carried out by managers of enterprises and the township director. After 1992, the party directly undertook economic management and administrative tasks. In many enterprises, the party secretary was also the factory manager. After 4 June incident of 1989, the party's ideological role to oppose bourgeois liberalization was stressed and had created an atmosphere of caution in economic work. But after Deng's southern tour in early 1992 and the Fourteenth Party Congress, the great majority of party members showed enthusiasm for more active initiative in economic work. Cadres, who were hesitant beforehand, now took bold steps inviting foreign capital, promoting private business and diversifying production.

The principle of differentiation of party, government and enterprise management still operated in theory. Party leaders insisted that they did not interfere in the management of enterprises and that they only gave advice and evaluated the latter's performance. They pointed out that in the past, whenever a party member made mistakes, he/she was penalized. The new work style was to encourage party members to make bold experiments and, in the case of mistakes, help them to learn and improve. There was no case of severe punishment as in the past. According to the township party authorities, in 1993, only three members had been expelled during the previous year on charges of economic crime or sexual misdemeanour. As Zhang Weinan puts it, 'For sometime we have to continue with the interlinked system uniting Party, Government and Management to achieve our economic and political goals, eventually however they should be differentiated'.[18] All indications pointed at this temporary arrangement continuing for a long time.

The township party membership had risen to 1,200 in 1996, 30 per cent of whom were reported to be women. There were 48 party branches in all, 1 each in the 13 villages and the remaining in the relatively large enterprises. At the township party congress held in 1995, a new party secretary, Cao Yongnian, was elected; he was formerly the director of Hela Township. The strength of the township party committee remained the same at 11 which included 2 women as before. As usual, there were two deputy secretaries, one the township director and another in charge of political affairs.

As at the national level, the party congress always preceded the people's congress; at the township level too, the township party secretary presented the political report, giving an assessment of the previous year's performance and proposal for the forthcoming years' economic development. The central theme of the secretary's report in 1995 was that party's work should focus on economic development. This theme had continued throughout the reform period as the central focus in the 'one focus, two points' framework. But the party was entrusted with political and ideological work all the time. After 1992, when 'socialist market economy' was announced as the guiding framework, the party units were called upon to take economic development as their main ideological work. But at the same time, party–government differentiation was stressed as was government–enterprise differentiation. Enterprises were to be fully autonomous and respond to the market in their production activity. Government's main task was overall supervision, guaranteeing the value of fixed assets and increasing the value. The government was to ensure that the social situation should be stable and compatible with economic development. It was also expected to look after social welfare, education health and cultural needs of people. The party on the other hand while taking economic development as its principal preoccupation was concerned with ideological issues such as socialist market economy, Deng Xiaoping Theory of building socialism with Chinese characteristics, etc., besides policy-making and deciding on personnel. It would be noted that major appointments, transfers and promotion were made by the party leadership rather than the government. Even when enterprise managers were appointed, the enterprise party committee and the township party leadership played a role.

Thus, the party's role during the reform period has undergone changes from time to time. In the early 1980, the township director assumed relatively greater importance. In the later 1980s, the enterprise managers emerged as the key decision-makers with the party secretary and the township director losing political prominence. In the 1990s, the political order at the grass-roots level crystallized unambiguously, placing the party leadership in command followed by the township director and then the enterprise managers. The enterprise managers may earn more—actually most of them earn far more than the township director and the party secretary—but the political authority of the party committee especially the party secretary was at the top of township politics. In actual practice, they have to follow the national policy and central leadership's directives and show results in their economic performance. Therefore, they are dependent on each other. The party leadership alone could secure resources and approval from above. The township administration, especially the director, coordinated the overall economy of the villages and the enterprises and also had access to the higher-level suburban district and city governments. Above all, the enterprise managers had to show profit in their enterprises, in the absence of which the township director and the party secretary would be blamed for lack of results in the township. All of them were now subjected to the overall sociopolitical environment in the township and the suburban district as well as in the city as a whole. Peasants, workers, business people and technologists had now got related to one another through a variety of interest groups. The prosperous farmers, entrepreneurs and managers now constituted the powerful stratum in the rural areas with links at the party and the government levels. It was no longer the earlier situation of the party-led mass organizations, the trade union, peasant association, youth league and women's federation; while peasant associations disappeared after the commune period, the other three continued to exist. But they were wings of the party and not autonomous organizations.

In the new environment, therefore, the political leadership had to be responsive to the demands coming from various groups. Despite the mutual consultation framework between the CPC and the other parties and non-party groups and individuals, CPC at every level remained the final arbiter. Therefore, all demand groups tried to enter the party to achieve their objectives. Upcoming entrepreneurs and engineers aspired to become party members and party cadres. This was the new phenomenon in China, visible at the grass-roots level. The enterprise manager was also party secretary in many cases as I observed in the 1990s. They were also the new rich in the villages. The principle of party taking economic development as its central task had meant that the emerging prosperous elements in the society acquired crucial positions in the party. In prosperous Hela Township, the CPC cadres were also the economic elite.

There was the ideological campaign launched by the Sixth Plenum of the CPC in 1996 and reiterated by Jiang Zemin at the Fifteenth Party Congress in 1997 to orient these strata towards 'socialist ethics with Chinese characteristics'. Reviewing the party's initiative to 'comprehensively cover' society as a national model for party building, the emergences of non-governmental organizations (NGOs), party-organized NGOs (PONGOs) and a hybrid of civic groups and professional charitable organizations had started taking welfare activities/provisions under the aegis of party control. They not only depended on sponsorship but also supported local party committees and maintained active internal party cells that recruit and perform other core tasks.[19] In fact, the ubiquitous role of the party vis-à-vis the civil society in contemporary China produced a new trend of governance. Party cadre as the manager–entrepreneur leading the economic growth with full mobilization of social forces combining the elements of State, party and society was the phenomenon of the 1990s and 2000s. It did achieve spectacular economic growth, but it also saw social differentiation and high degree of corruption from the village to the top echelons of society, economy and polity. It is this situation that Hu Jintao began to address and Xi Jinping confronted with blunt initiatives.

Local and the National

From the days of Mao Zedong and Deng Xiaoping to the regime of Xi Jinping, there is one feature of the Chinese Communist Party which is common, namely the aspiration to encourage the local energy and initiative of people and provide them autonomy in the functioning of the system while at the same time demanding compliance with the central directives. This dialectic takes different forms in different times and in different areas. The talk of autonomy is not just on paper. The mass line principle of 'from the masses to the masses' is fairly internalized in the CPC's party culture. But power politics does play its role with interests, factions and opinion groups operating in full steam to mobilize their support base and get their interests fulfilled. So the 'unitary state' as stipulated in the PRC Constitution is a reality, while it is well known that provinces and counties in China exercise a great deal of autonomy.

The Constitutional system does provide autonomy, but the party rule centralizes the power process. Neither statement is a full description of the reality on the ground. The autonomy of the local leadership depends upon the economic resources of the region and political influence of a leader that region enjoys at the higher level. This is where the differences between the Communist Party regime and liberal democratic regimes almost disappear. However, there are times when a regime takes special interest in granting more autonomy to the grass-roots units. During the 1980s, when rural economy was booming with rural industries spearheading the trend of prosperity, there was a great deal of autonomy enjoyed by the townships and villages. In the 1990s, the drive to fulfil growth targets was so strong that the central directives ruled the system. During the early years of the Hu–Wen regime, especially during 2002–07, prior to the global financial crisis, there was a clear attempt to revive the rural economy, allowing more initiative to the local governments. But after 2008, this trend subsided and there was greater emphasis on central coordination to maintain a certain tempo of economic growth. Xi Jinping's policies of anti-corruption involving some major departures in policy such as on land rights, *hukou* reform and shift away from the one-child policy to two-children policy and the 'four comprehensives' in general involved centralized coordination. The anti-corruption drive, one of his trademark initiatives, made the CCDI go down to the provinces, counties, districts, townships and even villages. This was a different kind of centralization to build responsible, honest, efficient governance at every level. But it was centralization nevertheless, and it made local units extremely anxious and vulnerable.

It is this party-led State machinery which has been the main agency of China's success story. But these very successes prevent it from transforming itself into an effective agency of democratic transformation despite many serious initiatives such as those taken by Xi Jinping. Functional achievements of a stability-centric, centralized political system had its own problems resulting in the 'agency trap'. This experience we find in even greater detail in specific areas of society and people's lives such as the political economy of TVEs.

Notes and References

1. State theory has evolved in creative ways in recent years to note complex characteristics of the power process and interaction among economic, social, cultural and political forces. See Manoranjan Mohanty, *Contemporary Indian Political Theory* (New Delhi: Sanskriti, 2000).

2. Li Junru, a leading theoretician of the CPC, explains the annual protocol of policy-making. At the start of the new year, the CPC's politburo decides the focus of the task for the year and sets up study groups who submit their suggestions to the 'document drafting group'. A policy draft is put before the public for seeking widest possible suggestions both in social media and by conducting meetings at the local unit levels. On the basis of the suggestions received, the politburo formulates a proposal for the CC which holds an annual plenum in the last quarter of the year. At the plenum, the policy guideline is finalized and adopted. On that basis, the State Council and NPC Standing Committee pass the decrees and laws. Li Junru, *Everything You Want to Know about the Communist Party of China* (Beijing: Foreign Languages Press, 2012), 113–34.

3. The full quotation from Mao Zedong is usually never cited: 'Every communist must grasp the truth, "political power grows out of the barrel of a gun", our principle is that the party commands the gun and the gun must never be allowed to command the party'. Mao Zedong, 'Problems of War and Strategy', in *Selected Works of Mao Zedong*, vol. 2 (Beijing: Foreign Languages Press, 1965), 224.

4. *Resolution on CPC History (1949–1981)* recorded the evaluation of the Deng leadership of Mao. See Manoranjan Mohanty, 'Power of History'.

5. *Deng Xiaoping Theory of building socialism with Chinese characteristics*, therefore, has become a part of the key ideological line of CPC cited next to Mao Zedong Thought. See the report on Deng Xiaoping's daughter Deng Nan's speech in *South China Morning Post*, 'How My Father's Speeches Saved China's Economic Reforms'. Available at: http://www.scmp.com/news/china/article/1578453/how-my-fathers-speeches-saved-chinese-economic-reform-deng-xiaopings (accessed on 19 April 2017).

6. Jiang Zemin, *On the Three Represents* (Beijing: Foreign Languages Press, 2001). This is also a part of the CPC ideological line as 'the important thought of Three Represents' mentioned after Deng Theory in the CPC Constitution.

7. Xi Jinping, 'Improve Party Conduct, Uphold Integrity and Combat Corruption', 436–41.

8. Xi Jinping, 'Strictly Enforce Diligence and Thrift, Oppose Extravagance and Waste' in *The Governance of China* (Beijing: Foreign Languages Press, 2014), 399.

9. *Xinhua*, 'Xi Spells out the Party Codes on Strict Governance', *Xinhua*, 2 November 2016. Available at: http://news.xinhuanet.com/english/2016-11/03/c_135801399.htm (accessed on 19 April 2017).

10. Ibid. He went on to list Zhou Yongkang, Bo Xilai, Guo Boxiong, Xu Caihou and Ling Jihua as examples of such behaviours, citing both their economic and political misdeeds. It is implicit that similar officials were still around, engaged in conspiracies and corrupt practices.

11. 'As the people have given me this job, I must always keep them in the highest place in my heart, bearing in mind their deep trust and the heavy responsibilities that they have placed on me', Xi Jinping, *The Governance of China*, 458.

12. Chen Xitong, 'Report on Checking the Turmoil and Quelling the Counterrevolutionary Rebellion', *Xinhua*, in FBIS-CHI, 6 July 1989, 20–36.

13. See Zhu Jiamu, 'Chen Yun and Deng Xiaoping in the Initial Stage of Reform and Opening-up' Available at: http://www.cssn.cn/upload/2013/01/d20130111154110755.pdf (accessed on 8 June 2017).

14. Michael E. Marti, *China and the Legacy of Deng Xiaoping: From Communist Revolution to Capitalist Evolution* (Dulles, VA: Potomac Books Inc., 2002), 103.

15. Ibid.

16. This and the subsequent account of the party organization and functioning at the district and township levels are based on my field notes and interviews with various cadres.

17. If compared to India, the township party secretary combined the power and prestige of the block development officer and the panchayat samiti's elected chair. The big difference is that all the panchayat samiti leaders may not belong to the same party in India, whereas they are the CPC cadres in Chinese townships.

    For comparative studies, see Manoranjan Mohanty, George Mathew, Richard Baum, and Rong Ma, eds., *Grass-roots Democracy in India and China* (New Delhi: SAGE Publications, 2009).

18. Interview with the author in June 1987.

19. Patricia M. Thornton, 'The Advance of the Party: Transformation or Takeover of the Urban Grassroots Society', *The China Quarterly* 213 (March 2013): 2–3.

PART 3

Effects on People

6

TVEs as Catalysts in China's Success Story: Why Were They Abandoned?

After having a macro view of the evolution of the reform strategy and a micro picture of a rural area that underwent rapid urbanization and with an understanding of the way the State and the Communist Party operated in contemporary China at both the national and the local levels, we now examine some important aspects of the reform process in the rural society and economy. For that, we focus on one experience that once was the catalytic force for bringing about a dynamic transformation of not only the rural economy but also the country as a whole. This was the phenomenon of TVEs whose rise had shown enormous promise with a possible way out of the success trap. It had energized the growth process, raised peasant income by creating employment opportunities, supported public health and education and facilitated a degree of political participation. The subsequent policy to abandon its strategic role, in my view, caused widening rural–urban inequality, decline of social infrastructure in the countryside, rural unemployment, distress migration and many other serious problems.

TVEs as Catalysts in the Countryside

Why Were TVEs Important?

Reducing urban–rural gap and providing decent living conditions to people in both the cities and the countryside have been the aspirations of all modern societies. European Industrial Revolution presented the model of development that promoted a path of urbanization and migration of the rural population to cities. That perspective dominated the thinking of many leaders of developing countries. But there was another outlook, especially in Asian countries, which advocated transforming the countryside into units of self-governance, promoting in them equitable and sustainable development, making rural and urban interdependent on one another. Politics and economics of both these perspectives had been debated in India and China during the freedom struggle as well as after Independence. As the process of globalization spread in the 1990s, the urbanization and megacity ideology won the day, and the perspective of self-governing villages was relegated to the background. In India, though panchayats and urban local bodies acquired constitutional status in 1993, under the new global economic environment, they mainly became mechanisms of delivery of services rather than units of self-development.[1] In China, the people's communes reflected that outlook together with a drive to achieve ambitious targets in industrialization. As we have seen, for various reasons they were disbanded with the onset of reforms. But the perspective of developing rural and urban areas simultaneously continued to guide the first two decades of reforms. That experience is analysed here to show how the TVEs contributed significantly to the success story of China. Their decline from the late 1990s onwards became one of the reasons that created the rural crisis. The Thirteenth FYP of China which was adopted by the NPC in March 2016 focused on creating domestic demands. It was an irony that precisely this had been done when the TVEs were in their peak of success in the 1980s and early 1990s with increased peasant income and a thriving market in the countryside. TVEs provided employment to the surplus rural labour, raised peasant incomes substantially, provided support for the social sector development and contributed to financing of agriculture and rural infrastructure. After 1992, the new growth strategy shifted attention to urban enterprises and increasing production, targeting the global market. By 2000, the TVEs had lost their central role, rural development strategy of the 1980s had collapsed and the rural crisis was evident. The three rural problems were discussed everywhere. The rural–urban income gap had widened to over 1:3, with China becoming one of the world's most unequal societies. The fast-developing export-led economy, no doubt, raised China's GDP to an unprecedented high level, but with a cost, not only of social and regional inequalities but also increasing environmental degradation and multi-level corruption. Abandoning the TVEs meant seriously neglecting the countryside. So, the discussion on TVEs and the rural development strategy of the first decade and half of the reform period takes us directly to examining the development path that evolved during the reform period as a whole.

In this chapter, we discuss the rationale underlying the TVEs, get a concrete picture from some case studies and then examine the functioning of trade unions in these enterprises.

Rationale for TVEs

One of the notable developments in China's countryside in the 1980s was the expansion of rural industries which significantly contributed to the increase in peasant income.[2] Shortly after the rural reforms were launched in 1979, the government encouraged the commune (renamed *xiang* or township) and the production brigade (renamed *cun* or village) to set up rural enterprises under collective ownership at their respective levels. Later, many private enterprises and shareholding cooperatives also came up. Earlier, during the commune period (1958–78) too, diversification of rural economy had included a certain degree of industrialization. But the policy at that time had a focus on food grain production followed by sideline productions which were mainly animal husbandry and fishing. Those industries which were relevant to agricultural mechanization and food processing were also set up in many communes. In the 1980s, however, there was a big push towards setting up of rural enterprises to produce any kind of goods which would earn profit.[3] Interior townships started producing mainly consumer goods to cater to the demand in the local market. The enterprises of the suburban townships and villages in addition to producing consumer goods also started producing spare parts for the city factories. Enterprises in both suburbs and interior counties entered into contracts with city firms for processing their products or supplying spare parts of other inputs.

By the middle of the 1980s, the expansion of rural industries in China reached a high point. In 1987, the output value of rural industries surpassed the output value of agriculture. This trend contained thereafter, achieving still higher results.

The Chinese government's policy on rural industries was governed by three considerations: (a) utilization of agricultural surplus, mostly the savings of the collective at the local level; (b) generation of employment by expanded economic activity and absorbing surplus labour released from agriculture and (c) close integration of agriculture with industry and services as well as urban economy with rural economy.[4] As a result of the increase in the procurement prices of food grains by the State in 1979, the income of the peasants had suddenly increased. Under the family contract, production responsibility system, they worked hard to produce more and earn more profit. Peasants now had opportunities to buy new household goods and build houses and also make savings. The surplus available with the township and village was used to set up new industries.

Before proceeding further, we may pause to note how the term TVE came to be used in China. During the commune period the term used was rural industry or rural enterprises. From 1978 onwards, especially in the early 1980s, the two layers of the rural collectives, namely township and under it the village, were encouraged to set up enterprises. They were mainly collectively owned and managed. So, in 1984, the central leadership of CPC described them as TVEs. As we shall see later in this chapter, the trend of privatization grew fast and in provinces such as Guangdong and Zhejiang, private enterprises flourished. So, strictly speaking, they were no more township- and village-owned TVEs. But the phenomenon of rural enterprises spread so widely that the term TVE stuck, and the 1996 law on TVEs reflected it. But by 2000, the character of the rural enterprises had changed so fundamentally that the small and micro enterprises—SMEs—which was the term used globally, entered the official parlance in China.

In the 1980s, however, the rationale for TVEs was persuasive. While the peasants were asked to make a success of agricultural production on the pieces of land allotted to their families, the collectives focused their attention on industries. During the commune period, too, brigades and communes had owned and operated industries. But the overall framework of their operation was different. The scale was small and the funding was mainly out of the accumulation fund of the production teams. In the 1980s, it was a large-scale expansion of rural enterprises.[5] They procured their capital partly from their own fund and partly as loan from the banks with low interest as an incentive. This capital was to be used for making profit by an autonomous enterprise. The enterprises were exempted from paying taxes to the State for the first three years. In the course of their production, the enterprises made profits, a part of which was used for their own expansion. In the process, the income of the farmers continued to grow. The average income of Chinese peasants was 134 yuan in 1978 which rose to 1,926 yuan in 1996 with as much as 30.61 per cent coming from non-agriculture as against 7.92 per cent in 1978.[6]

Rural industries were a major channel of employment in the countryside. The household contract system of agriculture had released a significant proportion of labour from agriculture which had been underemployed during the commune period. At that time, all working members of the family used to report for work to the production team leader who would allot work to them in various places. Migration from one commune to another was difficult and migration to the city needed permission of the higher authorities. In the new context, a family would deploy only the minimum necessary amount of labour on the field and seek other avenues of employment for the rest of the members in the city. In the rural enterprises or in other self-employed pursuits, they would try to avail additional sources of income for the family. The rural enterprises thus provided a significant avenue for the released rural labour, especially for the youth. During the 1980s, the rural enterprises absorbed over 100 million rural labourers. However, this was only half of the total surplus labour in rural China. Even though the problem of potential unemployment for the rest remained, still the rural enterprises made a major contribution to the solution of this.

During the commune period, too, there was a linkage between rural and urban economies. But the rural income remained depressed. Because of the tight boundaries of rural and urban areas, their mutual reinforcement was not smooth. In the reforms framework, the two economies were linked through various channels. Rural industries now processed products of bigger enterprises of the city or produced semi-finished goods for them. Through them, the urban and rural economies interacted with each other. Most of the workers in the rural industries belonged to peasant families. Thus, their income from the enterprises contributed partly to the agricultural investments by their respective families on their pieces of land and partly towards raising the purchasing power of the peasants for buying industrial goods.

A new pattern of interaction between the city and the village economies began to take shape. Many city-educated technicians found employment in the rural enterprises. Peasants welcomed them because by using their skills, the peasant's own income would grow. The rural enterprises diversified their products and established connections with foreign firms. They would get semi-finished goods from abroad which they would process and market their finished products within China or abroad.

Political leadership at the urban and rural levels was now closely coordinated with each other, so also at the levels of industrial activity and agricultural activity. When rural China began to show better results, not only did the terms of trade between industry and agriculture begin to alter in a direction favourable to agriculture but also China's peasantry became a source of legitimacy for the Chinese political system. The expansion of rural industries along with the growth of agriculture production contributed significantly to this process. There were, no doubt, several problems. The rural industries experienced a mushroom growth in an unplanned way in most cases, consuming enormous amount of energy and producing goods of doubtful quality. Suddenly, they found no buyers for some of their products. Numerous anomalies appeared in wage and personnel policy. However, it has to be acknowledged that the rural industries contributed enormously to the growth of peasant prosperity and development of rural economy.

According to a report published by China's Ministry of Agriculture at the end of 1991, during the Seventh FYP (1980–90), nearly 31.5 per cent of the net increase in national social product and 67 per cent of the net increase in total rural social product were contributed by rural enterprises. Moreover, 50 per cent of the net increase in taxes also came from these enterprises, even though generally their tax rate was lower than the city enterprises. Many of the products of the rural enterprises were exported. This trend also had grown further and 30 per cent of the net increase of export earnings came from them during the Seventh Plan. What is more, over half of the increase in net per capita income for farmers resulted from the rural enterprises. As of 1991, over 60 per cent of the total rural social product was contributed by rural enterprises. They possessed fixed assets worth 400 billion yuan which amounted to over 80 per cent of total fixed assets in rural areas. Out of the 18 million rural enterprises in China, 60,000 units were exporting their products. The foreign exchange earned by them accounted for one-fourth of the country's total. Another indicator of their significance was that as of 1991, as much as 30 per cent of China's national income was contributed by the rural industries.[7]

Characteristics of TVEs

The term TVEs is widely used in the English language writings on China during the reform period, referring to the rural enterprises at the township (*xiang*) level and the village (*cun*) level. In Chinese, however, the literature refers to *xiang zhen qiye* or enterprises at the level of *xiang* or township and *zhen*, the comparable rural town. Below them are located the *cun*- or village-level enterprises.

There were several characteristics of the township enterprises.[8] Firstly, the initiative to set up an enterprise is taken by the township or the village itself. The local peasants and their leaders in the local government together decide about the launching and management of an enterprise. Secondly, the local government uses its own capital for investment in rural enterprises, and the enterprises use their own capital accumulation for their expansion. After 1985, the enterprises not only used their own funds but also started taking bank loans for their modernization and expansion. During the third phase in the 1990s, they went for many other kinds of investment such as shareholding and joint ventures. Thirdly, the enterprises are responsible for their own profits and losses. In that way, they are different from SOEs. Just as they were autonomous in decision-making in production, they had to fend for themselves in terms of their performance, by responding to the market. In the 1990s, many enterprises went out of business because they could not withstand market competition. The local government also did not come to their rescue except when it thought of intervening to make it a profitable concern. Fourthly, rural enterprises were part of a diversified economy. All rural enterprises were not industries. Besides industry, they engaged in commerce, construction, transportation, food services and many other economic activities, though industry was a major component of the enterprises. The idea of rural enterprises was based on the assumption that the working system of the employees was flexible enough to allow them to do both factory work and farm work, hence the concept of 'leaving agriculture without leaving the village' or 'going for industrial production without going to the city'.

For large, populous, agrarian societies, diversification of rural economy is essential. Only then the rural economy can absorb the expanding rural population without forcing too much migration to the cities. That was possible only if productive employment increased in the villages and living standards steadily grew competing with the cities. In 1991, for example, out of China's 1,100 million population, nearly 900 million were peasants. Unless agriculture and a diversified rural economy grew steadily in China's countryside, there would be serious dislocation of the economic process, causing social instability and political tensions. Therefore, rural enterprises were regarded as playing a crucial role in China's development. But this could not be done at the cost of agricultural development. After all, basic food needs of this vast population were also to be fulfilled.

At the end of 1991, nearly 96 million workers were employed in an estimated 19.08 million enterprises. In 1996, it had increased to 150 million employees.[9] In 1991, their total output value was 1,160 billion yuan, which was a quarter of the national figure and was 60 per cent of the rural output value. Of it, industrial output value accounted for 870 billion yuan, which was one-third of the nation's industrial output value in 1991 or equivalent to the total national industrial output value in 1987.

The export orientation of the rural enterprises was consciously developed in the late 1980s. By the end of 1991, there were about 65,000 export-oriented enterprises which earned US$18 billion foreign exchange. Over 3,500 enterprises made over US$1 million earnings, of which nearly 700 earning over US$5 million each. The establishment of foreign and local joint ventures at township level made rapid progress during the 1990s. Most of these were located in the developed east coast region of China from Liaoning through Beijing and Tianjin, Hubei, Shandong, Shanghai, Jiangsu, Zhejiang, Fujian and Guangdong.

According to a comprehensive account of the growth of TVEs, we get a sense of how widespread it was.[10] From 1978 to early 2003, the number of

TVEs in China grew 20 per cent annually, though the rate declined after 1995. By the end of 2003, there were 21.85 million TVEs employing 135 million people, generating 30 per cent of GDP, 49 per cent of industrial added value and 35 per cent farmers' incomes. These enterprises contributed significantly to agricultural and infrastructural development. By the mid-1990s, the collectives had been gradually transformed into private enterprises with many of them being small-sized, family-owned units. According to this study, only 167, 000 were 'running as modern enterprise systems'.

The trend of transforming the TVEs into 'SMEs' continued thereafter as well. By 2009, the number of such enterprises was put at 43 million, including 38 million privately owned businesses. According to the Association of Small and Medium Enterprises, in 2009, SMEs contributed to 58.5 per cent of total annual GDP of China, 50 per cent of tax revenues, 68 per cent of exports and 75 per cent of new jobs.[11]

But the TVEs in rural China in the 1980s and the SMEs that flourished after 1995 were not the same. The former was mainly a collective enterprise financed by local savings, enjoying concessional taxes and other incentives from the State and leading the income generation of the peasants and infrastructure development of the countryside. SMEs were private businesses with little commitment to local population's economic or social needs, and they served mainly the national process of capitalist accumulation with linkage with global market. Their growth gave rise to the formation of a new class of entrepreneurs, making quick profit in the expanding production process. Therefore, even though the number of SMEs rose, they could not maintain the pace of rural development in tandem with urban growth, and the rural crisis began to intensify.

With this broad perspective in mind, let us get an idea about the TVEs as they functioned in the height of their successful performance.

Some Case Studies

We now turn to a study of some rural industries in the place of our study, Hela Township in Wuxi. I had collected data on these enterprises in the course of my field visits ranging from two to six weeks in 1979, 1980, 1985, 1987, 1993, 1996 and 2003 and shorter trips in 2006 and 2015. In the course of the first two trips, the focus of my study was on old contract agriculture and launching of the rural industry programme. By 1985, the new system had stabilized and rural industries had been in full bloom. Two years later, while the momentum remained, adjustments on various aspects had been initiated.

Thus, the data of this period provide valuable insights into the strategy of rural industrialization in its critical phase of expansion.[12] In the subsequent years, their output grew further and steps were taken to tackle some of the emerging problems such as deficient quality, excessive energy consumption and declining competitiveness. By 1996, the changes in policy towards TVEs had set in with a shift of focus to major urban enterprises producing for export. By 2003, the TVEs were no longer a critical component of China's development strategy. In 2006, the new strategy of speedy economic growth was in full steam. By 2015, however, there were some murmurings among policy-makers at local levels about whether abandoning the TVEs was the right decision. But China had moved so far away from that strategy that it was impossible to return to that path.

This information was collected through open-ended interviews with cadres of enterprises, government and the Communist Party in their offices. Visits to factories and conversations with ordinary workers provided some additional information. We have chosen enterprises at three levels—township-run industries, village-run industries, both of which were collectively owned, and a State-run industry for comparative purposes.

A clarification may be in order on the nature of this sample. Jiangsu province is one of China's most prosperous provinces in both agriculture and industry and was leading the country in the growth of rural enterprises whose industrial output value exceeded half of the province's total output value in the 1990s. According to the information provided by the director of the Wuxi suburban district, 96 per cent the suburban district output value came from industry in 1986. These data present the picture of a successful region which had been held out as the model for developing rural industries in the backward regions like the western and central China. From this data, we can get some idea about the political economy of the rural enterprises and the methods of handling their problems in practice. The objective here is to indicate the nature of development of rural enterprises and the changes in the management structure and workers' role.

During the 1993–96 period, one major element of policy had stabilized; that was the State's macro control over the economy while developing the market forces. The Fourth Plenum of the CPCCC in October 1995 had clarified this perspective very clearly. Through this role, the State could tackle various hurdles with regard to the functioning of the enterprises that led to falling profits in many cases.

Here is a profile of the TVEs seen as SMEs. From 1978 to early 2003, the number of TVEs in China grew at 20 per cent annually. By the end of 2003, there were 21.85 million TVEs employing 135 million, generating over 30 per cent of GDP, 49 per cent of industrial added value and 35 per cent of farmers' incomes. These enterprises contributed significantly to agricultural and infrastructure development. However, most TVEs were small and were dominated by family ties. Only 167,000 of them were considered to be running modern enterprise systems.[13]

By 30 December 2009, China's TVEs were more than 43 million, accounting to one source out of which more than 99.8 per cent of the total number of businesses and 38 million were privately owned. In China, in 2009, SMEs contributed to 58.5 per cent of total annual GDP, 50 per cent of taxation revenues, 68 per cent of exports and 75 per cent of new jobs. Overall, SMEs employed more than 80 per cent of the labour force (China Association of Small and Medium Enterprises). But these are different in character and orientation from the TVEs which existed during the 1980s.

TVEs in Wuxi

In 1995, Wuxi had 16,000 rural enterprises in all, employing 930,000 workers. The total output value was 175.4 billion yuan with sales income of 130.3 billion yuan, of which exports accounted for 33.4 billion yuan or 28 per cent of the latter. There were as many as 3,200 joint ventures in Wuxi. In 1995 alone, 298 were approved. Out of a total amount of US$3.2 billion, investment of US$850 million for which contracts had been signed was utilized in 1995. The overall picture for Wuxi's demography and economy are given in Tables 6.1, 6.2 and 6.3.

Table 6.1:
Employment in TVEs in China

Years	Employment (Million People)
1996	135.08
2000	128.20
2006	146.80
2008	154.10
2010	158.93
2013	102.94

Sources: National Bureau of Statistics of China, *China Statistical Yearbooks*, 2001 (Table 5-1); 2011 (Table 4-1); Ministry of Agriculture of the PRC, *China Agriculture Yearbook*, 2014, 143.

Table 6.2:
Wuxi's changing composition of employed workforce 1980–2015

Selected Years	Employed Workforce (Total in Million)	Primary Industry (%)	Secondary Industry (%)	Tertiary Industry (%)
1980	2.056	49.6	38.3	12.1
1985	2.367	25.8	56.3	17.9
1990	2.449	22.2	58.6	19.2
1995	2.379	16.5	57.2	26.3
2000	2.210	22.7	48.1	29.2
2004	2.746	12.8	54.8	32.4
2005	2.892	11.8	55.1	33.1
2010	3.823	6	55	39
2012	3.891	4.7	57.5	37.8
2013	3.892	4.6	57.6	38.2

Sources: Compiled from Statistics Bureau of Wuxi City, *Wuxi Statistical Yearbook*, 2005, 47; 2011, 47; 2013 (Table 2-7).

Table 6.3:
Total number of TVEs (1980–2013; units: 10,000)

Year	China	Jiangsu
1980	142.46	—
1985	1,222.50	9.85
1990	1,873.43	11.31
1995	2,202.66	10.88
2000	2,084.66	90.34
2004	2,213.21	110.35
2010	2,742.46	65.29
2013	699.38	76.22

Sources: National Bureau of Statistics of China, *China Statistical Yearbooks,* 2001 (5-1); 2011 (Table 4-1); Ministry of Agriculture of the PRC, *China Agriculture Yearbook*, 2014, 143. Statistics Bureau of Wuxi City, *Wuxi Statistical Yearbook*, 2005 (Tables 15-1 and 15-2), 2014 (Table 15-3); He Kang, *China's Township and Village Enterprises* (Beijing: Foreign Language Press, 2006), 398. Ministry of Agriculture of the PRC, *China Agriculture Yearbooks*, 2004, 2009; Statistical Bureau of Jiangsu Province, *Jiangsu Statistical Yearbook*, 2000 (Basic Situations of Rural Townships Collective Enterprises; http://www.jssb.gov.cn/jstj/jsnj/2000/jsnj02/ym03.htm (accessed on 19 June 2017); 2001; 2009 (Table 7-24).

The rural enterprises played a significant role in Wuxi's economic development. They contributed 50 per cent to the city's GDP in 1995, 72 per cent of its foreign trade and 80 per cent of the city's industrial output value. Compared to the 1990 level when each township had an average output value of 200 million yuan, in 1995 it had increased more than five times to 1.5 billion yuan. Going down further to the average village output value, it had increased from 5 million yuan in 1990 to 40 million yuan in 1995. As per the average output value of a rural enterprise, there was an even higher rise from 1.8 million yuan to 10 million yuan. In 1996, Wuxi had the largest number of rural enterprises in the country and 46 per cent of Jiangsu province, of which 93 enterprises are regarded as national-level enterprises which have high-quality production using advance technology. This is directly supervised by the central Agricultural Ministry which allows them many preferences. Three of these enterprises are located in the suburban districts but none of them in Hela Township.

In addition to light industries and textile for which a solid foundation has been laid, new steps have been taken to set up electronic, mechanical, chemical and metallurgical industries. In Wuxi, rarely is any enterprise closed due to sickness. It is usually grouped with other industries and revived through diversified production. It may be leased out to private entrepreneurs for similar purposes as well.

In Wuxi, the restructuring of ownership had made some progress in the 1990s. Bulk of the enterprises were collectively owned or managed by the township or village, but following the manager responsibility system, 500 enterprises had been contracted to private entrepreneurs. Under this system, operation of the production process had been privatized, but ownership still remained with the township or the village. Usually, the contract was given through a process of bidding.

There were 1,500 shareholding rural enterprises in Wuxi. There were three kinds of shares in the enterprises: one, shares by the collective, namely the township, the village or the enterprise itself; two, shares by the workers of the enterprise itself; and three, shares by social legal entities. These could be individual organizations and companies from anywhere in the country or abroad. However, as of 1996, the shares of the collective were in majority; foreign shares were still not many.

In the rural industries, 60 per cent of the workers were male as of 1996. On the one hand, in some light industries, female labour was as high as 80 per cent or so; on the other hand, in enterprises such as chemicals and metallurgy, there were more men. The technological upgradation did affect women in some enterprises. But according to Wuxi's rural enterprises director, whenever there were surplus labourers in one unit, they were shifted to other industries. They also had the policy of adjusting the migrant labour component in various enterprises. In Wuxi, 35 per cent of the rural enterprise workers were from outside the city. In some enterprises, however, their proportion was as high as 80 per cent. Whenever a township or village wished to accommodate its own labour, it could lay off the migrant labourers. Thus, on the labour front, it was clear that women did get laid off on reasons of technical modernization and productivity and migrant labour had insecurity of tenure. The flexibility of rural enterprises, hence, had adverse conditions for gender and backward regions.

The average income of a worker in rural enterprises of Wuxi was 4,500 yuan and together with bonus and subsidies, it was nearly 8,000 yuan in 1996. Wages were part of the production cost. The rural enterprises continued to follow a policy of high accumulation. After paying 17 per cent of the income as national tax (*guo shui*) and 5 per cent as local tax (*difang shui*), the enterprise contributed 30 per cent of its net profit to the township government, another 30 per cent to its own rural enterprise expansion fund and remaining 40 per cent as its bonus. It may be noted that bonus was a big chunk of the profit which was distributed according to performance among the workers and managers. The policy of industry subsidizing agriculture continued to be emphasized in Wuxi in the 1990s. This was put into the production cost of the enterprises. Similarly, there is a contribution of the enterprise towards education, health and welfare of the workers. This is also considered as a part of the production cost. By this method, the burden on the enterprise is reduced and the profit is divided only between accumulation and bonus. The national tax is also included in the cost of production. In Wuxi, since the cost of material and technology was high and together with the wages and salaries, the production cost had risen to about 80 per cent of the total output value. Even then, 20 per cent profit was good enough for maintaining the tempo of economic progress.

Enterprises at the Township Level

In the public sector, there were three kinds of industrial enterprises in China: SOEs, collectively owned at the township level and collectively-owned at the village level. In the 1980s, various forms of privately owned enterprises also emerged in China as enterprises jointly owned by the State, collective and private entrepreneurs. There were joint ventures involving foreign firms as well. The State-owned industries could come within the jurisdiction of either a central ministry, a provincial department or the city government.

The rules and principles governing all of them were different from those applicable to the collective enterprises at the township or village levels. The latter were part of the rural economy giving employment to some members of the agricultural households and were linked to agricultural activities in many ways. They were a link with the collective economy of the commune years and had a responsibility for contributing to the overall development of their township or village. At the same time, they operated with new ethos of producing for profit, of reward for hard work, of working in response to the market and of sharing gains and losses. The production responsibility system made them accountable for their production performance to the next higher body. In the course of practice, however, the principles of management and wage determination became similar in the case of both rural and urban enterprises as a part of the general development of commodity economy.

Let us now look at some specific cases of enterprises from the early reform years to the high point of success of the TVEs. They demonstrated the rationale of having TVEs in a framework of mutually supporting rural–urban economy. It should be noted that the production system and the wage policy of the commune period were altered and a considered production plan that responded to the market and a wage policy that respected the skills of labour were put into force during the 1980s.

A Township Enterprise at the Early Reform Period: Hela Commune Agriculture Machine Plant

We get a picture of the transition from the commune system to the reformed structure, as far as rural industry was concerned, from the study of a commune-run factory in 1980. The Hela Commune Agricultural Machine Plant was transformed from an old-style collective enterprise producing agricultural and fishery machines to a new-style diversified plant producing many other machine parts for the city factories. The agricultural machine plant was set up by the Hela Commune in July 1966 on the principle that industry should support agriculture, and the big factories in the city helped certain communes to set up industries. Wuxi's Textile Machinery Plant helped Hela Commune by providing certain equipment. The commune also put in its own funds. It had started with a capital of 3,000 yuan and with 30 workers. With seven rather old machines procured from the textile plant, the commune enterprise started in the premises of an old temple (whether this had anything to do with the Cultural Revolution policy of going to the countryside or attitude towards religious places, one did not know). The workers of the enterprise were sent to the textile plant for training. To begin with, the commune plant only processed parts for the textile factory. The idea was that it would eventually promote the level of mechanization. The trained workers were available to repair the agricultural machinery used in the commune.

Subsequently, the State provided heavy machineries in order to enable the commune plant to produce agricultural machineries to suit the local conditions. Thus, they produced rice transplanters, thrashers and automatic pumps, with some parts manufactured locally and others procured from large factories. After 1973, the commune expanded its fisheries very fast. Accordingly, the commune plant was called upon to produce machineries for fishing purposes: aerators, multipurpose pumps, snell-sucker and grinding machinery. Some of them were also supplied to other communes through the State. However, the products of the plant did not generate enough profit. They were of a large variety and enough demand was not forthcoming; hence, the plant was asked to look for profit-making avenues. Hence, in recent years, it started processing products for the city plants; for example, it produced bicycle brakes for Wuxi Bicycle Factory and made considerable profit.

In 1980, the Hela Commune Agricultural Machine Plant had 330 workers, including staff. The workers were drawn from various production teams of the commune and were engaged in the factory at the same time. In the busy farming season, they went back to their fields to work and in the slack season, they worked in the plant. Whenever labourers were needed for intensive operations in vegetable farming and fishing, they were also released by the plant. Thus, there was flexible allocation of labour time among various branches of rural economy. The same people worked as peasants and workers on different occasions.

The Hela plant had 82 machines of different types with fixed assets amounting to 1.5 million yuan. The total output value of the plant was 2.24 million yuan in 1978 and 3.21 million yuan in 1979. Its gross profit was 480,000 yuan in 1978 and 1.04 million yuan in 1979 which was a noticeable advance. The average annual income of workers was 623 yuan in 1978 and 700 yuan in 1979. Maximum was 1,000 yuan and minimum 400 yuan in 1978 and 500 yuan in 1979. After deducting 20 per cent State tax and wages, the net profit was 200,000 yuan in 1978. In 1979, the profit increased to 820,000 yuan. The plant reinvested 180,000 yuan in 1978 and 200,000 yuan in 1979 for its own development, giving the rest to the commune for the latter's capital construction fund. Earlier, 50 per cent of the net profit was handed over to the commune. But in 1979, it was agreed to provide a larger proportion because the commune was planning expansion of enterprises. This was an interesting example of capital accumulation while providing for a substantial increase in the wages which reached an average of

628 yuan. In the commune period, however, such a large annual increase in wages was not permissible and there would have been even more contribution to the accumulation fund.

There was also a change in the mode of distribution of wages. Earlier, the plant calculated the work points and handed over the sum of wages to respective production teams, which in turn added these work points to those earned in agriculture by the peasants and paid the final amount to the peasants. After 1979, the plant itself paid wages directly to the workers. Earlier, it was a kind of subsidy given by the factory to the teams for having used their peasant's labour in the factory. For several years, the factory paid 123 yuan per worker annually to the team as compensation. The workers earned work points ranging from 13 to 17 for a day's work. They had 10 grades of wages with a difference of half work point in the ascending order. In 1979, the industry and commerce department of the commune had fixed the value of 10 work points as 1.45 yuan. Since the plant over-fulfilled the production quota that year, the value per 10 work points was increased to 2.2 yuan. Among the workers, 51 per cent were women. Nearly 40 per cent were having high- or medium-level skill and 20 per cent elementary level of technical training; 20 of them were apprentices. There was no special housing for workers; they all lived in their homes in their production teams.

From the brief account of a commune-run factory during the 1979–80 period, two things are clear. First, with the new autonomy in decision-making, the plant decided to produce spare parts that were in demand by the city factories and thus vastly increased its income. Second, a beginning was made in streamlining the accounting system of the enterprises, separating it from the agricultural sector, namely the production teams. With the introduction of the household contract system, this became even simpler. At the same time, taking advantage of the collective economy it was possible to allocate funds substantially to the accumulation fund while paying increased wages to the workers. The accumulation fund was used by the local government not only to improve the enterprise itself but also to support agriculture as well as education, health and social welfare in the rural area.

TVE at Its Peak: Hela Machine Tools Factory

The Hela Commune Agricultural Machine Plant was reorganized to promote diversified production and was renamed Hela Machine Tools Factory when I visited it in 1985. This township-run enterprise provided employment for 473 workers in 1985. Besides manufacturing products such as aerators for fish ponds and bicycle brakes, it also made brakes for the train coaches and developed some new products like tools for cutting metals. In 1985, this factory had six workshops including one foundry, one machine machinery and one brake-assembling workshop. Its products now included multi-purpose pumps and drilling instruments as well. In 1985, the reputation of these township-run enterprises had become nationally known. Three of its products were awarded prizes. Since 1975, it had won the 'Advanced Enterprises Title' for 10 consecutive years. The output value of this enterprise had made impressive progress from 3.7 million yuan in 1981 to 7.95 million yuan in 1985. Profit had also nearly doubled. Since 1983, the government had imposed a uniform tax of 55 per cent on the income of all the industries including this one. The employment, however, had only increased from 419 in 1981 to 473 in 1985, which included workers as well as staff members. This showed that the increase in output value did not necessarily lead to a proportionate or even a significant increase in employment opportunities. Actually, the approach was to raise the productivity of labour which increased from 9,801 yuan in 1981 to 24,322 yuan in 1984. Thus, it cannot be generalized to suggest that expansion of output value of rural industries necessarily led to a corresponding expansion in employment opportunities. Of course, to a certain extent it did happen. There has to be a balance between raising labour productivity and providing employment.

The average annual wages of the workers in the Hela Machine Tools Plant increased from 715 yuan in 1981 to 1,147 yuan in 1984 when the highest income of a worker was 1,800 yuan and the lowest 700 yuan. In this factory, 55 per cent of the workers were women. The retired workers got a pension of 30 yuan per month (Table 6.4).

Table 6.4:
Hela machine tools factory

S. No.	Categories	1981	1982	1983	1984	1985
1.	Output value (million yuan)	3.7	4.62	7.02	11	7.95
2.	Profit (yuan)	565,600	633,600	777,900	1,000,000	1,100,000
3.	Productivity per person (yuan)	9,801.09	10,851.64	15,531.93	24,322.83	—
4.	No. of workers and staff	419	426	452	473	—
5.	Annual wage per worker (yuan)	715	833.75	884.46	1,147.37	

Source: Fact sheet provided by the enterprise leadership in 1985.

This case showed how a collectively owned rural enterprise adapted itself to modern conditions. Thereby it increased its output value and wages significantly and contributed to the national construction process by paying as high as 55 per cent of its income as tax. Its contribution to local infrastructure and social sector also expanded in a major way.

Village-run Enterprises

Hela Toothpaste Soft Tube Factory was set up by the Hela brigade in 1975 taking a loan from the commune bank. The brigade had set it up as a part of the programme of diversification of rural economy. These soft tubes were meant for plants producing toothpastes. It employed 90 workers, 50 of whom were women. Output value in 1979 was 400,000 yuan, with a profit of 70,000 yuan. In 1980, its target was to achieve 700,000 yuan with a profit of 130,000 yuan. There was no State tax levied on this factory, as of 1980. The wages earned by the workers varied from 400 yuan to 800 yuan which were directly distributed to the workers in the factory.

In other words, the system of transferring the work points from the factory to the production team had been discontinued. The workers were given bonuses which were calculated seasonally as well as at the end of the year. It was a piece rate system. Those who produced more than their quota got higher wages. This factory operated under the leadership of the brigade (in 1980, the village was still called so).

Xishan Village Woollen Sweater Works

A glance at another village-run enterprise such as Xishan Woollen Sweater Works in 1985 gives an idea of the pace and character of expansion of the rural industries in Hela Township which had taken place in the early 1980s. As mentioned before, Xishan village was earlier called a brigade and was one of the 14 villages (*cun*) of Hela Township. It had 358 labourers in 311 households with a population of 1,244. Earlier, they were engaged in vegetable growing, pig raising and some industries. With their land taken over by State for urban construction, they were left only with a few industries. In 1985, the village had five factories for shoe making, plastic products, pump repairing and garments. Together they employed 221 male and 137 female workers. The production quota for these factories set for 1985 was 4.5 million yuan with an estimated profit of 560,000 yuan. They had, by August, already achieved the target and profit for that year. They had got a profit of 1.08 million yuan. The output value for 1985 was expected to be nearly 10 million yuan. This increase in output was attributed to the production responsibility system. The per-labour annual income in 1984 was 1,513 yuan and in 1985 was expected to surpass the wage level of the State-run silk factory by over 100 yuan. In fact, the wage in the village enterprise was much higher, namely 126 yuan per month in 1984 and 220 yuan in 1985. This was so despite the fact that these workers in the village industries were far less skilled than in the silk factory. Most of them were young people who had not even completed higher middle school.

The Xishan Woollen Sweater Works which was set up in 1980 had 75 workers in 1985 when I visited it. It used 25 machines made in China and 40 made in Switzerland. Its profit was 50,000 yuan in 1980 which had reached 90,000 yuan in 1984. It produced woollen as well as synthetic sweaters. Its sweaters were sold all over the country. In this enterprise, the annual wages increased from 800 yuan in 1980 to 1,513 yuan in 1984 and an estimated 2,300 yuan in 1985. The enterprise had a general profit rate of 20 per cent of its output value.

Xishan village had a large amount earmarked for its public reserve fund, out of which 253 retired peasants of the village were paid pensions. The average monthly pension was 19.5 yuan and it ranged from 13 to 48 yuan. This fund was also used for welfare in the village such as supporting school education, running nurseries for babies and building public toilets and water supply points. In the case of the sweater works, 5 per cent of the profit was used for the well-being of workers which included providing working clothes and entertainment facilities.

Hela Village Transformer Repair Workshop

This workshop catered to the urban and suburban needs, though it functioned under the village leadership. Set up towards the end of 1980, this workshop had increased its output value very fast. In 1980, its output value was 1.15 million yuan and profit 276,000 yuan. In 1984, they had grown to 3.2 million yuan and 540,000 yuan respectively. It originally employed 109 workers whose strength had risen to 120 in 1985 including 72 women.

It should be noticed that rural industries provided considerable opportunity for women's employment. The annual income per worker had also risen from 1,059 to 1,420 yuan. The highest was as much as 2,750 yuan and the lowest 700 yuan in 1984. Thus, in a specialized factory, the income differential could be quite large. In 1980, there was only one technical person who did both technical and ordinary jobs. In 1985, the workshop had a professionally trained engineer and two full-time technicians. The enterprise had paid a lot of attention to the quality of products. In 1985, there were nine full-time quality inspectors. The specialization level of the workers had also increased. Several of them had joined evening schools for technical education. From doing repairing works, the enterprise had moved on to manufacturing new products.

Two trends were noticeable in the rural political economy arising from the working of the rural enterprises. One was the big profit that the enterprises made in their production resulting in substantial rise in the income of the peasant workers, thus creating a dynamic and expanding market in rural China for industrial products. The other was a peculiar situation which did not require young people to continue school education and move to higher studies as they were getting high-income jobs with middle school training. This had a negative consequence in the long run. It more or less rewarded low skill with high dividends. But this could have been tackled by demanding higher-level skills with vocational education.

After studying township- and village-level enterprises and the role they played in developing a diversified rural economy and contributing to enhancing of peasant income, let us look at a higher level—city-run enterprises. They are different from collective-run enterprises and are in the category of State-run enterprises, but still some principles of the collective economy also operated here, even though the TVEs enjoyed far greater autonomy in wage policy and production planning than the State-run enterprises.

State-run Enterprises

Wuxi Silk Factory

Until 1980, the commune and brigade-run factories had distinct principles of management and production, different from those of State-run factories. As the reforms were put into operation, in the next few years, some common principles of production responsibility and market responsiveness came to be implemented in all enterprises. However, in terms of payment of State tax, flexibility in deciding the proportion of wages and investment fund and autonomy of managers, the rural enterprises enjoyed clear advantages over the State-run enterprises. A comparison with a State-run factory, therefore, is useful.

The Wuxi Silk Factory was founded way back in 1929 and was taken over by the State after liberation. This area had a long tradition of growing mulberry trees and producing raw silk out of the silkworms. Over the years, this factory had gone into the production of a variety of silks. In 1980, there were 1,700 workers employed in this factory as against 900 before the liberation, and as many as 80 per cent of workers were women. In 1979, the output of raw silk was 320 tons as against a maximum of 40 tons before liberation. As much as 90 per cent of its products were meant for export. The annual rate of growth of production in this factory was 4 per cent.

In an interview in 1980 with me, the manager claimed that the factory contributed US$10 million out of its profits to the State. The average wage of a worker was about 58 yuan per month, the highest being 89 yuan and the lowest 39 yuan. Despite the high rate of profit and income earned from foreign exchange, the wage was almost the same compared to the earnings of the rural enterprises. In Hela Commune Agricultural Machine Plant, for example, the average wage in 1979 was also 58 yuan. But in the succeeding years, the wages in the rural enterprises increased much faster than those in the State enterprises. It should be noted that the Wuxi Silk Factory directly operated under the provincial and the central authorities, conforming to the plans laid out by them. On the other hand, the rural enterprises had acquired a great deal of autonomy in production decisions.

In 1985, the Wuxi Silk Factory presented a new look after a thorough process of 'readjustment and consolidation' in the course of the reforms. Producing economic results was the focus. There was a new stress on the quality of products and welfare of the workers. The size of the plant however was not enlarged. There had been some technical changes with installation of new equipment for spinning process. The standards set by the State Council for production and management were now the basis of the factory's work. Production responsibility system had been implemented at the workshop level both in groups and for individuals, ensuring more wages for more and better work. The production quota was fixed by the State for the factory as a whole and the management had fixed quotas for each of the sections in the factory. The number of workers and staff had come down from 1,700 to 1,600, including about 100 cadres and staff members. This could be due to the fact that the improved technology dispensed with some labour and also the responsibility system enthused the workers to produce more. The proportion of female workers had also come down from 80 per cent to 75 per cent. It could be because of the fact that enough skilled women were not available to handle the new equipment.

The total output value of the plant had now reached 22 million yuan with a profit of 2.8 million yuan which was calculated after deducting 55 per cent State tax. We can notice the high tax rate of the State-run enterprises. The average monthly wage, however, continued to be 58 yuan, but now this was only the basic wage which was supplemented considerably by bonuses and other payments raising the average earning to nearly 100 yuan per month. The highest annual earning of a worker in the Wuxi Silk Factory was 1,600 yuan and the lowest was 800 yuan. Compared to the investment and scale of the operations, the average earning of these workers was lower than those of the workers in rural enterprises. This was explained by the factory manager in terms of the fact that the township or village did not hand over its profit to the State, whereas State-run factories did. The TVEs paid only a small tax and distributed their profits among their members, besides saving for reinvestment.

Wuxi City Elevator Factory

This city-run factory presented yet another contrast to the township- and village-run enterprises in many respects, especially at the operation of new principles of management and production. In 1985, there was a newly set up elevator factory under the auspices of the city government of Wuxi. As the city of Wuxi was fast growing and many multi-storeyed buildings were coming up, the government set up an elevator factory. It used foreign technology and entered the national market.

In 1985, the Wuxi City Elevator Factory had 350 workers, of whom 75 were women. Its output value in 1984 was 7.5 million yuan with a profit of 2 million yuan. Set up in 1977, this factory had produced over 500 elevators until 1984 and marketed them in 27 provinces. This figure showed that the production capacity of this plant was small. It made three types of elevators—for carrying people, for carrying goods and for carrying hospital beds with patients. It had four workshops for processing, cold treatment, maintenance and control panel. The factory employed 8 professionally trained engineers, 10 college graduates, 8 graduates from secondary technical schools and 90 from senior middle schools. The rest were junior- and middle-school graduates. This factory had a higher component of educated and technical staff than many others. As seen in other State-run specialized industries, the proportion of female workers and staff was relatively less.

The production responsibility system operated in this factory and wage was linked with profit. In 1984, the average annual income of a worker in this factory was 1,398 yuan. This included the basic wage of 720 yuan and 678 yuan as bonus and other extra earnings. At the end of every year, a proportion of the plant's profit was distributed as extra bonus, in addition to the usual bonus linked to higher profit every month. Before the reform in the wage system, there was a fixed gross wage and also a fixed growth rate of the wages. But after the reform of the workers, wages were linked with the magnitude of profit in every phase of work. Work of every individual and every section was evaluated. If the quota fixed by the industrial company of the city was over-fulfilled, then the plant got additional incentives by way of tax savings and special grants. In 1985, the management reported that whereas before the reforms the plant had produced 7 elevators every month, the output had been raised to 17 elevators after the reforms.

In this plant, too, the emphasis in production was on maintaining quality and responding to the market. It had shortened the production period and improved servicing as well as installation facilities. But this process had run into some problems by 1987. The State had ordered an investigation into the poor quality of elevators produced in this factory. In 1987, the factory management was seeking to diversify its production so as to use its capital and technology with better results. This case showed how the desire to make quick profit could lead to sacrificing quality. This phenomenon was not limited to TVEs and was also seen in the case of State-run enterprises. This was cited as a major reason for closing down many enterprises. But there could be efforts to raise the skill level and institute quality control measures, rather than abandoning the strategy of developing rural enterprises.

Managers and Workers

We continue our discussion on the TVEs in this chapter with focus on the changes in the management system and the role of the workers in the enterprises. The principle of socialist management with workers' participation was only a point of theoretical discussion. TVEs aimed at increasing production and profit, giving economic incentives to workers, thereby adding to peasants' income. This was the main point of departure from the Cultural Revolution approach of 'red and expert' perspective on enterprise management.[14] But the reform regime continued to change its management policy until the mid-1990s when private economy and the corresponding management principles stabilized.[15] In the process, peasant-workers who had not only benefited from the higher earnings from the TVEs but also had a degree of participation through the village collective found themselves in a peculiar situation of difficulties by the turn of the century. With the decline of the TVEs, sources of peasant income had shrunk. The collectives' support for education and health for their families had come down considerably. Above all, despite the elections to the village committee, the little amount of political role of the rural citizens in an important economic activity had disappeared. The changes in the management system and the trade union role therefore should provide us some insights into understanding this process.

The Changing Management System

The management system of enterprises underwent rapid change in China following the decision of the Third Plenum of the Eleventh CC in December 1978. The rural enterprises were the first to introduce the new system of management. Subsequently, the State enterprises carried out the management reforms. The new management system had three characteristics: (a) separation of enterprise management from the government on the one hand and the Communist Party control on the other, (b) appointment of a single manager in charge of an enterprise replacing the management committee and (c) limiting workers participation to institutional channels like Workers' Representative Conference (WRC) and trade unions. When these principles were put into practice, there was a great deal of variation from region to region and enterprise to enterprise depending on the concrete conditions. But the focus was on the production responsibility system, making the manager responsible for profit and losses and workers gaining dividends only when production increased. For this purpose, the enterprise was granted considerable autonomy in decision-making. The Third Plenum of 1978 had stipulated that 'it [was] necessary boldly to shift it (authority) under guidance from the leadership to lower levels so that the local authorities and industrial and agricultural enterprises ha[d] greater power of decision in management under the guidance of unified planning …'.[16]

This was in contrast with the practice during the Cultural Revolution when each enterprise was run by a revolutionary committee composed of workers, technicians and party cadres according to the principle of three-in-one combination. After 1978, this was renamed as management committee. The Cultural Revolution system also stipulated direct participation of workers in management which was inspired by the Anshan Charter. The whole approach came under severe criticism by Deng Xiaoping mainly on two counts. Firstly, according to Deng, production in enterprises suffered enormously due to lack of discipline in management. Secondly, enthusiasm of workers had not been mobilized because they did not get rewards for good performance. This perspective of Deng Xiaoping was the basis for replacing what was called 'iron rice bowl' system with 'production responsibility'. Under the latter system, incentive wages were paid for better performance. During my visits during 1979–87, all the enterprise managers were happily talking about the new wage policy and denouncing the old 'equalitarian' policy.

In the earlier system, production decisions were made by the higher organs like the concerned departments of the provincial or county government, and the enterprises were merely to implement them. In the day-to-day administration, the party committee at the factory level maintained a close supervision which amounted to frequent interference in the enterprise management. The enterprise party secretary was generally more powerful than the head of the management committee. In many enterprises, however, the same person held both the offices, the secretary and manager. The enterprise party committee took it upon itself to ensure that the enterprise management implemented directives from the higher level. All this meant little autonomy to the enterprise management in the old system. After the reforms were put into force, the enterprise management was given full autonomy to take production decisions and work for making profit. In other words, autonomy was accompanied by accountability and accountability was understood in concrete economic terms. The manager's salary, the workers' wages and the bonus of everyone varied according to the record of performance.

The relationship between the enterprise and the higher administrative organ was codified through an annual contract. A mutually agreed production quota was fixed by this contract. Under the contract, the higher organ agreed to provide certain infrastructural support including grants and loans which were subject to certain conditions to be met by the enterprises. The higher organ also supervised the balance sheet of the enterprise and the quality of the products. All rural enterprises of Hela Township were thus subject to supervision by the Wuxi suburban industrial company. It was a relationship of mutual persuasion rather than downward control. This was because the suburban county industrial company was subject to similar supervision by Wuxi city's industrial company and the latter by the Jiangsu provincial level. If the lower unit did not show good performance, then they could not impress the higher level and get their due bonuses and grants. So, every level had to help its lower level to produce more and better in order to keep the system going. But it also meant that each level had to depend on the support of the next higher level of leadership in fulfilling targets and justifying their performance. When the lower level was as important as the upper level was, there was greater accountability. In the late 1990s, when the TVEs came under increasing challenge while attaining high growth remained the principal goal of the regime, maintaining the support system involved more and more mutual gratification among cadres, managers and entrepreneurs. This became a source of corruption that spread from the grass-roots level to the county, province and even central levels. That phenomenon became so dysfunctional and such a threat to the system that Xi Jinping decided to make it one of his principal tasks to fight corruption. But the scale and nature of production and ownership had evolved in such a fashion in China after 2000 that it was difficult to restore decentralized production and management.

Under the new management system in the early 1980s the role of the party was considerably altered. The enterprise party committee mainly performed a political and educational role. The educational role involved conducting ideological classes and explaining central leadership's policies. These classes were much fewer than those during the Cultural Revolution. They were not to interfere in the production process. Actually, they became fewer and fewer during the 1980s until the party decided to emphasize ideological education after the Tiananmen incident of June 1989. In fact, during the period 1980–87, the manager of the factory assumed far more importance than the party secretary or the *shuji*. I had noticed that it was the secretary who received the visitors prior to 1980. Subsequently, it was the manager who did it. However, the party committee continued to exist and was given a relatively greater importance from mid-1989 until the Eighth Plenum in November 1991. After Deng's southern tour, once again the emphasis on the manager's role became conspicuous. During the 1980s, workers had little time to attend party classes. Every bit of extra time was used by them for more production and additional earnings. Between factory work and household work, there was little time left for anything else. Women seemed fully occupied between rural enterprises, agriculture and household work—of course carrying double burden of work outside and at home. But the atmosphere looked like providing work to all.

The change from the management committee to a 'single-manager system' was a major development, affecting the evolution of enterprises in China. In fact, the 'single-manager system' was introduced in many factories in China in the mid-1950s and early 1960s. This practice had prevailed in Soviet Union for many years and was advocated by a section of the CPC leaders for implementation in China. But this system was seriously criticized as a revisionist system by the followers for Mao Zedong who, instead, promoted the Anshan model. During the Great Leap Forward and the Cultural Revolution, efforts were made to introduce collective management system with direct participation by workers. Thus, like many other questions relating to the path of socialist construction, the issue of enterprise management had also become a focal point of intense ideological and political controversies in China. It was resolved in favour of the Deng Xiaoping line in 1978. Thereafter, the management system underwent rapid changes and the single-manager system came into force in industrial enterprises. But this system was very different from the single-director system as practised in Soviet Union or in China earlier. It was a part of the package of new policies based on the production responsibility system and development of market forces in China.

In many enterprises in Wuxi, I noticed the same person being manager as well as party secretary. This was a clever way to respond to changes in the policies of the Central government. But in larger factories, they were occupied by two cadres. There was a general feeling that during the Jiang Zemin period, the manager's role was pronounced. Workers' organizations including the WRC and trade unions had come under attack. The WRC was condemned because it had to follow certain procedures for election and it did not square with the principle of three-in-one combination (one-third party, one-third army, one-third revolutionary masses/workers). Under the latter system, the dominant local factions could put their supporters from the party or the army in charge of various enterprises. The WRC, on the other hand, was a smaller body of workers' representatives and its meetings were not attended by all workers. Its job was to discuss various issues relating to production and workers' welfare and make recommendations to the manager. Thus, the WRC was considered an inadequate and limiting institution by those who valued direct participation of workers in management.

Under the reformed management system, the WRC was put to work according to legal stipulations. It was elected once a year in a general meeting of workers and it met periodically—monthly to quarterly in various places—to advise the manager on various issues concerning the enterprise. Technically, the manager was responsible to the WRC, but in the new framework, the principles of production responsibility system governed everybody including the manager and the WRC. In other words, if the enterprise was showing profit and quality in production, the WRC could not criticize the manager. In fact, the manager evolved new methods of enterprise management and production in cooperation with the WRC. In practice, the WRC's role had been reduced to one of giving formal support to and legitimating the manager's work.

Trade unions of the enterprises had been criticized as bodies 'practising economism' by the Cultural Revolution leaders. They had been in effect disbanded having been charged that they were only pursuing demands for economic gains such as higher wages and better living conditions, rather than working for revolutionary transformation. Under the reformed structure, the role of the trade unions as protector of workers' welfare was restored. In socialist countries, trade unions were generally not allowed to engage in workers' agitation. It was believed that since a worker's state had come into being, trade unions did not have to engage in political struggles and fight for their demands. Therefore, it was argued in the present and erstwhile socialist countries that the role of the trade unions was, first of all, to popularize State policy among workers and secure better welfare conditions such as housing, health, education and childcare for workers. Hence, the trade unions that were allowed to exist were the officially sponsored unions in enterprises and were affiliated to the party. Each enterprise was permitted to have only one union whose leadership was nominated by the higher authorities. Thus, trade union leadership was part of the unified power structure involving government, party, enterprise management and mass organizations. In other words, as a mass organization, the trade unions were not autonomous organizations of workers.

This view was for the first time challenged in Poland by the formation of the independent workers' organization, Solidarity. Whatever be its later incarnations and political consequences, in the early 1980s, Solidarity emphasized an important theoretical point. After a socialist revolution had taken place, a process had begun to eventually build a workers' state through a number of political, economic and cultural measures of democratic participation. For this purpose, the autonomous organizations of workers through trade unions were necessary, so that in the name of managing workers' state, the party and government did not build bureaucratic authoritarian structures. But this issue has been the subject of serious controversies among Marxists. The Cultural Revolution leaders had denounced the All-China Federation of Trade Unions (ACFTU), and in fact the concept of trade union politics in general had introduced the 'right to strike' as a fundamental right in the Chinese Constitution of 1975. This was, however, dropped by the Deng

Xiaoping regime in the new Chinese Constitution of 1982. Thus, since the early 1980s, strikes once again became illegal in China. In 1989, in the wake of the student movement in April–June, several autonomous trade unions and workers' organizations sprang up in Beijing and other cities. The 'Autonomous Workers' organization of Capital Iron and Steel Company in Beijing was one of the prominent groups which took part in the Tiananmen demonstrations in Beijing. But all such organizations were declared illegal by the Chinese government and their leaders were arrested.

However, workers strikes became a recurring phenomenon in China after 2005 when economic problems began to accumulate in both the cities and the countryside. In 2012–15, workers' strikes in northeast China became so frequent that the CPC leadership had to rethink a number of its policies on wages, employment and welfare measures.

But during the reform period, as a whole, the trade unions in China's enterprise performed essentially a collaborative role with the management and thereby shared the gains of China's economic growth. While in larger enterprises they had major responsibility for looking after the welfare needs of workers, in the smaller rural enterprises their role was minimal. In many enterprises, there was no trade union at all. Only at the level of the township as a whole, there was a trade union to look after the welfare needs of workers of various categories.

Keeping these issues in mind, it may be interesting to analyse the concrete situation relating to management and trade union practices in some of the rural enterprises in Hela Township. They illustrate some of the general principles of the reforms in the period of success of the TVEs. There were interesting specificities in some cases in both management practices and wage policies which showed how certain kinds of changes in management policies paved the way for the rural crisis.

Trade Union and Management in Rural Enterprises

The Hela Toothpaste Soft Tube Factory which operated under the Hela brigade or village in 1980 did not have a management committee; it only had a director and a vice-director who were later called manager and deputy manager. There was no party branch either. The party members at the factory functioned under the leadership of the brigade party branch. It was interesting to note that there was no trade union in this enterprise. When I enquired about the trade union in the enterprise, I was told that since those working in the enterprise were all 'peasants', there was no trade union. This was not the case everywhere. In some other enterprises within the Hela Township, there were trade unions. This one was a relatively small enterprise with about 90 workers. That is why perhaps there was no trade union yet.

Even though the manager exercised considerable autonomy, still he/ she had to function under the guidance of the industrial and commercial department of the commune or township. In fixing production quotas and piece rate wages, the township leadership had the final say. The enterprise also had to generally abide by the regulations of the industrial bureau (later called company) of the Wuxi suburban district. Thus, the decision-making power of the enterprise management was subject to the line of command of the township and the district.

The village-run factory, the Xishan Woollen Sweater Works, had one manager (31-year-old young person), one deputy manager (35-year-old) and three heads for the financial marketing and technical sections. The manager of this factory was appointed by the township government. The manager earned a salary of 2,700 yuan per year and deputy manager 2,400 yuan per year which were relatively high at that time. This was 10 times more a decade later and had continued to grow further. In the case of over-fulfilling the quota, the managers as well as workers got higher bonus. The irony then was that the managers who had passed only junior middle school (6 primary + 3 years) got more salary than a university lecturer or an engineer in a State-run factory in China. (As against the manager's monthly income of 225 yuan, the lecturer or the engineer had a starting salary of about 150 yuan in the mid-1980s.) In the early 1990s, when the manager's income rose 3–10 times, the lecturer had barely doubled his/her salary.

The Hela Village Transformer Repair Workshop also had a manager and a deputy manager. The 44-year-old manager had been promoted in 1984 from his earlier position as the head of the production section of this plant. Here too, a great deal of emphasis was put on linking enterprise management to production responsibility. To improve the technical level of workers, considerable attention had been paid to training them in the evening classes. I checked with many workers and managers in Wuxi and elsewhere and got the impression that skill development of existing workers and new recruits was built into the operation and management of TVEs.

The commune- or township-run factory, too, had undergone transition from management committee to single-director system. In 1980, the Hela Commune Agricultural Machine Plant had one director, once vice-director and seven section heads. It is interesting to look at the way the sections were organized. They neither conformed to the Soviet pattern nor with the Western way of organizing factories.

The seven sections were planning and production management, technical and quality inspection, supply marketing and transportation, equipment and power, political work, security and administration and finances. A complete set of activities were carried out to manage the unit at the same level, though the manager functioned under the supervision of the next higher level, the district or the county director of industries. There was no trade union in this enterprise either. The explanation given was the same, namely that village-run enterprises had peasants working in them. However, there was a branch of women's federation in this factory. As mentioned earlier, 51 per cent of the 330 workers were women. But it was not an autonomous organization of female workers of the plant. It was a branch of the Hela commune-level unit, which was in turn a branch of the ACWF.

Since the size of this plant was relatively large, there was a party branch with one secretary and one deputy secretary and three members in it. Among the workers of the plant, there were 12 party members. After 1978, the party's role had been slowly differentiated from the work of the management. The enterprise manager was the deputy secretary of the party branch. In theory, the secretary was a political superior. But his/her role was that of an indirect evaluator. The party secretary was more concerned with political education rather than factory management. As discussed earlier, the role of the party was re-emphasized during the Xi Jinping regime. At the level of the local enterprise, more often this was done by having the same person as the party secretary and the enterprise manager.

The production plan of the enterprise was worked out jointly by the enterprise manager and the director of the township industrial department under the supervision of the suburban district industrial bureau. During 1980–87, the enterprise was encouraged to decide its own production plan but it was always subject to approval by the higher levels. From 1992 until 1997, it was gradually conforming to the plans handed down from above. The trend was clear. The new strategy envisaged the TVEs to serve the requirements of the export-led faster growth process, rather than the original goals which aimed at providing employment to local labour, using local resources and contributing to local development.

Even though there was no trade union, the enterprise management had taken a few welfare measures for workers. The enterprise had a doctor who could treat ordinary ailments. There was a system of cooperative medical service to provide support to workers who fell sick.

The township-run agricultural machinery plant later renamed as Hela Machine Tools Factory had undergone further changes by 1985. The director, now called manager, was appointed by the township government, and the manager in turn appointed the deputy manager and section heads.

The section heads appointed their subordinates. This new system of recruitment to managerial levels was justified in terms of the requirements of the production responsibility system. They were hired to show results. They could be demoted or transferred if they failed to perform. Their salary and bonus went up or down, depending on their unit's production performance. There was yet another consideration behind the new recruitment system. In the mid-1980s, there was a great deal of discussion on 'ending life tenures' and finding successors to the old leaders and promoting young to responsible positions. This outlook spread everywhere. Many young managers were put in charge of factories. In 1985, the management of the factory had been expanded to some extent. It now had two deputy managers.

The party branch continued to have five members—secretary, deputy secretary and three members, one of them being a woman. The number of party members among factory workers had increased from 12 in 1980 to 16 in 1985. There were five female members among them. The party branch now helped the workers in acquiring training in various skills. The section heads and other cadres were sent to Wuxi Cadre School to study enterprise management. In the mid-1980s, the enterprise cadres spoke of '18 methods of modern management' that they had been taught in their cadres' schools. Most of them were acquired from the Japanese management practices, while some bore marks of the American concept of scientific management. Some relating specially to the production responsibility system had been evolved by the Capital Iron and Steel Company, Beijing. This system of management operated in full steam right through the 1990s when modern American management practices using infra-red and robotic control of employees' attendance and performance took its place.

The Wuxi Silk Factory which was a State-run factory under the Wuxi Municipal Government had also undergone similar changes in the management system in 1980. It had a director who was appointed by the Wuxi Municipal Government. The government also appointed three deputy directors who were in charge of production, economic management and supporting services. Under the production section, there were four departments—production technology, quality inspection, planning and research. Under the section on economic management, there were three departments—finance and accounting, supply of raw materials, marketing of products and personnel. The section on supporting services essentially dealt with worker's welfare, raising their living standards and facilities such as health and housing.

The Wuxi Silk Factory had two levels of management, one at the level of the whole factory and another at the level of each of the five workshops dealing with the five processes of silk production. Each workshop had a director and a deputy director who had full management authority and was appointed by the factory management. Earlier, even the workshops' directors and deputy directors were appointed by the government. This system was changed. After the reforms, each director and deputy director was appointed by the manager of the factory for a two-year term, at the end of which their work was assessed and decision was taken on renewal of their assignment. This gave the manager much greater authority in factory management than before.

Since this was a big enterprise with over 1,700 workers, there was a slightly larger party committee with 9 members. Under it, there were 12 party branches. Each branch had a committee of five members. Whereas the secretary of each branch was a worker at the same time, the secretary and deputy secretary of the party committee were full-time party cadres. It should be noted that during the Cultural Revolution, even these high-level cadres were required to participate in factory work like ordinary workers. There were over 300 party members in the factory or nearly 17.6 per cent of the total workers; such high proportion of party membership among factory workers was explained by the fact that the factory had a long history and it had many veteran workers. The party secretary was not the manager of the factory. Here, the manager was a member of the factory party committee. The functions of the party committee at the factory level were (a) checking up implementation of party's general line and policies, (b) ensuring the fulfilment of quotas and helping in making future plans, (c) participating in the appointment of leaders of workshops and decision regarding transfer and resignation of cadres and (d) participating in the decision-making on capital construction of the factory, for example, purchasing new boilers, expanding workshops' building facilities such as hospitals and houses for workers.

It was interesting to note that in 1980, the manager of the Wuxi Silk Factory explained the prevailing management system as being consistent with the principles of the Anshan Charter, particularly the principles of leader's participation in physical labour and worker's participation in management. He, however, said that each factory had to implement these principles according to its concrete situation. It should be noted that the Anshan Charter was criticized and rejected during the reform period as promoting anarchy disruptive of production. By the mid-1980s, the factory-level cadres did no longer take part in labour, whereas the workshop-level cadres did. Prior to the Cultural Revolution, in Wuxi Silk Factory, there was a professional management system with one director in charge. During the decade of the Cultural Revolution, all the leading cadres had been subjected to political criticism. Instead of professional cadres, the leaders of the factory were appointed by rotation. The factory had then a centralized management system. The workshops functioned as units of the factory management. Reflecting upon the experience of the 1970s, a manager said in 1980, 'In such a system it was very difficult to sum up experiences. All work was in a mess'.

The Wuxi Silk Factory had a regular trade union which functioned directly under the factory party committee. As the trade union leader put it, '[I]ts main role was to help the party in implementing the party's task by educating the workers'. The trade union committee had 17 members who were elected by the workers. Each workshop had a branch of the trade union (*fen gong hui*) consisting of five to seven members. The factory trade union committee held fortnightly meetings to sum up the work situation and make future plans. It periodically carried out labour emulation campaigns to motivate workers to perform well, following model workers. It organized advanced workers to study further and become model workers for others to follow. It conducted workers education classes once or twice a month.

The Wuxi Silk Factory had a WRC which met twice a year. In 1980, there were 220 representatives who had been elected by the workers roughly on the basis of one representative for about five workers. As mentioned earlier, this factory had 1,570 workers (81 per cent women) and 130 staff members. Each member made a monthly contribution of 0.25 yuan to the trade union fund. New workers contributed 0.10 yuan. The worker's representatives presented their reports to the annual session of the Workers' Representatives Conference on which there was full-scale discussion. Production trends, plans and management practices were discussed and suggestions were made in the annual and mid-term congress of the WRC.

During 1970–80, nearly 500 workers of advanced age were retired and over 400 were recruited in their place in the Wuxi Silk Factory. There was great deal of stress on training these workers to raise their level of competence. In this factory, according to the prevailing rules, workers' retirement age was put at 50 which was rather low because they were still capable of doing work. One could even retire at the age of 45 on medical grounds. The retired workers got a pension of 75 per cent of their final basic salary in this case. This, too, was higher than in most cases. Probably, this was due to a package of measures for replacing old hands with new, skilled people. The newly recruited workers were all 25 years old or younger. The rest of the workers in the factory were between the age of 25 and 35. The factory had built dormitories and small flats for workers. The trade union leaders said in 1980 that housing was still a problem. By then, migrant workers from less-developed areas had started coming to Wuxi. In the 1990s, the migrant workers from Subei (Northern Jiangsu) had been the bulk of the workers in Wuxi enterprises. In the Wuxi Silk Factory, there was a nursery where working mothers could leave their children during the working shift. It did not charge any fee for single-child families. Similarly, medical charges for children were exempted in the case of the one-child families. There was a small medical clinic in the factory. The labourers had eight-hour working day, with one day off every week. Female workers were given 20 minutes break twice a day to feed their babies. After seven months of pregnancy, their working hours were reduced from eight to seven hours a day. After delivery, the women got 56-day maternity leave with full pay. In this factory, there was no difference of wages between men and women for the same work. But in other factories, the disparity of wages among men and women was conspicuous and growing. We discuss this issue in Chapter 8 on women.

These trends in the management of the Wuxi Silk Factory had acquired considerable significance by 1985 in the course of the structural reforms of the early 1980s. Without expanding the size of the plant, there was stress on consolidation and readjustment of production. This factory was the second group of enterprises in China where industrial restructuring had been introduced. Under this system, the director/manager assumed the responsibility for economic results. As before, the manager was appointed by the city government, and he/she in turn appointed the deputy. The quota-based production responsibility system was now operating more rigorously than before. The interaction between the management and the workers continued through the WRC whose strength was reduced from 220 to 100. The reduction in membership showed that the management wished to deal with a smaller number of representatives and acquire more authority for effective management and show results. By 1985, a new institution had come into being, namely Workers' Democratic Management Group, consisting of 30 members with 5–6 members in each workshop. This group met generally once a month to discuss production plans and financial matters. The WRC, however, met once in six months as before. It was said that the workers–management interaction had thus become streamlined and the Workers' Democratic Management Group had become its main channel. However, this practice did not seem to prevail in other factories.

The strength of the party committee at the factory level had come down from nine to seven with three women in it. After the mass retirement, the number of party members among workers had come down to 160. The role of the trade union continued to be the same with emphasis on workers' welfare and living conditions and also various personal problems of facilities. The trade union had a seven-member standing committee with a full-time secretary who drew a salary of only 80 yuan per month from the factory account.

Two points of difference between the rural enterprises and the State-run factories should be underlined. Firstly, in the larger State-run factories like the Wuxi Silk Factory, there was a four-dimensional management system involving the managers or directors and their deputies, the party committee and the party branches, the WRC and the trade union. On the other hand, in the township- and village-run enterprises, neither the trade union nor the WRC was in existence. Only in the township enterprises which had a sizeable number of workers, there was a party branch. But on the whole, enterprise managers had enormous power in managing the rural enterprises. No doubt they operated under the supervision of the concerned department of township, county and suburban district. But they had a great deal of autonomy in decision-making. This was their strength in so far as they could diversify, innovate and invest imaginatively to make profit. It also sometimes led to problems such as avoidable experiments, uneconomic investments and arbitrary wage fixation.

The second difference lies in the linkage of the enterprises with the national economy. While both the rural enterprises and the State-run urban enterprises generally conformed to the broad State plans, the State-run factories were far closer to the monitoring system by the government than the rural enterprises. Towards the latter, the government was deliberately more liberal so as to allow the township and village considerable autonomy in launching and managing enterprises. That was intended to employ surplus labour, utilize rural savings and raise the standard of living of peasants. It was not only meant to develop a rural market for the expanding supply of consumer goods but also to maintain peasant support for the regime. But on one thing they were on a common ground. There was no compromise on the application of production responsibility system whether it was the rural or urban enterprise.

In the 1990s, the management practices were further streamlined. The concept of group contract (*jiti chenbao*) was forcefully implemented. Every enterprise entered into contracts with various agencies and its profit depended on the returns. Within an enterprise, engineers, technicians, workers and divisional managers also entered into contracts with the general manager or director. Everyone's wage, particularly the bonus, varied with the degree of performance.

Under this system, managers had emerged as prosperous elements in the new economic system in medium-range enterprises; the annual income of a manager ranged between 50,000 and 60,000 yuan per year. In larger enterprises, it was much higher—in the range of 200,000–300,000 yuan. The engineers got less than the managers and the salaries and bonuses were based on their performance. Compare it with the incomes during the 1980s when 10,000 yuan (*yi wan* yuan) was considered as conspicuous. Now a new class had emerged. They were the new elites of China not only in the countryside but also in the urban areas where these households also had a foothold either through their economic transaction or through a family member.

The relationship between the managers and the party secretary in an enterprise has always been an interesting pointer to the prevailing political framework. As has been mentioned earlier, during the 1980s, the enterprise managers acquired prominence in the political framework at both the township level and the village level. During the second period, in the late 1980s, the party secretary re-emerged as the leader in an enterprise. This also was the period when in some TVEs, there were tensions between the party secretary and the manager. After 1992, the situation clearly developed in a new way. Now the party leadership was directly in charge of economic administration. Operationally, however, the manager of the enterprise at the township level was given full autonomy by the enterprise party branch. In a large number of enterprises at the township and village levels, the manager was also the secretary of the enterprise party branch.

The enterprise managers were required to follow the national policy on economic management of enterprises. In the post-1992 period, the focus was on improving the technology level, making economical use of natural resources and taking serious steps towards environmental protection. Hence, every enterprise had a research wing. The provincial environmental bureau had strict guidelines for checking pollution and advising corrective measures. In Wuxi, the expansion of rural industries had encroached upon farmland in a big way. Therefore, the suburban district government and the respective township governments had to constantly monitor the industrialization process and its effect on agriculture. For optimal use of farmland and scientifically planned agricultural development, every township government used part of the income from rural enterprise to support agricultural. The Wuxi Municipal Government also spent about 500 million yuan on developing agricultural infrastructure. But the major sources of agricultural investment came from the township and village reserve fund. The rural enterprise managers thus had a role in the larger development process in addition to showing growth and profit in their enterprises.

In the new system, they emerged as a new stratum of skill, wealth and influence in rural China. Together with the specialized households, they earned more than the workers and peasants, even more than the engineers and party cadres. In fact, the trend to the 1990s was the emergence of technically qualified party cadres put in the role of enterprise managers.

Significance of TVEs

This account of some rural enterprises in the suburbs of Wuxi highlights three trends in China's countryside. One is the diversification of rural economy in the direction of industrialization. It went much beyond the earlier notion of diversification which had meant adding forestry, animal husbandry, fishery and such other sideline productions. Now enterprises undertook to produce many new products ranging from elevators to design garments. Second is the reform in the wage system. The remuneration now depended on the quantity and quality of work performed by each worker, and every bit of additional performance was rewarded monetarily. Thirdly, the management system was transformed giving great deal of autonomy to the enterprise and its manager to produce results by responding to the market.[17]

Rural industrialization had been tried in China during the Great Leap Forward in 1958 when a programme of five 'small-scale industries' was launched. They were the small iron and steel works, small hydropower stations, small fertilizer plants, small cement factories and small kilns. But due to the lack of attention to quality of products and managerial problems, this programme was a failure and hence was abandoned. In 1978 too, the initial spur in the development of commune industries produced low-quality goods. Therefore, great care was taken in the 1980s to make the rural industries viable. Deng Xiaoping set the framework for the new approach to industrialization which included multi-level industries.[18] One of the prominent economists Du Runsheng who was a key adviser to the Deng regime on rural reforms emphasized in 1984 that the rural enterprises should be 'small but specialized' using high-tech methods of production.[19] That would make them competitive in the market. He also advised that they should use locally available raw materials. Even then there were reports of products of poor quality in many enterprises. The phenomenon of 'irrational industrial mix' was one of the subjects of discussion in 1992 which referred to enterprises using up excessive energy but producing low-standard goods. Therefore, a new agenda was worked out to develop the rural enterprises in the 1990s with focus on improved technology, better training of workers and more effective management methods.

Several new steps were taken to streamline the rural industries in the 1990s.[20] Firstly, in the Yangtze River Delta in East China, they were closely integrated with urban economy under a programme of coordinated economic development. The big and medium industries of the city, the local universities and research institutions were playing their role in this process to benefit. Secondly, enterprises were forming groups to take advantage of scale, improve technological level and develop together. By early 1992, over 40,000 such groups had come into being, some of them including a few State-run enterprises as well. Thirdly, some enterprises had started the shareholding system to raise additional capital, providing a profitable outlet to people in their areas who now had money to save. In Jiangsu alone, 500 such enterprises had come up. Fourthly, many rural enterprises were developing an export-oriented economy. Already there were 60,000 such enterprises. Of the 7,000 joint enterprises with foreign capital, 1,000 were in Jiangsu alone, involving US$500 million. Some rural enterprises had set up production units in foreign countries too. Fifthly, for reasons of quality production and higher profit, many rural enterprises were shifting from labour-intensive production to technology-based production, a process in which Jiangsu province was leading. All this is part of the process of making rural enterprises a key to comprehensive economic, cultural and social development of the rural areas. But this attempt was not pursued all the way and by the late 1990s, the key role of the TVEs in China's economy had diminished substantially.

The per capita real income of residents of rural China in 1978 was 255 yuan which increased by 2.1 times to 545 yuan in 1988 with an annual average increase of 11.8 per cent. In 1991, it went up further to 710 yuan. This dramatic rise was to a large extent due to the rural industries. This experience shows that for populous peasant societies, rural industrialization could be a catalytic factor in the rural political economy. But this cannot be done neglecting food grain production and other processes of producing for meeting the consumption needs of the population. That is why CPC General Secretary Jiang Zemin in his political report to the Fourteenth Party Congress in 1992 underlined the need to ensure that the output of grain and cotton increased steadily and then talked about 'vigorously expanding township enterprises', particularly in the backward central and western areas inhabited by minority nationalities. The new rural policies may have contributed to the increasing disparities in the countryside, consumerism and moral degradation. Still in terms of creating material conditions for better life for China's peasants, the rural enterprises had played a catalytic role. They raised the income of every rural household, contributed to agricultural development and supported primary education and health care of the rural population. That their products were of poor quality and were energy-intensive was true. But instead of tackling these problems while strengthening TVEs, the new growth strategy after 1992 decided to shift attention elsewhere.

During Hu Jintao regime, it was a balanced role between the manager and the party secretary. After Xi Jinping came to power, the party secretary's role was given more prominence.

Finally, the worker's role in the new framework changed in a major way. The Cultural Revolution practice of direct participation by workers in making production plan was abandoned. Earlier, all the workers of the factories used to meet frequently—in some places once or twice a week—to discuss various issues concerning the enterprise. They used to write 'big character posters' on factory walls and gates, commenting on the performance of the factory management and often criticizing management committee. All issues ranging from technology and products to wages and working conditions were taken up in these mass meetings called workers' assemblies. During the Cultural Revolution, all the prevailing institutions including the trade unions and WRCs were replaced by revolutionary committees which also denied institutional participation of workers. During the reform period too, workers' participation in decision-making had remained on paper. Independent trade unions, that is, those not affiliated to the CPC, were not allowed to be formed in China. The role of the trade unions is one of a welfare channel for recording and conveying to the authorities the difficulties faced by the workers. Otherwise, it is a mass organization where leaders are trained to take up positions of party functionaries later.

The Su Nan Model

Wuxi's experience with rural enterprises had been described as the Su Nan model (south region of Jiangsu province and also of Yangtze River model). The characteristics of this model were as follows: One, rural industries played the key role in transforming agricultural economy. Two, among the industrial enterprises, most were SMEs. Three, as for the forms of ownership, by and large they were collectively owned. Four, the investment for the enterprises came from within the rural economy which in turn supported agriculture.[21]

The rural enterprises transformed Wuxi's economy to such an extent that this area acquired a leading position in whole of China. The success in this effort had a chain effect on different sectors of the economy. It became a major source of capital construction for agriculture as well as new rural enterprises including the tertiary sector. By providing employment to a large section of surplus labour, it increased the family income of peasants. This had a particular significance for this region which is a densely populated area with limited land. Without the development of rural enterprises, it would have been impossible to upgrade farmers' living standards. As a Wuxi official put it, the rural enterprises had created 'a new socialist countryside'. For some years, it was perhaps true, after which the urban–rural gap widened.

Shift of Strategy and Abandonment of TVEs

During the mid-1990s, there was a full-scale review of the experience with rural enterprises in China. Questions were raised as to whether they had reached a plateau. In fact, an official in Wuxi admitted that there was a need to review the experience. The new points of discussion were how to emphasize quality in production, improve technology, follow more effective management practices and be more responsive to the market. It was realized that the advantage that the rural enterprises enjoyed vis-à-vis the State enterprises and many private firms during the initial period had disappeared. Now they could not compete with the latter, hence the need for improvement. In January 1997, the State Council of China sponsored a National Conference on Rural Enterprises. Following this, the CPCCC and the State Council issued a circular on the situation and future reform and development of rural enterprises in March. Thereafter, on 1 July 1997, a new law on rural enterprises was promulgated. On the whole, these measures sanctioned the continuous growth of rural enterprises. The law standardized the performance of the rural enterprises and protected the interests and legal rights of the enterprises and their employees. It called upon the enterprises to improve upon their management system, adopt democratic management, and upgrade efficiency and strength measures for labour safety. The stress on improvement of quality of products was conspicuous in these measures. The enterprises have been asked to reduce use of farmland. There are number of provisions asking the enterprises to conserve energy and check pollution. In 1996, 5,000 small paper mills, tanneries and dyeing factories along the Huaihe River were shut down because of serious river contamination. Most of them were rural enterprises.

There were two new measures that were highly publicized under the new policy. One was to promote clusters of rural enterprises by locating a number of them in one development zone or small town. This policy had already been put into force in Wuxi in 1993. Taking the country as a whole, more than 10,000 such special clusters had been created by the end of 1995, housing over one million enterprises. As mentioned earlier, in these development zones, roads and railway links were especially developed and energy sources were optimally utilized. Common service facilities including market and social amenities were also provided. Secondly, the rural enterprises of the developed east coast were encouraged to set up enterprises in the backward region of the west. Under this policy, 152 joint projects had been launched in 1995 and 1996 for which the Ministry of Agriculture and the Agricultural Bank of China had invested 5.1 billion yuan. In 1996, 15,000 agreements were signed between rural enterprises from the eastern provinces and those in the western regions with negotiated investment amounting to 35 billion yuan. The developed enterprises from provinces like Jiangsu provided financial investment and technology, while the enterprises in the western region used their natural resources and labour. This collaboration brought more profit to the eastern provinces while helping the development of the backward western region. This was also part of the national policy for eradication of poverty. In addition to the central allocation through the Ministry of Agriculture, a major role was played by the developed enterprises of the eastern provinces to help the development of rural enterprises, commerce, horticulture as well as agriculture in the western provinces (Table 6.5).

This scenario began to change further in the 1990s. Development of privately owned rural enterprises was a growing phenomenon in the 1990s in China. According to one estimate, nearly half of the collective enterprises

Table 6.5:
Total output of TVEs (1980–2013; 100 million yuan)

Year	China	Jiangsu
1980	678.32	—
1985	2,728.40	352.12
1990	9,780.34	951.36
1995	69,568.66	5,237.46
2000	116,150.27	11,388.49
2004	172,515.73	24,401.09
2010	112,232	82,469.06
2013	522,375.68	121,349.62

Sources: He Kang, *China's Township and Village Enterprises*, 403–04; Ministry of Agriculture of the PRC, *China Agriculture Yearbook*, 2014; Statistical Bureau of Jiangsu Province, *Jiangsu Statistical Yearbook*, 2000 (Basic Situations of Rural Townships Collective Enterprises); 2001; 2011 (Basic Indicators of TVEs, Table 10-22).

in the rural sector were converted to privately owned enterprises by 1995. The figures for Wuxi also showed the trend (Table 6.2). This was particularly encouraged because of the acute unemployment problem. The reforms in the SOEs would lay off several million workers. On the other hand, the rural enterprises were engaged in improving their technological level without adding more labour or shedding off surplus labour. It was expected that the private enterprises would be more innovative and would set up new ventures besides reviving sick units in the process, providing employment to some additional workers. The new entrepreneurs could diversify their production and use profit from one enterprise for investment in another.

There was a debate at the national level on the approach to the future of the rural enterprises. One line of thinking was to incorporate them into the multi-structured industrialization programme: multi-structured in the sense of ownership of different types, private, collective, joint sector, shareholding corporations and State. This view was reflected in the statement of Professor Qi Jiangsu of CASS: 'Township enterprises were a special product for a special time'. They point out the programmes of low-skilled labour, outdated management capital shortage, poor technology, excessive utilization of energy and low competitiveness which could not continue in their original shape for long.

The other viewpoint asserts the critical significance of rural enterprises in China's economic development. The vast surplus rural labour could be absorbed only through rural enterprises. In fact, nearly 130 million people had been employed by the end of 1997. The circulation of capital for developing a diversified rural economy by utilizing agricultural surplus for rural industry and profit from the latter for agricultural development and both sectors contributing to education, health and other infrastructure made rural development self-financing to a very large extent. Rural enterprises contributed substantially to the increase in peasant income, thus making rural China an expanding market for Chinese as well as world industry. The social and political stability in rural China which had resulted from this development was of enormous significance. Explosive migration and massive rural unemployment could have caused social tensions of a high magnitude. Keeping the vast rural population gainfully engaged in rural economy itself and improving their living standards was a major policy of Deng Xiaoping's China during the 1980s.

The cultural dimension of this policy should not be underestimated. Chinese peasants love their birthplace and hesitate to leave their village. Even when they left the village to take up a city job they invariably maintained a connection with their village. The modernization wave has taken a part of the family to cities within the country and overseas, while another part of the family may continue to live in the ancestral homeland (*laojia*). Thus, Fei Xiaotong's thinking on transformation of the peasantry in his book *Peasant Life in China*, originally presented in the 1930s and reiterated in the late 1970s, continues to be vindicated. Setting up rural enterprises and developing small towns were essential for China's rural transformation. Thus, though the rural enterprises had to be restructured and modernized from time to time, they had a possible role as an integral part of China's development process in the twenty-first century. But their central role was abandoned as China moved to adopt a different growth strategy stepped into a success trap.[22]

If India and other developing countries had to avoid a 'success trap' that might achieve high growth but with enormous cost in terms of inequality, distress migration and environmental degradation among others, then attention had to be paid to the rural economy.[23] There were three concrete lessons for India, none of which involved replicating the TVE experience. Firstly, every rural unit, block and even panchayat had to be encouraged to plan to set up rural industries that used both the local resources and the resources from outside. In China, they had used the surplus from agriculture and savings of the collective. With that, they took bank credit. The government facilitated that with low taxes. The collective economy also had to be complemented by private investment and management. But the principles of coordinated rural transformation under the initiative of the village committee had to be maintained. Financing rural development from the resources now available with devolution of funds in India had to be considered along with other sources of rural finance. Secondly, providing rural employment not just under relief programmes but also in profitable enterprises of many kinds had to be the goal. The way the TVEs went for very modern industries with modern technology and collaboration with city enterprises in the early years provides some clue to this. For this, the education and health systems in the rural areas were supported by the local government as also vocational training. Thirdly, rural development had to be a part of a comprehensive rural–urban development continuum with multiple tiers of cities and towns linked to villages. Unfortunately, the present outlook dominating leaders of both India and China is governed by megacity ideology of urbanization and high growth rates. 'Village and the city serving each other' was the perspective that guided China's early reform leaders and was the principle governing the China's economy during the first three decades as well. We may remember that it was also the perspective championed by many leaders of India's freedom struggle. But the TVE phase in China's reforms is now history. The CPC leaders moved in the direction of achieving high growth and managing problems accompanying it. How those policies created crises in China's countryside, despite signs of prosperity, is the theme of the next chapter.

Notes and References

1. This has been the central issue of debate on Panchayati Raj in India. See Mohanty, Mathew, Baum, and Ma, *Grass-roots Democracy in India and China*; Niraja Jayal, ed., *Local Democracy in India* (New Delhi: Oxford University Press, 2006) and Girish Kumar, *Local Democracy in India* (New Delhi: SAGE Publications, 2006).

2. The TVEs are characterized as fulfilling a 'historical mission', 'a leading force that has propelled China's market economy forward, a vital pillar of the rural economy and an important component of the national economy'. He Kang (ed), *China's Township and Village Enterprises*, 293. It also carries as appendix the law of the PRC on TVEs which came into force on 1 January 1997. By then, the TVEs had undergone many changes. But it legitimized their character. See also Xue Liang, 'The Evolution of Township and Village Enterprises (TVEs) in China', *Journal of Small Business and Enterprise Development* 13, no. 2 (2006): 225–41.

3. The first circular (*Zhongfa*) of 1984 (every year, the party centre issues its first circular on rural work on the New Year's Day) said:

   The existing commune and production brigade enterprises constitute the mainstay of rural economy and some of them are indispensable to large urban industries. They need to undergo continuous consolidation, establish and improve the responsibility system, improve management and operation, adopt appropriate techniques and raise economic results; and this will promote their healthy development.

   Liu Suinian and Wu Qungan, eds., *China's Socialist Economy: An Outline History 1949–1984* (Beijing: Beijing Review Press, 1986), 666–67.

4. CPC Central Committee Circular Concerning Rural Work in 1984 (1 January 1984). Appendix in Liu Suinian and Wu Qungan, *China's Socialist Economy: An Outline History (1949–1984)*, 656–71. See also 'How Township and Village Enterprises Developed' essay by the Editorial Board, in He Kang (Ed) (Beijing: Foreign Languages Press, 2006), 1–45.

5. In his Report on the Work of the Government to the Fifth Session of the Seventh NPC, Premier Li Peng said:

   Township and Village enterprises, which play a vital part in the rural economy, have become an important component in the economy as a whole…. The hope is that this will enable them as soon as possible to emerge from backwardness and to raise the living standards of their inhabitants.

   Li Peng, *News from China* 4, no. 21 (15 April 1992): 5–6. See also *Xinhua*, 'Rural Enterprises in China Getting Mature', Beijing, *Xinhua*, 26 April 1992, in *News from China* 4, no. 23 (29 April 1992).

6. Ministry of Agriculture, China, quoted in Kang, *China's Township and Village Enterprises*, 185.

7. Du Runsheng, 'More Village and Town-based Industrial Enterprises by China's Peasants' in *China's Economic Reform* (Beijing Foreign Languages Press, 1989,) 57.

8. The period of the rise of the TVEs was governed by the decisions of the CC and the State Council from time to time. Only in 1996, the NPC Standing Committee adopted the law of the PRC on TVEs that was effective from January 1997. It spells out the features and functional regulations.

9. Xue Liang, 'The Evolution of Township and Village Enterprises (TVEs) in China', *Journal of Small Business and Enterprise Development* 13, no. 2 (2006): 225–41.

10. Yongqiang Li, 'An Overview of Township and Village Enterprises in China during 1949–2009', in *Proceedings of the 2nd International Conference on Corporate Governance*, 240–261. Available at: https://www.researchgate.net/publication/265315175_An_Overview_of_ Township_and_Village_Enterprises_in_China_during_1949-2009 (accessed on 30 July 2017).

11. Ibid.

12. We get an idea of the range of industries collectively owned by the *xiang* from the following list of 19 enterprises provided by the Hela *xiang* director in 1985:

    1. Wuxi Shi Elevator Plant
    2. Wuxi Shi Vehicle Parts Plant
    3. San-mica Plant
    4. Foam Leather Factory
    5. Wooden Products
    6. Paper Boxes Factory
    7. Metal Products Factory
    8. Fodder Plant
    9. Construction Station
    10. Electronic Device Factory
    11. Woollen Works
    12. Transportation Station
    13. Cold Storage
    14. Long March Pharmaceutical Plant
    15. Electric Metres Plant
    16. Fish Breeding Machinery Plant
    17. Hela Radio Components
    18. Garment Factory
    19. Machine Tools Factory

13. Zhu Shousong, Deputy Chief of Economic Division Rural Enterprises Bureau of Wuxi in an interview with the author on 9 October 1996. See also Jiang Wandi, 'Optimistic About Township Industry', *Beijing Review,* 40, no. 47 (17–23 November 1997), 18.

14. One of the three essays of Deng Xiaoping which were criticized by the media controlled by the Gang of Four during the last phase of the Cultural Revolution (1974–76) was the essay on enterprise reforms. Deng Xiaoping, 'Some Comments on Industrial Development (18 August 1975)', in *Selected Works of Deng Xiaoping 1975–1982* (Beijing: Foreign Languages Press, 1984).

15. Pamella Yatsko, 'New Owners: Privatisation comes to China's Township Enterprises', *Far-Eastern Economic Review* 161, no. 6, 5 February 1998). This is a case illustrating the new trend. A snicker manufacturing unit in Yangyang Township in Jiangsu province which incurred losses was taken over by Xu Fazhen and her husband who already ran a

kitchenware business. They turned it into a metal products factory showing considerable profit.

16. *Communique of the Third Plenary Session of the 11th Central Committee.* Appendix in Liu Suinian and Wu Qungan, *China's Socialist Economy: An Outline History (1949–1984)* op. cit., 569.

17. For a comparative study of rural enterprises in four counties (*xian*), two less prosperous than the others, see William A. Byrd and Lin Qingsong, eds., *China's Rural Industry: Structure, Development and Reform* (New York, NY: Oxford University Press, 1990).

18. Deng Xiaoping, 'Some Comments on Industrial Development (18 August 1975)'.

19. Du Runsheng, 'More Village and Town-based Industrial Enterprises by China's Peasants'.

20. Zhu Shousong, deputy chief of Economic Division Rural Enterprises Bureau of Wuxi, in an interview with the author on 9 October 1996.

21. He Kang, *China's Township and Village Enterprises*, 335–37.

22. Manoranjan Mohanty, 'China's Success Trap' (Foundation Day lecture, Madras Institute of Development Studies, Chennai, 18 April 2013).

23. Manoranjan Mohanty, *TVEs in China's Success Story: Lessons for India* (The 7th V. B. Singh Memorial lecture, Giri Institute of Development Studies, Lucknow, 25 July 2016).

7

Prosperity and Problems in the Countryside

Transformation of Rural China

The story of the Chinese village during the reform era illustrates China's success story and the success trap. People in the countryside shared the growing prosperity having new houses, living amenities including all modern household gadgets, new roads to the village and malls in the local shopping centre that sold foreign goods and many such things. The food basket had undergone a drastic change with people eating more meat as that was seen as a sign of progress. The common refrain in public conversations became something like this: In Mao's China, one ate more rice and vegetables with a touch of pork; in Deng's China, you ate pork as the main meal with a little vegetable to supplement. In fact, the living standards, according to all the usual indicators, of all villagers had improved substantially during the reform period. The per capita annual income on a standard scale increased more than 10 times during 1990 and 2015 from 686.3 yuan to 11,421 yuan. Out of this income, in 1990, a major proportion came from household operations including agriculture (518.6 yuan), and the income from wages and salaries was only 138.8 yuan. This structure of income underwent vast changes by 2013 when incomes from both these were close, with 3,793.2 yuan from the household operations and 4,025.4 yuan from wages and salaries.[1] Similarly, in 2015, income from wages and salaries constituted 4,600 yuan.[2] With the growth of enterprises, the sources of income changed. Among the remarkable success stories of China's countryside the most important one is the substantial reduction in poverty (Table 7.1 and Figure 7.1). As per one Chinese official estimate, it came down from 250 million people or 30.7 per cent under poverty line in 1978 to less than 15 million or 1.6 per cent in 2007. On a revised norm for poverty alleviation in rural areas, the official 2013 figure was put at over 82 million or 8.5 per cent of the total population,[3] and 55.75 million or 5.7 per cent in 2015 year-end. As per this calculation, the number of poor was estimated to be over 500 million in 1980 and that came down to less than 100 million over the 30-year period. At the Twelfth

Table 7.1:
Poverty in rural China

Years	Poverty Population (10,000 People)	Poverty Headcount (%)
1980	22,000	26.8
1985	12,500	14.8
1990	8,500	9.4
1995	6,540	7.1
2000	3,209	3.5
2005	6,432	6.8
2010	2,688	2.8
2013	8,249	8.5
2015	5,575	5.7

Sources: National Bureau of Statistics of China, *China Statistical Yearbook,* 2014, 206; 2015, 170; 2016 (Table 6-35).

Note: In 2010, rural poverty alleviation standard was fixed at 2,300 yuan at 2010 constant prices per person per year.

Figure 7.1:
Poverty in rural China

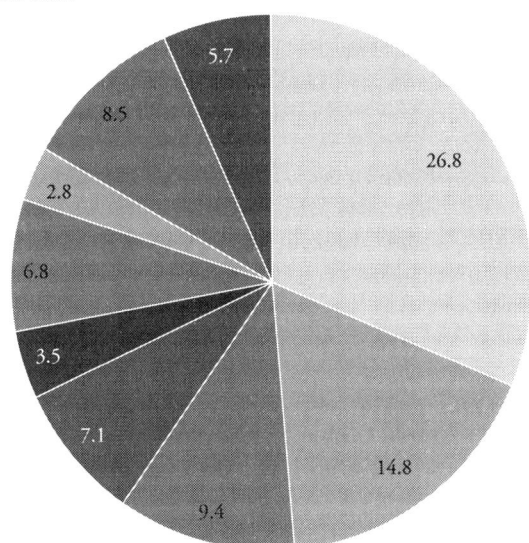

Sources: National Bureau of Statistics of China, *China Statistical Yearbook,* 2014, 206; 2015, 170; 2016 (Table 6-35).

Note: For year and population data, refer to Table 7.1.

NPC in March 2017, Premier Li Keqiang reported that 12.4 million people were lifted above the poverty line in 2016 and the plan was to help 10 million every year so that by 2020, the remaining 43 million would be out of poverty.[4] Table 7.2 showing urban–rural inequality also shows this steady improvement. But that is a part of the story.

The other part of the story is the distress in rural China. Agricultural production was no longer remunerative and employment opportunities in rural enterprises did not meet the needs of people. So, millions of rural workers

Table 7.2:
Progress in rural China

Items	1990	1995	2000	2005	2010	2013	2015
Per capita annual income (yuan)	686.31	1,577.74	2,253.42	—	5,919.01	9,426.6	11,421.7
Per capita annual expenditure (yuan)	548.6	1,310.4	1,670.1	—	4,381.8	7,485.2	9,222.6
Major durable goods per 100 households							
—Washing machines (unit)	9.1	16.9	28.6	40.2	57.3	71.2	78.8
—Refrigerator (unit)	1.2	5.2	12.3	20.10	45.2	72.9	82.6
—Motorcycle (unit)	0.9	4.9	21.9	40.70	59	61.1	67.5
—Air conditioner (unit)	—	0.2	1.3	6.40	16	29.9	38.8
—Computer (unit)	—	—	0.5	2.10	10.4	20	25.7
—Colour TV set (unit)	4.7	16.9	48.7	84.08	111.8	112.9	116.9
Per capita consumption of major foods							
—Grains (kg)	262.1	256.1	250.2	208.5	181.44	178.5	159.5
—Meat poultry and processed foods	12.59	13.56	18.30	22.42	22.15	22.4[a]	23.1
—Milk and processed products	1.10	0.60	1.06	2.86	3.55	5.7	6.3
—Aquatic products	2.13	3.36	3.92	4.94	5.15	6.6	7.2
—Fresh vegetables	134	104.6	106.7	102.8	93.28	90.6	88.7
—Fruits and processed products	5.89	13.01	18.31	17.18	19.64	29.5	32.3

Sources: National Bureau of Statistics of China, *China Statistical Yearbooks*, 1990, 1995, 2000, 2005, 2010, 2013, 2015.

Note: [a]2013 data for annual per capita poultry consumption was 6.2 kg, and in 2015, per capita pork consumption was 19.5 kg.

migrated to the cities. These migrant labourers' estimates varied from 250 million to 500 million—worked almost as second-class citizens in the cities as they were denied access to education, health and welfare facilities in the city. Moreover, the mechanization of agriculture also laid off many rural workers and consolidated farmland in rural countryside.[5] They retained their rural *hukou* in the village. Even though there had been some changes in the relaxation of *hukou* rules—the Third Plenary Session of 2013 under Xi Jinping's leadership opened up intermediate cities for treating them at par with the city residents—still the system discriminated against the rural citizen.[6] So, men migrated to cities, while women and children stayed behind with old people. Education and health facilities in the countryside lagged far behind those in the cities. Rural–urban inequalities of income and living conditions continued to grow or remain high (Table 7.2). The 'three rural problems' that the CPC acknowledged around 2000 were low productivity in agriculture, low income of the peasants and low state of rural infrastructure. Thereafter, 2003 onwards, the party announced a rural development plan called 'building a new socialist countryside'. But after 2010, both these items nearly faded away from public discourse. The new mantra along with economic growth was 'new urbanization'.

As mentioned earlier, the Thirteenth FYP adopted a techno-business-oriented modernization plan for rural areas. Firstly, to ensure the required amount of grain production—550 million tons for 2017—some land was designated as 'permanent basic cropland' with improved inputs in every respect. Secondly, integrated development of agriculture, industry and services were vigorously pursued with maximum use of modern technology and IT-driven business strategy, linking local with the national and global market. Thirdly, land rights of different kinds were recognized within the existing framework of collective ownership. Fourthly, a number of social security policies for rural residents, especially women and children, and migrant workers in the cities were announced. The plan of awarding urban residency to 100 million migrant workers in the Thirteenth Plan (2016–20), expanding access of migrant workers to education and health facilities, were some other measures.[7]

The National New Urbanization Plan (2014–20) was launched in March 2014 and that governed the path of urban–rural development in contemporary China. New urbanization aimed at synchronized or balanced development, layout optimization, sound ecological planning and cultural richness.[8] As an idea, the perspective was unexceptionable. But underlying the plan remained the logic of the reform strategy that had unfolded during the past decades. The urban population that stood at 54 per cent in

2013 is expected to reach 60 per cent by 2020 and that trend will continue. Therefore, building cities in the framework of 'reform and open door' by maintaining a moderate-to-high rate of growth and addressing the issue of rising urban–rural inequality and environmental problems with the declared goal of achieving a 'well-off society in all respects', was the policy perspective of the CPC. Following this line, the CPC leadership seemed to have opted for the megacity ideology that drives the current phase of global capitalist development where the 'global city' played the pivotal role as the centre of capital accumulation, advanced technology, innovation and trade and commerce. Within this framework, what we see is the continuing possibility of the problems of inequality, alienation and conflicts and therefore continuing need for centralized role of the party–State.

That the CPC leadership was aware of the serious problems in the countryside was evident from time to time. Under Xi Jinping's leadership, the Third Plenary Session of the CPC in 2013 decided on a three-pronged policy on 'integrated development of urban–rural area'. First, 'accelerating a new type of agricultural operation system' essentially by allowing farmers to subcontract to specialized households, form cooperatives, invite investment in agriculture and so on. Second, 'endowing farmers more property rights' under which they can mortgage land. Third, promoting equal exchange of factors of production by which the migrant workers would get equal wages for equal work, and allocating education, health care insurance and minimum living allowance among urban and rural residents equitably.[9] But much of it especially urban housing and social security network applied to those 'farmers who had registered as urban residents' under the decision, and it was not easy for migrant workers to get registered as urban residents.

In this chapter, we look at the process of change that the rural areas of Wuxi underwent with the start of the reforms. As the reforms proceeded, they became part of the city itself. The rural township became an urban district (*shiqu*) of the city, the village became a street (*jiedao*) or neighbourhood in the city district. Rural land owned by the village collective that was contracted to peasants for cultivation or fisheries became urban land owned by the State, used for real estate development, market buildings or offices or urban parks. There was compensation given to the villagers such as apartments for family members, space for shops and employment opportunities in some cases. The detailed account of the villages gives us an idea about the opportunities which they enjoyed before the pace of urbanization was accelerated and the later developments which brought them new sources of income, but accompanied by new problems. As said earlier, this area is a prosperous region in eastern China and the villages are close to the city. But this was the process that occurred throughout China even though the degree of urbanization was relatively low in some regions.

Village as the Basic Unit

A village or *nongcun*, meaning 'administrative village', was the production brigade (*shengcan dadui*), the intermediate level between the people's commune and the production team during the commune period. At that time, the production team comprising roughly the natural village or the hamlet was the key collective unit. In the course of the rural reforms of the 1980s and the early 1990s, however, the village emerged as the most significant unit at the grass-roots level in China's rural economy. The production team which was the crucial unit of ownership and accounting was practically dissolved and in its place 'villager's work groups' operated in many parts of China. In the new system, the production brigade was reorganized as the village, which became the lowest production unit supervising the family contract system in agriculture. It also managed rural industries and commerce at its own level. Operating under the overall supervision of the township government, the village assumed the charge of the direct management of the production process. After Deng Xiaoping's southern tour in 1992, as the momentum got generated for the growth of the market economic forces, the newly acquired significance of the village started declining. The collective economy at the village level gave place to private or joint enterprises catering to the expanding global market. That required centralized production plans involving investment and marketing strategies at the city and county levels for different sectors.

That comprehensively changed character of the rural economy and created serious problems which were officially described by the Chinese government as 'three rural problems' (*san nong wenti*) in 2000. The crisis had two sets of factors. Like in all modern agricultural systems using 'green revolution' methods, natural resources got depleted in China very fast. According to one report, 65 per cent of all water consumption in China was used only in agriculture in 2014.[10] Use of chemical fertilizers had reached such intensity destroying the quality of land that the State Council decided on a policy in 2017 to ban any increase in its use. Even more serious was the redirection of all the main factors of production from rural economy to urban, industrial economy.[11] Rural land was diverted from agriculture to industrial and commercial construction, thus decreasing the availability of land for cultivation. Even though the cultivated area is still above the so-called red line of 120 million ha—currently about 135 million ha—the situation is so alarming that the government had to declare a policy of 'permanent basic cropland'. As for rural labour, the trend of migration continued to grow. According to official data, the number stood at 277.47 million in 2015. But unofficial figures put it at much higher. The outflow of rural capital took place in two ways: by giving low prices for agricultural products and then through financial channels such as savings in banks. The former amounted to 0.5 trillion yuan during 1979–90 and the latter as much as 35.76 trillion yuan during 1995–2014.[12] This is how the accumulation process extracted surplus from the countryside to finance industrialization. In addition, there were new issues about the quality and quantity of food availability as well as food sovereignty in the context of globalization. Issues of poor conditions of social and physical infrastructure raised yet another dimension.

In this context, a number of initiatives were taken to respond to those problems under the programme of building 'a new socialist countryside'. In the meantime, the CPC had decided to introduce competitive elections at the village level, beginning experimentally in 1988 and regularly in 1998. That had induced a stream of political dynamism in the countryside even in the problem-ridden rural environment. So, in the course of the reform period, the emergence of village as a critical unit in China's grass-roots political economy and its decline with the rise of globalized market economy presented a useful reference point for all those who are interested in grass-roots democracy and equitable development.

In many ways, the reformed rural structure in the early 1980s restored the traditional system of rural administration in terms of the township and village. They also conformed to the pattern of socio-economic division of rural China in pre-liberation times. Township was a major unit of rural marketing structure. Village was a cluster of hamlets inhabited by certain clans and kinship groups. No doubt, during the preceding decades, a great deal of reshuffling had taken place in rural life in China. Yet, there was now a degree of convergence of traditional setting and modern institutions in China in the 1980s. The administrative and economic reasons for which there was a new focus on the village were no less conspicuous. After the dissolution of collective farming in 1979–80, land had been contracted to the families for cultivation. The size of the land depended on the number of labouring people in a family. To carry out this distribution process, the production team was too small a unit and the land at the disposal of the team was rather small in quantity. At the village level, distribution of land under the contract responsibility system was more practicable because of the larger amount of land under the village. At the same time, township was too large an area for effectively supervising family contract agriculture. This could be more closely done at the village level.

In addition to this, the size of the village was permitted to launch its own collectively run industries just as the township ran its own. If they had enough capital, as was the case with the rich villages in Wuxi's suburbs, they could set up industries in the same way as the townships did. Moreover, at the level of the village, the Communist Party and the Chinese government could have some presence. However, as a fully organized level of State and party in China, the township was the lowest administrative unit. Strictly speaking, the village was the lowest unit mainly as far as production management social affairs were concerned. In many villages, the chief official was described as 'Director of Agriculture, Industry and Commerce Company'. There were also a village representatives congress and village representatives committee which had the character of a mass organization rather than a State organ. Every village also had a party branch. Thus, in the reformed structure, the production management of the rural economy centred on the village.

Even though the village acquired an important economic role during the reforms, and after multi-candidate elections were introduced, it also enjoyed some political significance. Its formal institutional character remained one of 'mass organization'. Article 111 of the PRC Constitution said: 'The resident committees and villagers committees established among urban and rural residents on the basis of their place of residence are mass organizations of self-management at the grass-roots level'. On the other hand, the township and the town which had a 'people's government' were the lowest tier of the State. And for critical decisions on planning and political management, it was the county or the county-level city.[13] It is noticeable that in the 2000s and later, the Village was more often referred to as 'community organization' in the party documents and speeches of the leaders. But the village had the township above it and the hamlet or small village or the erstwhile production team below it. While in the 1990s, the focus of rural governance was the township or the county, before the reforms it was the small village collective that was the unit of production and mobilization.

The Team under the Village

As mentioned before, the production team was the lowest tier in the three-tier system of the commune, the production brigade and the production team. After the land reforms of the early 1950s, the mutual aid teams and the cooperatives operated more or less at the level of the village. If the village was too large, then it was split into two or three units as teams. Even though there had been frequent efforts to raise the collective unit of production to the brigade or village level for effective management as advocated by Mao, from January 1961 onwards, the production team remained the collective unit of agricultural production. In other words, people of a small village or part of a village together owned land around their village and shared income according to their labour. During the Cultural Revolution, there was a clamour for raising the collective unit to the brigade level again. But it was left optional to the communes. As the Article 7 in 1975 Constitution put it:

> The economic system of collective ownership in the rural people's communes at the present stage generally takes the form of three-level ownership with the production team at the basic level, that is, ownership by the commune, the production brigade and the production team with the last as the basic accounting unit.
>
> Provided that the development and absolute predominance of the collective economy of the people's Commune are ensured, people's commune members may farm small plots for their personal needs, engage in limited household side-line production, and in pastoral areas keep a small number of livestock for their personal needs.

Thus, when the 1975 conference on learning from Dazhai in agriculture took place, the emphasis was not on raising the collective level higher but on gradual mechanization of agriculture by consolidating the production team.

The commune system allowed clear authority to the production team in the following matters:

1. Keeping in view the State plan, the team decided what crops to grow.
2. The team had the right to work out its own policies and measures to achieve its targets.
3. The team had the right to pursue its own methods of management of industry and decide itself into groups and fixing quota for them.
4. The team could decide its principles of distribution and whether and to what extent give in cash or kind.
5. Not to blindly follow commands from above but to assert its own rights since law defined rights of each level.

However, the reform regime adopted a different approach. The households were made the primary units of agricultural production. Although land was still legally owned by the village collective, it was given on contract to households for cultivation on a long-term basis. The distribution of land was equitable as the quantum of land depended upon the number of members in a family. As mentioned earlier, the contract period was initially for 15 years, raised to 30 years and then indefinitely. What should be noticed is that below the village, there were still the traditional hamlets often as concentration of clans which were the former collective units, namely the production teams. As collective units, they became defunct from 1980 onwards. But in some concrete situations, they operated as work groups or small cooperatives which revived in the 2000s.

In places like Hela Township where fishing and vegetable growing were major occupations, there was a functional need for the team. Hence, the villagers formed work groups or villagers small groups (*cunmin weiyuanhui*) which were various kinds of labour and marketing cooperatives. But the team as the pivotal unit of agricultural production faded away and the next higher level, village, was considered to be a more appropriate level of the diversified economy and a viable economic unit.

The family re-emerged as the basic economic unit in the reformed economic structure in China. Even though there was no legal title to ownership of land, the long-term contract provided a piece of land which was seen as a symbol of a family's identity. Until now, it had the house site and the private plot besides the family's household assets and savings in the bank. The new land management system also changed the network of collective economic activities of the village. Earlier, the production team had managed not only grain production but also sideline production, commerce and industry. Moreover, it had a system of collective care for health, education and other welfare needs of the community. Now, the non-agricultural enterprises were run either by the village and township or by individual entrepreneurs.

In the earlier commune system, the family was also an economic unit. The labourers in the family—husband and wife and their adult working children if living with them—pooled their income together to run the family. Their savings were used for constructing new houses, buying new household goods, etc. It was not true that the family had ceased to operate as a social unit during the commune period. It was true that the family did not have the autonomy to reallocate to labour and invest in new undertakings. The team decided on the utilization of family labour. But when someone got education, he/she could go to the city for other jobs. He/she could join the army too. But such migration needed the team's sanction and the team leader's permission.

Both men and women earned albeit unequally wages from the team and contributed to the family income. Hence, during the commune period, the women had a higher status—only relatively than what they acquired after the rural reforms. Of course, the social ethos still placed men with better conditions of life and opportunities. In the reformed structure, now the land title belonged to the male leader of the household. The division of labour was also once again made unequally. In some areas, women stayed at home, did pig raising and the like, while men worked in the field. In Dongengshan, women worked in rural light industry and men did agricultural work. In some other teams, women worked in fields and men in city's sophisticated industries. In several teams, both men and women paid part-time attention to agriculture while earning their main wages from industry. In all cases, the family settled for 'lighter work and lower wages' in the case of women compared to men. This expression seemed to convey the prevailing thinking.

Did the new system of reforms foster individual freedom? To the extent the individual in the family was free to pursue new occupation, the answer could be in the affirmative. He/she could also migrate to the city for that purpose more freely. This indicated withdrawal of the State from the realm of family decision-making to some extent. But the individual was now left to himself/herself to find employment. The labour situation could be such that one could remain unemployed for a long time. The commune system had on the other hand engaged every adult, men and women, with some productive work in the field or in the construction of agricultural infrastructure. In the case of distress, the collective could draw from the commune fund and provide certain social security. But the turbulent years upset most such arrangements. Material conditions of freedom were created in both situations. But in the new situation, the differentiation in income and opportunity was much larger than before. There were rich households and the poor households. At the same time, with the growth of income, there was a rise in the standard of living. The savings of the family grew, enabling it to invest in new enterprises. The individual could perceive himself/herself as capable of pursuing new avenues of work in a wider environment. That is how many young peasants looked at the new situation. As for political conditions, the village collective had allowed the peasant more avenues of participation. The reformed system made peasant something of an autonomous entrepreneur but subjected him/her to the market forces over which he/she had little control. At the cultural plane, the peasant now saw himself/herself as a unit struggling in the larger market place far beyond the village. There was a loss of the cultural bond of the village, a loss of community. The vanishing team in China after the reforms heralded a new wave of alienation in the countryside.

Village Elections

When multi-candidate elections under a new law were introduced in China, there was much excitement within the country and abroad hoping that it was the beginning of the 'fifth modernization', that is, practice of liberal democratic form of multi-party politics.[14] But after more than two decades, it was clear that it was essentially a community engagement activity. But one must note that there is a logic of all institutional initiatives that have necessary consequences. Therefore, the introduction of statutory competitive elections at the village level had triggered a political process with democratic implications.[15] From our viewpoint, whether it could help China move out of the 'agency trap' was a moot question.

The first Organic Law for grass-roots government was enacted in 1987 that came into force in 1988 and was put into experimental use in some areas. In 1998, its amended version came into force all over China, leaving it open to provinces when they were ready to implement. By 2000, practically all provinces had their first round of elections to the villagers committee.

There are two sets of assessments of the grass-roots elections in contemporary China. One is a positive recognition of the realm of democratic space that it had created. The other takes it as a way of containing rural tensions and managing local interests under the party–State leadership. The first view sees it as a form of 'accommodating democracy in a one-party State' which has allowed rural citizens to exercise their 'right to participate' and use the occasion of election campaign to ask serious questions. Since the law provides 'recall' of villagers committee members with mass signatures, many villagers used the provision and succeeded in ousting some members.[16] As the social media has expanded exponentially and electronic media and movement of people have integrated the countryside with the urban areas, the local debates get publicity very fast. The presence of the foreign media has also made considerable difference. Therefore, all the issues of debate, ranging from corrupt practices involving land sale, pollution in the area and wage demands to campaigns against displacement caused by dams, industries and mining projects, come to public view. The village elections become the occasion for bringing many of these issues into the open.

The second view that considers it as a mechanism for local management rather than an institution of self-government points at the fact that the local elites have captured the offices at the village level, combining party, government and entrepreneurship, all in one. Many areas now continue to re-elect the same village leader who has been the party's nominee. Technically, there may be more than one candidate. Sometime, the higher party leadership suggests more than one, out of whom the villagers elect. They also point out that there was no indication of conducting the multi-candidate elections at the next higher level, the township level. Moreover, the village is considered only as a community organization and not as a political organ of State power at the grass-roots level.

On balance, the village elections have a political significance that should be recognized. Even if the elites maintain control and the new bourgeoisie in the countryside uses this institution to manipulate the village economy and dominate the sociopolitical scene, the election process itself opens up the political environment for discussion on important issues. As we see in the profiles of various villages, many important enterprises are located in the village. Even if they are owned now by private entrepreneurs, the issues come up for public discussion during the elections.

But at the same time, it is true that the village elections have produced mixed results. It has brought widespread cynicism among the populace, as it has merely become agent of the State to do the 'dirty work' of collecting taxes, implementing family planning policies and social stability issues.[17] There is no likelihood of this being extended vertically above village level in the coming years. Further, some critics point out that such democratization has led to anarchy, leading to poor governance and lack of consensus in the basis of local democracy. They think that far from being institutionalized, this has not actually strengthened competitive elections.[18]

Village elections may be a limited avenue for democratic politics, but they trigger a process of political significance. It may be interesting to note that Xi Jinping after becoming CPC general secretary frequently mentioned the fact that he served as the party secretary in a village (Liangjiahe village in Yanchuan county) in northwest China's Shaanxi province during the Cultural Revolution. So, the experience of a cadre working at the grass-roots level may be a very important milestone pushing him/her upwards for more responsibility.

Now let us take a closer look at some villages in the Hela Township. We take up two relatively developed and one less developed village. The focus is on the period between 1979 and 1993 when rural industries were the main driver of rural development and supported building of agricultural infrastructure as well as local health care and educational facilities. This account shows the nature of urbanization that took place at a fast pace in these and subsequent years not only in suburban areas such as this but also in interior rural areas where villages were getting integrated with rise of small towns. In all of them, the transformation of the economy and process of urbanization and their effects on people's lives are the points of our attention.

Hela Village

Of the 13 villages in the township, Hela village (as distinguished from Hela Township) and Lianhe village were two of the prosperous ones. The township headquarters which were originally located in Hela village had shifted to the sprawling complex in Lianhe village by 1985. The Qingxin village in the northwestern part of the township was a relatively less prosperous village. The two former villages had more rural industries contributing to their prosperity, whereas, in case of Qingxin, bulk of its productive income came from food crops. We will also refer to the fisheries village which is a collective enterprise operating through small work groups which was renamed Lihong village subsequently. They were still called village even after the township became town and then street.

Hela village had 1,081 households in 1980 which came down to 853 households in 1985, the corresponding population being 2,554 and 2,181. This reduction of households was mainly because several of them had become full-time workers in city enterprises or offices and were, therefore, not being counted as 'village households'. Some families had shifted to housing provided by the city. The others even while living in their own quarters were no longer part of rural economy. Thus, the village in a suburban area was partly a functional category and only partly a territorial category. In this, whether the jurisdiction of the city unit or the rural unit operated was the crucial factor. When a person worked in a village-run industry, he/she was a member of the village. Those working on land, of course, formed the bulk of the members of the village.

In 1980, Hela village was still called the production brigade. Several features of the commune system were still operating. It was basically a vegetable-growing brigade attempting further diversification of the rural economy. The Hela brigade had 15 production teams: nine vegetable growing, five vegetable growing along with silk worm breeding and one primarily silk worm breeding. Animal husbandry and poultry farming were also part of the collective production process. Already there was a trend towards looking for new economic activities because the brigade was losing more and more land to the city for the latter's expanding construction activity. At the same time, the brigade was also setting up industrial enterprises on its own land. Some land was also used for building new houses.

Between 1978 and 1979, the labour force and population of Hela brigade had come down from 1,400 and 2,800 respectively to 1,128 and 2,554. The area for vegetable growing had been reduced from 1,450 mu to 307 mu and for mulberry cultivation from 120 mu to 79 mu.

Vegetable production by the brigade was geared towards fulfilling the needs of the city population. With diversified production, the economy of the brigade had improved considerably. The per mu output value in the brigade's vegetable-growing area was 401.40 yuan. The performance in the year 1979 recorded a significant increase over the output value of 1978.

In 1979 and 1980, changes in the production pattern were already visible. Before the Third Plenary Session of the CPC in 1978, the focus was on grain production. As the brigade leaders pointed out, before the fall of the Gang of Four, the principle governing rural work was 'taking grain as the key link'.

An interesting but highly critical reference was made by local leaders to a reported remark by Vice-Premier Zhang Chunqiao, one of the Gang of Four during the Cultural Revolution, that peasants who engaged in vegetable grow-ing should not eat food grains. Everyone was expected to grow rice for their own needs as well as for the market. They pointed out that this had adversely affected vegetable production for many years. In the same way, setting up of rural enterprises was also banned. After the 'shift of focus' announced by the Third Plenary Session, there was a call to raise collective income and raise peasant income at the same time. That opened up the opportunities for diversified economy. Peasants undertook vegetable production in a big way. Silkworm production expanded fast, rural industries appeared on the scene and animal husbandry also increased gradually. The brigade leaders explained that the income from industry could be used for building agri-cultural infrastructure and also for medicare, education and other welfare purposes. The average income rose considerably. The per capita income (which included the aged and the children in the calculation) rose by a third. So did the per member income. The differential of income which was 2:7 in 1978 became 1:5. During the Cultural Revolution, there was a ceiling on income. No commune member was allowed to earn more than 200 yuan per year. The surplus was partly diverted into the public accumulation fund and was partly reserved for future distribution. After the Third Plenary Session, this ceiling was abolished. Under the reform perspective, there was no harm if some people became rich. This started a trend of social differentiation in Chinese society. Growing inequality was not a concern during these years for the goal was to raise production and profit.

In the case of industry, however, even in 1980, as much as 50 per cent of the profit was kept by the factory for reinvestments. The rest was distributed among workers in proportion to their labour. In 1980, the factories in Hela village were mainly engaged in processing work for the city. At this transitional stage, workers were given wages only through their production teams. The factory calculated a worker's wages and accordingly paid the relevant produc-tion team for further disbursal to the worker. In case the work-point value in the team was higher than that in the factory, then the team paid more to the worker after making a contribution out of its own fund. In case the team's work-point value was less than the factory's, it paid less. The latter dampened the enthusiasm of the workers. Incidentally, only the commune members engaged in agriculture had their personal accounting books, while the workers in enterprises had attendance cards as in State factories. This system was, however, streamlined in later years. Enterprise workers in the township and village factories were directly paid by their respective enterprises.

Hela Village after the Reforms

Five years after the reforms, the picture of Hela village had changed tremendously. Sun Ruide, who was the director of Hela brigade before, was now designated as the general manager of the United Agriculture, Industry and Commerce Company of Hela village. After the implementation of structural reform in 1983 in this area, Hela brigade had been turned into a joint company. Having lost even more land for construction to the city, this village was now mainly engaged in industry. The company was a comprehensive undertaking, 'combining industry and commerce with agriculture' in that order of importance in this village (Tables 7.3 and 7.4).

Table 7.3:
Rural–urban inequality in China: Per capita income and Engel's coefficient of urban and rural households (1980–2015)

Year	Per Capita Disposable Income of Urban Households Value (Yuan)	1978 = 100 Index	Per Capita Net Income of Rural Households Value (Yuan)	1978 = 100 Index	Engel's Coefficient of Urban Households (%)	Engel's Coefficient of Rural Households (%)
1980	477.6	127	191.3	139	56.9	61.8
1990	1,510.2	198.1	686.3	311.2	54.2	58.8
2000	6,280	383.7	2,253.4	483.4	39.4	49.1
2010	19,109.4	965.2	5,919	954.4	35.7	41.1
2013	26,955.1	1,227	8,895.9	1,286.4	35	37.7
2015	31,790.3	1,396.9	10,772	1,510.1	—	—

Sources: National Bureau of Statistics of China, 'People's Living Conditions', in *China Statistical Yearbook*, 2014, 158 (Table 6.4); 2016 (Table 6-16).

Table 7.4:
Hela brigade production trend

Products	Unit	1978	1979	Increase (%)
Vegetable production per mu yield	Dan	—	132	9.53
Value per mu yield	Yuan	—	401.40	11.25
Silkworm cocoon pieces	Jin	57.6	60.6	5.21
Mulberry leaves per mu		59.1	75.5	26.46
Pigs sold to State	Nos.	1,149	1,453	26.46
Brigade enterprises output	Yuan	471,800	854,800	81.18
Profit from enterprises	Yuan	104,000	200,400	92.69
Output value not including enterprises	Yuan	946,500	1,047,800	10.7
Team's production expenditure	Yuan	181,100	147,700	18.8
Public accumulation fund—60% Welfare fund—40%	Yuan	154,400	185,100	19.88
For wage distribution	Yuan	610,200	715,000	17.17
Per capita income	Yuan	208	276	32.69
Per member wage		410.60	545	22.73
Minimum		200	300	
Maximum		700	1,500	

Source: Interview with Hela brigade leaders in June 1980.
Notes: Dan = 50 kg; 1 Jin = 0.5 kg.

Hela village still had 10 production teams engaged in vegetable growing. But the bulk of the population was engaged in industrial work. Out of the 559 workers and staff members, 400 were engaged in the nine factories in the village. The rest were involved in the 10 production teams, two livestock and poultry farms, four small restaurants and one department store. Out of the nine factories, two were hardware factories, one plastic factory, one textile factory, one machine bearings factory, one knitwear and socks factory, one radio components factory, one vehicle repairing workshop and one furniture workshop. While some of them catered to the needs of big factories in Wuxi, others produced consumer goods mostly for the city markets. Thus, along with these industries, the village had in all 26 production units, covering a variety of productive activities.

The total output value of the village had reached 13.06 million yuan in 1984 as against 1.05 million yuan in 1979. This was mainly because of the rapid expansion of the rural industries. Industry accounted for 11.34 million yuan in 1984 as against 0.85 million yuan five years earlier. An interesting aspect of the sharp increase in industrial income was its contribution to agricultural development. Out of the reproduction fund in 1984, the village company had paid 50,000 yuan to support agriculture and 30,000 yuan for the expansion of pig raising. In 1984, industries in the village showed a profit of 1.89 million yuan out of which 471,300 yuan was used for distribution as wages and 649,600 yuan, that is, almost one and half times of the wages amount, was given to the company for reproduction purposes. A little less than the wage amount was paid as tax to the State. A very high amount was also earmarked for public welfare facilities such as health, education and recreation. Thus, it is noteworthy that in the reformed structure, the rural industries had a high accumulation rate and did not disperse bulk of their income on wages (Table 7.5).

Wages accounted for about a quarter of the profit made by the industrial enterprises, whereas more than a third was made available to the company for reinvestment. Out of this latter fund, the company could develop irrigation facilities and build new infrastructure and even launch new productive activities.

The State collected a good amount (22.63 per cent) as tax which was actually lower than in the case of many urban enterprises where it was 25–35 per cent. Hela village being in the suburbs of a prosperous city like Wuxi had to pay considerable attention to the provision of medical facilities, building of parks, maintaining schools and other public welfare activities. Hence, a significant share of the profit went to public welfare.

In 1984, the average annual income of a peasant in the village was 1,481 yuan, more than three times the average wage of 1978. For the factory workers in the village, the average income was 1,403 yuan. In Lianhe village, the

Table 7.5:
Allocation of profit of Hela village industries

Head	Amount (Yuan)	Percentage of Profit
Wages	471,300	24.90
Tax to the State	428,300	22.63
Public welfare	343,000	18.12
Contribution to company for reproduction	649,600	34.33
Total profit from industry	1,892,200	

Source: Interviews in Hela in 1985.

highest income of a peasant was 3,100 yuan and the lowest was less than 1,000 yuan. There were one or two households in the village whose family income crossed the mark of 10,000 yuan, earning them the title *wanyuanhu* (10,000-yuan families). Thirty years later, this looked too small an income as many hundred-million-yuan families (*wanwanhu*) appeared in such villages. According to the information provided by a village leader, a majority of the families of the village in 1984 earned about 3,000 yuan per year. A few families who had less number of people to work or whose members had poor health had relatively lower income in the range of 1,500 yuan per year. Usually men worked for the village and women worked in the light industries in the city. Thus, men earned about 2,000 yuan per year, while women less than half, namely, 800 yuan. This discrepancy of wages according to the leaders was due to the poor health and low productivity of female labourers.

Let us look at a team or a small village collective under the Hela village at the start of the reforms.

Shanglidong team in the Hela production brigade presented an interesting comparison in 1980. Being a purely vegetable growing team, it had certain special characteristics. Even though it had a population of 209 with 96 household, it had only 60 members in the team because many villagers worked in the township or city-run factories. Actually, every time some land was taken over by the State, the team negotiated and secured a fixed number of jobs for the villagers in the factory. Thus, between 1978 and 1980, the farmland of the team had shrunk from 125 mu to a mere 26 mu.

The production team of Shanglidong focused on producing vegetables to meet the increasing market demand for it thus working according to the current state directive to respond to the market. There was an agro-scientific research station at the Hela brigade which worked under the advice of the research department of the suburban district. The team secured regular advice from the station about the scientific methods of vegetable growing. The team was divided into two work groups (*xiao zu*) for carrying out production tasks. But they worked under the unified leadership of the production team. Already the competitive system was introduced in 1980, according to which higher production performance earned them greater income.

The per capital income of the team had moved from 220 yuan in 1978 to 253 yuan in 1979. The average annual income of a team member was much higher. It was 480 yuan in 1978 which increased to 620 yuan in 1979. The per capita calculation brought down the figures because many children and old people were left in the village, whereas their earning members worked in the city. It should be noted that their city income was not included in the team income.

Like in the other teams, the work points were calculated according to differentiated evaluation of work. The team leader distinguished three kinds of work-point calculation:

1. The Dazhai type: Depending on the higher social consciousness of the peasants. The work points were distributed more or less according to the number of members in a family. So, uneven performance of the peasants did not matter.
2. Calculation according to the quality and quantity of work done by the peasant: A peasant who tilled more land in one day would get more. There were complicated methods of calculating this. The highest work point earned by a man was 15 and by a woman was 12, whereas minimum per day were 10 and 8 respectively.
3. Responsibility method: The work points were calculated according to the output value of the production work done by a group. This was an incentive to get higher output. This was the system adopted by Shanglidong team.

The 1980 picture of household income at the Shanglidong team was one of rising prosperity as well as differentiation:

1. Thirty-five per cent households above 800 yuan.
2. Forty per cent households above 600 yuan.
3. Twenty-five per cent households above 400 yuan.

But it was still a situation when a family with more working members earned relatively more.

In Shanglidong team, they had a team committee with three members in it at that time. (It was stated that usually there was a woman in the committee, but she had gone to take up a job at that time and had not been replaced.) The committee had 3–5 members. There were three party members in the team who formed a small group (*xiao zu*) that met once a week.

The variation in organization and activity in different villages even within the same township meant that the team—the lowest unit of population and management—had considerable autonomy in the old system.

The story of Hela village depicts the nature of urbanization in contemporary China. It had three elements. Firstly, there was a clear shift in production relations from collective economy to corporate economy with principles of private enterprise, maximization of profit being the governing norm. Slowly, this trend saw the takeover of enterprises by private owners which was complete by the late 1990s. Secondly, the diversification of the rural economy acquired great momentum. Agriculture had already been diversified with many different crops and animal husbandry and fisheries. Industries of all kinds, old and modern, came up along with what was called the 'third industry or *san ye*' such as commerce and tourism. Thirdly, land was handed over to the city for industry and real estate and this trend unfolded nationwide. Thus, starting as a 'self-development model' of rural development of Hela village, indeed most of rural China became a source of extraction for urban development through market economy. This resulted in the neglect of agriculture, rural infrastructure, rural health and education, causing the steady process of migration to the cities. However, in the case of this suburban village, the village was fully integrated with the city and became an urban street or *jiedao* under the urban district. In the 2000s and later, the former Hela village had shopping malls, electronic factories and multistoreyed buildings, smarting the new boom in real estate in contemporary China. In a smaller degree, the same process was on in all parts of rural China.

Lianhe Village

The picture in the neighbouring Lianhe village was not very different. The focus of production had shifted from agriculture to industry. The village had an integrated company (*tonglian gongsi*) like Hela taking full advantage of the scenic beauty of the Taihu Lake and the famous gardens in this part of the suburban district. The village had set up a hotel in 1984 which continued to modernize and develop in the subsequent years. It had 11 teams engaged in vegetable growing, poultry and pig raising and developing orchards and flower gardens. In 1984, the village company had a total profit of 830,000 yuan and after the deductions for tax and other heads amounting to 600,000 yuan, they were left with 230,000 yuan for distribution as wages. In this village, 70 per cent of the output value had been spent on expenditure related to production. High savings for investment and production expenditure marked the early phase of reforms. Even when the wages were raised substantially in the later years, the amount of public investment from collective savings remained high.

The village company gave a number of incentives to peasants to raise the production of vegetables. It provided advances to peasants to grow vegetables. It also gave subsidies and bonus to the peasants. The township would set the quota for the village, and the village would set the quota for each peasant. In Lianhe, for example, the peasant was expected to produce 80–90 tons of vegetables per mu. The village took into account the production trends of the previous year. It had also evolved methods of checking the quality of vegetables. If the quota was fulfilled by the peasant, then he/she would get the remunerative price. If the quota was surpassed, they would get a higher incentive price. Considering the land size necessary for vegetable growing, the Lianhe village company had allotted 3–5 mu to each labouring person. It should be noted that in Lianhe, the village company did not enter into contract with the family but individual peasants. The policy on production responsibility system had allowed such local adjustments in different parts of China. Thus, the incentive policy which was a hall mark of Deng Xiaoping's economic philosophy was put into full use in the village.

Diversified production in the village included industry, vegetable growing and orchards as well. Lianhe village company had set up an orchard for growing tangerines, peaches and grapes. Even though it was a collective farm belonging to the company and managed by a production team, the team signed contracts with peasants for plantation and nurturing of trees in the orchards. The combination of collective ownership with individual farmer's production responsibility under an intermediate level of management seemed to function well in Lianhe.

Lianhe Village in the 1990s

Lianhe village had continued to make advance in industry and commerce. In 1995, the industrial output value had gone up to 50 million yuan, and in 1996 to 60 million. Since 1993, four new factories had come up; the most prominent of them was run jointly with a Taiwan investor producing leather goods, most of which was meant for export. The nature of expansion of industrial production in this suburban village can be understood from the list of following nine village-run enterprises:

1. Wuxi City Environment Protection Engineering Equipment Corporation
2. Lianhe Cotton Clothes Factory
3. Wuxi–Lianhe Comprehensive Production Factory (making coal ovens for cooking)
4. Electric Voltage Control Board Factory
5. Automobile Repair and Maintenance Company (joint venture with Mitsubishi)

6. Wuxi Plastic Products
7. Printing Press
8. Decoration Products
9. Plastic Metal Spring Unit

It may be noted that while the textile, coal oven and plastic products were relatively older production units, leather, environment engineering items and automobile engineering were new enterprises with sophisticated technology and high investment. They were all autonomous enterprises governed by the production responsibility system under the ownership and control of the village. As noted earlier, the village had been transformed into an integrated industry–commerce–agriculture corporation running the industrial enterprises. The leader of the village, Hou Huizhong, who continued in the leadership position in 1996, combined the party, administration and management leadership roles. He was the secretary of the village CPC branch, head/director of the village people's committee and general manager of the United Village Corporation. The trend of differentiation between the party, administration and management which was a policy decision at the 1978 Third Plenary Session and was visible in the 1980s seemed to be replaced by a new trend of unified local leadership. The difference, however, was that it was not the political outlook of the local cadre but the capacity for enterprise management which mattered from the mid-1990s onwards. The local cadre was to show high production results to get commendation.

Lianhe's commerce also continued to grow. It had now expanded the shopping complex near *Hengshan* (straight hill) with 60 shops. Its sales volume in 1995 was 10 million yuan. The village also ran a restaurant and a fruit market. Out of the labour force of the village, over 800 were in industry and nearly 20 in commerce.

The village grew vegetables in 400 mu. This was contracted to 110 families, all of whom had migrated from north of Yangtze River and had been provided accommodation by the village to live in Lianhe. They lived in large halls partitioned into cubic cells and dormitories. Lianhe was short of labour for agricultural production, but it had been assigned a production quota for vegetables by the township government. Thus, the village decided to welcome migrant labour from northern Jiangsu which was a relatively backward area. According to the information given to me by the village head, during the preceding five years, their living conditions and incomes had improved considerably from 5,000–6,000 yuan per couple per year to over 10,000 yuan per year. Their children went to school in this village. This phenomenon of intra-province regional migration from relatively backward areas to developed areas where labour was in demand was a noticeable trend in the 1990s. After 2000, when the rural enterprises declined and big urban industrial units were the focus of production to cater to rising global demands, such migration stopped. The rural labour then started moving to cities for work. The floating population in the cities continued to surge.

In Lianhe village, the management of production was organized, giving responsibility to cadres for particular sectors. Under the village leader who was the general manager, there was a deputy general manager, in charge of agriculture and commerce, while the leader looked after industry. The workers engaged in agriculture were divided into five production groups which were guided by leaders from this village. In the course of my discussions in 1996, the village leaders pointed out that industry was now subsidizing agriculture. With the production quota being abolished in 1993, there was a different situation now. Even then industry and commerce sectors annually invested 300 yuan per mu towards payment of salaries of personnel managing agriculture, payment of agricultural tax and building infrastructure in farmland. This was done to continue vegetable production and maintain some balance in the composition of the sectors of production. People's attitude towards agriculture was noticeably changed as it did not generate enough income, whereas industry did. It was so not only in suburban areas like Hela Township but also in interior rural areas. The system's inability to maintain a remunerative agriculture and simultaneously develop agriculture, industry and services was already showing on the ground.

In 1996, Lianhe had a population of 2,700, of whom 1,100 were peasants and 1,600 were residents. These residents lived in the buildings constructed in village land. They included 300 residents from Lianhe village and about 500 migrants who worked in the various enterprises. Out of the total workers, 60 per cent were women. As explained earlier, men generally went for heavy industries and city jobs and women worked in light industries. The average annual income of working members in Lianhe in 1995 was 6,000 yuan which was expected to increase by 1,000 yuan the following year. But this took into account income only from village enterprises and farming. In addition, family now engaged in private commerce and other productive activities besides having members working for productive units outside the village. For example, 300 local workers came from 300 households of the village, thus clearly having members working elsewhere or engaged in commerce or other activities. The families did not even reveal all their sources of income to the villagers committee. According to the village leader, there were a few families which had more than 1 million yuan income per year.

Thus, the phenomenon of million yuan household (*baiwan hu*) had already appeared in the late 1990s.

The development experience of Lianhe by and large reflected Hela's general model. Before 1979, the priority was on agricultural production. If there was failure in showing the targeted grain output, then the party secretary risked dismissal. From 1980 onwards, there was simultaneous emphasis on agricultural production and industrial development. Continuance of a cadre as party secretary was dependent upon clearly demonstrating industry's good performance. After 1988, development of industry and commerce was the crucial task of the village leadership. To finance this development process, accumulation from the village's own profit was the main source. In the 1980s, Lianhe put aside nearly 70 per cent of profit from enterprises as accumulation funds. While self-accumulation continued as a principal source, introduction of capital from domestic and foreign sources was encouraged for various projects. It was this trend which brought in joint sector enterprises and shareholding in ownership of industries. It may be stressed that high rate of self-accumulation was a common factor during the commune period as well as the first decade of reforms. While the rate of accumulation was usually between 30 and 40 per cent during the commune period, in places like Lianhe it went up to as much as 70 per cent during the early 1980s. This was because of the fact that profits from these enterprises had gone up in a big way and already high wages were given to the workers of the enterprises.

The relationship between the township government and the village enterprises had also undergone considerable change in the 1990s. The township, for that matter the suburban district government, was mainly concerned with macro guidance or management of overall system and not with arranging funds or making production plans for which the village had full power and responsibility. From the late 1980s, this trend towards autonomy of enterprises had been encouraged throughout China.

However, as regards taxes, the higher levels exercised considerable influence. Every enterprise gave local taxes (*di shui*) to the village and township's local government and also national taxes (*guo shui*). In 1995, Lianhe village gave 750,000 yuan towards 13 kinds of fees, contributions and taxes to Hela Township. In 1996, it went up to 900,000 yuan. The village enterprises used 40 per cent of their profit to pay local and national taxes which included 17 per cent towards national taxes. Some joint ventures were exempted from taxes for a certain period. Some handicraft units also enjoyed tax concessions. So, when the national government decided to abolish agricultural taxes in 2007, it came as a great relief to the peasants and workers in rural China, especially the village governments.

According to the village leaders, the living standards of the residents had increased considerably during the reform period. Unlike the pre-1979 situation, every household had colour television, refrigerator and washing machine, and nearly 50 per cent had air conditioners. In 1996, 20 per cent of the households had telephones, which was increasing every day. About 70 per cent of the families had rebuilt their houses after 1979 and built new houses again in the 1990s. About 10 per cent of the families owned private villas with luxurious courtyards and lawns. During these years, 80 per cent of the families had gone for interior decoration of their houses which was rare in the pre-reform period. As many as 40 per cent of the families had luxurious houses.

From the discussions with village cadres and people whom I had met in earlier visits, it became clear that everyone was oriented towards securing a comfortable living with better material conditions. In that process, a stratified society was already emerging in rural China, some families becoming richer and richer while some remaining far behind.

Qingxin: A Rice-growing Village

Whereas Hela and Lianhe villages had set up a number of rural industries that brought them most of their income, there was at least one village in the township even in the 1990s where agriculture was the principal occupation. That was Qingxin village in the far northwest part of the township. This village was also on its way to industrialization but in that, comparatively speaking, it was way behind Hela village or Lianhe village.

In 1985, Qingxin village had a population of 1,698 including 900 labourers. Like the other villages, it had also lost land (400 mu farmland) in 1984 for the construction of township-run factories. After that, it was left with 1,052 mu farmland out of which 727 mu was used for rice cultivation, 115 mu for fruit orchards and forestry, 105 mu for water oat, 55 mu for watermelon plantation and 50 mu for vegetable growing. Until two years earlier, this village was growing only rice and wheat. Now they had gone for cash crops. During the period of 1983–85, they had launched some industries as well. They now had six village-run industries. In 1984, the total output value of the village industries was 1.7 million yuan and of agriculture was 577,500 yuan. Thus, already industrial output value had surpassed agriculture as far as the collective economy was concerned. In other words, the agriculture figure did not include the private income of the peasants. Put together, the per capita income of peasants in Qingxin was 254 yuan, whereas the per labour income was 853 yuan. This was far below the corresponding incomes of Hela and Lianhe. However, they had made considerable progress over the 1984 level of the per capita income of 173 yuan and per labour income of 418 yuan.

In 1985, the Qingxin village industries were expecting a big boost, raising the output value to 3.5 million yuan. To begin with, this village had only a hardware factory and a stone quarry. In recent years, it had a strong glass plant, a pre-fabricated components plant; it also produced oil ink for carbon paper and it engaged in printing on polythene. A soda factory which the village had run for some time had gone bankrupt. So, it was turned into an alcohol factory. The hardware factory was also turned into a machine-building factory. The profit made by the rural industries in 1984 was 280,000 yuan which was to rise to nearly 800,000 yuan in 1985. Out of this, 30 per cent was paid as tax to the State, 30 per cent was paid to enterprises for reproduction and welfare and 40 per cent was earmarked as distribution as wages.

The combination of agricultural and industrial activity operated in a specific way in this village. The 457 households of the village were divided into two groups, one group consisting of families whose members were mainly working in factories, the other group having none engaged in industries. For the first group, a small piece of land was allotted to each family with 0.06 mu per person for cultivation for purposes of their own consumption. For the others, some more land—additional 1 mu per person—was allotted to grow grains and hand over a certain quota to the State. The village company organized this distribution of land on the basis of its knowledge of the conditions of the families.

In practice, what happened was that at least one member of the family was left to look after the land, while rest of the family worked in factories. Usually, all the members did some agricultural activity in their spare time. In Qingxin, mostly women and elderly people were found working on the land. In 1984, the yield of rice per mu in this village was 1,107 jin and wheat 717 jin. The purchasing price for quota rice by the State was 27.20 yuan per quintal and for wheat 31.60 yuan per quintal. If the peasant could sell beyond the quota, the State paid 50 per cent more as an incentive price for the grain. In this village, the company or the collective provided several common facilities to the farmers, such as ploughing the field and providing irrigation and drainage. Individual farmers, however, planted rice seedlings and took care of the plants by putting fertilizers, insecticide and other necessary inputs. The township administration was itself keen to help this backward village. The township had given 2,600 yuan in 1984 to build a 'greenhouse' for growing rice seedlings. The village had also got a 100,000 yuan loan from the township credit bank. Thus, slowly this backward village was developing with the help of the more advanced areas of the township. This is an interesting example of the collective economy of the village helping the individual household on the one hand and a higher level collective supporting a backward village to bridge the gap on the other.

The picture of Qingxin village had changed only marginally by 1987. With the State having taken more agricultural land for construction purposes, the land for agriculture had come down from 1,200 to 800 mu (the village was paid a compensation of 1,500 yuan an mu, 15 per cent of which was given to the township fund). Out of the 800 mu, half the land was used for rice cultivation and the other half for watermelons and vegetables. The farmers grew two crops a year, one rice crop and one wheat and not three crops as was the case in 1979–80. At that time, intensive cultivation was encouraged but it was abandoned later since it affected the productivity of land. The focus of the economy in 1987, however, was on expanding the rural industries, though no new ones were set up during the previous two years.

The output value of the industry had grown from 3 million yuan in 1985 to over 4 million in 1986 and nearly 8 million in 1987. The profit from the rural enterprises for the corresponding years was 600,000 yuan, 800,000 yuan and 1,000,000 yuan respectively. In other words, industries were picking up in this backward village.

In agriculture, the total output value in 1987 was 300,000 yuan. The entire agriculture had now come under the family contract system. Agriculture, however, did not generate any profit to the village and the surplus from industry continued to support agricultural development. In such conditions, people were keen to work more and more in rural industries, rather than being totally preoccupied with agriculture. As before, the factories contributed at least 20 per cent of their profit to the village.

In 1987, as many as 960 people of Qingxin village were engaged in agriculture and 300 in industry. The average income of the workers had risen from 1,100 yuan in 1985 to 1,250 yuan in 1986 and further to 1,300 yuan in 1987. The highest income of a labouring person was 10,000 yuan. Even though land was contracted to families, they were grouped in 10 teams in this village for coordination in production. However, these teams were no longer the collective units like the production teams of the yesteryears.

The experience of Qingxin has several interesting features having significant implications for rural transformation in developing countries. Firstly, it combined positive elements of a collective economy with individual and family-based agriculture. The village collective developed infrastructure for agricultural activity, while the families paid attention to their respective pieces of land. Secondly, the key to development of this backward village was the diversification of economy, making full use of the local resources. Grain production was expanded to vegetable growing and developing orchards. Industrial enterprises were also set up. Some of them used the stone reserves of the area. Thirdly, interdependence of regional units contributed to development of the backward regions. The massive profits from the rural industries of villages like Hela and Lianhe had generated surplus, part of which remained at the disposal of the higher level, namely the township government. This could be diverted to the backward regions for developing their productive capacity. At the same time, people from one village could get employment in rural industries in other villages, even though preference was given to the people from the village itself.

The Fisheries Brigade

An interesting link between the old commune system and the new reformed structure was the fisheries brigade or fisheries village. It was a collective enterprise; at the same time, under the new system, it operated as an integrated fisheries farm. In 1985, it had evolved into a comprehensive enterprise of diversified economic activities.

Hela Township is full of ponds, rivulets and water channels merging into the Taihu Lake. Soon after 1976, the commune had carved several ponds out of the lake, making 1,155 mu of water available for fish ponds. Out of this, 903 mu was used for breeding good-size, marketable fish and 252 mu for breeding fish seedlings. Several ancillary activities were also launched to support fish breeding. In 1985, they had farms with 156 pigs, 123 cows and 20,000 ducks. The livestock and poultry were meant to serve fish breeding because cow dung and excreta of pigs and dogs were used for fertilizing the pond water for growing fish. The weeds growing in the ponds are also eaten by the fish. This cycling of the waste was environmentally conducive and helped sustainable development.

From fishery and animal husbandry, the farm now had expanded its activities to industry and commerce. It had five companies: (a) fish breeding, (b) livestock and poultry, (c) industrial company for processing duck meat and processing cocoons (they had some mulberry trees around the ponds), (d) travel agency company (having hotels, 5 tourist coaches, 10 cars, 1 excursion boat and 1 restaurant, all catering to the tourist economy of the Taihu Lake) and (e) a commercial company (for selling products of the farm, having its own department store and other channels of marketing). This indicated that there had been enormous diversification of production in this brigade. Profit from fishing had been invested in activities such as industry and tourism, giving good dividends.

The brigade or village had continuously improved its fishing technology based on its own research and the findings in the nearby Asia-Pacific Fresh Water Fisheries Research Institute at Wuxi. Until a few years ago, the yield of fish per mu used to be 500 or 600 jin. In 1984, it had increased to 2,000–5,000 jin. The reason was that they had introduced good variety of seedlings from Mozambique and also from Egypt. These were high-protein good-size fishes. Another variety developed in Canton yielded 10,000 jin per mu. They had done many kinds of cross-breeding. For example, the famous Cushion Carp variety of fish from Osaka had been developed into Hela's Silver Cushion Carp. The production of fish had grown from 0.1 million jin in 1976 to 1.45 million jin in 1984, making a profit of 1.02 million yuan. After paying the staff and State tax, the net profit was 850,000 yuan. According to China's tax laws, fishery, livestock and poultry farming involved very little income tax, whereas for industry, commerce and tourism, substantial income tax was paid. Over the years, average income in the fisheries village had increased from 960 yuan in 1980 to 1,850 yuan in 1984. The highest per labour income in the fisheries village was 6,000 yuan per year, out of which he/she earned 4,000 yuan from the fishery farm and the rest from other activities in other villages. The average earning in various branches of the farm was as follows: fish breeding—2,400 yuan, poultry—2,300 yuan, tourism—1,650 yuan, commerce—1,800 yuan, industry—1,900 yuan. Work in fish breeding was regarded as tough work; hence, the wages there were higher. Poultry and piggery involved longer working time and dirtier work; hence, they earned relatively more than in the rest of activities. There were 500 workers in the integrated fisheries farm, out of whom 30 per cent were women. Mostly, men were engaged in fishing, while more women ran tourism. In industrial work, there were both men and women.

The farm which was formally called Integrated Enterprise General Company operated under the production responsibility system. It entered into contract with branch companies in specific spheres of activities and with production teams in the case of fish breeding. There were five production teams, each having only 20 per cent women. One of the teams was especially meant for breeding seedlings. The township entered into contract with the integrated enterprise which, in turn, fixed quotas for branch companies and teams. If they over-fulfilled the quota, they could distribute the excess among themselves. If the team could not fulfil the quota, the deficit was deducted from their income. The team worked as a collective, but there was an internal assessment of labour which earned differential wages. Thus, it was a combination of the collective system with differential wage determination. The advantages of collective accumulation facilitated expansion of new production activities. Wages also continued to increase as the collective's income grew.

Fish Brigade Renamed Lihong Village

The Fish brigade was now renamed as Lihong village with more areas added to it. I visited it in 1996, 2001 and 2004. The interesting point about this village is the development of fisheries into new level of commercial venture while simultaneously developing rural industries and commerce. Moreover, it had started special fishery projects in 1977, which had grown into a major enterprise.

With a population of 3,500 (50 per cent women) and 1,100 households, it had a labour force of 1,220 in 1996. Of them, 470 worked in industry, 260 were engaged in fishery and 50 in commerce. In addition, there were 500 migrant workers working in this village. Among the workers, 60 per cent were women. More women worked in electronics and more men in machinery. Among the management personnel, there were very few women. According to the village leadership, they followed the rule of same pay for same work. But they added that it depended on the skill and performance which meant that since women's performance was less than men's, they earned less. During China's Seventh and Eighth FYPs, though rural industries and commerce gradually developed, priority was given to fisheries in this village. It implemented and accomplished the goals of the SPARK Programme[19] in 1987. From producing 65 kg per mu, it had reached 1,030 kg. In 1995, it had a fish yield of 1,000 tons with sales volume of 10 million yuan. But the fish pond area had been reduced from 1,400 mu to 1,150 mu because of construction of industries. However, village industries output value was high with 230 million yuan and commerce 60 million yuan. After paying 17 per cent national tax and 33 per cent local tax, the profit in 1995 was 13.79 million yuan. In 1995, the annual average income of farmer-workers was 8,000 yuan.

Because of the higher income, the conditions of life had improved. Instead of coal oven, every family in this village now had liquid gas in their kitchens. Nearly 50 per cent households had telephone connections.

The target during the Ninth Plan was to accelerate economic development and also pay attention to 'culture and education'. Even though the latter was talked about, that the emphasis was on achieving high production objectives was evident. Their target was to achieve total output value of 1 billion yuan by the year 2000 and farmer-worker annual average income, 25,000 yuan. Following the Fifth Plenary Session guidelines of 1995, the village wanted to improve the level of technology, invite foreign capital and produce marketable goods. The village leaders were already negotiating with firms from Australia, Singapore and Malaysia, seeking investment and collaboration. Some big national enterprises were also invited to collaborate with the village. The three-point plan of this village was to (a) steadily develop fisheries, (b) rapidly develop industry and (c) develop tertiary enterprises with great effort. The village had worked out its plans for market-friendly development in several spheres. The aquatic products market was linked with the city's production and marketing companies. At the same time, taking advantage of proximity to the city, it set up and expanded the agricultural and commercial trading centre. Moreover, a large complex was under construction in 1996 for wholesale marketing of sideline products.

A dock had been constructed on the waters linking Liangxi River to the Taihu Lake to provide cargo facilities. In addition to these, the villagers committee was engaged in building fish ponds and facilities for processing, packing and refrigerating fish. Its research division was breeding special categories of fish which were highly priced and profitable when marketed outside the township, though they may be in less in quantity. The village was closely working with the Jiangnan Light Industry University and other research institutes of Wuxi and had engaged talented experts to help it in achieving its targets. It had links with big corporations within China and abroad, inviting them to the village for setting up enterprises utilizing cheap land and labour force of this area.

In the late 1990s, the village leadership often talked about 'emancipating the mind', meaning the need for giving up hesitations in adopting market methods. This was the nationwide trend after Deng Xiaoping's southern tour speeches in 1992 calling for boldly developing market economy. Local leaders referring to this frequently meant that some people in the village were probably still reluctant to change the collective ownership system into shareholding system. The dissidents may also be objecting to the new system of differentiating wages strictly according to a worker's output or an enterprise's performance. The village leadership had now firmly decided that payment must be linked to performance with rewards for higher results and deduction for failures. The village leadership was keenly following the 'two shifts' in the government policy on rural reforms in recent years: one from labour-intensive to technology-intensive production and the other from traditional (read collective) economy to market economy. The way these two shifts in policy were implemented by the local leaders had many serious implications. Firstly, the drive for adopting higher technology for promoting production often caused unemployment. Women were the first to be retrenched in such situations. Secondly, what was mentioned as traditional economy was actually collective economy whose replacement by market economy could create imbalances on many fronts. When cadres were asked about this, they said that these problems were the worries of higher authorities. The village was asked to enforce these two shifts to increase production and profit. To coordinate the production activities throughout the village, a village management group had been set up which was different from the villagers committee. Its main task was to achieve the economic targets. The experience of Lihong village shows how the policies to develop market economy to accelerate China's economic growth were put into full force by the top party leadership led by Jiang Zemin during the late 1990s. These no doubt achieved the economic objectives irrespective of its social and environmental consequences.

Thus, the Hela Township benefited out of a wide range of production activities. The advanced-level rural industries in Hela and Lianhe villages, agriculture in Qingxin village and the prosperous fisheries village represented the development profile of the Hela Township. The activities at the level of the various villages were coordinated by the township administration, and its common fund could be utilized for the villages according to their needs.

Fisheries development had acquired such a significance in the Hela Township that a Pond Fish Research Institute was set up by the township of which Hela Township's former director Liu Weiping had become the director in 1985. This was part of the SPARK Programme launched by the Science and Technology Commission of China. Liu Weiping who had considerable expertise in fish breeding and had won many awards before was put in charge of further expansion of fisheries.[20] Under a 1986–90 plan, 93 ha area of fish pond was to be developed. The target of production for 1990 was 15 ton fish per ha or one ton per mu. It was indeed over-fulfilled and the fisheries economy of Hela continued to prosper throughout the reform period.

Political Organization and Management

Our discussion on the villages in Hela Township has shown how political organization at the village level underwent major changes in the course of the reforms from the 1980s onwards. From the brigade revolutionary committee of the 1970s, a transition was made to the brigade management committee and then to a system of village company manager. Thereafter, an elected villagers committee was in charge of administration with different enterprises having their autonomous management. There was a party branch throughout this period. Revolutionary committee of the Cultural Revolution period was a high-powered leadership organ directing collective agriculture. The management committee of the early 1980s still catered to the needs of a largely collective economy. With the full implementation of the HRS, the management system underwent a change. Now there were individual managers in charge of every sector of the economy, every rural enterprise responsible for generating profit in its respective sphere of production. Accordingly, the role of the party was restricted. The village party leaders were no longer encouraged to interfere in the day-to-day production process. At the same time, the control of the higher level, namely township administration, was also reduced. In the mid-1980s, the village enjoyed much greater autonomy than before. However, since the village was dependent on the township administration in many ways, it had to be a cooperative relationship. But the national policy of decentralizing decision-making power in the production process gave a fair degree of autonomy to the village. The village in turn gave more autonomy to the peasant households. However, despite the fact that HRS was a successful institutional innovation, it had some limitations. The autonomy led to fragmentation of land, as each individual household was allocated land as per their family size, and it differed from place to place depending on the fertility; some land was wasted for making paths and boundaries.[21] These anomalies had hindered the possibilities of mechanization and development of agricultural infrastructures in many provinces.

In 1978, the Hela brigade revolutionary committee (*geming weiyuanhui*) was converted into the brigade management committee (*guanli weiyuanhui*). Before 1967, this was the system as well. In 1980, there were seven members in the brigade management committee including two women. It was interesting that three of these members were also members of the dissolved revolutionary committee. According to the brigade leaders, no serious mistakes had been committed by the earlier leaders in this village; hence, no one had been removed. Three of the old members had been transferred to other assignments. The brigade had a hundred-member representatives conference (*daibiao huiyi*) which was elected by the team members. The management committee was elected by the representatives conference and gave an annual report to the latter. This election was based partly on informal consultation among the representatives and partly on the concurrence of the superior-level leadership. Discussion on the annual report at the annual conference was an occasion for the grass-roots-level worker's close interaction with village leadership.

In 1985, the brigade now renamed village had a general manager of the United Agriculture, Industry and Commerce Company. This office replaced the earlier office of the head of the management committee. Then there were managers for specific enterprises. The management committee was replaced by this new system of managers who were to operate in consultation with the villagers committee (*cunmin weiyuanhui*) and the representatives conference. In 1985, the Hela village representatives conference had 170 members out of whom 25 per cent were women. The villagers committee had 18 members out of whom only 2 were women. Already there was a stress on giving leadership position to relatively younger people. In this committee, the average age was 45. Incidentally, the villagers committee had three members who were exclusively engaged in management activities rather than in production. Thus, some amount of professional management was introduced at the village level in the 1980s. Later, this trend became conspicuous with grass-roots cadres going for administrative training and spending time in party schools at various levels.

In Lianhe village, too, the system was the same. There was an integrated company which operated in consultation with the villagers committee. It is important to note that in the case of both Hela and Lianhe, the head of the villagers committee was not the same as the general manager of the United Company. In the same way, party leader was a third person. This was to give full autonomy to the general manager who was to take decisions on production plans in their enterprises and show results to meet the nationally determined priorities. In theory, they worked in consultations with mass organization, that is, the villagers committee and the local party unit. Later, when all three posts were held by the same person, the local leader became the new 'manager cadre' of the party focused on economic results. This phenomenon persisted in most parts of China in the late 1990s and early 2000s. The Lianhe villagers committee had one director and four other members including two deputy directors, one of whom was a woman. In December 1995, the village had its three-yearly elections. The migrant families living here did not have the right to vote. They were expected to go to their original places to take part in the village elections.

In 1996, Lianhe village had 55 members of the CPC including 27 women. They were all relatively young people within the age group of 40–51. The five-member party branch had one secretary, two deputy secretaries (including one woman) and two other members. The 49–year-old Mr Hou Huizhang, who had received me in this village in 1985, had continued to lead this village. It indicated how he had adapted with the new demands on his leadership during the past decade.

The Lihong villagers committee had five members including two women in the age group of 30–50. It was clear that every new committee had a higher educational and technical level. The membership of the committee was based on (a) 'cultural level', meaning educational qualification of the member; (b) 'practical experience' or active role in some sector; (c) 'relationship with the party', that is, recommended by the local and higher party cadres and (d) 'capacity to represent the village' or common people's impression that the member was interested in the upliftment of the village. This village also had its election in December 1995. All people aged 18 or above participated in elections. Any 10 people could propose one candidate. The panel usually has one or two more candidates than the required number to be elected. After the five members are elected, they in turn elect the village leader or director of the villagers committee in their first meeting. The village leaders told me frankly that the township leadership guided the whole process. This made all the difference. Until recently, before the competitive election law was enforced, the nomination of the village leader was made by the township leadership. Now the township leadership only 'guided' the process. Although this meant a large degree of control by the upper level over the election process at the lower level, it could not be arbitrary for two reasons. Firstly, the township leader himself/herself had to show good performance in the enterprises of all the villages. So he/she needed the support of the enterprise managers and village leaders. They in turn depended on their workers' performance and local cadre's contribution. Besides, some villages were rich and powerful, wielding much influence over the higher level. Secondly, the movement for democracy in China had its widespread impact. Multiple candidates for single post were emerging as a democratic alternative. In the December 1995 elections in Lihong, this was the case. Thus, one had to understand the nature of the political process that involved consultation between higher and lower levels of the party, the party monitoring the overall political process and seeking legitimacy in the eyes of the non-CPC groups and common people.

There were 52 CPC members in Lihong with 40 per cent of them women, a rather high proportion perhaps due to the expansion of the service economy where women got more employment. However, the party branch had seven members with only one female member among them. All of them were at least senior middle-school graduates. The two deputy secretaries were engineers. In this village, the party secretary was the general manager, and one of the deputy secretaries was director of villagers committee besides being manager of the fishery corporation. Asked about the national policy of differentiating party, government and management functions, the Lihong village leader said that such policy applied to the township government and higher levels. The village was a grass-roots organization where it was hard to make such differentiation. In this village, collective ownership was still the predominant form in 1996. But the village was getting ready to introduce shareholder companies gradually. By 2003, the transition to private or joint ownership of enterprise was nearly complete.

In Qingxin, too, there was the United Agriculture, Industry and Commerce Company, but in this case, the general manager was the party secretary as well. One wonders if this was meant to pull up the backward region with concerted efforts, or was it a simple question of finding appropriate personnel. Qingxin's general manager was assisted by two deputy managers. The villagers committee consisted of the leaders of the 10 teams. The representatives conference consisted of the team leaders and four representatives from each team, thus 50 in all. The villagers committee had one head and two deputy heads.

The Party at the Village Level

In the initial years of reforms, the political role of the CPC was redefined at the grass-roots level. In the sphere of production, the local party unit did not interfere or take over economic management role. Still, the local unit of the party continued to play its role as the principal articulator of the national-level decisions. It also remained as a check point for the enterprise managers and village company managers to ensure that they operated within the national policy framework. At the practical level, however, this fine arrangement did not always work. Personnel were constantly shifted from party positions to enterprise management and vice versa. Moreover, holders of the key positions in enterprises and village companies were also functionaries in the party. Usually, a village head or an enterprise manager was the deputy secretary of the corresponding party unit. It meant that politically the party secretary was superior to the manager or the director. In matters of administration and management, the others were in full charge. In the mid-1980s when increasing production and raising income were the principal preoccupations everywhere in China, the local party leaders maintained a low profile. The managers and directors left no doubt in the minds of visitors that it was they who called the tune and not their party secretaries. After 1992, there was a shift of focus to the role of the party, but the party cadres themselves became managers of enterprises.

In 1979, Hela brigade had 58 members of whom less than one-third were females. The party branch (meaning branch committee, but the term committee was used for levels from township upwards) had seven members and none out of them was a member of the higher party committee at the township level, implying that either a different faction was in power at the higher level or none of them was experienced enough to deserve a position in the higher committee. The branch met three times a month. The leaders of various teams in Hela brigade were not all members of the party branch. In 1985, the party membership was 55, that is, three less than in 1979. It did not necessarily mean resignation or expulsion. It could also be due to transfer to other units (Figure 7.2). The party branch had now five members, two less than before, for streamlining its functioning (Figure 7.3).

Sun Suide, the general manager of Hela United Agriculture, Industry and Commerce Company, was deputy secretary of the branch. The secretary was a 39-year-old woman leader, a farmer, who had been the secretary since 1978. The party held a general conference of members periodically.

In Qingxin, in 1985, there were 33 party members including 7 women. The party branch had five members including one woman. In 1987, however, the party membership figure stood at 34. The average age of the party branch members was 50 years. The educational level was somewhat low in this case. None of the members had got university education. One had passed higher middle school and two had middle-school education.

There was a convergence of party and management leadership in the fisheries village. In 1985, the 37-year-old Xi Fumin was both the secretary of the party branch and the general manager of integrated company. Each branch company had a manager. There were about 30 party members in the fisheries village. The party branch had five members including one woman who was also the head of one of the four sections in the headquarters of the company. In September 1985, the two leaders who were interviewed by me were Rong Fulin, deputy secretary, party branch, and Jiang Rongkun, who was earlier the manager of the fish farm and had recently retired at the age of 67. From the experience of the fisheries village, one gets the idea that not everywhere was the differentiation between party and enterprise management enforced in China.

Figure 7.2:

Organizational structure at the village level after 1980

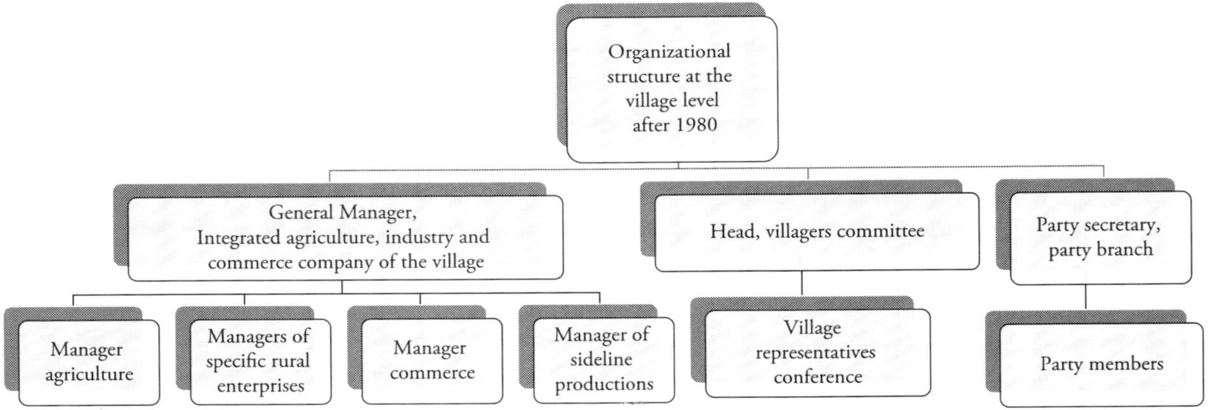

Figure 7.3:

Organizational structure at production brigade level before 1980

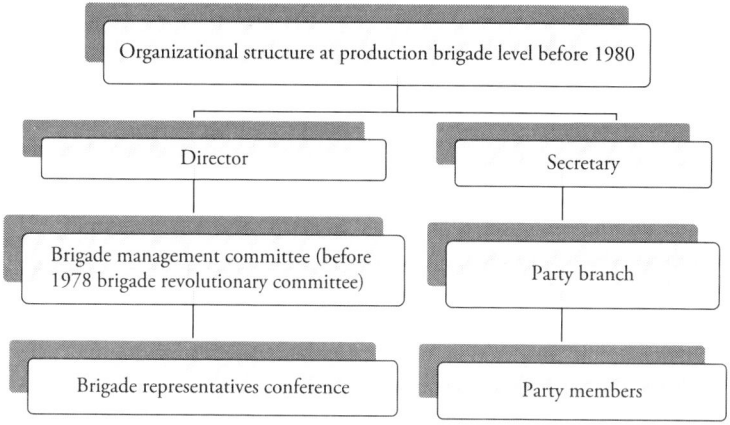

Rise and Fall of the Village as the Focus of Rural Transformation

Even though Hela, Lianhe and Qingxin were all suburban villages of Wuxi and may not be accurate samples of interior rural areas of China, still we get significant pointers to the structural changes that took place in China during more than three decades of reforms since 1979. During the first decade and half, the development strategy at grass-roots level was operated by the village. It played the critical role in diversifying the economy, growing cash crops along with food grains and developing rural industries and animal husbandry along with agriculture, commerce, tourism and every possible productive activity that the village was free to launch. The bottom tier, namely the production team, had been practically dissolved and family contract agriculture had come into force. However, families could still come together in work groups or villagers small groups (*cunmin xiaozu*) for purposes of cooperative use of labour or some inputs. Organizationally, the party's interference in production management was curbed. In every sphere, a manager was in charge of operating the production responsibility system. As a critical functional unit, the village was allowed to exercise a great deal of autonomy by the State. Even the higher-level leadership in the township respected the village and provided the needed financial and administrative support. Transforming the production brigade of the commune period into a company was a significant conceptual change because it entailed a major change from what was a peoples' mobilizational institution into a producers' profits-making enterprise. The mobilizational orientation of the earlier period was replaced by a system of competitive production that was coordinated at the village level. The cultural break, however, was not as sharp as political discontinuity. As mentioned earlier, village after all was the traditional administrative village.

At the end of the 1980s, especially after the Tiananmen episode when the rural policies were streamlined, certain changes took place affecting the functioning of village. The village economy was to closely follow the framework of the overall economy. Thus, the State laid out the overall framework and maintained its supervisory powers. The county's control over the township and the township's control over the village were increased to a large extent. Production plans, especially diversification and investment proposals, were now to be approved by the higher level. The party's role at the corresponding levels was emphasized to promote adherence to the party ideology and political education. Still, the basic framework of the rural reforms focusing on the village and the family contract system continued to operate.

After the Fourteenth Congress of the CPC in 1994 and especially after the Fifth Plenary Session of the CC in 1995, the long-term policy framework was clear. It formally assigned autonomy to the lowest production units but stressed the need for compliance with policies under socialist market economy. This meant that the State carried out macro-level coordination. The introduction of competitive elections at the village level had conveyed a message to the world that grass-roots democracy was taken seriously in China. Thus, from 1979 until about 1995, the village rose as the basic unit of both production and political participation in rural China.

But its decline began soon thereafter as both the grass-roots production unit and a base of local democracy. When the rural enterprises under the collective ownership of the village underwent structural transformation, the village's resources dried up. As mentioned earlier, many TVEs were closed because they did not have the capacity to compete with the big enterprises. Many others did not meet environmental regulations. Several enterprises were closed because their products failed the quality tests. After Deng Xiaoping's call for accelerating market economy or privatization in 1992, many big investors from within China or abroad came in to take over some of the TVEs. They enjoyed the concessions granted by the Central government as incentives to promote industries in the countryside. The village's high income and the practice of high rate of savings to develop the enterprise, contribute to agriculture and promote health and education which we saw in all the villages of Wuxi was a thing of the past. The main function that remained with the village was to manage the land within its territory and administer the HRS. It had to decide on cases involving subcontracting of land if the household was engaged in other trades in the city. When some households decided to entrust their land to a specialized agricultural household, the village leadership was to consider giving permission. Having lost opportunities to lead the comprehensive development of the village, the village leadership now focussed on making profit out of land. Hence, transferring land for real estate development and setting up industries or commercial zones became the village leadership's main preoccupation. In many instances, deals were struck by the village leadership with a corporate interest that was not acceptable to the villagers in general. Either such deals violated environmental norms or were seen as cases of corruption indulged in by the local leaders. As a result, land disputes emerged as a major source of conflict in China's countryside in the 2000s and later. According to one estimate, 60 per cent of the 'mass incidents' were attributed to land disputes. At the same time, the rural health and education systems got deprived of regular support from the local government. Thus, by the early 2000s, all the three rural problems (*san nong wenti*)—low productivity in agriculture because of lack of adequate inputs, low farmer income because of lack of employment and wage disparities and backward infrastructure in both physical facilities and social sector—had come to the fore. Village remained only a land administration unit. The much publicized multi-candidate election became an arena of local entrepreneurs together with party factions to create and maintain islands of power and influence. Ironically, except for collective land ownership, China's village became closer to India's panchayat, devoid of economic resources except what it received from above, but an arena of political activity. In the case of India, the reservations and political mobilization at the village level provided the possibility of panchayats becoming an institution for democratic struggle. In the case of China, even that possibility had become remote as the leaderships in higher echelons would consider that as disruptive of economic growth. Thus, the rise of village as a political and economic unit of development and democratization and its fall into an agency of land management and rural control through the household registration system has many lessons for the world.

How did this process of restructuring of the political economy under the reforms affect women? That is our interest in the next chapter.

Notes and References

1. National Bureau of Statistics of China, *China Statistical Yearbook 2014* (Beijing: China Statistics Press, 2014), 165.
2. National Bureau of Statistics of China, *China Statistical Yearbook 2016* (Beijing: China Statistics Press, 2016).
3. National Bureau of Statistics of China, *China Statistical Yearbook 2014*, 170. However, on a different standard, low income as identified in 2008 was 10.2 per cent in 2000 and 2.8 per cent in 2010. On a further refinement called 2010 standard, called poverty alleviation standard, the 2010 figure was put at 17.2 per cent and in 2013 it was 8.5 per cent.
4. Li Keqiang, *Report on the Work of the Government*, 19.
5. Zhao Chen, Ming Lu and Pengtu Ni, 'Urbanization and Rural Development in the People's Republic of China'. ADBI Working Paper 596, 19 September 2016. Available at: https://ssrn.com/abstract=2853330 (accessed on 13 June 2017). See also F. Liu, 'A Study of the Conditions of the Scale Operation of Farmland and of the Effect Thereof: Taking the Northeastern Countryside as a Case', *Management World* 9, no. 1 (2006): 71–79 [in Chines].
6. China's *hukou* system that evolved in imperial China to control rural migration and continued in contemporary China may be different from the Indian caste system, but it is discriminatory and exclusionary. Caste is a social structure based on the cultural ideology of Brahminism while *hukou* is a political framework enforced by rulers that also restricts rural people's right to freely move out of your area. For its cultural dimensions, see Cai Fang, 'Migration Obstacles, Human Capital and Mobility of Rural Labour Force in China', in *Inequality, Mobility and Urbanisation*, ed. Amitabh Kundu (New Delhi: ICSSR and Manak, 2000), 77.
7. *The 13th Five-Year Plan*, Part IV; *NDRC Report to 12th NPC* (5 March 2017), 33–34.
8. Central Committee of the CPC Compilation and Translation Bureau, *The 13th Five-Year Plan for Economic and Social Development of The People's Republic of China (2016–2020)*, (Beijing: Central Compilation and Translation Press, 2016). Also available at http://en.ndrc.gov.cn/newsrelease/201612/P020161207645765233498.pdf (accessed on 31 July 2017).
9. Central Committee of the CPC Compilation and Translation Bureau, *Documents of the Third Plenary Session of the 18th Central Committee of the Communist Party of China* (Beijing: Foreign Languages Press, 2013), 94.
10. China's Ministry of Water Resources, China Water Resources Bulletin 2014 quoted in Zhou Li, Fang Ping and Wang Caihong, 'Dancing with Three Hands: The Identical Root of Chinese Agricultural Miracle and Crisis'. Unpublished Monograph, Renmin University School of Agricultural Economics and Rural Development, 2017, 9.
11. Li Zhou et al. formulate this problem succinctly as outflow of three elements—labour, capital and land. Ibid.
12. Ibid., 10.
13. The panchayat in India is regarded by some as the lowest tier of the Indian state with functions given to it under the 73rd Amendment of the Indian Constitution and statutory requirement for five-yearly elections. See George Mathew, 'Local Government System in India and China: Learning from Each Other', in *Grass-roots Democracy in India and China: The Right to Participate*, eds Manoranjan Mohanty, George Mathew, Richard Baum and Rong Ma (New Delhi: SAGE Publications, 2007). But in my view, Panchayat is at

the confluence of state and society as the latter operates through the gram sabha (village assembly).

14. The Carter Center, Atlanta, that monitors elections around the world and the International Republican Institute (IRI), Washington, DC, which trains people in discharging their role in electoral democracy in different parts of the world have published number of reports on the village elections in China.

15. Common people and local cadres felt encouraged to take advantage of this environment and took initiatives to expose corruption and criticize decisions by local leaders and resorted to protest actions which Kevin J. O'Brien calls 'boundary-spanning contention in China'. O'Brien, 'Boundary-spanning Contention in China', 107–08.

16. Kevin J. O'Brien and Lianjiang Li, 'Accommodating Democracy in a One-party State', *The China Quarterly* 162 (June 2000): 465–89. On the 'right to participate' as a new human right in global discourse, see Manoranjan Mohanty, 'Introduction', in *Grass-roots Democracy in India and China: The Right to Participate*, eds., Manoranjan Mohanty, George Mathew, Richard Baum and Rong Ma (New Delhi: SAGE Publications, 2007).

17. Kerry Brown, 'The Future of Village Elections in China'. *The Newsletter* 53, (Spring 2010). Available at: http://iias.asia/the-newsletter/article/future-village-elections-china (accessed on 13 June 2017).

18. Richard Levy, 'Village Elections in China: Democracy or Façade?' *New Politics* XII, no. 4 (Winter 2010). Available at: http://newpol.org/content/village-elections-china-democracy-or-fa%C3%A7ade (accessed on 13 June 2017).

19. The SPARK Programme is the first programme approved by the Chinese government to promote the development of rural economy by relying on science and technology and is an important component of plans for the national economic and scientific and technological development. The purpose of the programme is to introduce advance, appropriate technologies into the rural areas and lead the farmers to rely on science and technology in the rural areas, promote rural productivity, and expedite the sustainable, rapid and healthy development of agriculture and rural economy. Available at: http://ie.china-embassy.org/eng/ScienceTech/ScienceandTechnologyDevelopmentProgrammes/t112842.htm (accessed on 13 June 2017).

20. Liu Weiping was the leader of Hela Township in 1979 when I first visited Hela. He retired from that role in 1984 and was put in charge of fisheries programme. In 1984, he was succeeded by Zhang Weinan who played a key role in Hela's urbanization plans during the next decade and more.

21. Fu Chen and John Davis, 'Land Reform in Rural China since the Mid-1980s', *Land Reform, Land Settlement, and Cooperatives* 6, no. 2 (1998): 123–37.

8

Clearing Clouds in Half the Sky: Women in the Success Trap

Debating Impact of Reforms on Women

China's 2010 Census had a disturbing result relating to the phenomenon of 'missing women'. Men constituted 51.27 per cent of the Chinese population and women 48.73 per cent. The trend of falling sex ratio continued unabated. For every 100 females, there were 119.45 males in 2009. Among the new born, for every 100 female children, there were 118.6 male children in 2010 which was worse than the situation 10 years earlier in 2000 when the corresponding figure for male children was 116. At this rate, it was predicted that in two decades, as many as 15 per cent of young Chinese men will not find female partners in China.[1] The fact that the practice of one-child policy and the attendant steps taken by families to abort female foetus or new-born female babies, despite a legal ban on it, which had largely caused the gender imbalance—the phenomenon of 'missing women'—was serious enough. But more than that, this finding represented a host of socio-economic trends arising from the policies pursued in China during the reform period which had adverse effects on women. Despite the worldwide praise for China's economic rise, these results had many embarrassing implications for China besides having lessons for the rest of the world. Even though the one-child policy was replaced by a two-children policy which came into force in January 2016, still the consequences of the previous policy were going to impact society and economy for at least three more decades.[2]

In discussing the women's prospects during the China's reform period, three issues have emerged as critical points of debate. First, the view that has dominated the thinking of policy-makers in China and India since the reforms is that achieving high rate of economic growth was important in itself, irrespective of its social consequences. They argue that only after products and services were available in adequate quantity could they be distributed fairly among the various groups. It is said that growth will put more resources in the hands of the State to spend on welfare measures including health and education. Above all, economic growth invariably led to improvement of living conditions of households from which everyone, including women, benefited. The counterview is that the very pattern of growth creates its social, political and environmental consequences; therefore, issues of social justice, gender equality and environmental sustainability should be an integral part of the choice of development strategy right from the beginning. Welfare of women should be seen as women's rights instead of either patrimonial support or 'welfare' policy arising out of subjective decisions of leaders or parties. During the decade of Hu Jintao's leadership, this question came to the fore and several initiatives were taken to direct attention to social and environmental issues under the formulation 'Scientific Outlook on Development'. But for his critics, this was a dilution of the growth strategy, slowing down the rate of growth. The literature on globalization and gender overwhelmingly suggested that the dominant pattern of economic growth governed by the market economy created many new adversities for women, even though it created new opportunities for women in some sectors. The many achievements of women in China during the past three decades were recounted by the women deputies at the NPC in March 2014. But on this occasion, they were boldly eloquent about the serious problems faced by women. Chen Xiurong, NPC Standing Committee member, quoted profusely from the third survey on Chinese women's status released in October 2011 and pointed out many indicators of gender inequality and discrimination despite the fact that the State had a policy on promoting gender equality.[3] How the growth profiles of the economy suffered from deficiencies of statistical methodology because it did not have adequate gender statistics in it was pointed out by deputies.[4]

The second issue emerges from the perspective of socialist feminism, especially as it was pursued during the Mao era. The Yan'an legacy—the ideological line promoted during the anti-Japanese War 1937–45 when the CPC evolved many of its creative ideas on revolution and transformation—had stressed the value of gender equality. After 1949, it was put into action through many policies. The Marriage Law of 1950 was a progressive step protecting women's choice. (In 1980, it was revised incorporating many new provisions protecting women's rights.) Women were released from household work during the commune period and many socialized services were provided to facilitate this. But women's status during this so-called '17-year period' 1949–76 had been subjected to much debate among feminist scholars and activists during the reforms.[5] Critics of this period point out that the distinct character of the female gender was not taken into consideration by the leadership during this period.[6] However, the negotiation of class and gender continues to raise new questions. But on the whole, the fact that an attempt was made during the Mao era to provide universal education and health care to all Chinese men and women and the work opportunities were made available to both sexes had a permanent value as it opened up possibilities of gender equity in future. But disparities in wages persisted through reduced work points for women. And women carried double burden, one in the workplace and another at home, because the patriarchal culture had not changed and the women were still expected to perform their role as wives and mothers at home. From the Yan'an period onwards, this phenomenon had been pointed out by the party's feminist ideologue Ding Ling in many of her essays and stories.[7] Moreover, very few women reached the top-level leadership even during the Mao era. In other words, even though some of the structural conditions were more favourable to women during the Mao era in contrast to the market economy of the reform period, patriarchal domination in the State and society persisted.

The third issue concerned the central agenda of women's liberation, namely development of women's agency or the capacity of women to change their life conditions. At one level, it involved promoting autonomy of women in every sphere in family, society, economy and politics through a variety of means. Some of it was to be done through autonomous organizations of women, allowing women's movements to critique State policies, social practices and economic trends. Some agency resulted from education and health care and employment opportunities. A great deal of emphasis is put on women's political participation and share in leadership and decision-making. Whether traditional practices were so patriarchal that they did not provide any space to women or some of them could be used to serve as contributing to the women's agency is another area of debate. The discussion on women's agency in the feminist literature is rich and varied and has been applied to the Chinese situation in many ways.[8] But a one-party State that does not allow autonomous women's organizations and a political leadership that insists on giving priority to economic growth and a cultural milieu where patriarchal practices galore the prospects of women's agency developing at a fast pace are rather low. Yet in China, from the revolution onwards and in the world as a whole that has seen continuous growth of women's rights movement, historical processes create their own momentum and the dynamic progress of women's liberation cannot be prevented.

It should be noted that the Fourth World Women's Congress was a landmark event held in Beijing in September 1995. This was an evidence of China's rising status in world affairs.[9] This status was mainly the product of the economic successes achieved in China during the period of reforms after 1978. The hosting of the World Women's Congress indicated a certain sense of confidence of the Chinese leadership in their performance even on the women's front in the course of the reforms. It also demonstrated openness on the part of the Chinese regime to share their achievements as well as failures in promoting women's development. A decade later, in 2005, the Chinese government released a White Paper on Women giving details of the progress made on this front. In 2007, *Beijing Review* published an article entitled 'Clouds over Half the Sky', with obvious reference to the famous slogan from Mao Zedong 'Women Hold up Half the Sky'.[10] The article used recent survey data of the UNDP and World Bank to report on the extent and dimensions of the gender gap in China in spite of remarkable improvements in women's overall social status. By the end of the Eleventh FYP in 2010, China's success trap in respect of women's development had become even more conspicuous. No doubt, women had been beneficiaries, along with men, of the enormous improvement in living standards of families and the vast new infrastructural development during the reform period. But at the same time, because of the commitment of every leadership to continue the growth-oriented reform strategy, the State and the party seemed to have decided to live with some of the iniquitous consequences of the development process. The adverse sex ratio, the unfavourable employment situation, the gender disparity in wages and the absence of adequate representation in political leadership were some of the indicators of the *clouds in half the sky*.

Right from 1979, I had tried to observe the conditions of women in Wuxi through my discussions with officials as well as villagers. When I interviewed women cadres in Hela Township and various villages in 1993, they were unaware of the impending World Congress of Women in 1995. But when I visited this area in 1996, the leading cadres both male and female knew that this was held in Beijing and was addressed by CPC General Secretary Jiang Zemin and thousands of women from all over the world participated in it.[11] So, the Fourth World Congress of Women had at least one major outcome for Chinese women. It highlighted women's issues and contributed to the growth of consciousness about women's rights. But as far as the substantive situation in terms of women's employment, representation in decision-making bodies and cultural attitudes was concerned, much remained to be done. Ten years later, in 2006, Wuxi wore a new look of a fast-growing modern metropolis and much of Hela Township had been converted to high-rise apartment buildings or industrial sites. Families had become substantially richer. But the gender disparities remained conspicuous.

The women's movement in China has not been the kind of social movement in mass scale which has taken place in many Third-World countries such as India. It is conducted mainly through mass organizations under the leadership of the CPC. The ACWF is a mass front of the CPC with branches in various regional levels such as the province, city, township, *zhen* (town) and the lowest level, the village. There are women's federation (*funu lian hehui*) units at all these levels as also in functional units such as the enterprises. The party, through the women's federation, is supposed to develop opportunities for women and advance their cause. The ACWF inherits the major legacies of twentieth-century movements in China to promote the cause of women's liberation. Women's participation in the democratic and nationalist movements during the May Fourth Movement had set in motion the forces of women's liberation in China. The major ideological sources of China's women's movement were the Marxist tradition and the worldwide currents of women's liberation whose meanings evolved through the political practice of the Chinese revolution. After 1949, both these currents formed the basis of the CPC policies on the women's question from time to time.

It is noteworthy that China's opening to the outside world and the force of world opinion on promotion of women's rights has had a serious influence on Chinese government's policies on women and on the rising consciousness among women in China. As a result, at every level, one can see evidence of debates on policies and their consequences for women. Despite being a party front, the ACWF has emerged as a relatively autonomous watchdog organization striving for realization of women's rights. Its monthly organ *Women of China* publishes many articles that provide evidence of gender disparities and are critical of government policy. Intellectual activities emanating from gender studies centres in universities and research institutes, as well as the emergence of numerous women's NGOs, have drawn attention to women's status in a significant way. Thus, debates continue and even gain occasional momentum on the effects of the post-Mao reforms on the status of women asking whether socialist market economy has expanded the conditions of women's liberation.

During the early 1980s, many analysts thought that the overall impact of the reforms was adverse to women's interest.[12] They pointed out that under the HRS, much surplus labour was withdrawn from agricultural work. Consequently, men migrated to nearby towns and cities seeking employment; some set up their own shops and service centres. But women were mostly left to perform household activities and farming. Even though they did take part in agriculture, in a fast-growing, competitive, market-oriented situation, men undertook the more serious jobs in the agricultural process ostensibly to ensure greater productivity. On the other hand, the commune system that existed until 1978 had utilized the labour power of women in agriculture and had set in a process of emancipation of women from traditional family structures. Hence, this trend in the early 1980s signified a reversal of that process.

This impression of the early years of the reforms, however, did not go unchallenged. With the expanding diversification of rural economy, there were greater job opportunities for both men and women. The activities ranged from grain production and growing cash crops to fisheries and other sideline productions and above all rural industries. Together, they expanded the scale of employment opportunities in the countryside tremendously. In some rural industries, women occupied a majority of the jobs. In suburban areas such as Wuxi, men chose to concentrate on specialized farming, and industrial and commercial activities, leaving women to look after agriculture. This was evident in Hela Township. Thus, the new agricultural system worked both ways, sometimes pushing women out of agriculture, sometimes assigning them a crucial role in it.

De-collectivization of agriculture also meant a degree of withdrawal of public support for health, education and other social services in the villages. Earlier, the people's commune provided health care facilities and funded the schools, childcare centres and local education programmes. The township in the new context maintained only part of that responsibility. Now the families had to pay substantially for these services. Thus, health care for women was partly privatized. Even though the family planning efforts were sustained by the government, still the decline of public action in social sector had negative effects on women's health conditions.

At the same time, since the family income increased considerably, there were now new gadgets in peasant households. For example, the washing machines reduced women's work in the households to some extent. So did some other electric appliances. Colour TVs and refrigerators generally improved the ambience of day-to-day living. New houses were built leading to dispersal of joint family to nuclear households. For many a daughter-in-law, this meant greater freedom in managing a household. As savings rose, some women set up small household enterprises earning additional income. The reforms period also saw tremendous emphasis on expansion of education, especially non-formal education in vocational fields. The TV universities— a system of higher education through radio and TV started in 1979—was China's main open learning system, allowing women to avail inexpensive education. At the same time, the right of women to avail education in all streams of regular education was also pursued as a policy.

The new situation saw the emergence of several new social trends affecting women's status. The divorce rate increased considerably. Since the stress on socialist ideology had declined and influence of Western ideas had spread, the institution of family underwent a process of weakening. Such a process was not necessarily adverse to women. Theoretically speaking, if women found themselves in a situation of adequate economic opportunities and political rights, the weakening of the traditional family may be a positive trend. That weakening may actually remove some constraints of the patriarchal social order and provide new conditions of freedom. But in the situation obtaining in China with inadequate economic opportunities for women and political institutions dominated by men, the weakening of the family institution was generally unfavourable to women. Men took advantage of the new situation at the cost of their family obligation. The traditional family bond between husband and wife and parents and children that had provided a degree of mutual support and recognition of each other's needs had declined as a result of the influence of the market and modernization. Men migrated to the cities in large numbers leaving women behind in the villages. The family allocated its labour mainly to make profit, rather than trying to engage both men and women in work. Since male labour was utilized either in specialized farming or in skilled jobs in industries or in profitable family enterprises, many women were left to doing the household chores.

The large-scale migration of rural labour to the cities had many adverse consequences for women. Often, only the men migrated to the cities leaving women and children back in the village. This was for three reasons. First, the employers in the city mostly required male labour in construction jobs and since urban infrastructure was the booming sector, men found opportunities. Moreover, as manufacturing for the world market increasingly involved technological skill, the demand for skilled male labour expanded. Second, since the *hukou* system continued to operate and the rural migrant did not qualify for the educational, health and other facilities that the urban resident availed, the rural people needed to maintain their rural residential registration.

Third, the one-child family had created a situation where the family wanted give good care to the child. On the one hand, it did not have adequate income in the village. On the other hand, the migrant labour could not take the child to the city where the child could not get admission to the city school or the migrant worker did not have proper housing. In that situation, the male migrant often left his child and wife in the village. In many cases, the couple migrated leaving their child with grandparents or relatives. The cultural tradition of 'son preference' that is widespread in Asian countries also worked in this situation. More girls were left behind than boys. This is how the phenomenon of 'left-behind women' and 'left-behind children' emerged as one of the most serious problems in contemporary China with many economic and social consequences.

The left-behind women in rural China were now in charge of cultivating their contracted land. This gave rise to 'feminization of agriculture' not as a well-thought-out programme, but as a side effect of migration. This not only overburdened women with dual responsibility of agriculture and childcare but also did not ensure full productivity of agriculture. Women did unpaid labour or low-paid work. This system disrupted their marital life, making them vulnerable. In this process, women 'experienced new and deeper form of exploitation of their labour, paying a heavy price for the development of China'.[13] Was it a 'hard choice' for the sake of China's development?—it is difficult to accept.[14] Similarly, the problem of 'left-behind children' is equally disturbing. Their number as per the 2010 Census was 61 million. It is not confined to underdeveloped areas of central and western China. In developed provinces such as Jiangsu, Zhejinag and Guangdong, this phenomenon exists because migrants to cities leave behind their wives and children as well as elderly parents. Studies reveal rise of mental health problems, suicides, crime and suffering from many diseases including HIV/AIDS in the case of such children. Separation from father and/or mother—sometimes meeting only once or twice a year—had many psychological problems for parents as well as children.[15]

Thus, the situation during the reform period was full of contradictory trends. On the one hand, the successes in the growth process, especially increased income, new amenities of modern life and interaction with the outside world, opened up many opportunities for women all over China. On the other hand, the pattern of industrialization, neglect of the countryside, decline in government support in health and education and the technological choices made by enterprises created many obstacles for women's development. The most conspicuous positive trend trying to promote women's freedom was the continuous spread of consciousness about rights among women. The impact of the worldwide movement for women's rights in China was evident from the change in the discourse on women's development. The reports and advocacy on women's issues, especially on rural women, the language and the concepts used by the women's federation activists and scholars, underwent a noticeable change in the late 1990s, becoming closer to the global discourse, particularly Third-World feminist discourse.[16] After the World Congress, the ACWF monitored the process of women's development rather closely. The women's federation units at every level right down to the township and the village were required to give detailed reports to the higher level, and the annual country report submitted to the UN was based on them. It is also true that many patriarchal attitudes and practices persisted alongside the much talked-about economic successes. Thus, one can say that on the whole, the reform process had activated new sources of potential development for the emancipation of women while at the same time putting women in many adversities. These adversities were similar in character to the impact of neoliberal reforms on women in all countries of the world including India and other developing countries. But unlike in India and elsewhere, the scale of growth was so vast and the pace so fast in China that much more opportunities were open to women. But at the same time, the disparities were much larger and the effects on sociocultural sphere were much deeper. The cultural degradation that accompanied the economic successes showed not only persistence of patriarchal attitudes and new forms of exploitation of women's labour and women's body but also exposed high magnitude of corruption involving officials and business magnets who exploited women. This is the view I gather from my field investigation of the rural reforms in Hela during past three decades as well as from the study of reports and findings from other areas.[17]

Rural Women at the Start of the Reforms

We can get a picture of the conditions of the rural women in China, especially in the suburban areas, from interviews with local women leaders in June 1979. Even though technically the reform had been launched after the Third Plenary Session of the CPCCC in December 1978, still the policies had not yet been implemented at the grass-roots level. Thus, we may consider this as a picture of rural China prior to the reforms period. In June 1979, Ms Shen Jianchen, aged 27, was the chair of the Hela Commune Women's Federation. She had a steady rise thereafter. In 1987, when I met her again, she was a vice-director of the township government. Along with Ms Shen, in 1979, I had also interviewed Ms Wang Shuizhuan, age 33, who was the chair of the Hela Brigade Women's Federation. In 1993, while Shen continued as vice-director, Wang had succeeded her as chair of Hela Township Women's Federation. The commune women's federation had been set up when the people's communes were formed in 1958. It operated under the commune party leadership. Each production brigade and each team had a women's group which was a branch of the ACWF. Besides mobilizing women for farming, the women's federation paid special attention to the task of spreading literacy among women. After the fall of the Gang of Four in 1976, the focus shifted to carrying out the four modernizations (in agriculture, industry, science and technology and defence).

According to the information provided by Ms Shen in 1979, about one-third of the workforce in the commune and brigade enterprises, that is, approximately 2,100 workers, were women. Bulk of the women, however, were engaged in farming, especially in the fields where food grains were grown. As for wages which were calculated in work points during the commune period, in some places, women got the same number of work points as men, namely 12 work points for a day's work. In some other places, women got less than men, that is, eight to nine work points. Although the value of work point differed from team to team depending on its total income, the average value of 10 work points in vegetable-growing areas was 1.30 yuan. In grain-growing areas, 10 work points fetched 1 yuan. It is to be noted that gender disparity in wages for the same number of hours persisted during the commune period as well as in the reform period.

In the vegetable-growing areas, women did the sowing, picking up vegetables, spraying insecticide and also general field management. In the rice-growing areas, they did transplantation, application of chemical fertilizers, spraying insecticide, thrashing (generally with machines), carrying, cutting and also nurturing of seedlings.

There were still no women tractor drivers in Hela in 1979. Women bus drivers were visible in the city. Men did heavier jobs such as transportation and carrying manure to the fields and grain to the thrashing grounds. They also levelled the land. There was a slack season after harvesting wheat and transplanting rice. At that time, besides nurturing plants, women got busy with sideline activities such as poultry and pig raising. In these activities, 80 per cent and 70 per cent of the workers were women respectively. In 1979, sericulture was an important activity in Hela. Sericulture was a women occupation with nearly 95 per cent of its workers being women. They were mostly middle aged. In fishery, 55 per cent were women. Women procured grass and collected clam from water. Pearl culture was a cent per cent women's activity. In forestry, which in Hela was mostly horticulture, 30 per cent of the workers were women.

In rural industries, the average monthly wage was 36 yuan for women and 45 yuan for men. As we shall see later, this increased almost six fold by the mid-1980s and continued to increase thereafter. The difference of wage was explained by the cadres as being generally due to the differing degrees of hard work and skill of male and female labour. Female labour was predominant in some enterprises such as the garment factory where 80 per cent of the workers were women, tea industry had 70 per cent women and electrical equipment plant also had 70 per cent women.

Thus, the employment situation in the early reform period was quite favourable to women despite the differences in wages. They were engaged a variety of agricultural and industrial activities.

During the commune period, because both men and women went to work, the children were left in nursery or in kindergartens, which were maintained by the production brigades. In Hela brigade, each team had a nursery. In Hela commune too, by and large, that was the case. When men and women went back home at the end of the day, generally the man took care of the child, while the wife did the cooking and other household chores. In case there was an old member, he/she took care of the child. It should be noticed that despite the talk of the socialization of services during the commune period, it was limited to childcare at nursery and kindergarten. The main burden of the household work still fell on the women, who also worked in the fields or factories to earn an income. The women carried this double burden even during the reform period, though now they had higher incomes to rely on and therefore more access to household gadgets. Only in the case of some prosperous peasants, some women stayed home exclusively for managing the household.

The educational profile of Hela women in 1979 appeared more encouraging than any comparable suburban scene in India. As many as 50 per cent of women were graduates of junior middle school, while 10 per cent had passed the senior middle school and 30 per cent were primary-school graduates. About 10 per cent of women of Hela Township were illiterate. In 1977–78, six women from Hela had gone to the university.

The family size in Hela was three to four. Married couples generally lived with their parents. If the house was too small, then the young couple moved out. As a brigade woman leader put it, 'in order to avoid contradictions most of them preferred to live separately from parents'. On the whole, the young people extended their support to their parents, though there were isolated cases of 'ungrateful children'. But public opinion was against such people. In case there was a genuine problem due to which a handicapped child could not support his/her parents, then the collective gave a monthly allowance to them. The phenomenon of 'ungrateful children' became widespread in the subsequent years when the young couples were keen on increasing their incomes. There were campaigns to appeal to children to take care of their old parents. As life expectancy increased and the number of the aged continued to rise, there were new efforts by the government to provide old age care besides family support.

The institution of marriage had acquired many new characteristics by the end of the 1970s. According to the township woman leader, 90 per cent of the marriages were love marriage after courtships lasting for two–three years. In some cases, the courtships were as long as five years. There was no consideration of clan or kinship in matrimonial decisions. Even the boy and girl could belong to two different provinces speaking different dialects. However, most of the marriages were local. As far as divorce was concerned, it did exist but was a rare phenomenon. During the previous three years (1976–79), there were only two cases of divorce in Hela commune.

It was pointed out by the women leaders that divorce was rare because the choice of partners was made by the young people themselves. The two divorce cases of Hela were both cases of arranged marriages which turned out to be no congenial. In the case of the quarrels in the family, when the matter became serious, the team leader intervened and tried for reconciliation. Sometimes it went up to the commune authorities as well. (In fact, Lao Mo or old Lady Mo, in whose house I stayed for a few days in 1980, was in charge of social mediation as a part of the Civil Affairs Department of the Hela Township. By 1993, she had retired.) Unlike the situation before liberation, widow remarriage was very common. Only if a widow had some serious disease, remarriage was difficult.

While the picture I got in 1979 and 1980 gave a glimpse of the women's conditions obtaining at the end of the commune era, my visits during 1985 and 1987 showed the nature of the impact that the vigorous implementation of the reform policies of that period had on women. However, during 1989–91, attempts were made to introduce measures of caution after the Tiananmen demonstrations of April–June 1989. But Deng Xiaoping's 'southern tour'—his visits to Shenzhen and other SEZs in early 1992—once again restored the tempo of reforms and in fact gave impetus to high-speed market-oriented development. When I visited Wuxi for another round of fieldwork in August 1993, the Deng-inspired acceleration of reforms was the talk everywhere. The decade of the 1990s witnessed the quick expansion of private enterprises and export-oriented production process in China. That was the decade where the attention was fully focused on achieving high growth rate and issues such as gender were given low priority. In 2001, it was Jiang Zemin's important thought on Three Represents which gave a boost to the status of entrepreneurs in the country, opening door of the CPC membership to them. At the Sixteenth Party Congress of the CPC in 2002, Jiang Zemin's Three Represents was codified in the party constitution as a part of the party ideology. This congress elected the fourth generation of CPC leadership led by Hu Jintao as CPC general secretary and president of PRC and Wen Jiabao as premier who sought to bring in some concern for social issues including gender. Right from the beginning of their term, they seemed to have caught the imagination of local cadres and common people who were pleased not only about the process of smooth transition in party leadership but also about their proclamation of several 'pro-people' policies. I witnessed the high point of the Jiang Zemin era of economic growth during my fieldwork in 2001. Subsequently, during my visits in 2003 and 2006, I saw the continuing growth process with much talked-about people's interest which was the reality of the success trap during the Hu–Wen regime. During the Hu–Wen regime, the logic of the open-door reforms persisted vigorously, despite the studious efforts by the party in implementing Hu Jintao's 'scientific outlook on development'. In the attempt to focus on social development along with economic development, some attention was paid to reducing income inequality and regional disparity, but gender inequity did not get any priority. The Eighteenth Party Congress in November 2012 put Hu Jintao's perspective into the CPC Constitution and elected Xi Jinping as the new general secretary. Xi's stirring call for realizing the 'Chinese dream through rejuvenation of the Chinese nation' provided a general framework for pursuing his policies combining the economic growth with a strong anti-corruption campaign among other things. But gender or for that matter other social inequities did not figure prominently in his plan outlined at the Third Plenary Session of the Eighteenth CC in November 2013. The relaxation of the one-child policy at this plenary session, however, indirectly had implications for the life and status of women which we discuss in a subsequent chapter.

Women's Gains during the 1980s

The first decade of reforms clearly showed a uniformly positive trend of rising status of women in terms of economic opportunities and social welfare, even though gender gap in wages and social practices continued in many ways. The income from agriculture, employment in the rural enterprises and the expansion of local funds for education and health were mainly responsible for this. During the second decade, especially after 1992 as the TVEs gradually showed a decline and rural funding for health and education also stagnated or declined, women faced new difficulties. Enterprises had to struggle to remain in the market and that required technological upgradation with more investment and asserting managerial autonomy. Under this system, usually the women were the first to be retrenched. This is the story we see in Wuxi's suburbs. In the interior areas of rural China, this rural crisis was even more intense.

After the reforms had been in full operation for over five years, I witnessed significant changes in suburban Wuxi through field observation and interviews in September and October 1985. During the period 1979–85, there had been a considerable shift of focus from agriculture to industry.

This was primarily because even more agricultural land had been taken over by the State for industrial or commercial construction. Hence, some peasants worked either in city-run or in township-run factories. Of the 8,611 labourers in the township, 4,545 or 53 per cent were women. Women now had got more opportunities in rural enterprises. As much as 60 per cent of them were employed in factories and 40 per cent in agriculture and other non-industrial activities. However, the average income of a female labourer was far below the average income of a male labourer in Hela Township. The average annual income of a female labourer was 800–900 yuan, whereas the average for commune members, that is, male and female labourers together, was 1,410 yuan. The lowest annual income of a female worker was 500 yuan and the highest was 3,500 yuan. This meant that the male workers earned far more than female workers.

This process continued in the late 1980s and the early 1990s. As the leader of Hela Township Women Federation Wang Shuizhuan put it, in the 1970s, women stepped out of home to work; in the 1980s, they took part in economic construction; and in the 1990s, their perspective was to 'take part in economic competition and upgrade their status still further'. What she meant was that in the process of this upgradation, women had to face new challenges caused by retrenchment and make adjustments in their life conditions. They were either reconciled to staying at home or look for new avenues of work. Thus, from the 1990s onwards, as the market economy flourished in China, its demands outweighed all other considerations such as women's employment.

In the mid-1980s, the expansion of rural industries had clearly provided greater employment opportunities to the women. The demand for recruiting workers for rural enterprises expanded so fast that the youngsters dropped out of school after finishing junior middle level, that is, class nine, to take up jobs. Many did not even complete middle school. However, there was a drive to impart technical education to women; factories encouraged their workers to join evening schools.[18] There was a campaign to train women in 10 fields, most of which indicate stereotypical occupations for women though with a few new areas added. They were (a) agro-technician, (b) finance official: managerial and accounting, (c) medical worker, (d) family planning propaganda personnel, (e) legal system popularizer, (f) sanitary supervisor, (g) personnel for elimination of pests and house flies and disposal of waste and night soil, (h) kindergarten teacher, (i) nursery teacher and (j) public facility workers for laying out pipe lines, constructions of public toilets, etc.

Some of these areas of training opened up new opportunities for women. For example, not many women earlier were agro-technicians or finance officers. Many other areas of training were meant to utilize women's services in familiar spheres in local areas but in a more systematic way. All these items involved simple training programmes conducted by the women's federation. As far as training of women in industrial skills was concerned, that was left to the industries themselves. This was a conscious intervention by the women's federation to utilize women's services at a time when production responsibility system had led many women back home to take charge of agriculture. Thus, increasing employment of women in rural enterprises and additional training for rural socio-economic activities contributed to the rising of family income in Hela.

That situation had changed in the early 1990s. In the early 1990s, especially after the 1992 impetus on market reforms, the women's federation took several steps to relate their programme with the new pace of the reforms and to help women in facing the new situation. They organized special training programmes for retrenched women or aspiring women to enable them to handle new technology in the factories. The federation took an initiative to set up some enterprises including restaurants to be run by women. Under the new dictum of optimization of use of enterprises through new technology when factories retrenched workers most of whom were women, the women's federation intervened trying to find them new jobs and training them in new skills.

But the general trend of increasing family income continued without interruption. Most families bought domestic electric appliances, refrigerators and washing machines besides TV/tape recorders. Many people now had motorcycles. They ate more nutritious food. The new prosperity was seen in people's clothing. Women now wore more fashionable dresses and jewellery. As a women leader put it, for modernization and competition, the Chinese women should 'look decent and modern'.[19] It may be recalled that this was in sharp contrast to the dress code during the Cultural Revolution when the stress was on simplicity in clothing—the famous Mao suit for both men and women. When I first visited China in 1979, that was still the scene everywhere, but by the early 1990s, women's dress was full of variety and colour.[20]

By the mid-1980s, almost 80 per cent of the households had built new double-storeyed houses. In 1993, I noticed yet another wave of house building with modern facilities. Many families now had telephones installed at home. Most families were able to save. The number of joint accounts in the banks had increased. Many women leaders confirmed in 1985 that with rising income, there was a trend of women staying home and looking after the household. But in 1993, there was a reverse trend. After staying at home for a year or two, they approached the women's federation to help them find work. Work outside homes was considered necessary for having a sense of fulfilment and raising their status.

I was told by many informants that husbands usually turned over their income to their wives. As one leader put it, 'Most of the wives were ministers of internal affairs'. But obviously this was not enough for enlarging the conditions for freedom of women. In some spheres, opportunities opened up for women, whereas in some other spheres, their potentialities for creative activities were constrained. But there was an evidence of positive development of women's leadership at various levels. Yet the progress in women's political participation in China in the course of the over three decades of reforms was rather tardy.

Women in the Political Structure

Even though there has been steady improvement in the presence of women at the local institutions, the picture at the national level is not impressive. The top decision-making body, namely the Standing Committee of the CPC Politburo, has had no female member. The Eighteenth Party Congress elected only 10 female members to the 205-member CC in November 2012, while its 25-member Politburo had only 2 women. Actually, the representation of women in the CPCCC declined from 2002 to 2007. In the NPC, the representation had increased from only 12 per cent in the first NPC in 1954 to 22.6 per cent in 1975 and had hovered around 21 per cent thereafter.[21] This is a positive phenomenon in international standards. While the NPC with its over 3,000 members met annually in a relatively ceremonial fashion, its more functional, law-making organ, the Standing Committee, had much lower representation of women, 11–17 per cent. However, there were always one or two women vice-chairpersons of the Standing Committee.[22] At the local levels, however, the picture was different. In 2010, as many as 68.2 per cent county-level leaders were women, marking a 20 per cent increase over 2000 and 42.5 per cent of civil servants were women.[23]

In 1979, the Hela commune still had a commune revolutionary committee—the institution of the Cultural Revolution which was disbanded shortly afterwards. It had 12 members, 4 of whom were women. Since 1973, there were only two women on it to which two were added in 1978. At the higher level of the Wuxi Suburban Revolutionary Committee, there was one female member since 1978 as well. The Hela Commune Party Committee had two female members since 1975. Thus, it was clear that in the second half of the 1970s, there was a general trend of increasing women participation at administrative as well as party levels.

At the level of the production brigade too, there was some women representation. Out of the seven members of the brigade revolutionary committees, two were women; in the case of the smaller brigades, at least one was a woman. On the Hela Brigade Party Branch, of the five members three were women. At the level of production team, however, there was not a single female team leader in any of the 95 teams of the Hela commune in 1979. But in the 'leading group' operating in every team, there were one or two women. In other words, at the operative levels of production activities on the ground, there was no women leadership as yet.

Women formed almost a third, actually 35 per cent, of the party members of Hela commune, the total membership being 491. In the Hela brigade, the proportion of female members was even higher, that is, 40 per cent. It showed that the political and education level of women in this suburban area was fairly high. It was also due to a degree of effective mobilization of women by the women's federation.

The ACWF had its branch at the commune level. As mentioned earlier, the 11-member commune committee of women's federation was headed by Ms Shen Jianchen since 1977. This was yet another evidence of continuous rise of this woman activist of Hela. In fact, before 1977, she was the general secretary of the Commune Youth League. Her predecessor in the commune women's federation had moved up to become the chair of the suburban women's federation. According to Ms Shen, the main functions of the women's federation were (a) to help party branch in carrying out ideological education among women, (b) to solve problems regarding socialization of household chores to enable women to go out to work, (c) to promote family planning and (d) to help resolve contradictions in families.

It should be noted that during the 1980s, the focus of the women's federation activities shifted to economic construction which did not figure prominently in the above list. The stress on family planning acquired even more importance during the next decade. However, socialization of services such as collective-run nurseries, old age homes and some medical and education facilities declined in the late 1980s and the 1990s, thus leaving individual families to make their own arrangements.

During the 1980s, several steps had been taken to put younger people in charge of women's federation units. In addition to this, in practically every village, women had been assigned some leadership roles.

The change of leadership in women's federation was described as 'reconsolidation'. Lianhe village had a new chair of women's federation in 1985 who was 29 years old. The 60-year-old leader of Qinlongshan Village Women's Federation had been replaced by a 30-year-old woman who had passed senior middle school. In Meiyuan village, the chair of the women's federation had become the director of the village administration. She was 37. Another young person, a 40-year-old kindergarten teacher, had succeeded her. Similarly, the women's unit leader of Liqiao village at 35 had taken over as the director of a factory. Now it had a new leader who was 29. These changes also showed mobility of women to positions of political, administrative and managerial responsibilities.

In a village-by-village check-up to identify women in leadership positions, it was noticed that there had been significant developments during 1979–85.

1. In Hela village, the person who was the leader of the women's federation in 1979 got promotion and later became the secretary of the party branch at the age of 38.

2. Longshan village also had a woman leader since 1979 who was both the party secretary and the director of the village economic cooperative. This village had many other women cadres including the social security director and the barefoot doctor. The director of the village or the village committee head, however, was a man.

3. The accountant in charge of financial management in Lianhe village was a 34-year-old woman.

4. The former chair of the women's federation in Meiyuan village in 1985 had moved up to become the director of the village. Considered very active in the region, Ms Chen Chuanzhen, who was 37, was one of the few women who were heads of village administration. In Meiyuan village, they had two female barefoot doctors.

5. In Daqi village, the deputy director of economic cooperatives was a 42-year-old woman. A graduate of senior middle school, she was also chair of the village women's federation.

6. In Qinlongshan village, the former women's federation leader was now party secretary at the age of 45. There was yet another cadre who was both deputy director of the economic cooperative and the chair of women's federation.

7. In Wujin village, the leader of the women's federation was also the village accountant. The agro-technician of the fruit orchard was also a woman.

8. In Qingxin, the grain-growing village located at one end of the township, the director was a woman, a 36-year-old junior middle-school graduate. The agro-technician there was also a woman.

9. The accountant of Xishan village was also a 41-year-old woman.
10. In the relatively better-off Xiemin village, there was a female director since 1979. (Her annual income had reportedly increased from 800 to 3,500 yuan by 1985.) The accountant and the medical worker there were also women.
11. Liqiao village had a female director who had moved as the manager of the village-run socks factory. Her successor was also a woman, as were the accountant and the medical worker of the village.
12. The director of Sunjing village was also a woman. The accountant and two medical workers were also women.
13. Finally, in the fisheries village, there was also a 30-year-old female director besides the accountant and the receptionist. As mentioned earlier, one of the Vice-Directors of the Xiang was a woman. But there was no woman Deputy Secretary of the Party Committee at the township level, let alone a Secretary.

Thus, in 1985, the heads of as many as six villages or village administrations were women which was a conspicuous evidence of expanding women's leadership at the grass-roots level. Party secretaries in three villages were women as well. Only in two villages, women were agro-technicians. But in as many as seven villages, women worked as accountants, a job that involved responsibility but desk work with computational and accounting skill. This was considered by some as an 'appropriate' job for women.

In the late 1980s, the political administration of the village was fully integrated with economic management. The village committee head became the general manager of the integrated complex of agriculture, industry and commerce. After that was done, out of the 13 villages in Hela Township, women were general managers only in two, that is, Hela and Longshan, in 1993. Both, however, were very successful villages, each making an annual profit of over 100 million yuan. In six others, deputy heads were women. There was no female manager in any township-run enterprise, though there were some in the lower-level village-run enterprises. There was a woman as one of the three deputy secretaries of the township party committee who was also one of the four deputy directors of the township government.

As for the Hela Township as a whole, the women's federation had its township-level representatives conference. In the two-day conference of May 1987, for example, there were 80 members representing the 13 villages. In 1993, the women's federation had a 38-member representatives committee which was elected once in three years. Each village sent one representative— the rest coming from factories which had more than 30 female workers.

One member represented the 'educated circles' and one other represented the township government. Every village had a women's federation unit with a committee consisting of three–seven members. The annual conference discussed the progress of reforms in Hela Township and also deliberated on the special problems that women faced. The unit at the village and enterprise levels held monthly meetings.

Women's representation in the CPC leadership at the top level has been meagre or almost non-existent. In the Fifteenth CC Politburo elected in 1997, there was no woman among the 19 full members and Wu Yi was the only woman elected as one of the two alternate members of the Politburo. There was no woman elected to the six-member Standing Committee of the Politburo which is the all-powerful decision-making body in China. In fact, there has not been a female member of the Standing Committee of the Politburo CPC so far in the history of the PRC. After the Sixteenth Party Congress, the CC elected Wu Yi as a member of the Politburo; there was hope that this would set a trend. But there was no female member in the Politburo of the Seventeenth CC elected in 2007.

At the grass-roots level, the normal practice is to have a woman as one of the deputy directors of the township. There were a few directors at the village level. As for the managers of enterprises, there was none that I could identify in 1996. This was despite the fact that in several light industries, women constituted the majority of the workers.

Many years later, in 2011, the Chinese government announced a new decision-making; it was obligatory to have at least 30 per cent women among the members of the village councils and 10 per cent among the directors or heads of the village councils. This was part of the Outline of National Plan for Women's Development 2011–20 announced by the State Council on 9 August 2011. Contrast this to the initiative in India. Statutory representation of women under the 73rd Constitutional Amendment in India created a favourable situation for women. They now occupied at least one-third of the leadership posts at the panchayat samiti or block level (equivalent to a township in China) and panchayat level (equivalent to the village). One-third representatives in all the local bodies in rural and urban India (urban under the 74th Amendment) had to be women. Beginning in 2009, many Indian states went a step further and provided for 50 per cent representation of women at the local government levels. The relevant laws were to be amended to make it as the all-India norm. However, the initiative for amending the Constitution of India to provide at least one-third reservation in the Parliament and the state legislatures was still awaited to be passed by the Lok Sabha, the lower house of the Indian Parliament.[24] In China, however, there was no statutory representation for women at any level until 2011. It was left to the local leadership of village, township and the suburban district to decide on appointment of women into political offices. But the fact that the existing leadership was highly male-dominated itself made it difficult to increase the share of women in leadership. This is where one has to acknowledge the significance of statutory provision for representation, though that by itself may not secure substantive power for women and this had to be supplemented by structural measures in securing women's access to productive assets, employment, education and cultural measures. On these fronts, no doubt a number of measures were initiated in China in the course of the reforms. But they were not adequate to achieve gender justice and equality.

Thus, there was a significant measure of women's presence at the local leadership level. But it was uneven in every sphere, namely party, administration and enterprise management, all of which were man-dominated, even though there were female leaders in office. There was no formal quota as in the case of India's local bodies under the constitutional requirement of having at least one-third women as members and in leadership positions. But there was an informal rule to have at least one woman as one of the deputy leaders. The official approach was to promote women's rights and women's welfare through the women's federation. But this was structurally flawed as the local unit of the women's federation was working under the leadership of the local party unit. The autonomy that the ACWF has exercised was the cumulative result of the total situation domestic and international rather than specific role played at particular levels. This becomes clear when we look at the mobilizational role that it played at the grass-roots level and how it could hardly respond to the challenge of the market economy.

Family and Income Trends

In 1987, the women's federation had proclaimed a new plan of action for its units all over China. The plan consisted of 'two tasks and four extensions'. The two tasks were to (a) organize women to read rules under the land laws and (b) raise women's educational level. This was to be further realized through the Four-point Extension Programme: (a) ideological education, (b) application of science and technology in childcare, (c) knowledge of law and (d) knowledge about women and child health. These tasks and programmes had to be carried out not only through lectures to women but also by concrete activities.

This perspective was further reinforced after the Tiananmen demonstrations of 1989. But in 1992, after Deng's 'southern tour', once again the stress was on accelerating growth and modernization of life along Western lines.

In part, the 1987 perspective reflected a tilt towards ideological alertness after the emergence of the student movements in the late 1980s. In January 1987, Hu Yaobang had been replaced by Zhao Ziyang as the general secretary of the CPC. The CPC leadership had launched a campaign against 'spiritual pollution'. At the same time, stress on science and technology education, which was a characteristic of the reforms period, was added to the women's programme. But it was noteworthy that the federation was still focusing on women's household role and childcare. To a query on this issue, the Hela Township Women's Federation leader asserted that the women's federation acted as the backbone of the process of releasing women from household work for outside work. She, however, added that good family relationship was necessary for promoting modernization.

In Hela, majority of women had passed junior middle school or nine years of education. Very few went to higher middle school. None from this township was in the university in 1987. But in 1993, there was considerable improvement. Nearly 30 per cent women had got senior middle-school education. Over 20 were studying in the university, and illiteracy had been eliminated. There were some special educational programmes to provide technical education and education in law, health and childcare for women. Those who passed the childcare examination were permitted to work in the nursery.

In 1987, the picture regarding women's employment had improved a great deal. Majority of women workforce, that is, 55 per cent, were employed in township- and village-run industries, 35 per cent in agriculture and 10 per cent were engaged in the city industry. Average income of women was 1,200–1,300 yuan per year as against 800–900 yuan the year earlier. The leader of township women federation confirmed in November 1987 that women's wages were lower than men's by about 20 per cent. Only in technical jobs there was equal pay for equal work for both. But, one may add, the number of women technicians was small.

Generally, the piece rate system[25] operated in the enterprises. The managers claimed that those women who performed as well as men got equal wages as men, or even better wages than some men. In the enterprises where piece rate system did not apply, the situation was different. Normally, women were assigned lighter jobs than men; hence, they got lower wages. The management paid different grades for different kinds of work and under the production responsibility system, it graded workers according to performance.

Persistence of disparity of wages between men and women was thus evident during the reform period beginning 1979. Prior to that, during the commune period too, women earned less work points than men. However, two new aspects were present as a result of the reforms. First, the general level of the economy had improved vastly, thus raising the incomes of all. Second, women's education and skill were considerably expanded, now enabling them to avail greater opportunities in the economy. This was the case in the developed areas such as Wuxi. In the backward regions, however, the scenario was different. Opportunities for women were much less. Thus, whether it was a collective economy or market economy, unless special efforts were made to reduce women's inequality, it would persist in various forms.

As in most other places in China, the retirement age was different for men and women in Hela too. Men retired at 60 and women at 55. This had been explained by the fact that through child bearing and other physical problems, women were weaker in old age than men. This, however, had been contested by many studies in different parts of the world which proved that aging and debility were not primarily determined by gender. In any case, there were controversies on this issue. The differential retirement age for China's men and women has perhaps more to do with cultural belief than with rational decision. The same belief could also explain the lower wages for women.

The pension system applied to both. It was determined by the annual wages that a person earned and the number of years he or she had worked. Hence, the women's pension was lower than men's because of their lower wages and early retirement.

The social scene was changing slowly. In 1985, the new marriage law had come into force. Under it, women's status had been raised to some extent. The law had prescribed the minimum age for marriage as 20 for women and 22 for men. In Hela, the average age of marriage was 22.5. In recent years, the number of divorces had increased. As against two cases in 1985 and seven in 1987, it was put as one in 1,000 couples in 1993. According to the women federation leader, the reasons were diverse and complicated. In some cases, there was the lack of warm feeling for one another; in some, there was a third person in the picture. In yet other cases, the women looked forward to doing larger things and when marriage was seen as a constraint, they broke it up. These developments by themselves could not indicate any positive or negative trends. There was definitely a sign of departure from the traditional moorings. In some situations, the family expanded the opportunities for women. In some others, it could create obstacles. At any rate, increase in divorce rate was still too small to warrant any generalization.

The party put emphasis on the value of the family which it regarded as an important cell of society. Party cadres invoked traditional virtues of Chinese family as being an institution of love, sharing and mutual support. As the women's federation leader put it to me in 1993, on the one hand the wife pinned high hopes on the husband for his achievements and was prepared to make sacrifices for that end; on the other she wished to achieve things for herself—this was a serious contradiction. The social milieu was still such that the former aspect, wife sacrificing for the sake of the husband, dominated. The patriarchal aspect of the traditional Chinese family—husband–wife relationship was one of the five principles of Confucius—was in a way reinforced in the new achievement-oriented situation of the market economy. But as it became clear in the late 1990s–2000s this cultural backdrop was used to rationalize the trend of increasing domestic role of retrenched women.

As indicated earlier, one of the interesting aspects of the workforce in Hela Township was the preponderance of women. About 60 per cent of the workers were women because they were in great demand in textile industry which was one of the major productive activities in this area. In other industries and in commerce and fisheries, generally men did most of the job. In agriculture, involvement of men and women was almost even, whereas in vegetable growing, women were predominant. From this picture, it was noticeable that in relatively more skilled jobs, women's participation was still limited. In textile industry, however, women had maintained a lead. But as was seen in the case of city-run silk factory, as technological modernization progressed, the proportion of female workers had fallen. In the case of vegetable growing, women were deployed mainly to take continuous care rather than for any skilled job.

With the development of the electronic industries, however, new opportunities had been opened up for women. An example was the Wuxi Microelectronic Factory which as a joint venture of the Wuxi city government, Hela Township and Hela village. There were 800 workers in this factory, 80 per cent of whom were women. This factory produced parts for radio, TV, tape recorder, cassettes and telephones. It engaged in compensation trade with several foreign companies from the USA, Germany, Japan and Singapore. In this factory, there was the piece rate system of wages, therefore no differential wages for men and women. The new workers were put on probation for three months, getting 1.40 yuan per day the first month, 1.60 yuan per day the second month and 1.80 yuan thereafter. For production beyond quota, there was additional remuneration. There was a guarantee of living wage of 60 yuan per month for every worker. Very often the bonus was more than wages. Average total earning in the factory was between 125 and 175 yuan per month. It should be noted that these wages were relatively lower than many of the township- and village-run factories. For example, the sweater works gave an average wage of 220 yuan per month in 1985.

The economic trend during the 1980s unquestionably created greater opportunities for women. Diversification of agriculture and expansion of rural industries generated new avenues of employment and income. There was also evidence of selective utilization of women workforce with sophisticated technology, attracting more men than women. This reflected the prevailing structure of education. It was also due to some traditional cultural norms which did not encourage women to acquire industrial skills.[26] But there were signs of change as well. Women were coming up as agricultural technicians, medical scientists and teachers. But there was a paradox in women's education. Young girls graduating from junior middle school after nine years of education could easily find jobs in the expanding rural enterprises and earn more than the better-educated workers and staff in the cities. But they remained with low-level education and low-level skills. In other words, there were no economic or other incentives for going into higher middle school and beyond. In political and management positions, however, there was a clear sign of increasing representation for women.

There were women in charge of village administration, women as party secretaries and as managers in village enterprises. During the 1980s, the political rise of women cadres was a clearly discernible trend. This was partly due to the vigorous role played by the ACWF and partly due to the worldwide campaign for women's rights. An equally important role was played by local women leaders like Ms Shen Jianchen of Hela. But this political trend could be perhaps more true of economically developed regions like suburban Wuxi. In the interior village and less developed areas, the picture was not necessarily the same. In any case, even in this area, reforms and modernization brought mixed blessings for women. As for the representation of women in political structure, there was no consistent pattern to indicate that the momentum of the 1980s would be protected.

Women and the Expanding Market Economy

It is well known that after Deng Xiaoping's 'southern tour' in 1992, a powerful momentum was built up all over China to increase production and profit through the reform and open-door policy without hesitating to pursue capitalist methods. This meant going all out for private investment from home and abroad, upgrading the level of technology, exercising even greater autonomy in hiring and firing of workers and doing everything necessary to respond to the market. The preoccupation of all the cadres thereafter was raising production and profit by any means—a trend that continued until 2002. In the new milieu, social issues such as gender were relegated to the background. My interviews in Wuxi in 1996 and 2001 confirmed the paradoxical situation of great economic achievements alongside widening gender gap and other adverse trends. During my visit in 2004, discussions with women federation leaders revealed many serious dimensions of this situation. On the one hand, the Beijing World Congress had alerted the CPC leadership about the need for women's development; on the other hand, the preoccupation with economic growth had been re-emphasized as the one-point 'focus' which outweighed all other considerations.

Moreover, the primary focus on economic construction and profit had its adverse effects on many social objectives including the goal of securing gender equality in day-to-day life. In many enterprises, when steps were taken to modernize technology and improve competitiveness, many workers were laid off, most of whom were women. But this situation forced the families to plan their own life. Discussing the case of 45 women laid off recently, township women federation leader Li Qing told me in October 1996 that the ones with heightened consciousness joined new employment schemes. She said that even if a family earned high income, the newly conscious women found it unacceptable to stay at home and do only housework. They would look for new jobs or set up their own business. Since by and large they were one-child families, women were freer to plan their work. This was the new trend in the economically advanced areas of coastal China. Having accepted market economy and the enterprise management's right to fire, women had to cope with the situation through their own efforts. They had to reconcile their new awareness about their own creative potential, with the competitive market economy focused on growth. But many women said that they found this new dynamic economic environment more hospitable to their carrier prospects. As in many other countries, economic reforms of this kind had a great deal of adverse consequences for women, even though many women found new opportunities opened up for them.

The traditional notion of women looking after the household and family members staying at home was also revived in the case of wealthy families. But this was a minor trend in the Wuxi region as new consciousness about the value of women's work had spread widely. Here, the milieu of money-making had its effect as well. No matter how rich was a household, women's work could add further to the family's earning. This also propelled women to go out and work.

The new cultural climate affected the institution of family in many ways. Family was no doubt still a valued social institution in Chinese society. The new economic policies actually consolidated the family institution. Land was contracted to the household. Incidentally, still it was in the name of male head of the household.[27] In the new diversified economy, the members of the family planned their employment with some working in agriculture, some in industry, some in commerce and all putting their income together for a higher standard of living. Thus, the development of market economy in rural China supported the institution of family which was a key institution in traditional China. Even after a son or a daughter grew up and got married, usually they lived with the boy's parents. But there was an increasing trend of a newly married couple setting up a separate household. Even then the family relationships continued to be strong. Three of the five relationships that Confucius had talked about related to the family. They helped each other in achieving prosperity even after staying apart.

But the divorce rate was slowly increasing. This was mainly due to two reasons. One was incompatibility in jobs or one person not accepting the other's choice; the other was one of them developing friendship with another person. Divorce was no longer seen as a calamity in the new milieu. The township's Civil Affairs Department was authorized to handle family problems. If the two sides had decided to divorce on mutual consent, then the civil affairs cadre would negotiate their terms of divorce including division of property, custody of child and such other things. The approval of the township government was the conclusive step and there was no need to go to a court of law in such cases. Only if one party disagreed with other, it was necessary to go to the court.

Two pieces of data could be cited to indicate women's life condition. At the district level, the male work participation rate was much higher than that of female. Out of the total of 86,000 workers in the Wuxi suburban district, 56 per cent were men and 46 per cent were women who were engaged in various economic activities. At the lower level, in Hela Township, however, women constituted a little over 50 per cent of the labour force. This cannot be the basis of calculating the sex ratio as there could be more old women and female children and many self-employed women who may be left out. These are the categories that are not included in the categories of the female workers of the suburban district. The other piece of data is about life expectancy in Hela Township in 1996 which was 70 for men and 74 for women.[28] It is an irony that despite higher life expectancy, women retired five years earlier than men.

The township women federation committee had 11 members in 1996 with an average age of 39 years. All of them were at least senior middle-school graduates, some from vocational secondary schools. Only one of the 13 villagers committee directors was a woman. That was in Longshan. Deputy directors in five villagers committees were women. In other words, not every village leadership had a woman even as a deputy. As for the party leadership at the village level, only in one case (in Hela village) the branch secretary was a woman. In three other villages, there were deputy secretaries of the party branch. There was only one woman manager in the township-owned factories. In the village-run factories, there were several. As mentioned earlier, one of the vice-directors of the township was a woman. But none of the township party committees deputy secretaries was a woman. One of the deputy chairpersons of the township people's congress was a woman. In addition, the township party discipline committee also had a woman as one of its deputy leaders.

According to the data provided by the township women federation leader Li Qing in October 1996, at least 45 women had been laid off during the current year. Some of them stayed home getting their basic wages while waiting for new jobs. In 1995, 300 women had lost jobs; some of them found new avenues on their own. The women's federation took the initiative and arranged with Da Qishan village to employ some. Only 10 of them had been re-employed. The proportion of re-employment was low, according to the woman leader.

The problem of women's employment acquired serious dimensions as marketization proceeded vigorously in the 2000s. The Third Survey on Chinese Women's Status released in 2011 brought out many details of this situation. It revealed that the proportion of urban women who lost job opportunities based on gender considerations or encountered gender discrimination in the work place was four times that of urban men.[29] Women's work participation rate declined in China during this period (Table 8.1). In the countryside, the number of female labour had increased due to migration of men. According to one study, there were 47 million 'left-behind wives' in rural China, suffering not only economic hardships but also high depression and other ailments.[30]

The women's federation had been asked by the central party leadership to publicize Jiang Zemin's address to the Beijing World Congress and stress three national policies: one, family planning; two, man–woman equality; and three, economic development. However, in the course of the discussion

Table 8.1:
Labour force participation by sex and location (%)

Categories	1982	1990	2000	2010
Total	78.7	78.8	76.9	64.2
Male	86.45	84.6	83.0	51.26
Female	70.56	72.6	70.6	48.73
Urban	77.8	75.7	65.9	49.95
Rural	78.9	79.9	80.6	50.05

Sources: Margaret Maurer-Fazio, James Hughes and Dandan Zhang, 'Economic Reform and Changing Patterns of Labor Force Participation in Urban and Rural China', *William Davidson Institute Working Paper*, Number 787 (August 2005): 34; World Bank Data available at: http://data.worldbank.org/indicator/SL.TLF.CACT.ZS/countries (accessed on 15 June 2017). China: Population by sex and geographical coverage, available at: http://www.ilo.org/ilostat/faces/home/statisticaldata/data_by_country/country-details/indicator-details?indicator (accessed on 15 June 2017).

with the women federation leader, it was clear that gender equality was not a priority in the contemporary order of things. She clearly stated that economic development was the government's top priority which she seemed to accept happily. For the women of rural China, whether the economic reforms secured greater emancipation or more freedom in terms of material, political and cultural conditions of self-realization, there is no clear answer.

After the adoption of the framework of a socialist market economy and Deng Xiaoping Theory of 'building socialism with Chinese characteristics' in October 1992, marketization was widened and deepened in China. Its effects on women were mixed and perhaps positive in some ways. But the efforts to secure women's rights were confined to the political initiative of the women's federation which functioned under the party leadership. Women did not have political rights to organize themselves in pursuit of their rights. Under the theory of mass organizations, workers, peasants, women and youth had their organizations only as wings of the party. Thus, in the economy, there emerged the market forces promoting free enterprise, incentives and competition; but in the political sphere, autonomous political organization and movements were still not allowed. The party defended this situation as a requirement of political stability which was needed to promote vigorous growth. Yet, there were indications of growing consciousness among women about their rights and positive developments on that front in employment and political representation. Socialist feminism as a dimension of socialist freedom was absent in the reform discourse. What dominated was the preoccupation with achieving economic growth by developing a socialist market economy, that is, market economy under the leadership of a Communist Party.

There is general acknowledgement within China that the phenomenon of 'one low and three small' (*yi di san shao*) persisted even after the achievement of high standard of living and economic advancement. One low referred to women's low participation in politics and the three small referred to the presence of small number of women in high-level decision-making bodies, position as heads of institutions and in key sectors.[31] The Third Survey on Chinese Women's Status conducted in 2011 jointly by National Bureau of Statistics and ACWF found many reasons for this. One was that women said that they did not have self-confidence for political role. More than half believed that men should do public jobs and women should work in the household. What is remarkable is that such a view increased over the figure of 2,000. In a case study of Township in the Xi Prefecture in Henan province in 2006, as many as 87 per cent of rural women and 54 per cent of urban women did not take any part in political activities or civil organizations or associations. They cited overload of home duties as the main reason for this. Yet, an overwhelming number of women, 83.5–88.6 per cent, felt that women's capabilities were not worse than men's.[32]

In addition to 'left-behind women' in rural China, the phenomenon of 'left-behind' women as a general trend in terms of age and employment was another trend. Especially in the cities, women in the new milieu went for higher education and jobs and postponed marriage. When they were ready for it, they did not get proper match. The cultural environment of China did not support them to tackle such situation effectively.[33]

Has the ACWF shown adequate capacity to play the role of the main agency to meet the challenge of the persisting phenomenon of gender inequality in China? Unfortunately, it has to be pointed out that despite its increasingly active and autonomous role since the 1995 World Congress, it is clear that its capacity has remained limited. It is a mass organization of the party to prepare women to implement party policies rather than be the main champion of women's rights, though its role as the latter has become more pronounced gradually. Its president is at best a member of the party CC rather than the Politburo. At the Eleventh National Congress of ACWF held in October 2013, the outgoing president became a vice-chairperson of the NPC. ACWF leaders have not been part of the top echelon of the party. Addressing the Eleventh Congress on behalf of the party, Wang Qishan called upon women to work for the 'realization of the Chinese dream and contribute to the development of the motherland'. Describing ACWF as a strong link between the party and women, he asked it to 'build a warm home which was a popular slogan among women all over the country'. Vice-President of ACWF Song Xiuyuan followed the same tone in her report to the congress and said that 'in the next five years, further efforts are needed to give women more opportunities and resources in economic construction, to improve their abilities in administrating national and social affairs and to help them play a more important role in cultural development'. She dedicated the ACWF to implementing the National Programme for Women's Development 2011–20.[34] Between this congress and the NPC session in March 2014, we already notice more specific steps on many issues such as women's land rights and curbing sexual abuse.

In three areas, concrete initiatives were visible in response to the mounting concern over gender inequality in contemporary China. Firstly, survey, research and documentation by governmental and non-governmental agencies on the conditions of women had expanded steadily, even though questions about statistical inadequacies remained. There were three national surveys conducted jointly by ACWF and the State Statistical Bureau in 1990, 2000 and 2011 in addition to several large-scale studies by the Institute of Sociology of CASS and Peking University. These were the basis for the annual reports submitted by the Chinese government to the UNIFEM and later UN Women. The All-China Young Scholars Gender Study Forum and the Chinese Women Studies Society became more and more active, producing study reports and campaigning for women's rights.[35] Secondly, National Policy on Women's Development was announced in 2010[36] and several new initiatives launched following that. The China Association of Women Entrepreneurs became more active and made specific proposals from time to time. So was the Association of Chinese Scientific and Technological Workers. ACWF had set up task forces and made proposals to governments. Under its leadership, a serious campaign had been launched to make legislative provision for women's land rights. The HRS gave the contract to the male member of the household. Since women generally moved to men's villages after marriage, they lost their share. When divorces took place, women suffered more due to the lack of land rights. The other issue that had acquired attention was increasing incidence of sexual abuse on which ACWF had demanded strict action. The issue of double burden taken by the woman, both in work place and performing household duties, continued to be a major preoccupation of the women's organization. The third area in which a new level of consciousness was visible in contemporary China was treatment of the women's issues in the media. Cases of violation of women's rights were promptly reported and government's response was closely monitored.

The number of women in the media had increased considerably. The cultural representation of women was more complex than before.

But the cumulative effect of all three positive responses did not seem to be adequate to contain the tidal wave of marketization of gender relations in Chinese society. Inequalities continued to rise and violence against women and gender discrimination persisted. An authoritarian system protected the broad policies to maintain the market-led growth and therefore the women remained victims of the success trap.

Confronted with the world discourse on women's rights which saw a high point at the World Women's Congress in 1995 and which continued to grow globally as well as in China, these issues were bound to be debated sharply. But clouds still persisted in half the sky not only in China and India but also in the world as a whole, though consciousness on gender equality had grown everywhere to continue to clear the clouds.

Notes and References

1. Isabel Hilton, 'China May Grow Old before It Grows Rich', *The Guardian* (London) 28 April 2011. Available at: https://www.theguardian.com (accessed on 28 July 2017).
2. A senior scholar from the CPC Party School even advocated abolition of family planning policy in China. Liu Lili, 'China's Two-child Policy: One Year On', *Asia Times*, 19 April 2017. Available at: http://www.atimes.com/writer/liu-lili/ (accessed on 23 April 2017).
3. Song Xiuyan said:

   > Women in China are still facing many problems and challenges in sharing the economic resources and economic income distribution. For example, women are mainly in a lower level of employment in the labour market. And there is still gender discrimination and income gap between men and women.

   Tracy Zhu, 'China Loans US$28.9 Billion to Female Entrepreneurs', 23 May 2014. Available at: www.womenofchina.cn/html/womenofchina/report/173126-1.htm (accessed on 28 May 2014).
4. Fan Wenjun, 'Female Deputies Answer Questions on Women's Development, Rights Protection', at a press conference on the sidelines of the NPC on 12 March 2014. Available at: www.womenofchina.cn/html/womenofchina/report/171211-1.htm (accessed on 28 May 2014).
5. 'Women entered society shaped by male standards' during the Mao era, said Li Xiaojiang, Director, Gender Studies, Dalian University, to a group of Indian feminist scholars in 2005. Mary E John, 'Women and Feminism in China and India: A Conversation with Li Xiaojiang', *Economic and Political Weekly* 40, no. 16 (16 April 2005): 1596.
6. It is widely believed that women's liberation was advanced in a substantial way in the immediate post-1949 period. Ravnai Thakur says: 'The first decade in the communist party's history truly attempted and to a large extent succeeded in undoing centuries of

gender subordination'. Ravnai Thakur, 'Women Studies in China Today', *Economic and Political Weekly* 41, no. 42 (21 October 2006): 4457. Yet, the CPC's perspective on women's liberation was considered somewhat narrow by some scholars in the 1980s. They thought that such an approach 'tended to treat women as an invisible category whose individual agency and distinct, complex subjectivities are sacrificed to the patriarchal state's priorities and socialist ideology'. But Dong Limin thinks that it was more complex than that if seen as a deeper feminist dialogue with history. Dong Limin, 'Historicizing Gender: A Study of Chinese Women's Liberation from 1949–1966', *Differences: A Journal of Feminist Cultural Studies* 24, no. 2 (Summer 2013): 93–108.

7. Ding Ling, *Collected Works of Ding Ling* (Beijing: People's Publishing House, 1982).

8. Li Xiaojiang put it thus: 'It should be possible to form their own self while creating something for society—something their mothers for instance have never known'. John, 'Women and Feminism in China and India', 1596. Li elaborates this perspective further in Li Xiaojiang, 'The Progress of Humanity and Women's Liberation'. *Differences: A Journal of Feminist Cultural Studies* 24, no. 2 (Summer 2013): 22–50.

9. Interestingly, the then CPC Politburo Standing Committee member Hu Jintao who assessed the preparatory work for holding the World Women's Congress said that holding of this congress demonstrated that 'the world status of China under the opening up drive and reform had been improving'. According to Foreign Minister Qian Qichen, it would show to the world that 'reformed, open China was now enjoying social prosperity'. 'China Prepares for World Women's Congress', *News from China* 7, no. 15 (13 April 1994). See also 'China Actively Prepares for World Women's Conference', *Beijing Review* (28 February–6 March 1994). Chen Muhua said in her speech at the opening session on 4 September 1995 that 'raising the status of women was the call of the times'. Chen Muhua, *Beijing Review* 38, no. 38 (18–24 September 1995): 10.

10. Wang Hairong, 'Clouds Over Half the Sky', *Beijing Review* 50, no. 52 (27 December 2007): 24–25.

11. Some of the negative consequences were pointed out in Elizabeth Croll, *Chinese Women since Mao* (London: Zed Press, 1985); Govind Kelkar, 'PRC: at Forty: Women and the Land Question in China', *China Report*, 26, no. 2 (1990), 113–31; Shirin M. Rai, '"Gender", Education and Employment in Post-Mao China: Issues in Modernization', *China Report* 29, no. 1 (1993), 10–14.

12. Some of the negative consequences were pointed out in Croll, *Chinese Women since Mao*; Kelkar, PRC; Rai, '"Gender", Education and Employment in Post-Mao China'.

13. Huifang Wu and Jingzhong Ye, 'Hollow Lives: Women Left Behind in Rural China', *Journal of Agrarian Change* (15 September 2014). Available at: http://onlinelibrary.wiley.com/doi/10.1111/joac.12089/ (accessed on 23 April 2017).

14. Sarah Cook and Xiao-yuan Dong, 'Harsh Choices: Chinese Women's Paid Work and Un-paid Care Responsibilities under Economic Reform', *Development and Change* (July 2011). Available at: http://onlinelibrary.wiley.com/doi/10.1111/j.1467-7660.2011.01721.x/full (accessed on 23 April 2017).

15. Wei Lu, 'Left-behind Children in Rural China: Research Based on the Use of Qualitative Methods in Inner Mongolia' (PhD thesis, Department of Social Policy and Social Work, University of York, June 2011). Available at: http://etheses.whiterose.ac.uk/1546/1/Wei%27s_thesis.pdf (accessed on 23 April 2017). See also *Melissa Hellmann*, 'Dark Corner of China's Rise: A Surge in Trafficking of Children', *The Christian Science Monitor, 27 July 2015*; 'China to Protect Migrant Workers' "Left-behind" children', BBC, 15 February

2016. Available at: http://www.bbc.com/news/world-asia-35581716 (accessed on 23 April 2017). Also CNN story by April Ma reporting on sexual abuse suffered by left-behind children. April Ma, 'China Raises a Generation of "Left-behind" Children' (5 February 2014). Available at: http://edition.cnn.com/2014/02/04/world/asia/china-children-left-behind/index.html (accessed on 15 June 2017).

16. Tamara Jacka, 'Approaches to Women and Development in Rural China', *Journal of Contemporary China* 15, no. 49 (November 2006): 585–602.

17. My interview data is constantly compared with the official reports as well as scholarly studies.

18. See William Lavely, Xiao Zhenyi, Li Bohua and Ronald Freedman, 'Rise in Female Education in China: National and Regional Patterns' *China Quarterly*, no. 121 (1990).

19. For a study of perceptions of womanhood in the West and China, see Patricia Uberoi, 'The Chinese Woman in the Construction of Western Feminism', *China Report* 26, no. 1 (1990): 71–88.

20. See J. C. Robinson, 'Of Women and Washing Machines: Employment, Housework and Reproduction of Motherhood in Socialist China', *China Quarterly*, no. 101 (1985): 32–55.

21. Benxiang Zeng, 'Women's Political Participation in China: Improved or Not?' *Journal of International Women Studies* 15, no. 1 (January 2014): 136–50.

22. In the NPC Standing Committee elected in March 2013, there were 24 female members and 2 vice-chairpersons.

23. Zeng, 'Women's Political Participation in China'.

24. All the major parties, the Congress, the BJP and the left parties had accepted the proposal. But two North Indian parties, the UP-based Samajwadi Party and the Bihar-based Rashtriya Janata Dal representing backward classes or middle castes vehemently opposed the proposal alleging that the reserved seats for women would be taken mostly by upper-caste women who were more educated and conscious. This accusation is however exaggerated as the political process will most likely take care of this danger.

25. Piece rate system meant that you were paid according to the number of pieces of the items you produced, and not according to hours or days of work.

26. A professor at Peking University had once confided to me unhesitatingly that girls should study Arts rather than Science and Technology. Ironically, thanks to the changing milieu, his own daughter decided to go for biochemistry and made a career in it. There were signs of change in that direction as well.

27. A small measure to emphasize female role in a family's food security was taken in India when the Food Security Act 2013 made the provision to have the household's ration card in the name of the eldest woman of the household.

28. Interview with township director.
    Interview with Li Qing, chairperson, Hela Women's Federation on 11 October 1996. She said, 'gender equality in now our national policy' [*nan nu pingdengshiguoci*].

29. Fan Wenjun, 'NPC Deputy Pushes for Gender Equality, Training for Rural Women', 10 March 2014. Available at: www.womenofchina.cn/html/womenofchina/report/171093-1htm (accessed on 28 May 2014).

30. Jinyao Yi, Bin Zhong and Shuqiao Yao, 'Health-related Quality of Life and Influencing Factors among Rural Left-behind Wives in Liuyang, China', *BMC Women's Health*, no. 14 (2014). Available at: https://bmcwomenshealth.biomedcentral.com/articles/10.1186/1472-6874-14-67 (accessed on 31 July 2017).

31. Zeng, 'Women's Political Participation in China'.
32. Ibid.
33. Adam Taylor, 'China's "A-Quality Women" Are Getting Left Behind', *Business Insider* (30 January 2013). Available at: http://www.businessinsider.in/Chinas-A-Quality-Women-Are-Getting-Left-Behind/articleshow/21409046.cms (accessed on 23 April 2017).
34. www.womenofchina.cn/html/womenofchina/report/168638-1.htm (accessed on 7 June 2014).
35. The forum and the society in their annual meeting in Beijing on 23–24 May 2014 came up with many proposals to address the problems faced by Chinese women; www.womenofchina.cn/html/womenofchina/report/171093-1.htm (accessed on 28 May 2014).

	Women and CPC Party Congresses							
	(1997) 15th		*(2002) 16th*		*(2007) 17th*		*(2012) 18th*	
Party Organs	*Total*	*%*	*Total*	*%*	*Total*	*%*	*Total*	*%*
Women in Party Congress	344	16.8	382	18.1	445	20.1	521	23.0
Politburo	0	0.0	1	4.2	1	4.0	2	8.0
Central Committee (CC)	8	4.1	5	2.5	13	6.4	10	4.9
Alternate Members	17	11.2	22	13.9	24	14.4	22	12.9
Central Commission on Discipline Inspection (CCDI)	14	12.1	14	11.6	17	13.4	13	10.0

Source: Tabulated from various party congresses; *People's Daily Online*; http//news.xinhuanet.com/newscentre/2007-10/22/content (accessed on 31 July 2017).

Congresses	*Total Deputies*	*Women Deputies*	*%*	*Women in NPC Standing Committee*	*%*
1954	1,079	147	12.0	4	5.0
1959	1,076	150	12.2	5	6.3
1964	2,492	542	17.9	20	17.4
1975	2,232	653	22.6	42	25.1
1978	2,755	742	21.2	33	21.0
1983	2,346	632	21.2	14	9.0
1988	2,344	634	21.3	16	11.6
1993	2,352	626	21.0	19	12.6
1998	2,329	650	21.8	19	12.7

Congresses	Total Deputies	Women Deputies	%	Women in NPC Standing Committee	%
2003	2,381	604	20.2	21	13.2
2008	2,987	634	21.2	29	16.6
2013	2,987	635	21.3	26	15.29

Sources: Women in National Parliaments, 'World Classification', situation as of 1 March 2013. Available at: http://www.ipu.org/wmn-e/arc/classif010313.htm (accessed on 2 June 2014); 'Twelfth NPC Standing Committee'. Available at: http://www.npc.gov.cn/npc/cwhhy/12jcwh/node_24674.htm 29 May 2014; Niu Tian Xiu, The Study of Women's Political Participation in Contemporary China: A Gender-Justice Perspective (unpublished doctoral thesis, Nanjing Normal University, 2013).

36. The White Paper released in 2005 by the State Council titled 'Gender Equality and Women's Development in China'. Available at: http://www.china.org.cn/english/features/cw/140980.htm (accessed on 15 June 2017).

9

Social Sector Achievements and Crisis: Health, Family Planning and Education

Growth at the Cost of Social Development

China's most important achievements since the founding of the PRC in 1949 have been in the arena of human development. Life expectancy has doubled to 70 years, and the infant mortality rate which was 300 per 1,000 live births in 1950 had come down to 31 in 1999.[1] Even during the reform period, there were significant improvements in the health situation. Life expectancy increased from 63.2 years during the 1970–75 period to 72 years during the 2000–05 period and infant mortality continued to come down from 85 per 1,000 in 1970 to 23 in 2005.[2] In 2015 year-end, life expectancy at birth stood at 76 years, and infant mortality at 9.2 per 1,000 live births.[3] Same was the case with education. Adult literacy rate increased from 77.8 per cent of the age group 15 and older in 1985–94 to 90.9 per cent in 1995–2005 and 96.4 per cent in 2005–15 period.[4] In the case of youth literacy, it was still higher, 94.3 per cent and 98.9 per cent respectively,[5] and 99.7 per cent in 2005–15 for both males and females.[6] One can mention many other indicators to show the achievements of China in the spheres of health, education and social welfare. These records of performance are remarkable when compared to India's and those of other developing countries. But what we see during the reforms period is the relative neglect of these sectors and new sources of health crisis and considerable inequalities of access and quality among rural and urban areas and among different social and regional groups.

We wish to point out that the growth-centric policies in China had their most serious impact on the social sector. A country that had taken pride in making health care available to all its population at the grass-roots level until the mid-1980s found itself in a strange situation in the 1990s and thereafter. The public health system in the countryside had collapsed, while private clinics sprang up. Public hospitals in townships and counties had less personnel and beds and now charged money for services. Peasants who could not afford to pay found themselves in a distress condition, and for many the new health situation turned out to be a cause of their poverty. The general sanitation and health care environment in the villages and small towns deteriorated due to reduced public investment in the rural areas. The extent to which the public health and sanitation system in rural areas had broken down was abundantly exposed when SARS broke out in 2003. Even in the cities, the poor and the unemployed faced a similar situation, though the urban health condition was far better than the rural. The migrant labourers who had left their rural habitat and had landed in the cities in search for jobs had no easy access to city hospitals because they did not possess the *hukou* or the residence registration in the city.

In education too, a similar trend was noticeable. The investment in rural elementary schools and middle schools declined or remained stagnant. There was a stark reduction of primary schools from 917,316 in 1980 to 668,685 by 1995. The number of students enrolled in primary education declined from 146,000,000 in 1980 to 122,400,000 by 1995, but with a marginal increase in number of primary teachers from 5,499,000 to 5,582,000 respectively.[7] Even kindergartens which were a showpiece for all visitors to China's countryside now looked less colourful. From the mid-1980s onwards, China's new education policy was addressing the issues of professional quality and standardization to meet the growing demands of China's economic growth and international trade. Quality schools with special facilities and select students came up in every county. Private groups were allowed to set up private schools which catered to the requirements of the newly rich families. Thus, bulk of the public schools which had relied on the funds provided by the various levels of government and where still the vast majority of the rural children studied were now impoverished.

The main reason for this crisis in the social sector was the breakdown of the integrated rural political economy. During the commune period as well as during the first decade of the rural reforms, the three-tiered rural economy at the village, township and county levels had regularly generated surplus and invested a significant part of it for health, education and social welfare. The Commune Welfare Fund was the main source until 1978. From the early 1980s, it was the profit from the TVEs which was used by the rural government at each level to finance education, health, old age homes as well as substantially improving agricultural infrastructure. A major part of the profit of the rural enterprises of course was given to the workers as enhanced wages. Rural financing worked in a framework of 'self-financing and self-managing development'. As we will see later, village clinics, township health centres and county hospitals were competing with each other to show off their facilities, specialities and how good was their health care. The school performance was also assessed from time to time under 'production responsibility system', giving higher bonus to teachers corresponding to better results of students in examinations. Local governments were proud of taking visitors to show their old age homes, disability friendly facilities, cultural centres and infrastructures that they had built out of their own funds.

The expenditure on public health has been greatly diversified in the recent years with individual expenditure reaching 60 per cent in the year 2001 and then slightly coming down to 52.2 per cent during the Hu–Wen regime. Government expenditure was estimated to be 15 to 17 per cent during the 1999–2005 period.[8] Tables 9.1 and 9.2 and Figure 9.1 show how health care covered by enterprises and other non-governmental agencies constitutes more than a quarter of the expenses.

> Social health expenditure refers to non-government budgetary capital input, mainly referring to health insurance. It includes expenditure on health institutions run by enterprises and rural collective entities; and health expenditure of government employees in excess of that which could be covered by the government health care system but borne by government units.[9]

This implies that the expenditure on the still surviving hospitals and clinics in villages and townships are included in the category of 'social expenditure'. But the quality of the services available in the rural clinics and hospitals had deteriorated enormously during the 1990s.

Table 9.1:

Expenditures for public health 1980–2015 (100 million yuan)

Item	1980	1985	1990	1995	2001	2005	2010	2015
Total expenditure	143.23	279	747.39	2,155.13	5,025.9	8,659.9	19,980.39	40,974.64
Government budgetary expenditure	51.91	107.65	187.28	387.34	800.6	1,552.5	5,732.49	12,475.28
Social health expenditure	60.97	91. 96	293.1	767.81	1,211.4	2,586.4	7,196.61	16,506.71
Resident individual expenditure	30.35	79.39	267.01	999.98	3,013	4,521	7,051.29	11,992.65

Sources: National Bureau of Statistics of China, *China Statistical Yearbook*, 2007, 875; 2016 (Table 22-19).

Table 9.2:
Per capita health expenditure in rural and urban (1990–2014; yuan)

Item	1990	1995	2000	2005	2010	2014
Total	65.36	177.93	361.88	662.30	1,490.06	2,581.66
Urban	158.82	401.28	812.95	1,126.36	2,315.48	3,558.31
Rural	39.31	101.48	214.93	315.83	666.3	1,412.21

Source: National Bureau of Statistics of China, *China Statistical Yearbook*, 2016 (Table 22-19).

Figure 9.1:
Expenditures for public health (1980–2015; 100 million yuan)

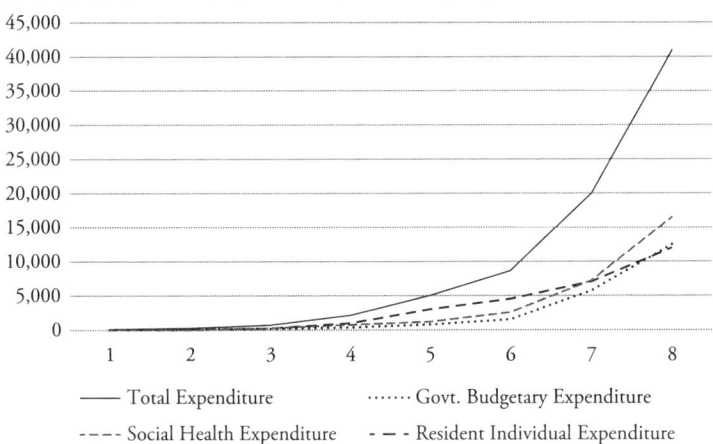

Source: China Statistical Yearbook, 2016: (Table 22-19).

The Ministry of Health itself admitted in 2003 that even though the amount allocated in the budget for public health was rising for a decade, the proportion spent was steadily declining. As per WHO, in 2000, China's input on public health was only 2.7 per cent of its GDP which put China well below in the global rankings, 144 in the world in terms of the general level of public health and 188th in terms of fairness in the distribution of public health resources.[10] According to one estimate, 70 per cent of China's population in rural areas consumed only 30 per cent of the country's medical resources. Rural–urban disparity in health services continued to widen during the 1990s. On the one hand, the cooperative health insurance which had continued from the commune days declined after the introduction of the rural reforms; on the other hand, government expenditure on health came down from 32 per cent in 1978 to only 15 per cent in 1999.[11] In 1999, while 49 per cent of the urban dwellers had health insurance, only 7 per cent of the rural residents had it.[12]

Besides the rural–urban disparity in health care, the rising trend in the infectious diseases in the 1990s was of serious concern. After the founding of the PRC, health campaigns had successfully contained cholera and other epidemics. There was improvement in sanitation and immunizations as well as in health education during the 1950s and 1960s. But in the 1990s, as many as 60 million rural Chinese were suffering from endemic diseases such as leprosy, goitre, plague, malaria and schistosomiasis—a disease caused by snail vector. According to a report, the incidence of TB which had not been reported in 1994 was 39.03 per 1,000 in 1999 and rose to 44.06 in 2001 and 71.95 in 2004.[13] Death rate from infectious diseases which had stood at 188.62 per 100,000 in 1991 and had grown to 203.68 in 1994 had declined to 197.63 in 1999 but again rose to 235.85 in 2004.[14] The emergence of HIV/AIDS, Avian Flu and SARS posed new threats to people and exposed the fact that the previously existing collective structures of health care had largely collapsed, thus weakening the capacity of the State and the community to respond to such epidemics. But the CPC leadership quickly mobilized the necessary public response in 2003 and contained the spread of SARS after initial postures of the health administrators which hided the actual magnitude of the outbreak of SARS.[15] New epidemics like the Avian Flu are connected with the environmental degradation, pollution caused by coal-based industries and others and the living conditions in the countryside. The World Bank estimates that by 2020, unless there are policy changes, China will be paying US$390 billion to treat diseases indirectly caused by burning coal.[16]

While farmers' suicide in India has got prominent publicity during recent years, the high rate of suicide in rural China is less known. Suicides in rural areas are three times that in urban areas. It is high among elderly and women.[17]

During the 1990s and later, the nature of the rural health crisis had become clear. Two things had happened. First, the capacity of the township governments to finance rural health services had considerably declined. Second, some of the practices of the commune period which were discredited had been abandoned. The community financing of rural social services had been a continuing feature during the commune and the early rural reform periods. According to one author,

> [T]his community financing and organization model of health care was believed by many to have contributed in a significant way to China's success in accomplishing its 'first health care revolution' by providing prevention

and primary care to almost every Chinese and reducing infant mortality rate from about 200 per 1,000 live births (1949) to 47 in 1973–75, increasing life expectancy from 35 to about 65 years.[18]

The cooperative medical system that existed until the early 1980s was financed by the cooperative medical fund to which every peasant family made an annual contribution which was supplemented by the collective welfare fund at the production team level and then the village and commune levels and subsidies from the higher government levels. But after the dismantling of the communes, there was a steady decline of public investment in health. Even though the size of the health budget continued to increase, the allocation on health in the budget was 2 per cent in 1979, rising to 3.2 in 1983 and declining to 2.88 in 1999, and subsidies to the cooperative medical system declined from 34 million yuan in 1979 to 22 million yuan in 1988.[19] Thereafter, the township hospitals were neglected and facilities at the health clinics in the villages became poor. This is when private medical practitioners appeared on the scene. Their fees were generally high and only the better-off families could afford their services.

The practice of having 'barefoot doctors' which was a celebrated feature of local health care system during the commune period and was considered as one of 'new born socialist things' during the Cultural Revolution was derided during the reform period as an unprofessional fixture—a hangover of the old period. The concept of 'barefoot doctor' was mainly to have a cadre of trained para-medical staff from among the villagers who could provide emergency care to the patients and more importantly look after sanitation and preventive health care in their area and lead the various public health campaigns. Like production and education drives, they made health an important programme of socialist construction (Table 9.3).

The rural health crisis became an important issue of national and international attention in the period after the outbreak of SARS in 2003. During the Hu–Wen regime, several new steps began to emerge in different parts of China. In Wuxi, there were efforts in 2006 to invest more money in health care and revive the township hospitals. In some villages, barefoot doctors were appointed by giving training to local youth. The new breed of 'barefoot doctors' were better trained and got more remuneration from the local authorities, even though the kind of public service commitment seen in the earlier years was not conspicuous now.[20] In the newly visible general milieu of discussion on the 'three rural problems', some townships now built up their reserve fund and allocated more money to township hospitals, appointing two or three doctors in each where their number had come down to one. The health station—actually it was only a room in most villages—was revamped somewhat as were the health clinics. The village health station provided

Table 9.3:
Structure of health services in rural China

Unit	Commune Years	Post Reforms in the 1980s	1990s Onwards
Village	Health station/clinic Full-time health worker Barefoot doctor Public health campaign Sanitation and immunization campaign	Health station/clinic Part-time health worker	Clinics (public and private) Part-time staff Private clinic staff Revival of campaigns in 2003 after outbreak of SARS
Township	Commune health centre Full-time doctors	Township health centre Full-time doctors	Township health centre Private clinics, diagnostic centres and specialized hospitals Primary health care and supervision of clinics
County	County hospitals Larger medical centres Specialized services	County hospitals Larger medical centres Specialized services	County hospitals Larger medical centres Specialized services Referral cases Private hospitals and modern diagnostic centres in county towns

Source: Author.

medicines to the patients and billed a portion of it to the city hospital, while the patients paid a part of the bill for treatment and the medicines.[21]

During the recent years, the Cooperative Medical Insurance was revived with new terms. A household could join it by a small monthly contribution—the amount varied from area to area—and avail 70 per cent coverage for treatment in hospitals and expenses on surgery and pay 30 per cent from own resources. In many factories, the trade unions managed health insurance as a part of the 'four deductions' from the wages—medical, housing, unemployment and old age.

By the early 1990s, Chinese economy had grown into a new stage mainly trying to increase production for exports and attract foreign investment to facilitate that process. During the 1980s, even though the collective economy and social welfare had been dismantled, still the surplus generated from the TVEs and the diversified economy had financed the social sector. That situation vastly changed with the decline of the TVEs and loss of local support for the social sector. Wherever the TVEs were privatized, there was no obligation on them to contribute to local social development. The tax that was collected by the local government from them was too little to provide any substantial support to schools and hospitals. Thus, the framework of a self-financed, self-directed development which had operated in China's countryside as a national policy now practically collapsed. Once again the rural economy was engulfed in a crisis of agricultural stagnation and backward infrastructure. Only in 2005 when the Central government woke up to the crisis of what was called the 'three rural problems' (low production, low peasant income and backward countryside) and proclaimed a response strategy of 'building a new socialist countryside', it was not easy to make up for the damages already made. Even the large sums of money for rural infrastructure announced by Premier Wen Jiabao from 2006 onwards could barely finance the expenses to maintain the rural governmental structure. Even the education budget earmarked for the poor rural counties was inadequate to revive the schools. Only in some of the areas in the western provinces, some schools and hospitals got a face lift under the Western Region Development Strategy. But on the whole, the base of China's social sector in the countryside had weakened seriously during the past two decades. This was mainly because of the reduction of social development responsibility of the State and decline in public action.

The Issue of Public Action

One of the basic dimensions of the welfare State in the modern era was public action in the sphere of community health. In other words, the State undertook the role of providing medical facilities, taking preventive measures to avert epidemics and creating conditions favourable to longer and healthier life expectancy. Charitable institutions like religious missionary bodies did provide a degree of public action, but they were inadequate. Hence, the positive intervention by the State on behalf of society as a whole was felt. In socialist systems, such public action was at the core of State policy and was the responsibility of various levels of public bodies, namely the Central government, provincial government, county and *xiang* level administration as well as the collective enterprises. Thus, every commune and later *xiang* had its own hospital and health services which were used in conjunction with the facilities installed by higher organs. The question was to what extent the individual households should pay for the services. Should it not be the function of the welfare State and in the case of China, a socialist State, to provide health services free? This debate has gone on in the West in the recent decades over the privatization of public health services in UK and elsewhere. In China too, the trend during the reform period was to charge peasant households for medical services. This was interpreted as the decline of the extent of public action in China.[22]

The argument advanced by the Chinese reformers, however, was that with the increase in the income of the peasant households, they had the capacity to pay for the health services. In this way, the collective or the State could accumulate funds for modernizing the health services and improving their quality. It should also be stressed that the extent of medical facilities and the allocation for health in the national budget continued to rise. Moreover, several distinct features of the Chinese medical system which had evolved after liberation continued to operate even after the reforms. But there is a widely shared view among experts that China's health care system has developed into a serious crisis during the recent years mainly due to the breakdown of the collective and State-led health care system.

Evidences show that there were significant disparities in mortality rate, including infant and maternal mortality, between rural and urban areas.[23] Between 1989 and 1999, whereas the overall death rate in China remained at 5.5 per 1,000 and the same in the cities declined by 4.7, the death rate in the rural counties increased by 1 per cent.[24] Overall mortality and life expectancy show higher death rates and lower life expectancy for rural, poor and western provinces compared to the more urbanized provinces. Guizhou, for example, had 6.35 deaths per 1,000 and life expectancy of 65.96 years against Beijing's 5.4 and 76.10 respectively. In infant mortality, the contrast is even sharper: 23.8 against 4.8. Resurgence in infectious diseases, growing threats of HIV/AIDS and Avian Flu show how the new situation of reduced public action had serious consequences in the recent years.

In this chapter, we examine the health situation at the grass-roots level during the period of reforms. First, let us get a glimpse of the health situation as it obtained in Hela, in 1980, early in the reforms, from interviews with several barefoot doctors and officials in the Hela *xiang*.

Health Situation in 1980: Health—A Collective Responsibility

Hela *xiang* had one hospital and two branch hospitals in 1980. There were 63 medial workers and 50 beds in all. It had several departments—internal medicine and paediatrics: 11 medical workers, surgical: four, gynaecology:

four, dentistry: four, ENT: two, X-ray: three, Chinese traditional medicine: five and laboratory–pharmacy: six. Besides, there were 12 nurses and 2 people for massage and some others for administrative and other work. It should be noticed that there was a fair amount of specialized medical service available at the *xiang* hospital. It is possible that because Hela was a suburban *xiang* it had specialized services which could be difficult to ensure in interior rural areas. Another noteworthy feature of any hospital in China is the existence of Chinese medicine alongside the Western medicine. Like Ayurvedic and Yunani systems of India, the Chinese traditional systems produced medicines out of herbs and minerals and had developed a variety of methods of treatment including acupuncture. Practically, every doctor trained in one system had considerable knowledge of the other. The doctors always started their treatment with Chinese medicines which the patients also preferred.

Actually, in the last years of the commune period, every member gave an annual subscription to the commune's cooperative medical care that enabled the peasant to avail free treatment up to a limit of 200 yuan. In 1979, a new system was introduced which made medical service free except for 5 fen registration fee. There was a new practice of providing general check-up for all the members and special check-up for women. The commune got 200 patients on an average per day.

The system of barefoot doctors (*chijiao yisheng*) of China attracted worldwide attention during the Cultural Revolution. Unable to employ sufficient number of trained doctors in rural areas, the Maoist leadership had encouraged the appointment of medical personnel who had undergone short training courses and were familiar with China's traditional medicine system. The term 'barefoot' was put in contrast to the modern doctors who had got Western medical training. It was a mode of utilization of local wisdom with only marginal support from the State. During the Cultural Revolution, however, the Gang of Four and their supporters exaggerated the role of barefoot doctors by putting them above the trained doctors. As many activists in Hela pointed out, this was a part of their campaign against intellectuals. After correcting that perspective, the reform leaders nevertheless saw the utility in continuing this institution. In 1980, Chen Muhua, China's minister who was in charge of health and family planning at the Centre, gave a call to train 1.5 million barefoot doctors and praised their role. The new emphasis, however, was on training them in modern medical science to a reasonable degree. During the Cultural Revolution, the slogan was 'serve the people'. But it had no perspective on improving the quality of the services. Hence, each county had undertaken to train the barefoot doctors in medical schools. In Hela, every barefoot doctor was called upon to complete the six-month course. On passing the examination, they got a certificate which entitled them to a higher salary and responsibility.

The Family Planning Programme

At the start of the reforms period, the family planning programme had been re-emphasized as a national priority and the one-child norm was proclaimed as a national policy. Those with one child did not have to pay tuition fees for their child's education. This was an important incentive in view of the increased tuition fees in the new context. Another incentive was to double the share of private plot. It should be recalled that during the commune period, each household was allowed to retain a private plot for purposes of kitchen gardening. This was retained in the reform period in addition to agricultural land for cultivation. In the same way the one-child family was granted additional living space when the *xiang* or the provincial government had to allot accommodation. Besides, there was an additional 40-yuan bonus annually for every one-child family. As against these incentives, there were many disincentives in the case of families having more children. Families with two children did not get these incentives. Those with three children were not eligible to buy food grain at the concessional price; they had to pay a higher price. They did not enjoy free medical care either.

The health workers pointed out that the main method for promoting family planning was education and persuasion. Since Hela was close to the city, the social consciousness on this issue was very high. In 1979, the rate of population growth in Hela had already come down to 10 per 1,000. And in 1980, they were confident of bringing it down to 9 per 1,000.

The most popular method of birth control was the use of pills. The single high-potency pill effective for a whole month had already been produced, but only a few people used it as it was available in small quantity. Most women used loop to prevent conception. Several informants confirmed that vasectomies were still rare. Apparently, there was a feeling in the minds of both men and women that operations adversely affected health. Whenever they went for operations, it was mostly the women going for tubectomy. In Hela *xiang*, there were 150 operations in 1979. The medical workers took special care to reduce side effects of operations.

It should be noticed that the family planning programme was an arena where government's political and economic perspective on birth control had to reckon with social beliefs and attitudes of the population. More and more people appreciated the fact that without checking the birth rate, China could not achieve economic development and social progress. But they would not accept surgery for birth control. Even women believed that men should not go in for vasectomy for it might reduce their sexual vitality. Many families still preferred to have a male child and a few even dared to forgo incentives for the one-child family.

The leadership of the *xiang* stressed the link between family planning on the one hand and prosperity and good life on the other. The life expectancy in this Hela commune had grown continuously. In 1978, the average life expectancy was 66 years where female averaged 6 years more at 70 years than males at 64 years only. Thus, there was an anachronism that while the women lived longer in Hela *xiang*, female workers retired five years earlier in the rural enterprises.

Much attention was paid to childcare. According to barefoot doctor Ding Maosheng, there were only three cases of infant mortality in Hela brigade since 1968, that is, during the previous 12 years. Equally important was the programme for hygiene and sanitation in the villages. This was linked to the cultural levels of the peasant. Therefore, the campaign for elimination of illiteracy was used to raise the level of consciousness on health and hygiene among the peasants.

The Picture in the 1980s: Focus on One-child Family

Health and family planning programmes were further integrated with the economic agenda in the course of the reforms. In 1985, the growth rate of population in Hela *xiang* had further come down to 6.9 per 1,000 which was 3.1 down in five years—a significant check of population growth. Madam Shen Jiangchen, deputy chairperson of Hela *xiang* and the leader of the women federation, gave these figures in the course of an interview in September 1985. The women federation played a special role in looking after the health situation in the area with particular focus in family planning. It monitored the health condition of women, especially of pregnant women, child births, childcare and ailments, and the death rate of people in the *xiang*. It also had the responsibility to promote movement for 'good family with five merits'. 'Five merits' were as follows: respect the old, love the young, deal well with one another, maintain harmony with the neighbourhood and have good relations within the family. The woman leader asserted in 1985 that as many as 86 per cent of the families of Hela *xiang* had achieved the 'five merits'. In addition, there was a national campaign for 'three good': protect environment, maintain social order and impart good service. This was to relate cleanliness and living habits with social harmony and peace and ensure good services on every front including the health front. One can ask as to why health and family planning and also protection of social harmony and environment should be the special responsibility of the women organization. But the CPC had assigned this role to the ACWF which continues to stress this as a part of its core programmes.

On the basis of the interviews with the family planning official of the *xiang* and other responsible people, we get a picture of the trends during 1980–85. In 1980, when the population of the *xiang* was 19,672, as many as 250 babies were born during the year. That year, the birth rate was 12.8 per 1,000. The total number of death was 152. In 1980, the prevailing family planning policy still allowed two children per couple with the requirement that there should be a gap of three years between the children. Thus, several families had two children. But in 1980, as many as 71.6 per cent of the newly married couples were one-child families. Among the 250 babies born in 1980, as many as 179 were first babies.

In 1984, the number of babies born in the *xiang* was 164, the birth rate being 8.5 per 1,000. The number of deaths was 144—only 8 less than in 1980. In 1984, the number of the one-child families among the newly married couples had risen to 98.2 per cent. Out of the 164 babies, as many as 161 were first babies; only 3 were second babies (apparently, their first child had some disability, so they were 'permitted to have' a second baby). It was pointed out that people in the rural area still had feudal ideas such as the feeling that more children meant more labour power. They did not pay attention to quality of labour and happiness in a small family. Many parents preferred boys to girls because boys had better prospects of employment and would take care of them. That the girls were equally talented and could provide the same security to the parents was still not convincing to many. Until the national campaign acquired momentum in 1983, many families remained somewhat indifferent to the one-child drive. Thereafter, all the newly married couples in Hela had only one child. As of 1985, 56.4 per cent of the total households of the Hela *xiang* had one-child family. It should be noted that still a large number of families had more than one children (Table 9.4).

Throughout the 1980s, the emphasis in the promotion of family planning programme continued to be on propaganda and education work. The government used the broadcasting media to popularize the family planning

Table 9.4:
Households with one, two or more children in Hela (1985)

Number of Households	*Number of Children*
1,933	1
1,045	2
358	3
98	4 or more

Source: Interview with local officials.

programme. Every household had a speaker to carry the broadcast from the *xiang*. Radio and television programmes were used for this purpose. Every rural enterprise had wall magazines and big-character posters. The traditional folk method of telling stories in an entertaining manner (*xiao hua*) was a popular method of conveying the family planning message.

Special meetings were organized to explain the policy of the party and the government on family planning. January of every year was the month for promotion of family planning. During this month, various meetings, cultural performances and educational drives were carried out. Mothers with one child—both young mothers and old mothers—were given certificates of appreciation. Meetings of young people were organized to persuade them to go for late marriage and delay in child birth. Young people who had reached the age of fertility were taught various methods of contraception. Various propaganda teams performed plays and musical events. The cultural performances were very effective in the countryside. A very popular opera was staged widely which spoke about a grandmother changing her attitude towards her daughter-in-law whom she had earlier reprimanded for giving birth to a daughter. Recreational activities in the winter time included a number of items on family planning. There were clubs of one-child families. They conducted many games and tournaments such as table tennis and tug of war. Family planning workers were rewarded for their innovations and achievements. The *xiang* government allocated 5,000 yuan for the family planning propaganda work which the family planning officials considered substantial.

Every female worker was entitled to maternity leave of 90 days from the date of delivery of the baby. One-child mothers got special gifts. The women federation leader personally visited the mother and greeted the family. The mother got a certificate entitling the one-child family to several privileges. During the period of maternity leave, a woman got 200 yuan per month which was the average income in Hela *xiang's* enterprises at the time. Female workers were given lighter work in their units during the period of pregnancy. At home too, they were spared of heavy work. But there was no practice of giving special diet or vitamins to pregnant women. Except for elite families, this was perhaps a common feature as far as the masses of the Third World were concerned.

All child deliveries were conducted in the hospital in Hela. In interior villages, however, there were cases of delivery at home with the help of midwives. All factories and villages had their own nurseries where parents put their children during work time. After the introduction of production responsibility system, whenever the women got an abortion done, they were out of work, losing wages during the period of rest. The enterprises did not have any normal scheme for this situation. The women federation came in to alleviate the hardship to some extent. It would arrange to get her work done in the farmland, factory or even in the household. The women federation's expression of warmth and concern made women happy.

There were exceptions to the one-child norms in some cases. In 1985, 12 couples in the Hela *xiang* were 'allowed' to have their second baby—but this had to be approved by the Municipal Family Planning Department of Wuxi. Later, three of them actually changed their mind and did not go for a second child. In the case of one of the couples going for a second child, the first one was a mute baby.

The Chinese government's main defence of the one-child norm was that the child could avail a better-quality life and the country's population pressure will be under check. Among the people, however, there were differences of opinion on this. Many people felt that the single child in the family would be a spoilt child, always pampered by the parents and grandparents. This phenomenon of 'little emperors' (or *xiao wang* referring to pampered children) has been much discussed in China. Many population experts have also warned that the age structure of the Chinese population in future could be highly distorted as a result of this policy. At some point, there will be a high percentage of old people living in China. The government, however, considers the problem of population explosion too serious to relax the one-child norm. As for the spoilt child syndrome, there were many educational steps including lectures on the psychology of young children and of the one-child parents.

The system of incentives and disincentives, introduced in 1979–80, had been further strengthened in the 1980s. The disincentives for the second child included an annual fine of 120 yuan for seven years. Investigation in 1985 and 1987 revealed that many newly prosperous families found it quite easy to pay the fine and have another child.

Table 9.5:
Family planning methods used in Hela (1985)

Methods Used	Number of Users
Vasectomy	16 males
Tubectomy	585 females
IUCD (loop)	2,006 females
Injections or long-term pills	145 females
Short-term pills	273 females
Condoms	55 males
Use of external medicine	11 females
Use of personal method such as safety period	123 females

Source: Interview with local officials.

In the mid-1980s, there was a slight change noticeable in the use of contraceptives. The use of IUCD or loop had become more popular, while the use of pills had declined because the latter was said to cause adverse side effects. The newly married couples were generally encouraged to use contraceptives. But if they insisted, then the loop was recommended to them. For those ladies who could not wear the rings, pills were suggested. After child birth, women used rings. Table 9.5 provides the extent of use of various methods by 3,390 women in the fertility age which was defined from the time of marriage to the age of 49.

It should be noted that in contrast to India, very few males went for operation for sterilization. More than a sixth of fertile-age women opted for operation. But generally, one-child mothers were not encouraged to go for operation. They were advised to use the loop, which was the most popular method used by a little less than two-third of women in Hela. The use of long-term injection or pill was still very meagre. Surprisingly, the use of condom was also not very popular.

There were enough indications in Hela of the powerful national drive to check population explosion of China. The policy entailed a comprehensive approach that linked health care with family planning, women and childcare with population control drive, and education and propaganda with a system of incentives and disincentives. It has often been asked as to whether China's family planning programme was a coercive campaign. The answer, very clearly, is that the campaign did not involve physical coercion. Undoubtedly, there were moral and political pressures by the State, party and mass organizations. A social climate had been created which caused embarrassment to families with multiple children. The approach mainly centred on economic incentives and organizational pressure. In the course of an interview, in June 1979, with a woman deputy to the NPC and also a neighbourhood committee leader of Beijing's Zhuangta Street, the lady introducing her family of five children said: 'I committed a historical mistake'. There were numerous incentives for the one-child families, whereas those having more children suffered material losses through fines, loss of priority in allocation and so on. As the reforms progressed, this policy had clearly produced dividends.

Health and Family Planning in the 1990s: Towards Professionalization

Whether reforms had adversely affected the health care situation had been a point of discussion not only abroad but also in China. Local cadres were more than emphatic in saying that government continued to pay much attention to health care. But whether objectively the nature and scale of public action in the sphere of health had declined will continue to be debated. In Hela, my investigation showed that public action had not been abandoned, though the proportion of investment in health sector had declined. Medical services were no longer completely free. But the fees were not exorbitantly high. On the whole, the health situation had continued to improve.

In 1996, Mao Dingshen, now the chief medical officer or the head doctor of the *xiang*, clearly stated that the cooperative health care system had continued in the villages, though in the city there was a new trend of having medial insurance. He pointed out that there was a periodic educational campaign in the villages about paying attention to health. The slogan was 'without good health, there would be no economic development'. This was a policy propagated by the party as well as the State organs. Indeed, the crucial role of health and education in China's economic development cannot be exaggerated. They popularized the understanding that the indicators of economic development are measured in terms of better health and education which in turn are instruments for achieving higher growth and better quality of social development.

The WHO programme of preliminary health care system or health for all by the year 2000 had been achieved already in Hela in 1995. This was a case of several *xiangs* in the economically prosperous region of Jiangsu province.

The cooperative health care system was undergoing a change with prices being fixed for certain health services. Earlier, all services were provided by the *xiang* hospital or the village health station. To finance this, the *xiang* government and the village committee used to make an annual contribution from their income to the hospital. At that time, 10–12 per cent of the hospital expenses were charged to the individual patients and the rest was funded by the *xiang* or the enterprises. It should be noted that in addition to the *xiang* or the village committees, the factories also made contribution to the health fund at the *xiang* or the village level. In 1995, the Hela *xiang* government allotted 300,000 yuan or 3 per cent of its income for health. In addition to this, the contributions from the village committees amounted to 700,000 to 800,000 yuan.

Hela now had two *xiang*-level hospitals, one of which had the famous orthopaedic section specializing in reconnecting fractured limbs. For their renovation, the *xiang* government occasionally made special contributions. In 1994–95, each hospital was provided two million yuan towards buying new equipment and other renovation. One of the branch hospitals had now grown into a full-fledged hospital. In addition, each of the 13 villages had a health station with a doctor and some paramedical staff. These doctors were less qualified than the *xiang*-level hospitals. All the doctors and the paramedical staff were trained in both Western medicine (*xiyao*) and Chinese medicine (*zhongyao*). The barefoot doctor (*chijiao yisheng*) was no more a very popular concept because the new policy insisted on raising the level of technical knowledge of doctors and nurses. But the essence of the concept survived. Firstly, they had absorbed local wisdom of the Chinese people on health matters together with the modern Western medical knowledge. Secondly, the doctors at the village level were still called upon to be motivated by 'serve the people' orientation and they were very accessible to common people. But since public funding for the medical centres had been subject to restrictions of these facilities, doctors also had started charging fees. Eventually, the concept of the barefoot doctor may disappear. The contemporary policy-makers in China say that this was relevant to a time when trained medical doctors and scientific medical facilities were not available at the village level. Now that it was increasingly possible, to have these barefoot doctors was an outdated concept. Others, however, point out that the approach underlying the scheme of barefoot doctors was significant because it emphasized proximity to the people and a commitment to public service besides using traditional medicines together with modern. As medical knowledge grows, barefoot doctors can acquire greater expertise in modern medicines. The idea thus was still relevant. The modern policy-makers, however, spurn it as a wastage of public resources as unqualified personnel caused risks to the ailing people. But at the same time, it was clear that the trend of privatized medical care makes modern health facilities more accessible to the prosperous sections of society than to the common masses. In Hela, this phenomenon was already rising. There were no private doctors or clinics as yet in Hela *xiang*. But in some parts of the suburban district, they had already come up and, of course, all expenses were to be borne by the individuals in the case he/she went to a private clinic.

In China, there has been a great deal of emphasis on prevention of diseases than curative measures right from the yearly years of the PRC. Accordingly, health education has been imparted through schools and in public discourse. This approach was further reaffirmed in the 1990s. The party and the State have health committees at the *xiang* level who periodically review the health situation in the *xiang*, especially the preventive measures. The annual report of the *xiang* director always has a section devoted to health. In Hela, every newborn baby's health is closely monitored until the child is seven years old. In fact, during the pregnancy of a woman, nutritional and health care advice is given by the health personnel of the village. Inoculations are given according to schedule until the age of 7. Every child has a health card on which the records are kept. Preventive measures include, besides vaccination, street cleanliness drives and environmental upkeep.

The *xiang* had reached negative population growth rate as is the case in many developed countries of Europe. The health cadres are happy about it, considering the need for China to further reduce the population growth rate. According to health officials of the *xiang*, there is 100 per cent population control for the peasant households of Hela *xiang*. This however was not true for the migrant labour families who did not come under their health jurisdiction. Like everywhere else, migrants were partly covered and partly excluded from the health care system. They availed local facilities by paying fees. Ostensibly, they were under the welfare jurisdiction in their original village.

The common diseases in the *xiang* were cold, flu and stomach ailments. As for causes of death, they were mainly due to cancer, blood pressure and heart attack. This also made it comparable to the situation in the developed countries.

Towards 2020: Social Development Trends

The social development trends in Wuxi and in China as a whole were full of contradictions as the country was getting closer to the target of achieving a 'well-off society' in 2020—a goal set in 2002 at the Sixteenth Congress of the CPC. Even more pronounced was the widespread discussion on the 'two centenaries' (*liangge yibai nian*), that is, the centenary of the founding of the CPC in 2021 and of the PRC in 2049.[25] But the irony was that in the media and public discussions, the focus was on the economic and military strength of China and how it was spreading its influence around the world, meeting the challenges of the big powers. The focus was not on social development, that is, on health, education, social welfare, reduction of inequalities and regional disparities. In these sectors too, the orientation was to achieve advanced standards of health care and educational institutions comparable to Europe and the USA. The acclaimed goal of the CPC was to achieve a 'well off society in all respects' by 2020. The 'Scientific Outlook on Development' also meant to achieve 'coordinated, balanced, development in economic, social, political, cultural and ecological sectors'. But the actual trends in the social sector did not seem to be in consonance with that commitment.

However, two critical decisions of the Xi Jinping regime created a degree of support for paying greater attention to social sector issues. One was to declare a moderate rate of growth (moderate to high, strictly speaking, i.e., 6–8 per cent) and not a high rate of growth (around 10 per cent and above) as the new normal for the foreseeable future.[26] This was expected to orient the policies towards creating domestic demands, provide employment and better wages. The commitment to 'modernize education', build a 'learning society' and a 'healthy China' as spelt out in the Thirteenth FYP for 'economic and social development', as the plan is called, did indicate the regime's desire to develop these sectors (Table 9.6 and Figure 9.2). This could lead to allocation of more resources for health and education, even though there were not enough evidence to show a significant trend. The second measure was the

Table 9.6:
Number of students per 100,000 people by level (1990–2015)

Year	Pre-education	Primary Education	Junior Secondary	Senior Secondary	Higher Education
1990	1,725	10,707	3,426	1,337	326
1995	2,262	11,010	3,945	1,610	457
2000	1,782	10,335	4,969	2,000	723
2005	1,676	8,358	4,781	3,070	1,613
2010	2,230	7,448	3,955	3,504	2,189
2015	31,118	7,086	3,152	2,965	2,524

Source: National Bureau of Statistics of China, *China Statistical Yearbook*, 2016 (Table 21-32). Available at: http://www.stats.gov.cn/tjsj/ndsj/2016/indexeh.htm (accessed on 29 March 2017).

Figure 9.2:

Number of students per 100,000 people by level (1990–2015)

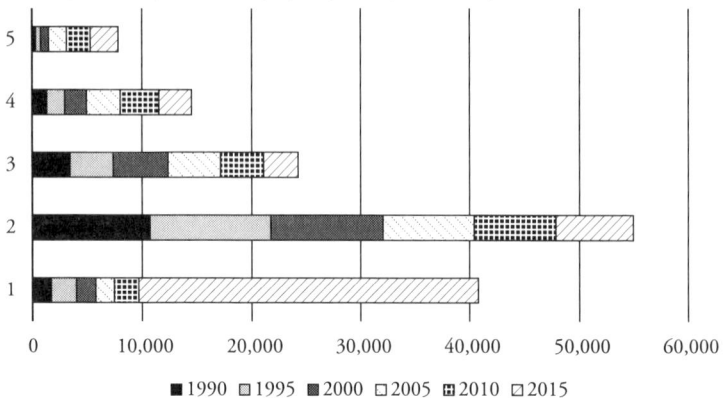

■1990 ▨1995 ■2000 □2005 ▦2010 ▨2015

Source: See Note 27.

decision at the Third Plenary Session in 2013 to relax the one-child norm and allow two children for a large number of categories. There may have been some positive results out of the one-child family by substantially reducing the rate of population growth during the reform period. But the negative consequences had much long-term impact. The structure of the population developed a trend that saw a shrinking of the working-age population at a very important period of history and an expansion of the old-age population which was going to cause serious social crisis. The phenomenon of female foeticide and infanticide due to the cultural milieu of son preference was another matter of great concern. Scarcity of brides for eligible young men is a growing problem. Therefore, the two-children norm was welcomed widely within and outside China. But the one-child norm had created a new urban preference for most working couples and this was bound to have continuing effect on the population structure. However, the campaign for women's rights and rights of the girl child was having its positive effects as well.

Xi Jinping's robust anti-corruption campaign had its favourable effects on social development too. Cadres at every level can no longer ignore the allocations for health and education (Tables 9.7 and 9.8). Earlier they would divert funds for economically gainful programmes, even though the budget had provided otherwise.

Yet, the situation with regard to health and education in contemporary China was far from satisfactory. Public hospitals were crowded and private

Table 9.7:
Government expenditures on education (100 million yuan)

1980	1985	1990	1995	2000	2005	2010	2014
114.2	226.8	462.5	1,193.8	2,562.6	5,161.07	14,670.06	26,420.58

Sources: Compiled from National Bureau of Statistics of China, *China Statistical Yearbooks*, 1990, 1995, 2000, 2005, 2010, 2014.

Table 9.8:
Health indicators: India and China (2015)

Indicators	India	China
Total health expenditure as % of GDP (2014)	4.7	5.5
Public expenditure as % of GDP	1.4	3.1
Per capita expenditure in health (in $; 2014)	75	420
Out-of-pocket expenditure as % of private expenditure (2014)	89.2	72.3
Life expectancy at birth	68	76
Infant mortality rate (IMR; 2015)	38	9
Maternal mortality ratio (MMR) (2015)	174	27
Incidence of tuberculosis (per 100,000 population) (2015)	169	68
Physicians per 1,000 population (2011)	0.7	1.5

Source: http://data.worldbank.org/topic/health (accessed on 19 June 2017).

hospitals were extremely expensive. The State was taking the route of providing insurance to the people of various categories with subsidies. That was inadequate. Hence, people remembered the universal health care facilities during the commune period and the 1980s when the local government had enough resources for providing health care and education for all. Hence, the reforms had brought economic growth for the country, propelling Chinese nationalism, but it also caused serious gaps in social development, exposing the nature of the success trap that China had got into.

In March 2016, Yuan Guiren, then minister of education, in a press conference at the Twelfth NPC's Fourth Session outlined that China's educational development had entered a mid–high level in the world in the Twelfth FYP (2010–15) period.[27] In the same press briefing, the minister also conceded that rural education was facing serious hindrances because of a lack of quality teachers and had resulted in the rural–urban regional gap. The major essence of future reforms still focuses on at least four characteristics—universal access, free, balanced and compulsory. The

Thirteenth FYP (2016–20) has also re-emphasized on these features and gives thrust to make vocational education free by 2020 and raise enrolment rates at all levels from pre-primary to high school.

Notes and References

1. Ian G. Cook and Trevor J. B. Dummer, 'Changing Health in China: Re-evaluating the Epidemiological Transition Model', *Health Policy* 67, no. 3 (2004): 329–43.
2. UNDP, *Human Development Report* 2007–08 (New York, NY: Palgrave Macmillan, 2007), 262–63. Under 5 mortality rate also declined sharply from 120 in 1970 to 27 per 1,000 in 2005. In 2005, maternal mortality was 45 per 100,000 live births for China as against 450 for India.
3. World Bank, *World Development Indicators*, 2012, 2014, 2015 (updated on 16 February 2017).
4. UNDP, *Human Development Report 2016: Human Development for Everyone* (29 March 2017). Available at: http://hdr.undp.org/en/content/download-and-read-latest-human-development-report-2016-human-development-everyone (accessed on 30 March 2017).
5. UNDP, *Human Development Report (2016)*, 270–71. India had reached 61 per cent for 15+ years of age and 76.4 per cent for the youth in 2005.
6. UNDP, *Human Development Report 2016*, 231.
7. National Bureau of Statistics of China, *China Statistical Yearbook*, 1996 (Tables 18.1, 18.4 and 18.5).
8. National Bureau of Statistics of China, *China Statistical Yearbook*, 2007, 875.
9. Ibid., 877.
10. T. J. B. Dummer and Ian G. Cook, 'Exploring China's Rural Health Crisis: Processes and Policy Implications', *Health Policy* 83, no. 83 (2007): 1–16.
11. David Blumenthal and William Hsiao, 'Privatization and its Discontents: The Evolving Chinese Health Care System', *New England Journal of Medicine* (2005): 1165–70, doi:10.1056/NEJMhpr051133
12. Dummer and Cook, 'Exploring China's Rural Health Crisis', 8.
13. Ibid., 5.
14. Ibid., 6.
15. Cook and Dummer, *Changing Health in China.*
16. Matt Walker, 'A Nation Struggling to Catch Its Breath', *New Scientist* no. 2549 (2006): 8–9.
17. Dummer and Cook, 'Exploring China's Rural Health Crisis', 8.
18. Yuanli Liu, William C. L. Hsiao, Qing Li, Xingzhu Liu, and Minghui Ren. 'Transformation of China's Rural Healthcare Financing', *Social Science and Medicine* 41, no. 8 (1995): 1085–93.
19. Ibid., 1087.
20. Interview with township director, 2006.
21. Field interview, 2004.
22. Ibid., 6.
23. Ibid., 8.

24. Ibid., 3.
25. *Xinhua*, 'Xinhua Insight: CPC's New Governance Theories Steer China on Fast Track to "Two Centenary Goals"', *Xinhua*, 4 May 2016. Available at: http://news.xinhuanet.com/english/2016-05/04/c_135334465.htm (accessed on 19 June 2017). Although this concept was first articulated at the Fifteenth CPC Congress in 1997, it however became popular only after Xi Jinping became the general secretary in 2012.
26. *The 13th Five Year Plan for Economic and Social Development of the People's Republic of China 1916–2020* (Beijing: Central Compilation & Translation Press, 2016) See Chapters 59 and 60 on education and health.
27. Ministry of Education of the People's Republic of China, 'Chinese Education Minister Discusses Education Reforms and Development at Press Conference', Ministry of Education of the People's Republic of China, 15 March 2016. Available at: http://en.moe.gov.cn/Specials/Specials_Spotlight/Spotlight_News/201603/t20160315_233577.html (accessed on 7 April 2017).

10

Learning from China's Development: Lessons for Global Transformation

The Main Argument

China's reform path will continue to unfold along with the problems that accompany it. Chinese leadership will continue to attend to these problems creatively and competently. Chinese people will celebrate the two centenaries of 2021 and 2049 with fervent nationalist pride and would be recognized as a great power by the world. Whether they fulfil the goal of their revolution of becoming a socialist society and achieve the values of the Chinese civilization is an open question. As we find in our study, the reforms have achieved remarkable economic progress in China with vastly improved living standards for people. But with it have come serious problems of social inequality, regional disparity, environmental degradation and social alienation. The argument that emerges from this study is that this pattern of economic success with social and ecological problems is likely to persist. That is China's success story and the success trap. The pursuit of a 'socialist market economy' has been exceedingly successful in achieving economic growth and has maintained relative stability of the sociopolitical system. But it has transformed China into a fast-developing capitalist society with unique features. The unique features are the leadership of the Communist Party, the State-led market economy, the centrally coordinated but highly decentralized economic process, a centralized political system with one-party rule engaging in an elaborate system of consultation and a built-in process of innovation in all spheres. These features allow the leaders to formulate new policies from time to time, take decisive steps in the face of crisis situations or negative trends and continue to maintain the system. In the face of new technological, security, social and economic challenges at home and abroad, every country sought new ways of grappling with them. We have seen this process not only in Wuxi but also as a general phenomenon in China.

Deng Xiaoping set the main framework as 'reform and open door' but emphasized the need to evolve policies as circumstances demanded, 'crossing the river by feeling for the stones'. Jiang Zemin vigorously developed market economy after Deng's southern tour in 1992 had reasserted the role of the market. Jiang's Three Represents extended the framework by incorporating capitalist forces within the party framework. From 2002, as the problems began to appear sharply, Hu Jintao addressed them through his 'scientific outlook on development', stressing social justice and sustainability. But he did that without relenting on the growth priority and China achieved the status of the second largest economy in the world in 2010. Xi Jinping clearly reoriented growth strategy declaring medium-to-high rate of growth—not high rate as before—as the new normal and promoted his 'four comprehensives' and some major international initiatives for 'balanced, coordinated, open, green and shared development'. This illustrated the creative capacity of the Chinese political leadership to provide continuity and develop further on the reform path. From 2009 onwards, there was a clear trend in China to take the entire post-1949 period as a whole rather than celebrate only the reform period. Xi Jinping continued the new discourse beginning with inauguration of the Exhibition on National Rejuvenation in November 2012 at the Chinese History Museum where the history of the PRC, the CPC and anti-colonial revolutionary movement was on show.

Therefore, while learning lessons from China, one has to keep in mind the totality of the Chinese development history, not only the period after 1978 but also the entire period since the birth of the PRC, and put them in the context of the anti-colonial struggle and the broader history of Chinese and global civilization.

First, let us recapitulate the innovations made during the reforms in China.

Innovations in China's Reforms

Contract of Land

The first innovation was in the realm of land ownership. After communes were dismantled, land was contracted to households in proportion to the number of working people in the household. This was not the same as privatization of landholdings because the legal title to land remained with the village under collective ownership. But as in the case of private holdings, this contract was a long-term contract and could be succeeded from generation to generation. It could also be subcontracted to other households for a specific period. This system combined the advantages of private ownership with those of public management. The members of the household could rationally allocate their labour, releasing some family members for non-agricultural work. They could also give their best to agriculture to earn maximum profit. Because land belonged to the collective, the village committee could make overall plans for agricultural development, link agriculture with other activities and also make public investment for irrigation and other aspects of agricultural development.

This innovative form of land management seemed to give high dividends during the two decades of reforms as was evident from the rate of growth of agricultural output. But it also brought out certain problems. Many households found that the piece of land at their disposal was too small and gave so little dividend that it was a burden to maintain it. Many problems of small farmers' agriculture familiar in developing countries were seen also in China. Rather than engaging in agriculture, they would go for commerce or industry. The policy-makers were aware of this situation and therefore legally allowed subcontracting so that while the original right to cultivate remained with the household, it could engage in other economic activity by assigning its land to another villager for cultivation. Another policy response was to develop specialized households who could take a large piece of land on contract and engage in profitable agriculture using modern technology. Another problem with this form of ownership was from the side of the collective, the *cun* or the *xiang* administration. Under pressure of showing profit, they were not always able to invest sufficiently in agriculture. The collective would rather invest in commerce and economically flourishing enterprises. But this situation changed fast in the 1990s when peasants began to migrate to cities. In such a situation, therefore, political leadership of the State and the Communist Party had to play an important role to ensure a certain level of food production in each area. But it had to do it without curbing the enthusiasm of the farmers to diversify economy and increase their income. The new initiatives under the Thirteenth FYP on management of land rights by separating ownership from contract and use were meant to tackle this situation.

Rural Industrialization

The second major innovation in the course of China's rural reforms was the reconceptualization of rural economy as a diversified economy with sectors interconnected with one another and with urban economy. Here, development of rural industries played a key role in the diversification and development of the rural economy. The contours of rural industries expanded to include sophisticated modern technologies—electronic and chemical industries—as are seen in Hela. At the same time, some of the traditional industries producing agricultural tools and processing agricultural goods, animal husbandry and fishery products continued to operate. It aimed at bridging the gap between the city and the countryside. But as we know, this situation was changed drastically in the 1990s when TVEs were abandoned or transformed.

The economic calculus of rural industrialization was mainly based on two things. One was to absorb surplus rural labour as much as possible within the countryside so that cities were not clotted with unemployed labour. The second was the generation of a rural market by increasing the income of rural households. On both these counts, China achieved considerable success. This is where Chinese rural reforms of the 1980s presented an alternative path to the developmental experiences of Europe and the USA where peasantry migrated en masse to the city to work in factories and agricultural mechanization was resorted to for maintaining the growth of agricultural production.

Industries and other rural enterprises were not set up by State funding from above. In the late 1970s and early 1980s, they came out of the township's accumulation funds. In other words, the surplus generated from within the commune was used to finance the establishment of industries. Since each *xiang* was let free to plan its own development, it could take decisions according to the availability of its natural and agricultural resources and investment funds and take risks in marketing its products for profit. Gradually, they expanded their operations and took bank loans for investments. But much of their capital construction took place out of the savings from their own profit. Thus, development of China's rural enterprises was essentially financed from within rural China. After they flourished to become a critical sector of China's national economy contributing much more than what agriculture did, they became attractive stations for national and international investment. Hence, in the 1990s, the government decided to promote shareholding system in rural enterprises. This system could not only gather more capital for investment but could also constantly put the enterprise to the market test so that it was compelled to show dividends and keep the shareholders happy. In case an enterprise failed to show profit, it had to rectify its production policy. Continuous failure might lead to it being declared bankrupt and shut down.

Problems with unlimited diversification were mainly two. One was creating imbalance in the economy in terms of certain products being produced in plenty and certain other products not being produced because they did not earn sufficient dividend. In a vast populous country, there may be a clear need for certain products for social consumption. It is a fact that food grains production in China has actually fluctuated and the State has intervened to fix quota of production for each zone in response to this fluctuation. The periodic phenomenon of overheated economy, that is, showing high output of products irrespective of the demand situation, has resulted partly from the diversified rural as well as urban economy.

The second problem relates to the trend of high degree of differentiation within the rural economy. Those who produce modern goods and market them will become rich quickly and those who produce food grains remain poor. The fisheries and animal husbandry products may come in between. No doubt, families plan their own response to this differentiated situation, some members working in agriculture some members working in industries. The assumption here is that all families have access to acquiring skills, investible capital and motivation. In reality, families may not always be able to diversify skills of their members and may not succeed in getting distributed across the sectors of industries, commerce and agriculture. Hence, diversified economy has also contributed to growth of inequalities in rural China during this period. Development of the market economy has accentuated this process.

Responsibility System

While the first innovation was in the realm of structure of agrarian relations and the second regarding the production system involving variety of economic possibilities using capital, labour and technology, the third innovation was in the realm of economic management by ubiquitously introducing the responsibility system. This principle was devised by Deng Xiaoping initially as a reaction to the large-scale disruption of economic activity during the Cultural Revolution. Later on, it acquired the status of a central principle of reforms. The application of this principle made every unit of production at every level from the household to the big State enterprise, including the emerging forms of private and joint stock companies to link performance with dividends.

Responsibility system cannot be equated with the notion of profit motive in a capitalist economy. While the former has the goal of making profit in production, the norms of performances assessment are not the same as in the private enterprise. In the case of the Chinese rural enterprises as well as the farming households, the norms are set through negotiations between the production unit and the relevant higher level of production and the political leadership. Whenever a production quota is fixed, it is decided through mutual negotiations. In many cases, the fixed quota is the average of the three preceding years. If the units produced more than the quota, they would get higher bonus and additional income through such measures as tax concessions, higher wages and special rewards.

Responsible to whom and about what has been clearly enunciated through a number of polices through the reform period. Firstly, responsibility is located in the managers of enterprises and heads of production units within each enterprise. In other words, responsibility is not an abstract collective function of a production unit. It rests on the manager and the other leading personnel. If the enterprise shows profit, the manager gets a higher bonus personally, and the workers also get higher bonus. Similarly, the punishment for loss in production and violation of norms is also given to the manager. This assignment of personal responsibility of the manager for production was a major change from the collective responsibility system of the revolutionary committee or the managerial committee during the Cultural Revolution period.

Secondly, the production unit was responsible to (a) the market, (b) the economic leadership, (c) the political leadership and (d) its constituent members. Responsibility to the market meant that it had to respond to the supply-and-demand situation for its products and resources. With the development of the market economy in China, this had become concrete. There were appropriate economic bodies to whom every unit was responsible. Each rural enterprise in the Hela *xiang* was responsible to the *xiang* industry bureau headed by the vice-director of the *xiang*. And they together were responsible to the suburban district industry bureau. In addition, there were the quality control bureau and the environment bureau as well. Thirdly, more important was the political leadership, namely the *xiang* director, the *xiang* party committee and the suburban administration and the suburban party committee. Now that the party itself had become an essentially economy-oriented organization, it was ruthlessly applying the responsibility system of assessing performance and delivering rewards and punishment.

Finally, every unit of production was responsible to its membership. The *cun* representatives conference would discuss the performance of managers and their managers of enterprises and leaders of integrated corporation of agriculture, commerce and industry. The *xiang* people's congress discussed the work report and thereby the economic performance of the enterprises. A milieu gets created by these discussions as to whether certain enterprises were doing well or not. Ideas are exchanged in the course of such meetings, members and cadres helping one another to cope with pressures and improve performance.

The responsibility system was based on the premise that those who worked hard, improved performance quantitatively as well as qualitatively and made innovations in production were materially rewarded. This was in contrast with the ideological motivation underlying the Cultural Revolution. Even though during the reform period sentiments of Chinese nationalism and patriotism were invested for building a strong and prosperous China, the main emphasis was on economic rewards for performance. Each family was called upon to join this process and earn more so that it enjoyed better comforts of life. This was in contrast to the policy of the so-called 'eating from the same big iron bowl' or the hardworking person getting the same wages as the lazy, incompetent worker.

Can the responsibility system work in a capitalist market economy or is it peculiar to a 'socialist market economy'? The answer may be yes because capitalism is based on the principle of paying more for hard work. But the Chinese responsibility system sought to ensure by a number of measures that better performance earn better wages, whereas in the capitalist system it is only a formal principle. Capitalist competition may not always allow the payment of just wages for hard work. In the contemporary Chinese system, there is a certain party–State institutional arrangement operating the responsibility system. Here too, the role of political leadership at every level becomes critical to operate the responsibility system. The CPC Committee at each level watches the economic process closely to see that the responsibility system is implemented correctly.

The responsibility system has contributed to the steady growth of production and rising per capita income in China. But at the same time, it has caused a new hierarchy of power centres operating often through nepotism, arbitrariness and corrupt practices. The power of the manager and division heads in a factory has increased enormously. They evaluate the performance of workers and decide who should get higher wages than the others. Frequently, they are guided by *guanxi* arising out of personal relationship, kinship and factional, territorial and such other linkages. It is in this kind of situation that criminal gangs operate under direct or indirect protection and patronage of managers and leaders. Commercial deals are struck secretly and in violation of norms. The party and the government leaders are very much aware of this phenomenon, and that is why the anti-corruption drive has been strengthened during the last five years and ethical conduct and education have been stressed. The party and the State have taken steps to standardize evaluation of performance at various levels. But since democratic management has been subordinated to economic performance, the system of director-centred management persists. Thus, responsibility system has further contributed to growing social inequalities and a persistence of political authoritarianism and has constrained the growth of democratic politics in China. Theoretically, however, a responsibility system is not inconsistent with democratic institution building in a socialist framework. Only if there are institutional safeguards against arbitrary decision-making and nepotism and there is a collective involvement of the workers in implementing the responsibility system, both can be realized together.

Let us now take up a few issues of political economy from the Chinese reform experience that may suggest recasting of questions in development theory.

Recasting Development Questions

Accumulation versus Consumption

One of the central issues of development theory in modern times has revolved around the question of generating surplus for investment. Initially, Industrial Revolution in Europe was financed by the surplus generated from agriculture. Once industrialization got stabilized, it generated surplus for its own expansion besides contributing to agricultural development. That was a normal process which evolved over a long period of time. The situation, however, was different in countries which started late on the path of industrialization. They had to take strong measures to generate savings from agriculture so that they could divert them to industry. This was also necessary for supplying food grains to urban areas. Moreover, capital accumulation was needed for developing irrigation and other infrastructural facilities for themselves. But high rate of accumulation meant that less was available for distribution and hence consumption, hence the dilemma of balancing accumulation with consumption.

The socialist countries faced the problem of finding adequate resources for industrial development. The Communist Party of Soviet Union and the CPC after coming to power opted for high rate of accumulation. The USSR enforced the system of collective farms during the First FYP in 1928–31. The PRC introduced the system of people's communes in 1958. It has been said that the peasantry having supported the communist parties to come to power was forced to make substantial sacrifices for building a strong nation state. In response to this observation, the communist leadership argued that it was necessary to promote industrialization and build strong national defence without which the socialist regimes would have collapsed under imperialist threat much earlier.

The Chinese rural reforms presented an alternative method of resolving the contradiction between accumulation and consumption. They discarded the commune method of having a large proportion earmarked for accumulation fund and the reserve fund in agricultural production. Under the household contract system, the contract fee was nominal and agricultural tax was abolished in 2006. On the other hand, by increasing the purchasing prices of food grains by the State agencies and eventually making them comparable to market prices, they ensured higher income for peasants. Rural industries and commerce were used for capital accumulation at a high rate. As we have seen earlier, only about 35 per cent of the profit was distributed as wages, almost comparable to the commune situation. But it did not hurt the peasants because their earnings from agriculture had increased considerably and were not taxed. The expansion of rural industry was so fast and their profits in the 1980s so significant that they added considerably to the average peasant income. As we said earlier, savings from agriculture financed rural industrialization. This was done by using a part of the quota procured from the peasantry for industrial investment. Of course, the collectives already had a significant amount of savings at the time of the start of the reforms which they used for launching rural industries. Thus, rural industries were financed originally by agriculture and later they contributed to infrastructure building, social welfare and agricultural development of the *xiang*. At the same time, through the taxes on the collectives and rural enterprises and fixing quotas of agriculture products at each level, the State acquired resources from the *xiang* for provincial-level and national-level development. Thus, the reforms refrained from direct bureaucratic method of extracting surplus from the village. While procuring surplus, it consciously facilitated the growth of consumption as has been evident in the steadily rising living standards in the rural areas.

Whereas taxation and quotas represented direct accumulation, the rural reforms as a whole contained in them many others ways of indirect accumulation. The expansion of the rural market provided impetus to production of several consumer goods within the country. The profit that the manufacturing unit obtained also had a component of savings for capital construction and other development. With the increase in family income, there was not only a new prosperity enabling people to purchase new consumer goods but also saving for future comforts. Thus, voluntary savings as a phenomenon also grew in the prosperous areas of the coastal provinces such as Wuxi. It was in this milieu that shareholding became a new form of ownership.

Now consumers were prosperous enough to buy shares and contribute to accumulation.

Increasing integration with the world economy created opportunities as well as constraints. Opportunities came in the form of direct foreign investment in China's countryside. Goods manufactured abroad also found their way to the Chinese rural market. Overseas Chinese played a major role in reaching out to China's countryside. But the constraints also came along in those spheres where the local Chinese had to match their investment with those of the foreign investors. Local enterprises had to sometimes face foreign competition prematurely and they failed to maintain technological standards. In the process, several rural enterprises lost out and closed down. Some were sold to private enterprises, particularly those who could afford to modernize and compete. This became so serious that 'three rural problems' intensified in the late 1990s. As we have seen, an imbalance began to grow in the 2000s with accumulation proceeding steadily but rural income not rising as fast. Therefore, there is a need to re-examine the traditional understanding relating to accumulation. What started as a fair combination turned into an extractive process. *Accumulation by extraction* from the peasants became evident in China. This phenomenon took various forms in other areas where development projects caused displacement of local people, often tribals or indigenous communities. However, the rural reforms in the 1980s showed a possibility of handling the problem of accumulation in a rational and fair way.

Rural–Urban Linkage

According to Mao Zedong, socialist construction aimed at resolving the three great differences (*san da chabie*) between the city and the countryside, the mental labour and the manual labour, and the worker and the peasant. The reform leaders did not talk about this objective for long. Only after the rural–urban inequality produced massive flow of migrant workers into cities, the issue attracted some attention. Following the European experience with Industrial Revolution, the assumption was that the countryside had to transform itself into the model of the city; manual labour should progressively become unnecessary with mechanization of work and peasant ought to become a worker. Socialist practice in the Soviet Union more or less adopted this framework of transformation. But China under Mao Zedong's leadership had a tortuous experience through the revolutionary movement, Great Leap Forward and the Cultural Revolution trying to project an alternative model. This alternative was to emphasize equal significance of the town and the countryside, the mental and manual labour, the workers and the peasant. Deng Xiaoping, however, questioned Mao's model and took a position on urbanization that was a unique perspective different from both Mao's and the European model. But that operated until about 2005 after which moving towards the European model of urbanization became the general policy. Ultimately, that was reflected in the China's 2014 policy on new urbanization.

The Deng approach to resolving the three great differences hinged on introducing science and technology and market forces to the countryside without shifting the population from the countryside to the city. Households and families as institutions continued to operate and in fact got reinforced in the course of the reforms. They had actually been considerably weakened during the commune period. The family ties with land (*laojia* being ancestral home owning land) continued to operate. Rural industries and commercial and other enterprises flourished extensively to employ bulk of the population in the countryside itself. Rural industries contributed to the modernization of the rural economy by bringing more capital and improving science and technology. To a very large extent, the difference between the city and the countryside was reduced in several respects in coastal provinces. The concept of the peasant-worker became real in the new situation in China. Even when someone worked in a high-tech electronic factory in the *xiang*, because he/she came from a peasant household in a *cun* which contracted land for agriculture, the worker considered himself/herself as a peasant. No doubt, the commune system had turned every peasant into an agricultural worker (*nongye gong*) and such workers earned 'work points' as wages. In the new situation of reforms, however, it was different. The agriculture worker became a peasant again because now the household was in full charge of a piece of a land for agricultural purposes. But at another level, the rural labourer's credentials as workers increased manifold because they were now part of a modern economy that was more organized than ever before. They were technologically developing from one stage to another. Thus, a family would have its members as both peasants and workers in the same village. Therefore, the reforms accomplished a serious advance in reducing the worker peasant dichotomy. In the 1980s, average peasant income surpassed the average urban income. In the 1990s, it fell behind. But together with the provision for each family owning a house and kitchen garden and multiple sources of income, all of which is not computed for statistical purposes, the peasants particularly in coastal provinces enjoyed comfortable life comparable to that of the skilled workers in the city. If problems of urban pollution, transport clogging and crime are taken into account, then of course the countryside could be preferred by many Chinese.

The policy of the Chinese government on declaring an area urban also contributed to this situation. It scrupulously avoided indiscriminately designating rural areas as urban. As we have seen earlier, turning the rural county (*xian*) to city (*shi*) and township (*xiang*) to town (*zhen*) is done with a great deal of care. Even though it irritates the rural units who are anxious to be declared urban so that they become entitled to industrial infrastructure, the government has usually gone slow on it in order to be able to enforce agricultural production plans in rural areas.

Treatment of the peasantry in Marxist political economy has evolved through several polemics and policy shifts in socialist regimes. Karl Marx's critique of the French peasantry as conservative, isolated and traditional—'a sack of potatoes'—underwent some change in Lenin's analysis of development of capitalism in Russian agriculture. He showed that dynamic linkages did exist in the rural economy which produced capitalist elements. Mao Zedong's analysis of the peasant movement in Hunan affirmed a revolutionary capacity of the peasantry to challenge landlordism as well as political power of warlords. His theory of people's democratic revolution proved the viability of an agrarian revolution against feudalism as well as imperialism. This perspective had its echoes in other colonial situations such as Vietnam and India. Thus, the peasantry's capacity to pursue revolutionary politics and transform the political economy acquired acceptability within Marxism.

M. K. Gandhi in India had proved a similar potency of peasant power through anti-colonial struggles in India. Gandhi rejected the Industrial Revolution paradigm comprehensively first in *Hind Swaraj* (1908) and consistently upheld this line throughout his life. He propagated the model of rural self-governance for common good (*sarvoday*) based on the unity of manual and mental labour, human existence and nature through a mutual sustainable process. In his scheme of things, villages should be interdependent in managing the political economy through a system of oceanic circles. Critics have rightly pointed out that this model ignored the contradictions between landlords and peasants as also the upper castes and the lower castes which raise a number of problems in pursuing this line.

Thus, the debate initiated by Chayanov and renewed by Theodor Shanin on transforming the peasantry for integrated industrial development has to be put in a fresh perspective in the light of the Chinese experiences first during the commune period and later during the reform period. Capitalist transition in the rural economy does produce differentiation, that is, class stratification of peasants. That formulation continues to be relevant as seen in the case of China's rural reforms. Indeed, there has been the emergence of a rich peasant class in China in the course of the reforms. But the mode of surplus extraction from agriculture through collectivization or through the pricing policy in capitalist economies need not be the case always. The rural reforms in China showed a variety of processes by which the rural economy and the urban economy exchanged their surpluses. Thus, the terms of trade which were always tilted in favour of industry and the city could be altered in the direction of establishing a degree of even transaction between rural and urban economies. Thus, the 'traditional' peasantry was no longer isolated. Through the rural enterprises and technology integration, the Chinese peasant was now part of a national political economy. The party organization and the people's congresses of course are institutions through which all sections of the society and all areas of the country are integrated. But the new political economy was both more differentiated and integrated on the ground.

The new urbanization plan after 2014 put a clear stamp on the future shape of China's growth. That formation of cities, big and small, was the goal and that urbanization was the essential feature of modern transformation became evident.

But the early reforms in China's countryside had presented a fresh conceptualization of spatial spread of humans. They could be in various spaces with degrees of urban–rural features—coastal, inland hilly, pastoral and other regions. But it was possible to recognize the value of their work, knowledge and culture and accordingly develop appropriate forms of economic activities.

State, Market and the Reforms

During the last quarter of the twentieth century, one of the most prominent dichotomies that surfaced in world scale was the one between the State and the market. As State-led economies in the socialist countries and much of the Third World ran deep into crisis, the Western capitalist countries unfurled the flag of the market and gradually revamped their economy into a position of strength. Thereafter was unleashed a process of globalization and structural adjustment involving retreat of State and expansion of the market. The Chinese reforms, however, preceded the initiative of the World Bank and global capitalist institutions. As we have seen in the case of rural reforms, the Chinese policy-makers also cut down the role of the State in economic management and the production process. But the 40 years of reforms clearly indicate that the Chinese reformers do not accept the dichotomy between the State and the market. This is reflected not only in the economic policies but also in their concept of socialist market economy and Deng Xiaoping Theory of building socialism with Chinese characteristics.

Socialist market economy is different from the capitalist market economy in many respects. The most important difference centres on the role that the State plays in macro-coordination of the economy to protect the socialist system from various pressures and steer the system in the direction of socialist objectives, especially reduction of disparities. Here, the assumption is that State power in China rests with the 'people' or the United Front of workers, peasants, petty bourgeoisie and national bourgeoisie in the context of people's democratic revolution and the Communist Party represents them in the exercise of State power. Strictly speaking, the phase of people's democracy is over and the State during the socialist phase theoretically is a workers' State—workers in alliance with peasants. But the CPC has appealed to the nationalist sentiments of the entire Chinese society to rally behind its leadership for building a strong and prosperous China. Therefore, the social character of the State may have undergone a change; objectively, the CPC-led State has promoted market economy and newly differentiated class society. As we have seen in Wuxi, a class of rich peasants and capitalists has grown. Some of them are autonomous and partners of foreign capital. Subjectively speaking, the party leadership has consciously tried to protect the autonomy of the Chinese entrepreneurs and safeguard sovereignty of the Chinese State and take measures to reduce poverty and disparity. The most important role that the government plays is to intervene in the case of disproportionate growth, overheated economy, economic consequences that cause social disequilibrium and so on. There is this contradiction between the objective social formations and the subjective political role. But it is a conscious policy that seeks to utilize the capacity of the market and public institutions at the centre.

There was a sharp difference in understanding the nature of the market between Mao Zedong and Deng Xiaoping. For Mao, market was a feature of the capitalist epoch; it promotes accumulation through ruthless profit orientation; it generates antagonistic contradictions in capitalism. Hence, according to Mao, socialism had to progressively reduce the operation of market forces and facilitate the transition to communism where market ceased to operate. Deng Xiaoping rejected this line of thought. In what is now called the Deng Xiaoping Theory, market is regarded as a feature of the modern age which is an era of increasingly interconnected exchanges. Like technology and management, according to Deng, market is by itself neither capitalist nor socialist, for in both systems there would be demands and supply influencing each other. Deng emphasized that when production is mainly based on administrative decisions of the State, it is likely to be less efficient. For the State agency may either have a distorted view of the overall situation due to lack of adequate information or may take reductionist decisions from its ideological belief. Deng wanted that all units of production should have capacity to relate themselves directly to the economy through their right of assessing the market. The concept of responsibility system was based on the principle that every producer and enterprise must be responsive to the market. At the same time, there is a need for public support through the State agencies so that crisis situations are managed and progress is made in the direction of social goals. Thus, for Deng, market can be used by the socialist State under the leadership of the Communist Party.

China's reforms have given rise to many institutional innovations that forbid the State–market dichotomy. For example, the village collective which monitors agricultural production and guides the village enterprises is a small, local-level collective that is not the same as the State. Under Chinese law, it is actually a people's committee with the characteristics of a mass organization. The *xiang* is legally a State unit—the lowest administrative State unit in the countryside. But the relationship between the *xiang* administration and the enterprises management is a relationship of contract rather than control. Hence, the legal economic entity of the enterprise is neither that of a State enterprise nor of a private enterprise. In the contemporary context, it is not even a collective enterprise in the strict sense. In a collective enterprise, the norms of performance assessment and distribution are closer to the commune system. In the reform context, they are different. With the emergence of shareholding system, the nature of the composition of shares would determine the extent of influence in the corporation. But it is not even that simple. The party committee or party branch in a production unit continues to play the supervisory role, and through the party network the leadership coordinates and directs the production process. But party units are forbidden to interfere in economic decision-making. They have to respect the autonomy of the manager. At the same time, the entire party has been subjected to 'emancipation of the mind' or abandoning the hesitation to develop market economy; thus, there is a multi-pronged arrangement to utilize productive initiative of all kinds, individual, family, cooperative, collective, joint stock company, Chinese-foreign joint ventures, State enterprises and other possible forms. At the same time, coordination and leadership role is assigned to various public agencies including the conventional agencies of the State. This arrangement is flexible enough to respond to the information dynamics in national, regional and global scale; it is at once capable to act as a centralized system to cope with internal and external challenges. That there were multiple agencies in society outside the State and the market was illustrated in the Chinese experience.

Socialism with Chinese Characteristics

'Deng Xiaoping Theory of building socialism with Chinese characteristics' which is now enshrined into the CPC Constitution has been regarded by many as defining the Chinese model or China path of development. Until the Cultural Revolution, the Chinese model was associated with the Maoist model of development as against the Soviet model. But the Deng's line of reforms has produced great economic successes for China; therefore, the contemporary China model refers to his ideas. But some of the questions raised by Mao Zedong about building socialism cannot be wished away.

One strand of thinking that was articulated during the youth demonstrations in Tiananmen Square in April–June 1989 was a desire to define socialism as socialist freedom. There were of course many other strands including a powerful strand of promoting liberal democracy to replace the prevailing socialist system. In addition, there were Maoists, conservatives and anarchists of various kinds. Those who upheld both socialism and its superior claims to democracy and freedom against capitalism's claims were hoping to work for a new order that was materially, politically and culturally fulfilling for a new stage of social development. The creation of material conditions laid the foundation for democratic self-governance and a culture of equality and creativity of human beings. They were not sequential as was often the case in socialist system where the communist leadership wanted to achieve economic progress 'before granting democratic self-governance and cultural rights' to various identity groups. The material, political and cultural conditions of freedom are interconnected and simultaneous in building socialism.

The reforms in China have been based on a new assertion of a sequence. Economic growth and increasing income are given top priority. It is said that political stability is a precondition for economic prosperity; therefore, political freedoms, right to dissent, right to compete for political offices and right to criticism of basic policies are disallowed in the Chinese polity. These are dismissed as liberal democratic freedoms of capitalist societies. In recent years, however, there are gradual trends of democratic politics at the village and *xiang* levels and in some respects at the national level as well. But it is still a minor trend. On the cultural front, a great deal of freedom has been allowed to promote one's lifestyle and in the sphere of art and other cultural forms. Together with economic liberalization and close intercourse with the West, it has meant an explosion of consumerist, atomistic, sensate values. The moral order of socialist values has no salience in contemporary China after four decades of reforms. This has such serious implications that the CPC leadership itself was worried about the possibility of ethical degeneration subverting and destroying the socialist system.

We have noted that from 2002 onwards, first under Hu Jintao and then under Xi Jinping's leadership, a number of steps had been initiated to address the problems that arose in the course of the reforms. Xi's focus on a 'new development philosophy', reorienting the growth path towards domestic demands and stress on green technology and taking a longer historical and civilizational view to guide the development process together with his many crucial initiatives on governance including the anti-corruption drive are signs of a positive future of China. At the same time, there are areas of anxiety flowing out of the firm commitment to the overall Industrial Revolution path, taking US economy and technology as the model as for transformation though under party leadership, aspiration to become the leading world power by pursuing the current reform path makes it difficult to adequately tackle the serious tensions in the development experience. It should be stressed that under one-party rule that inherits great revolutionary and civilizational legacies and pursues a particular development path and mobilizes its people on national rejuvenation, there is less likelihood for change of development path. Hence, there is a dilemma. Therefore, it is through debates in the country and in the party that new policies can be formulated.

Socialist market economy that Deng Xiaoping initiated in China had one clear assumption that the Industrial Revolution path that developed in Europe from the late eighteenth century onwards had no alternative in the modern era. He thought that Marxism supported that line of thought. On this, he differed fundamentally from Mao Zedong. Mao Zedong may have erred in underestimating the role of the market in building socialism. But the past 200 years of capitalist development in the world and the four decades of reforms in China had proved two things. The logic of capitalist accumulation created more and more inequalities, environmental degradation and need for controlling people's choices through different ways. The achievements of the capitalist era notwithstanding—in the spheres of technology of medicine and communication particularly—after two centuries of capitalist development, the fault line of the capitalist path had become clear. The high-energy, high-consumption, high-speed, high-rise urban-centred human civilization that it had created was unsustainable. Deng devised many ways of making the capitalist policies work through party–State control, giving a role to the State to guide the market, rooting present policies in cultural and civilizational milieu and maintaining the strong leadership of the CPC. He described them as 'socialism with Chinese characteristics' which gave a great deal of opportunities to his successors who sincerely tried to address the problems that arose out of the reform's successes that are adored around the world. But these were problems of the fault line of the path of capitalist Industrial Revolution that is under scrutiny all over the world.

Glossary

ACFTU	All China Federation of Trade Unions (Zhōnghuá quánguó zǒng-gōnghuì 中华全国总工会) in short zǒng-gōnghuì (总工会)
ACWF	All-China Women's Federation (Zhōngguó fùnǚ lián huì 中华全国妇女联合会）in short fù lián（妇联）
AIIB	Asian Infrastructure Investment Bank
APCs	Agricultural producer's cooperatives
APEC	Asia-Pacific Economic Cooperation
Barefoot Doctors (Chìjiǎo yīshēng 赤脚医生）	Medical personnel with elementary training assigned to villages to provide health services during the Great Leap Forward—a practice abandoned during the reforms on the charge that it promoted quacks and unsafe treatment
BJP	Bharatiya Janata Party
Brigade or Production Brigade (Shēngchǎn dà duì 生产大队)	Formed in 1958, the Collective unit below the Commune, renamed cūn（村）or village after 1978
CASS	Chinese Academy of Social Sciences (Zhōngguó shèhuì kē xuéyuàn 中国社会科学院）
CC	Central Committee
CCDI	Central Commission for Discipline Inspection (Zhōngyāng jìlǜ jiǎnchá wěiyuánhuì 中央纪律检查委员会）elected by the Central Committee of the CPC
Chinese Dream Zhōngguó mèng (中国猛)	Announced by Xi Jinping in November 2012 calling for the rejuvenation of the Chinese nation
CITIC	China International Trust and Investment Corporation
Commune (gōngshè 公社）	People's Commune formed in 1958 renamed Xiang or Township after 1978
CPC	Communist Party of China (Zhōngguó gòngchǎndǎng 中国共产党)
CPCCC	Communist Party of China Central Committee
CPEC	China–Pakistan Economic Corridor
CPPCC	Chinese People's Political Consultative Conference
CSD	Council for Social Development
Cultural Revolution	Great Proletarian Cultural Revolution (wúchǎn jiējí wénhuà dàgémìng 无产阶级文化大革 usually mentioned as Wénhuà dàgémìng 文化大革命）Launched by Mao in 1966 against what he called capitalist roaders in the party, terminated by his successors in 1976 who regarded it as a catastrophe

Cūn（村）	Village
Dǎng zhèng qǐyè fēnkāi（党政企业分开）	Party-government-enterprise management differentiation
Deng Xiaoping Theory (Dèngxiǎopíng lǐlùn 邓小平理论)	Deng Xiaoping theory of building socialism with Chinese characteristics to develop socialist market economy
FYP	Five-year plan
Gang of Four (Sìrénbāng 四人帮)	Four leaders of the final years of the Cultural Revolution led by Mao's wife Jiang Qing with Wang Hongwen, Yao Wenyuan and Zhang Chunqiao
GDP	Gross domestic product
GNP	Gross national product
Great Leap Forward (Dà yuèjìn 大跃进)	A multi-pronged development strategy aiming at quick results based on mass mobilization in 1958
Hela	The one-time township and village in Wuxi pronounced as *Hela* in Wuxi dialect though in *pinyin* (official roman script) its formal name is spelt as *Héliè*（禾垾）
HRS	Household Responsibility System (Jiātíng zérèn zhì 家庭责任制) Also known as Family Contract System—a rural reform measure since 1979 giving village-owned agricultural land on contract to households making them responsible for using that land for profitable production
Hùkǒu (户口)	Household registration (户籍 hù-jí)—a residency certificate that entitles a resident to access public education, health, housing and other welfare facilities, an instrument used by the regime to control migration from rural to urban areas
ICS	Institute of Chinese Studies
ICSSR	Indian Council of Social Science Research
Iron Rice Bowl (Tiě fànwǎn 铁饭碗)	(Eating from an) Iron Rice Bowl—a principle of equal wages for the workers irrespective of the quality of their work
Jiāoqū (郊区)	Suburban District
Li (lǐ 里) or *shili*	A traditional unit of length in China equivalent to 0.5 km
MAC	Military Affairs Commission
Mu (Mǔ 亩) or *shimu*	A traditional unit of an area in China equivalent to 0.165 acre
NDA	National Democratic Alliance
NDRC	National Development and Reforms Commission (Guójiā fāzhǎn hé gǎigé wěiyuánhuì 国家发展和改革委员会) that replaced the State Planning Commission during the reform period
New Urbanization (Xīn chéngshì huà 新城市化)	A policy announced in 2014 to develop multi-tier cities that are environmentally sustainable, culturally compatible, socially equitable and with technologically advanced, comfortable amenities

NGO	Non-governmental organization
NPC	National People's Congress (quánguó rénmín dàibiǎo dàhuì 全国人民代表大会) China's Parliament with nearly 3,000 Deputies, elected every five years—discusses the annual Work Report of the Premier and other State organs, passes the budget and enacts important laws.
NPCSC	National People's Congress Standing Committee
One child policy (Dú shēng zhèngcè 独生政策)	A family planning policy strictly enforced during 1979 and 2014 allowing couples to have only one child—though there were some exceptions allowed for minorities, handicapped, etc.
Party Plenum (Dǎng zhōng-yāng quánhuì 党中央全会)	Generally refers to the Plenary Session of the Central Committee of the Communist Party of China
Party Congress	National Congress of the Communist Party of China (zhōngguó gòngchǎndǎng dàibiǎo dàhuì 中国共产党全国代表大会), elected and convened every five years
PLA	People's Liberation Army (Rénmín jiěfàngjūn 人民解放军)
PONGOs	party-led NGOs
PRC	People's Republic of China (Zhōnghuá rénmín gònghéguó 中华人民共和国)
Reforms and Open Door (Gǎigé kāifàng 改革开放)	Political line adopted by the 11th CPC Central Committee at its Third Plenum in December 1978
Renminbi (Rénmínbì 人民币)	The PRC currency
Residents Committee (Jūmín wěiyuánhuì 居民委员会)	Also known as Neighbourhood Committee below the Street Committee—lowest level administrative unit in a City
Responsibility System (Zérèn zhì 责任制)	A principle enforced during the reform period to make remuneration of a manager or worker in every enterprise determined by the gains or losses incurred by the unit making every member responsible for production performance
Revolutionary Committees (gémìng wěiyuánhuì 革命委员会)	An institution introduced during the Cultural Revolution that replaced government committees as well as Party Committees in most places from the Provincial level to the Commune level
Sannong Wenti (sān nóng wèntí 三农问题)	Three Rural Problems
SARS	Severe acute respiratory syndrome
Scientific outlook on development (kēxué fāzhǎn-guān 科学发展观)	Hu Jintao's formulation in 2007 stressing comprehensive and balanced development taking people as the basis

SCPB	Standing Committee of the Political Bureau (of the Communist Party of China: Zhōngguó gòngchǎndǎng 中国共产党) (zhèngzhì jú chángwù wěiyuánhuì 政治局常务委员会)—the supreme decision-making body of China
SEZs	Special economic zones
Shi 市 (Shì) City	The same character can refer to provincial-level municipality like Shanghai, to prefecture-level city like Wuxi or county-level city, Jiangyin
SMEs	Small and medium-sized enterprises
Socialist Market Economy (Shèhuì zhǔyì shìchǎng jīngjì 社会主义市场经济)	Adopted at the 13th CPC Congress in 1987 as the governing line to develop an economy encouraging market forces to operate while maintaining the guiding role of the state
SOE	State-owned enterprise
Standing Committee of the NPC (Quánguó réndà chángwěi huì 全国人大常委会)	The nearly 150-member committee of the National People's Congress with a Chair and a dozen or so Vice-Chairs that meets almost every month to formulate most of the Laws and Regulations of China
State Council	(Guówùyuàn国务院) China's Council of Ministers
Street Committee (Jiēdào wěiyuánhu 街道委员会 ì)	Also called sub-district, a unit level committee that is a division under a metropolitan district of a city
Sunan model (Sū nán mofan 苏南模范)	A collectively owned, rural industrialization model followed in the southern region of Jiangsu Province, south of the Yangze River
Three Represents (Sān gè dàibiǎo 三个代表)	Jiang Zemin's formulation in 2000 on the need for the party to represent advanced productive forces, advanced culture and interest of masses
Tiananmen Demonstrations (tiān-ānmén shìwēi yóuxíng 天安门示威游行)	Student and Youth Demonstrations beginning in April 1989 in Beijing's Tiananmen Square demanding democracy and freedom that was crushed by the PLA on 4 June on Deng Xiaoping's orders
Taihu (Tàihú 太湖)	Literally meaning Great Lake—China's second biggest lake surrounding Wuxi on three sides
Team or Production Team (Shēngchǎn duì 生产队)	Formed in 1958 generally inoperative after 1978, emerged later as Work Groups
Ten Major Relationships (Shí dà guānxì 十大关系)	Mao's 1956 formulation on the general perspective on the whole gamut of policies that was referred to appreciatively by Deng Xiaoping and the reform regime before Mao moved towards radical positions of the Great Leap Forward
Twelve Major Relationships (Shí'èr dà guānxì 十二大关系)	Jiang Zemin's formulation on various policies in 1994 inspired by Mao's Ten Major Relationships

TVE	Township and Village Enterprises (Xiāngzhèn qǐyè 乡镇企业)
UPA	United Progressive Alliance
Villagers Committee (Cūnmín wěiyuánhuì 村民委员会)	The managing committee at the village level below the Township
WRC	Workers Representative Conference (Gōngrén dàibiǎo dàhuì 工人代表大会). Elected by the workers in an enterprise every three years
WTO	World Trade Organization
Xian (Xiàn 县)	County which is below a prefecture of a province
Xiang (Xiāng 乡)	Township which is below the county
Xiaozu (Xiǎozǔ 小组)	Small Work Group—in various forms such as labour collective, multi-purpose cooperative—below the village level equivalent to the Production Team of the Commune period
Yu mi zhi xiang (Yúmǐzhīxiāng 鱼米之乡)	Land of fish and rice
yuan (Yuán 元)	Unit of *Rénmínbì* (人民币), the currency of PRC; one yuan (one hundred *fen*) was equivalent to about US$ 0.15 in 2017 May
Zhen (Zhèn 镇)	Town, can be at the township level or at the village level
zhou (Zhōu 州)	Prefecture below the province

Index

About the Author

Manoranjan Mohanty is a renowned political scientist and China scholar whose writings have focused on theoretical and empirical dimensions of social movements, human rights, the development experience and the regional role of India and China. As Vice-President of the Council for Social Development (CSD) and Editor of CSD's social science journal *Social Change*, published by SAGE, he brings a wealth of experience from both policy and practice perspectives. He is also Chairperson, Development Research Institute, Bhubaneswar, and Honorary Fellow, Institute of Chinese Studies (ICS), Delhi. Until 2004, he was Director, Developing Countries Research Centre, and Professor of Political Science at University of Delhi where he taught until his retirement. Former Chairperson and Director of ICS and former Editor of *China Report*, he has been on visiting assignments in several universities and research institutes in India and abroad including University of California, Berkeley; Institute of Far Eastern Studies, Moscow, Oxford, Beijing, Copenhagen, Lagos; University of California, Santa Barbara; and the New School, New York. Professor Mohanty has been a part of the founding and evolution of ICS, the Developing Countries Research Centre at University of Delhi and Gabeshana Chakra and Development Research Institute in Odisha. He has also been closely involved with the People's Union for Democratic Rights, Delhi, and the Pakistan–India People's Forum for Democracy since their inception. He was part of the founding process of the Boao Forum for Asia in China and REGGEN, the Third-World sustainable development network in Brazil. His other contributions include 'China's Reforms: The Wuxi Story' in *China after 1978: Craters in the Moon* (2010), *Ideology Matters: China from Mao Zedong to Xi Jinping* (2014), 'Political Discourse on Public Sector Reforms in India and China' in *Public Sector Reforms in China* (2014) and 'India, China and the Emerging Process of Building a Just World' in *Building a Just World: Essays in Honour of Muchkund Dubey* (2015).